THE MINNEAPOLIS RECKONING

The Minneapolis Reckoning

RACE, VIOLENCE, AND
THE POLITICS OF
POLICING IN AMERICA

Michelle S. Phelps

PRINCETON UNIVERSITY PRESS
PRINCETON & OXFORD

Published by Princeton University Press
41 William Street, Princeton, New Jersey 08540
99 Banbury Road, Oxford OX2 6JX

press.princeton.edu

All Rights Reserved

Library of Congress Cataloging-in-Publication Data

Names: Phelps, Michelle S., 1983– author.
Title: The Minneapolis reckoning : race, violence, and the politics of policing
    in America / Michelle S. Phelps.
Description: 1st book. | Princeton : Princeton University Press, [2024] |
    Includes bibliographical references and index.
Identifiers: LCCN 2023036206 (print) | LCCN 2023036207 (ebook) | ISBN
    9780691245980 (hardback) | ISBN 9780691246000 (ebook)
Subjects: LCSH: Police—Minnesota—Minneapolis. | Police
    brutality—Minnesota—Minneapolis. | Police administration—Citizen
    participation. | Black lives matter movement. | BISAC: SOCIAL SCIENCE /
    Discrimination | POLITICAL SCIENCE / Public Policy / General
Classification: LCC HV8148.M56 P44 2024 (print) | LCC HV8148.M56 (ebook) |
    DDC 363.232—dc23/eng/20231012
LC record available at https://lccn.loc.gov/2023036206
LC ebook record available at https://lccn.loc.gov/2023036207

British Library Cataloging-in-Publication Data is available

Editorial: Meagan Levinson, Erik Beranek
Jacket: Katie Osborne
Production: Erin Suydam
Publicity: Alyssa Sanford (US), Kathryn Stevens (UK)
Copyeditor: Michelle S. Asakawa

Jacket Credit: (top) photograph of Minneapolis City Hall by
Tony Webster / Flickr, (bottom) Majority World CIC / Alamy Stock Photo

This book has been composed in Miller.

Printed in the United States of America

10 9 8 7 6 5 4 3 2 1

To my students, who have taught me so much.

May you remake the world as a better place.

CONTENTS

ON MAY 25, 2020, officers with the Minneapolis Police Department (MPD) killed George Perry Floyd Jr. at 38th and Chicago, kneeling on his neck, back, and legs as he lay face down on the pavement for over *nine minutes*. The officer who held his knee on Floyd's neck, Derek Chauvin, was white, a department veteran and field training officer with a history of misconduct allegations, while the two men at his waist and legs were rookie officers, one white and one biracial. A fourth officer, an Asian American man, stood between the crime in progress and a growing crowd of distraught onlookers, including a teenage girl recording on her cell phone who would soon release the video of a murder committed by police in broad daylight to the world.[1] Coming on the tail end of the "lockdown" measures intended to slow the COVID-19 pandemic, Americans had nowhere else to look. As the crowd of digital witnesses grew, protests swept the city and country, reaching far-flung corners of the world.

In the aftermath, some would call Floyd's killing a lynching, evoking the long history of racist violence against Black men in America. Yet unlike the lynchings of earlier decades, where white audiences jubilantly cheered the spectacle,[2] Floyd's death was witnessed by a multiracial (and majority Black) crowd of residents, described later by the prosecutor as a "bouquet of humanity," who stood watching in horror and outrage. They included a nine-year-old girl, the teenage cashier who had dialed 911, an off-duty firefighter with emergency medicine training, a martial arts expert, an older man who had tried to help calm Floyd initially, and a 911 dispatcher watching the cameras who saw something unusual happening at 38th and Chicago. And unlike so many of the lynchings of yesteryear, the murder of George Floyd would spark outrage across the racial, geographical, and political differences that so divide our country—prompting what became known as the summer of racial reckoning.

During the heat of this reckoning, the MPD's 3rd Precinct would be torched alongside swaths of the city as unrest swept the nation. All four involved officers would be fired and criminally prosecuted, with Chauvin facing murder charges and a lengthy prison sentence. But organizers in Minneapolis were thinking bigger—accountability didn't mean the prosecution of "bad apple" officers (or even the torching of one precinct building); it meant an end to policing as we knew it. Staging a march to the home of Mayor Jacob Frey, activists demanded a yes or no answer: Did he support defunding the MPD? Drawing boos from the crowd, Frey declared that he would *not* abolish the MPD.

Unlike the mayor, however, many city council members were ready to say *yes*. The day after the march to Frey's door, on June 7th, nine of the thirteen city council members held an outdoor press conference at Powderhorn Park, just down the street from 38th and Chicago. Standing on a stage emblazoned with giant letters that read "DEFUND POLICE," the council members read this pledge:

> Decades of police reform efforts have proved that the Minneapolis Police Department cannot be reformed and will never be held accountable for their actions. We are here today to begin the process of ending the Minneapolis Police Department and creating a new transformative model for cultivating safety in Minneapolis. We recognize that we don't have all the answers to what a police-free future looks like, but our community does. We are committing to engaging with every willing community member in the City of Minneapolis over the next year to identify what safety looks like for everyone. We'll be taking intermediate steps towards ending the MPD through the budget process and other policy and budget decisions over the coming weeks and months.[3]

The Powderhorn Pledge concluded by promising that the city council would stand with city residents to fight together for a "safer community." It was a powerful ending to what had been two weeks of turmoil in Minneapolis, written across the headlines of the city's newspaper of record (see figure P.1).

In the weeks that followed, council members would work to push forward the primary policy tool to "end" the MPD, a ballot initiative to amend the city charter that would strike out the section on the MPD (which included a mandatory minimum number of officers per capita) and replace it with a new Department of Community Safety and Violence Prevention (which *could* include officers). Advocates cheered, declaring that changing the charter would allow the city to finally reckon with its long past of racist, violent policing.

The Powderhorn Pledge was a stunning departure from the police reform proposals that had dominated left-leaning cities during the first wave of Black Lives Matter (BLM) protests after Michael Brown's killing in Ferguson, Missouri, and the non-indictment of Officer Darren Wilson in 2014.[4] In those early years, activists called for the prosecution of officers, as well as better hiring, training, and accountability policies to rein in police violence. After years of protest, police reform, and seemingly little change

FIGURE P.1. Two weeks of front-page news
Source: Star Tribune, digital print edition.

in police killings, the goals and tactics of the movement grew more radical. By 2017, while some activists continued to work toward the prosecution of individual officers and reform of policing training and policies, others began to build support for police defunding—moving dollars out of policing and into "life-sustaining" resources that would better address the root causes of poverty and violence. For abolitionist activists, the ultimate goal was the end of policing, framed as the only truly effective solution to police violence and the broader harms of mass criminalization and punishment.[5]

The charter amendment, however, would be blocked from appearing on the 2020 ballot by political opposition and procedural hurdles. The following year, the proposal was revived as a citizen-led ballot measure, eventually appearing on the 2021 election slate as "Question 2" alongside races for the mayor's seat and each ward's city council representative. Wrangling over the charter amendment produced a deeply contentious election season, as candidates, activists, community leaders, business elites, and residents fought over the future of public safety in Minneapolis—or what, exactly, might make "everyone feel safe."

By that point, Minneapolis was in a desperate bid to increase the number of police officers after a mass exodus in the wake of the unrest. The city was also more than a year into a historic spike in homicides that rivaled the period in the mid-1990s when it garnered the nickname "Murderapolis." This rise in violence gave defenders of the police powerful ammunition. As the MPD's Medaria Arradondo, the city's first Black chief, declared in a press conference: "We have an epidemic right now of unequivocal gun violence." As a result, "the biggest threat to public safety in our city, and particularly to our African American community, is not the police."[6] For the police chief, and the mayor who stood behind him, police were not the problem but the solution to the city's woes. In the end, city voters seemed to agree, reelecting Mayor Frey and rejecting the charter amendment. The national media headlines trumpeting that Minneapolis was set to abolish the police in 2020 were replaced in 2021 with bold declarations about the failure to end policing in the City of Lakes.

On the day MPD officers murdered George Floyd, I was sitting at home just two miles away, writing up the results of a study on policing and anti-police-violence activism in Minneapolis. I had started the project after the 2015 death of Jamar Clark, a Black man killed by police after a late-night confrontation with an ambulance crew. His killing prompted an explosion of protest in the city, including an occupation outside the local police precinct. Then, too, activists demanded accountability for officers' violence. Not for the first time in its history, the city attempted to revise how officers' misconduct was evaluated and enacted a series of policy reforms.

And yet, despite residents' outcry, in the years that followed, MPD officers' violence continued. So did the protests. In 2017 the victim was Justine (Ruszczyk) Damond, the only white woman killed by MPD officers during this period, who called 911 to report a possible sexual assault in her alleyway. In 2018 it was Thurman Blevins Jr., a Black man who police chased down an alleyway after residents called to complain about someone firing their gun in the street, and Travis Jordan, a multiracial man who had been the subject of a welfare check and came out of his home holding a knife. Both were killed in North Minneapolis, the same police precinct that took Clark's life. In 2019, still in North Minneapolis, it was Chiasher Vue, a Hmong man involved in a family dispute who had come to the door armed with a shotgun. And in 2020, in South Minneapolis, George Floyd was killed, one of the more than one thousand victims of lethal police violence that year across the country.

As I thought about the historic importance of the protests unfolding in Minneapolis and elsewhere, I started to wonder what it would take to really change policing. Why were cities seemingly unable to staunch the horrific repetition of state violence? And who or what could really change policing? Many policing textbooks report that police became more insulated from political influence as they professionalized in the mid-twentieth century. Yet policing and politics are still deeply intertwined.[7] As residents make political demands for policing services in the voting booth, protest leaders call for the prosecution of "killer cops," mayors depose the latest police chiefs, city councils set police budgets, and state legislatures revisit officer use-of-force statutes, politics remain essential to directing (and potentially limiting) police power. In addition, police themselves have since the 1960s become more savvy political players, directly intervening in local, state, and national crime politics through media appearances, lobbying campaigns, and even running for office.[8] To me, it seemed the answer of who or what could change policing therefore had to be connected to these politics, embedded in the ongoing struggle between city leaders, the police, activists, community and business leaders, and everyday residents.

Rather than studying the police, police violence, or even police reform, I realized what I was studying was the *politics of policing*. And to better understand these politics, in 2017, I and a team of students began interviewing the key players in Minneapolis, from residents to organizers and city leaders, trying to understand how each group understood the problems in policing and what it might take to change them. We also started observing public events, participating in protests and vigils, and showing up for hearings at city hall and the state capitol. By 2019, I thought my team had reached theoretical saturation—nearing the limit of what we could learn through these interviews and observations. And so it was that I found myself writing up our findings, trying to contextualize the Minneapolis case for a national audience. Then George Floyd was murdered and the 3rd Precinct went up in flames.

Instead of ending the study, I dove back into data collection in 2020, watching protests in the streets, city council hearings (now streamed online), and digital media coverage. It quickly became clear that everything I had learned earlier was not the end-point, but the prelude, to George Floyd's murder and its aftermath. You couldn't understand the headlines of summer 2020 without tracing the years (even decades) of activism that preceded it, laying the groundwork for the Powderhorn Pledge—from the elected officials on the stage (some of whom had been elected, in part, because of BLM activism) to the text they read to the crowd (which repeated language from the opening of a 2017 report written by a local police abolitionist collective). This prelude also explained the barriers advocates slammed against as they attempted to dismantle the MPD. And just as you had to go back in time to understand the roots of what happened in summer 2020, so too would it take several years to trace all of the complex outcomes of the murder and our summer of reckoning (some of which are still unfolding). The story told in the national media headlines, it turned out, bore little resemblance to the complicated political struggles on the ground.

A year after George Floyd's murder, I began writing this book in earnest, trying to answer the question reporters, students, and friends kept asking of me: *What happened in Minneapolis—and will anything ever change?*

THE MINNEAPOLIS RECKONING

Introduction

BEFORE SUMMER 2020, few might have predicted that Minneapolis would become the epicenter of a fierce rebellion against police violence. Unlike Ferguson, Missouri, where "Black Lives Matter" (BLM) transformed from a eulogy into a national movement against police violence, Minneapolis is a majority white city; less than 20 percent of its 430,000 residents in 2020 identified as Black or African American.[1] Yet the city is also a hotspot for left-leaning politics, with a long history of racial justice organizing, including a robust set of activist groups challenging racialized police violence. As a result, going all the way back to the 1940s, the Minneapolis Police Department (MPD) has been a test case for both the possibilities and limits of liberal police reform.

That Minneapolis had been the site of *generations* of police reform made the murder of George Floyd all the more galling. As abolitionists declared, the MPD was a "poster child" for reform, yet Officer Derek Chauvin still pressed his knee into the neck and back of a restrained Black man, prone in the street, for over nine minutes in front of a crowd of witnesses. If police could show such wanton disregard for life here, then it could happen anywhere. Conversely, if change could happen anywhere in the startling heat of summer 2020, it should have been in Minneapolis. As city council members pledged to "end" the MPD, the story of Minneapolis became inextricably intertwined with policing in America and calls to "defund the police." Yet by the close of 2021, with the "no" vote on the charter amendment to end the MPD, the moment to transform public safety seemed to snap closed, locking in the status quo that had so shocked the world. The same national media headlines that blared Minneapolis was set to "abolish" the police in 2020 were equally declarative about its failure in 2021.

The Minneapolis Reckoning goes past the headlines, asking how and why Minneapolis became a city on fire—and what, if anything, changed as the smoke cleared. As someone who had been researching policing, police violence, and anti-police-violence activism in the city for several years before Floyd's murder, I was struck by how rarely the headlines conveyed the nuance I was seeing on the ground. For example, the charter amendment to replace the MPD with a new department did not emerge out of thin air in summer 2020, but instead was the result of years (even decades) of organizing efforts. So too would activists ultimately run up against a familiar set of barriers, including a powerful officers union and state laws built by their political allies to enshrine police power.

But it was not simply officers' resistance, or the expected opposition from more conservative quarters, that blocked the charter amendment in Minneapolis. Nor was it just about white residents' voting patterns. As you will see, before and after the uprisings of 2020, the Black community in Minneapolis rarely spoke in one voice on police and safety.[2] Even residents all too familiar with the dangers of police violence often described wanting *more* (and *better*) policing in their neighborhoods. This complex set of attitudes, and how they were deployed by a diverse cast of city leaders, would form the most contentious core of debates over the charter amendment.

But I also knew that the "no" vote on Question 2 in 2021 was not the end of the struggle. Working inside and outside the bounds of city governance, new visions of public safety were just starting to take root. Rather than crown a victor, this book shows that both ardent supporters of the Minneapolis police and those seeking to radically transform public safety won some battles and lost others. The result was, as ever, a complex mix of policies and practices that continues to reshape the city as I write today. As shouts of "Justice for George!" were converted into political struggles, the results often strayed from the initial visions of the activists in the street. Nevertheless, these fights led to meaningful changes to policing policy and practice.[3]

For instance, the 2021 charter amendment never amounted to a wholesale reorientation of city governance; it would not have abolished the MPD, obviated policing in the city, or even mandated police defunding. Had it passed, it might have resulted in little but an administrative restructuring of city agencies (a new name for the same old department), depending on who held power in city hall. And despite the charter amendment's failure on the ballot, public safety policies in the city did change in important ways—Minneapolis created an Office of Community Safety and expanded alternatives to police. Further, though the MPD was never substantially defunded in the city budget, the size of its armed force stands significantly smaller today than in 2020.

To understand this more complex, but truer, version of the Minneapolis reckoning, we have to go back in time, unearthing the origins of the police in the city and across the country, especially the contested role police play in Black communities. In the early days of America's democracy, law enforcement and their proxies were mobilized to defend the power and privileges of white slave owners. In parts of the South, these slave patrols often transitioned into the police we now know.[4] Because of this history, visions of true liberation for some Black theorists and organizers, or what historian Robin Kelley describes as *freedom dreams*,[5] have demanded the abolition of police. At the same time, other voices in Minneapolis and elsewhere draw on different strands of radical Black thought, arguing that any vision of freedom must include state protection from both white vigilante *and* intra-community violence, in part through the form of the police.[6] Just because the roots of policing were racist did not, for these dreamers, mean that its future had to be racist too.

This book wrestles with these questions, tracing how mass mobilization for transforming policing crashed into the local politics of race, inequality, and violence in Minneapolis and, in the process, examining why attempts to end police violence have proved so elusive. In short, I argue that this cycle of outrage and reform is driven by the two competing visions of police—one that sees police as providing *the promise of state protection* and another that sees the police as representing *the threat of state violence*. It is not simply that police protect some by threatening others, but that the people and places most in desperate need of stronger state protection are also those facing the greatest risk of police violence.[7] These contradictions create the contested politics of policing described in this book, which in turn erect the barriers to more radical shifts in public safety even in left-leaning cities where elected officials declare that they are "listening to Black voices." Ultimately, it is this dilemma that we must resolve to create lasting changes: solving police violence, in other words, will require that we change much more than policing.[8]

Heroes or Murderers: Police in America

There are two stories about the police, depending on who you ask. The story that has been told in policing textbooks and many classrooms across the country is the valorous version: police departments emerged from more informal community watch groups as urbanization and migration patterns produced larger, less socially interconnected cities. Taking cues from Sir Robert Peel's innovations with the London Metropolitan Police, new city forces in the rapidly growing Northeast emerged to better prevent and manage crime and disorder.[9] Policing, in this account, was developed as a redistributive public good, using tax dollars to protect those at the greatest risk of victimization (and least able to pay for private security).

Indeed, early police officers often provided a range of governmental services, from the order maintenance roles we now see as essential to policing to welfare services like finding lost children, running soup kitchens, and providing employment assistance.[10] As police professionalized in the mid-twentieth century, their work came to focus more directly on crime prevention and response in efforts to "serve and protect" an increasingly diverse public.[11]

The other story, of course, is that police departments descend from institutions devoted to upholding chattel slavery and represent a throughline of anti-Black racism across US history. Long before the first police forces were formally established in the Northeast, places like Charleston, South Carolina, were organizing slave patrols—teams of white men who terrorized enslaved people and free Black Americans alike. Only through the Civil War was slavery abolished in 1865. Yet violence against Black Americans persisted, both extra-legal and that sanctioned by law. After the failure of Reconstruction, white legislatures across the South created new laws like the "Black codes" and "Pig laws" that criminalized Black Americans' survival and made them vulnerable to capture, servitude, and disenfranchisement. Police became the new enforcers of this racist legal order, funneling Black Americans into Southern courts to reproduce the bondages of slavery.[12]

While "freedom" ostensibly reigned according to the letter of the law in the post–Civil War North, in practice, police played a key role in maintaining racial domination there, too. Perhaps most importantly, police enforced *spatial* boundaries, as white police forces corralled newly enfranchised Black Americans, increasingly journeying to the North, into neighborhoods of concentrated poverty (which became today's "ghettos"). Rising ethno-racial tensions hit a breaking point in the race riots of 1919, or the "Red Summer," which saw mass white violence against Black Americans across the Northeast and Midwest. Put to the test, police either looked the other way, failing to protect Black residents, or joined the white rioters (who were often, like officers, first- and second-generation immigrants from Europe).[13]

Nearly half a century later, police remained central to the story of racism in America. While many of the pivotal civil rights struggles targeted institutions like public transportation and education, it was police who reestablished "order" on the streets, often by meting out brutal beatings to protesters—perhaps most emblematically at the 1965 "Bloody Sunday" attack in Selma, Alabama.[14] Not only was police violence the headline from that day's protest, but the killing of a Black civil rights activist (Jimmie Lee Jackson) at the hands of a white state trooper was the spark that set off the march.

Thus, many carceral historians argue, policing has always been a tool not for some neutral vision of "order" or the protection of society (much less its most vulnerable), but instead of racial domination and white supremacy.[15] There has never been a golden moment in our country's history, in other words, when policing *worked* for Black Americans.[16]

These two stories are not simply different interpretations of the historical record but also powerful heuristics for understanding the role of police today. Are police brutal enforcers of an anti-Black racial order? Or are they the physical embodiment of the state's obligation to serve and protect the public? One of the main contentions of *The Minneapolis Reckoning* is that to understand the politics of policing, we have to see both stories simultaneously, understanding the police as representing both the *promise* of state protection and the *threat* of state violence. And this duality of the police means that no matter the context, calls to reduce the size of the police are perceived by many Americans as a threat to their own safety, not only by white Americans buffered from the worst victimization rates, but also by many Black Americans. As a result, waves of anti-police-violence protests have often led to reforms that increased, rather than reduced, police power.[17]

Statistical evidence supports this complex story about race, policing, and violence. In numbers now grimly familiar to many Americans, Black people represent just 14 percent of the US population, but 27 percent of the roughly one thousand people shot and killed by police in recent years.[18] Estimates suggest that over the life course, one in every one thousand Black boys and men will be killed by police.[19] Black victims of police killings are less likely than white victims to be armed, adding evidence that the threshold for officers' perception of dangerousness is tainted by racial bias.[20] More quotidian negative encounters with police are also starkly unequal across race. Among the roughly 10 percent of Americans who will have a police-initiated contact with officers in any given year (most commonly a traffic stop),[21] Black Americans face a heightened risk of intrusive investigatory stops, demeaning language by police officers, vehicle and person searches, and non-lethal use of force, compared to white Americans, even when controlling for the person's behavior.[22] As a result, policing in poor communities of color is often defined not by the motto of "protect and serve" but by police maltreatment, including verbal harassment, racial profiling, slow responses to 911 calls, and violence.[23]

The other side of the coin is that these same communities face persistently high rates of intra-community violence, despite the seemingly pervasive presence of police.[24] This disparity is particularly clear when we look at lethal interpersonal violence; among the roughly fourteen thousand victims of homicide in 2019, for example, just over *half* were Black or African American.[25] And among Black boys and young men, homicide is the *leading* cause of death.[26]

With few state resources to call on to manage the crises of precarity, people in communities beset by high rates of disorder and violent conflict turn to the police, calling 911 to summon help.[27] High rates of victimization also fuel broader political mobilization in *support* of the police. Even amid the painful summer of 2020, for example, four in five Americans identifying as Black or African American told pollsters that they wanted the same or more police time spent in their area.[28] As I show in these pages, we cannot interpret this fact as a sign that Black America uncritically endorses the police. It is instead a result of deeply constrained choices and a beleaguered pragmatism that police are one of the few resources consistently available on demand. If there is a "Black silent majority" as some argue,[29] they are not *pro-police*, but instead deeply *ambivalent*, torn between competing desires for safety.

Why Cities Are "Cheap on Crime"

This state of affairs in poor communities of color, or what Jill Leovy's best-seller *Ghettoside* describes as *over-policing and under-policing*, is often framed as a paradox.[30] The answer, she argues, is to *recalibrate* the kinds of policing in such places, reducing police harassment over low-level offenses and increasing effective police responses to serious crimes, especially homicide. More recently, a new generation of scholars and activists has insisted that poor communities of color are not *under-policed*, but *under-protected*, deprived of the kinds of holistic support that prevents violence in thriving communities.[31] Rather than a "paradox," unjust and inadequate policing are thus better understood as two sides of the same coin—both extensions of the failures of the state to take the safety concerns of its most vulnerable residents seriously.[32]

As criminologist Elliot Currie writes, since the work of visionary Black sociologist W.E.B. Du Bois, scholars have understood why poor communities of color are continually beset by horrifically high rates of violence.[33]

Concentrated poverty, racism and exclusion, and meager social welfare programs make a uniquely lethal combination. That's why while the rate of lethal violence has ebbed and flowed over the generations—driven by socio-economic forces, trends in drug markets, and more—the broad story of racial disparities in violence has remained stubbornly persistent. It is also why most Black men are murdered not by white Americans, but by people who look like them—so-called "Black-on-Black" crime.[34] And though it is perhaps easier to see racism at work when a white police officer kills an unarmed Black man, it is no less a fundamental cause when young Black men kill each other. This violence is fueled by the racial injustices produced by the long afterlife of slavery, alongside America's love affair with guns, which has made it easy to lay hands on both legal and illicit weapons, from beat-up old pistols to "military-style" assault rifles.[35]

Real redress for Black America's vastly unequal exposure to premature death would require substantial state and federal investments in housing, education, employment, health care, and more. Yet as political scientist Lisa Miller documents, the people closest to the problem of violence—local residents in hard-hit urban cores—are often least represented in the federal policy arena, where there are the most resources.[36] Indeed, since the 1960s federal aid to cities and states for nonmedical services has shrunk, even as Washington's players incentivized more aggressive policing and tougher punishment. As local tax bases felt the impact of white elites fleeing city limits,[37] cities were left to manage racial and economic inequality (and the crime it produced) on their own.[38] And so city leaders turned to policing to manage high rates of interpersonal violence, one of the few tools at their disposal. Policing is also, relatively speaking, *cheap*. What cities pay in tax dollars to provide for policing services pales in comparison to the dollars needed for real economic redistribution, full and dignified employment, safe and affordable housing, responsive health care, and equitable education for all.[39]

Yet police are, at best, a last-stop measure against crime, disorder, and victimization. Police can *deter* (through their physical presence or the threat of apprehension), they can *remove individuals* (at least temporarily), and they can *deploy violence*. As policing scholar Egon Bittner argues, violence is not incidental to policing—it is its core. Police are called because they are the ones who can compel someone to leave an apartment or a corner, using either the threat or application of force, from handcuffs and arrest to lethal violence.[40] Finally, police can *solve crimes*, potentially preventing retaliatory violence that might have ensued otherwise. (Though, in practice, most police departments solve less than *half* of homicides, a rate that has been declining rather than improving over time.[41])

But police can't change any of the social conditions that beget endemic violence, nor are they typically very effective as managers of the myriad consequences of mental illness, homelessness, substance use disorders, and intergenerational trauma. And for each of the potential benefits of police intervention, there are tremendous social harms, including harassment and surveillance, the costs of arrests and conviction (including incarceration), and the persistent risk of violence perpetrated by officers.[42] As sociologist Patrick Sharkey concludes, police can at best maintain an *uneasy peace*, fueled by repression and control rather than community thriving.[43]

Black America's Demands for Safety

Communities of color are intimately aware of the limits of the police. Indeed, Black America's champions have long argued that they would be better protected not only by *more* and *better* policing but also through broader social investments in the community. Legal scholar James Forman Jr. traces this process in the context of Washington, DC, during the prison boom in his Pulitzer Prize–winning book *Locking Up Our Own*.[44] Over the decades, Black community leaders, elected officials, and justice system actors alike called for deep investments in communities to address crime and disorder, including more policing and punishment.[45] Yet, critically, they also demanded investments outside of the criminal justice system—like full employment and dignified housing. But instead of getting "all of the above," communities largely got aggressive policing and mass incarceration, a form of *selective listening* by city, state, and federal officials.[46] And, in a perverse civil rights victory, in the District of Columbia this punishment was now meted out by an increasing number of Black cops, prosecutors, and judges as racial segregation loosened its hold on the middle class.[47]

By the 1990s these choices came to haunt the country, with low-income Black communities beleaguered by pervasive surveillance, police enforcement, and punishment. The next generation of Black changemakers across the country critiqued the constrained choices of the past, calling for political leaders to reckon with the brutal system of mass incarceration it produced.[48] By the mid-2010s these critiques of mass incarceration had gained traction. In the context of historically low crime rates, mass incarceration began to seem like a policy *problem* rather than a *solution*.[49] Propelled forward by scholar-advocates like Michelle Alexander, left-leaning organizations began to articulate a critique of the criminal (in)justice system as racialized punishment or, in Alexander's words, *The New Jim Crow*.[50]

Before 2014 the police, however, were not subject to the same scrutiny as our country's prisons, either in public discourses or socio-legal scholarship—despite periodic unrest related to police violence. Indeed, even the Black Lives Matter slogan initially emerged not in response to police violence but to vigilante violence, coined by three Black organizers (Alicia Garza, Patrisse Cullors, and Opal Tometi) in 2013 after the acquittal of George Zimmerman for the killing of teenager Trayvon Martin. The following year, after the police killing of Michael Brown and non-indictment of former officer Darren Wilson, BLM exploded into a national movement centered on racialized police violence. What was *new*, however, was not police violence, or police violence targeting Black Americans, or even filming of police violence, all of which were continuations with the past.[51] (Think: Selma in 1965. Or, more proximally, the beating of Rodney King by the Los Angeles Police Department in 1991, caught on video by a bystander. Or Amadou Diallo, an unarmed twenty-three-year-old West African student shot and killed by officers with the New York City Police Department in 1999.) Instead of the previous generation's call for *equal rights*, as political scientist Deva Woodly writes, these new organizers made a more fundamental yet radical demand: make Black lives *matter*.[52]

Organizers in Ferguson—and, soon, across the country—drew on local networks and earlier radical movements for inspiration. Explicitly turning to women, queer, and transgender organizers to lead the movement, organizers deployed the new tools of social media to spread the word.[53] In the years that followed, BLM protests emerged across the country, often precipitated by local police killings.[54] And as protests grew into a movement, "Black Lives Matter" came to reference the national Black Lives Matter Movement (BLMM) group, including chapters of the Black Lives Matter Global Network, the broader Movement for Black Lives (M4BL) coalition, any anti-police-violence protests that drew on BLM slogans, and hashtag activism under #BlackLivesMatter and #BLM on social media.[55] Pushing forward public discourse, BLM protests increased the public salience of both specific instances of police violence and the ravages of racism and capitalism more broadly.[56] The protests also propelled local, state, and federal governments to consider police reform as a legislative priority.[57]

Yet, as you'll see in this book, increased consensus on the *problem* of illegitimate police violence has not meant agreement on its *solution*. Some BLM activists would come to fight for *police reform* as a form of harm reduction, pushing to transform the policies and practices of police departments.

For example, Campaign Zero, a public advocacy and policy initiative, was unveiled in 2015 by a team of organizers who had been on the ground in Ferguson. They demanded the country reduce the number of police killings to *zero*. Rather than the more moderate reform provisions enshrined in the 2015 "President's Task Force on 21st Century Policing" report commissioned under President Barack H. Obama and led by law enforcement themselves, these reforms were designed to be transformational, or more meaningful shifts toward just policing, including ending "broken windows" practices like stop-and-frisk, for-profit policing, and militarization, as well as implementing more powerful community oversight, stronger policies and accountability for use of force, and fairer police union contracts.[58]

Others would look outside policing, calling for money to be pulled away from policing and punishment and invested in "root cause" solutions—or *police defunding*. For example, when the M4BL released its first "Vision for Black Lives" in 2016, the coalition extended the Black Panther Party's demand to "End the War on Black People" by calling for divesting money from police budgets and investing in Black communities through reparations, health care, economic justice, and community control of government budgets.[59] This invest-divest strategy would become, by 2020, the call to #DefundThePolice, bolstered not only as a means to transfer public dollars but also as a pathway to *police abolition*, or the end of policing as we knew it. Reform, for abolitionists, was a dead-end, positioned only to entrench police power. Instead, the path forward, they argued, was "nonreformist reforms," or changes that would shrink the power, size, and legitimacy of the police.[60] And by 2020 this clash between police reform and abolition would explode, centered in Minneapolis.

Policing the City of Lakes

Minneapolis was not an early mover in urbanization or policing, nor is it an unusually large police department. By the close of 2019, the Midwestern city employed roughly 880 sworn officers for a ratio of 2 officers per 1,000 residents. (While this is an average rate for midsize cities, in the country's mega-cities, police forces can number ten thousand or more, with staffing ratios of more than 4 officers per 1,000 residents.[61])

Despite its unremarkable development and scale, however, Minneapolis has been a secret bellwether city for understanding race and policing in America. In the 1940s, for example, the city was among the first to require that police complete "race relations" training, an initiative led by Mayor Hubert Humphrey, who would go on to serve as a US senator and one of the architects of the landmark federal civil rights legislation. Minneapolis was also one of the many cities that erupted in protest during the "Long Hot Summer" of 1967, ushering in both a brief flourishing of radical experiments in community-led safety and a longer era of conservative policy-making. City residents, in fact, elected the head of the police officers association as mayor, cheering as he promised to "take the handcuffs off the police."[62] By the 1980s Minneapolis was firmly back under Democratic leadership, as a series of mayors (white and Black alike) promised to bring more safety to the city—including through police militarization and the War on Drugs. By 2015 Minneapolis was an early BLM protest site and adopter of the "21st Century Policing" model for reform.

And after the murder of George Floyd, the city came to represent the failures of generations of police reform. In 2021, voters would elect the first Black Socialist to serve on city council, Robin Wonsley (then Robin Wonsley Worlobah), whose central ward straddles the Mississippi and includes the University of Minnesota's young voters. A prominent voice for abolition, she would declare in 2022 that the MPD was "one of the worst-performing police departments in the country."[63] Yet while the city's police force was responsible for one of the most distressing police killings caught on video in our lifetimes, in other respects the MPD is worryingly average. It does not, for example, stand out among either peer departments or others in the state when it comes to the rate of lethal killings of civilians.[64]

What is perhaps most unusual about Minneapolis, in the end, is not that police violence happens, but that it happens *here*, in a place defined by its left-leaning politics and explicit commitment to racial equality. That reputation was not simply a façade; indeed, it is what built the strong networks of activists in Minneapolis and laid the foundation for a movement to end the MPD. Those networks meant Minneapolis would become national, not just local, news when its police force committed an egregious harm. And it is why many voters in the city understand themselves not as *liberals*, but *progressives*, positioned to the left of today's mainstream Democrats in their policy preferences, which made the debates over the charter amendment possible. But none of that, in the end, would prove enough to end the MPD.

Race, Space, and Place

Another way Minneapolis reveals the limits of liberal politics is through the legacies and present-day realities of racial segregation, which deeply shape policing. Indeed, as even a cursory glance at a map of Minneapolis

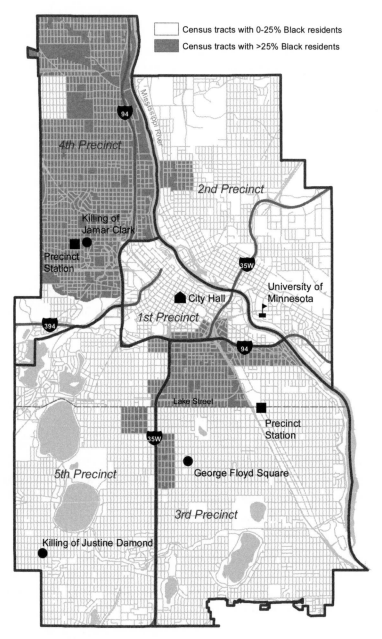

FIGURE I.1. Map of Minneapolis with police precinct boundaries, key protest sites, and racial demographics

Source: US Census Bureau. 2020 Census Redistricting Data (P.L. 94-171) - Table P1, Race. Washington, DC: US Department of Commerce.

illustrates, each of the city's five police precincts "protect and serve" notably different communities.[65] As shown in figure I.1, in the southwest corner of the city sit the wealthiest zip codes, dotted around the "chain of lakes" and policed by the 5th Precinct. It is these neighborhoods that have historically housed Minneapolis's white elite (and where Justine Damond was shot and killed by police in 2017). By 2021 this precinct would represent the staunchest opponents of the charter amendment to end the MPD.

On the other side of the city, just north of downtown and to the west of the Mississippi River, is North Minneapolis, or Northside, home to more than a third of the city's nearly eighty thousand Black or African American residents.[66] Policed by the MPD's 4th Precinct, North Minneapolis experiences a distressingly high and persistent rate of violence, with street corners peppered by memorials to the slain. In 2020, for example, *nearly half* of the city's homicides were reported in the 4th Precinct alone, representing a rate of death nearly three times the city's overall average.[67] North Minneapolis has also been the site of several police killings of Black men in recent years. In response to the 2015 shooting of Jamar Clark, activists staged an eighteen-day occupation outside the doors of the 4th Precinct station, a precursor to the torching of the 3rd Precinct. As the neighborhood most directly bearing the brunt of both police and community violence, North Minneapolis loomed large in the 2021 ballot initiative.

In between these two extremes are downtown and the more racially diverse neighborhoods of Central Minneapolis. In the heart of the city, right along the Mississippi, sits downtown, policed by the 1st Precinct; this is the city's cultural and artistic hub as well as its business center. Just south of downtown is Lake Street, a connecting throughway from east to west. It is home to many newer city arrivals, especially from Latin America and Africa, including a neighborhood known as "Little Mogadishu" for its high number of Somali immigrants, as well as a housing complex for the city's Native residents. The northeastern corner of the city is composed of a set of post-industrial neighborhoods now dotted by trendy condominiums along the river, policed by the 2nd Precinct. In the south end of this precinct sits the University of Minnesota.

Finally, just east of the massive I-35W highway in South Minneapolis sits the MPD's 3rd Precinct, with a territory stretching from the wealthier and whiter neighborhoods down near Lake Nokomis, into the mixed-income and multiracial neighborhoods around 38th and Chicago, an early site of Black settlement in the city that would later become memorialized as George Floyd Square. It was also where the charter amendment would find its strongest support.

The Politics of Policing

I began this project in 2016, trying to make sense of Black Lives Matter protests and how they might reshape policing in America. At the time, I was finishing a book entitled *Breaking the Pendulum*, in which Philip Goodman, Joshua Page, and I argue that if we want to understand how and why punishment changes over time, we must examine the actors and institutions that made penal history by fighting for change at the local, state, and federal levels.[68] So who, I wondered, was shaping policing—and how did they define the problem(s) facing the institution and their solutions? And what kinds of power did they wield to make change?

The question of who controls the police is surprisingly fraught. One line of thought says that police have increasingly co-opted systems designed to regulate their actions—for example, police unions growing their political influence over mayors and legislatures, ginning up fear of crime to promote the institution as essential, and protecting against outside influence or oversight from the public through the veneer of professionalization.[69] At the same time, during the early BLM protest years in Minneapolis, policing became the crux of mayoral races in the city, with candidates vying to see who was more "on the outs" with the police union and proving to the public that they would be the ones to rein in the police. And activists increasingly turned to city hall for change—demanding action and believing that elected officials could make a difference. Were these elections and campaigns a mirage, or could organizers effectively cajole local (and state, or national) elected officials to represent the interests of their constituents? And how should we understand the demands of "the people" when it comes to policing?

It is this set of people, institutions, and their interactions that I refer to as the *politics of policing*, as diagrammed in figure I.2.[70] And it is through these politics, I argue, that policing does (or does not) change. The politics of policing include the traditional political structure of the mayor and city council, who ostensibly direct and set police budgets, respectively. But it also includes the voters, who decide which campaigns to support and who to elect, how to vote on ballot questions, and whether and how to agitate for change. That means that a key player in these politics are people *outside* of city hall, including activists and social movement organizations who seek to change how we understand police violence and what to do about it. Policing, in other words, is not simply a top-down process of city officials and police leadership imposing their will; it's also bottom-up.

These political contests take place across many venues, including the voting booth as well as letters and calls to council members, direct actions

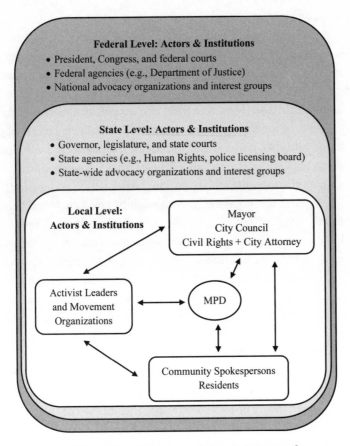

FIGURE I.2. The politics of policing in Minneapolis

like protests, and public debates and community forums. They also splay across the front pages of local papers, sometimes reaching national news outlets.[71] While news media have traditionally deferred to police narratives in shaping stories about violence, one of the goals of the BLMM has been to disrupt this coverage, using communications teams and protest mobilization to shift attention to the problem of *police* violence and spotlighting the concerns of protesters.[72] And, as we'll see throughout the book, residents, activists, the police, and city leaders all took to social media platforms (most prominently Facebook, Twitter, and Instagram) to shape the public narrative on the MPD. Though not all contenders had equal power, resources, or influence, they all played a role in the politics of policing.

Seeing this dynamic contestation over policing requires a local perspective—looking keenly at the history of a single place and institution and all of the policy battles and personality clashes. But local political struggles do not happen in a vacuum; instead, they are shaped by the broader political, social, economic, and cultural context of the city, state, and country. This includes state and federal laws, regulations, and policies—including requirements about police training and oversight, state and federal investigations into officers and departments, and protections for officers' discretionary use of force written into law. These statutes, regulations, and processes both constrain and enable local activists and city leaders in fighting for change. Zooming out further still, the politics of policing also includes the policies and practices, historic and contemporary, that create and maintain racialized patterns of poverty and violence (e.g., education, economic redistribution, health care, and housing).

To understand this dense set of relationships and structures, I couldn't just research a single group, issue, or moment in time. Instead, the research behind *The Minneapolis Reckoning* draws from an emergent case study of the politics of policing in Minneapolis from 2017 to 2023.[73] Readers will hear from the key organizers of Minneapolis's activist coalitions, elected officials, and everyday residents in their own words. While many of the stories in the first half of the book are drawn from interviews I conducted in 2017–2019 with a team of students, the second half of the book traces the political struggle in Minneapolis after George Floyd's murder, drawing primarily on digital observations of public meetings, investigatory reports, media coverage, and more.[74] And, finally, I turned to the historical record to go back in time, tracing how the MPD expanded alongside the city.

Throughout the research process, I was myself a resident of Minneapolis. I entered this racially laden space as a white woman, often asked by organizers, colleagues, and students to explain my own positionality (or the ways *who* I was affected my work). As the study went on, I increasingly became a participant in the struggle to define the problem in Minneapolis, answering reporters' calls after each case of police violence that went viral. In my personal life too, I experienced this cyclical interest in the MPD after each case. Friends, neighbors, and my kids' daycare teachers asked me how to make sense of the violence and what it would take to make it stop. This book is my attempt to answer their questions.

Plan of the Book

The Minneapolis Reckoning tells the story of the politics of policing in Minneapolis in two parts. Part 1, "Minnesota Goddamn,"[75] begins to explain why the state became the site of such wrenching anti-Black state violence and how both local activists and everyday residents made sense of this history. We begin in the past, unraveling the history of Minneapolis and its troubled police department in chapter 1. It is the legacies of residential segregation, the rise of the police officers union, and the failures to ameliorate racial inequalities inside and outside of policing that set the stage for BLM activism. Chapter 2 shows how the city's left-leaning politics fueled a network of grassroots activist groups contesting police violence, which exploded in 2015 following the MPD shooting of Jamar Clark. By 2017 the growing dissatisfaction with the limited gains of early efforts toward police reform would prompt the splintering of groups committed to police defunding and abolition—activists who would take center stage in summer 2020. I then turn to the voices of residents in North Minneapolis, the site of Clark's killing, in chapter 3. Long before George Floyd was murdered and activists nearly ended the MPD, Black residents in North Minneapolis told my team that they felt caught between police violence and community violence, wanting elected officials to do more to address both crises. Meanwhile, although white residents told us they were increasingly concerned about police violence against their Black neighbors, they debated how much really had to change in policing.

This ambivalence would reverberate in public attitudes after the murder of George Floyd, where Part 2, "In the Wake of Rebellion," picks up. Would a new Department of Public Safety make Black lives matter in Minneapolis? As homicides spiked in the city alongside a historic drop in the number of officers on the city's streets, attention turned from police violence to community violence. Chapter 4 shows how an unlikely coalition of white business interests and elites, Black community leaders, and even some BLM activists helped to defeat the ballot initiative to end the MPD, convincing enough voters that protecting Black lives *had* to involve robust police protection. This same political stalemate largely produced failure in local, state, and federal attempts to push forward "Justice for George" beyond the criminal cases against the officers, as I show in chapter 5. However, in the shadow of this perceived failure, a series of new alternatives to the police began to take root in Minneapolis. In chapter 6, I argue that while these new models face many of the same challenges as the police, they hold the potential to loosen the MPD's stranglehold on city politics—opening up more space for radical imagination.

The conclusion of the book meditates on the lessons learned from Minneapolis. Instead of picking one vision of the police in society, I ask what we might learn from taking seriously the police's role as both heroes and murderers. In a world rife with persistent racial segregation, economic inequality, and neighborhoods with high rates of interpersonal violence, the all-too-predictable result is under-protection and over-policing of poor communities of color. So too is the inevitable tug-of-war between public attention paid to police violence and community violence. This dynamic in turn fuels political stagnation, as city leaders inevitably turn away from the task of reform and toward bolstering police power to create "safety," sometimes just months after horrific police violence. The path forward for real and sustainable changes, I came to believe, therefore requires reckoning with violence inside and outside of policing in America.

PART I

Minnesota Goddamn

CHAPTER ONE

The Shame of Minneapolis

BY THE TURN of the twenty-first century, Minneapolis was widely regarded as one of the country's best places to live, with abundant natural resources, strong economic and educational opportunities, vibrant arts and culture scenes, and relatively affordable housing. And yet, these resources have largely benefited its *white* residents, an inequity economist Samuel L. Myers Jr. dubs the "Minnesota Paradox."[1] Indeed, despite boasting high quality-of-life metrics, Minnesota and its largest city have some of the greatest racial disparities in wealth, high school graduation rates, and life expectancy across the nation. The median household income, for example, among Black families in Minneapolis is less than half of white families, with an even larger gap in homeownership.[2]

Policing is no exception. A 2015 ACLU report revealed that Black and Native American people in Minneapolis were more than 8.5 times more likely than whites to be arrested for low-level offenses (the sorts for which police wield the most discretion).[3] Police violence evinces similar disparities. An explosive 2020 *New York Times* analysis published in the wake of George Floyd's murder found that from 2015 to 2020, the city's Black residents, representing just 20 percent of the population, endured nearly 60 percent of use-of-force incidents reported by the Minneapolis Police Department (MPD).[4] The city's Black residents also face much higher risks of being harmed by other community members—evidence of their lack of protection. In 2021 there was one homicide victim for every 150 Black residents in Minneapolis, more than twenty-five times the risk facing white residents.[5] These disparities are arranged by place as much as race, with the worst community and police violence con-centrated in Northside, located north of downtown and west of the

Mississippi River, and the highest quality of life and least police contact in the city's southwest corner around its famous chain of lakes.

To understand how Minneapolis came to be defined by this profound racial and spatial inequality, this chapter looks to the city's past. Along the way, we will see how pivotal moments in the country's history, from the foundational violence of settler-colonialism to the economic crisis of the Great Depression and the urban unrest of the 1960s, shaped one city. As Minneapolis grew, the MPD rapidly expanded from a small-town police force of just six officers to a major metropolitan force numbering in the hundreds. By the 1940s, it would even become a test case for liberal police reform under Hubert Humphrey, then Minneapolis's mayor (and soon to be a pivotal player in the struggle over civil rights in America). But as midcentury Minneapolis diversified, its new migrants were largely blocked out of the wealth-building policies that had so benefited previous generations of white families, building the patterns of inequality that would haunt the city.

Police were cast as the brutal enforcers of this unequal social order, creating an acute point of conflict between the city and communities of color. Successive generations of liberal political leaders following in Humphrey's footsteps would try to balance a seemingly impossible contradiction: how to rein in the MPD's "thumpers" while promising safety in the growing metropolis. In their struggles to reach a compromise, each generation would face its own moment of crisis with the MPD, the perennial "shame of Minneapolis" in the unforgettable words of a muckraker journalist. None of the MPD's twenty-first century challenges, violence, or reforms, in other words, were new. Yet each generation's crisis would leave its mark, redrawing the politics of policing.

The Violent Birth of a City

Home to the start of the mighty Mississippi River, the place we now call Minnesota has always been known for its many waterways. Prior to European colonization, the region was home to a number of Indigenous groups, including, in what would become Minneapolis, the Dakhóta (Dakota), who named the place Bdeóta Othúŋwe ("Many Lakes City"), and the Anishinaabe (Ojibwe), who called it Gakaabikaang ("At the Waterfalls").[6] Military troops entered the future territory in 1819, and by 1825 the US Army had completed building nearby Fort Snelling, attempting to establish dominance in struggles for power between Native groups and British-Canadian traders. In 1849 Minnesota became a territory, joining the "free" North in prohibiting the sale and enslavement of human beings.

Still, some of the families at Fort Snelling brought enslaved Americans to Minnesota (including Dred and Harriet Scott), an early marker of racial oppression and resistance in the state.[7]

In Minneapolis, the early white settlers included mostly Scandinavian immigrants, many who had initially migrated to New England, bringing Northeastern sensibilities to the Midwest. As a magazine would soon declare, Minneapolis was "a Yankee with a small Puritan head, an open prairie heart, and a great, big Scandinavian body."[8] The city was officially incorporated in 1867, just five years after the end of the Dakota War. While massacring the Dakota people, city leaders appropriated their words, merging Mníȟaȟa (waterfall) with the Greek word for city (polis). The MPD was founded the same year under the watch of its first mayor, Dorilus Morrison, an East Coast businessman who came in search of lumber. The town had over five thousand residents, with a police force of just six officers and a chief of police, for a staffing ratio just above 1 officer per 1,000 residents—a rate the city would maintain across the next century.[9]

Politics and policing were deeply intertwined from the start in Minneapolis and across the country. As police historian Robert Fogelson writes: "No institution which had so great an impact on the lives and livelihoods of so many citizens could have been separated from the political process. Nor, so long as the nation was committed to democracy and pluralism, should it have been."[10] In Minneapolis, as in many other cities, the city charter granted the mayor the power to appoint (and fire) the police chief.[11] Until the 2021 election, in fact, the city charter stipulated what was known as a "weak mayor" system in which the MPD was the *only* city department directly controlled by the mayor, with all other departments primarily under the direction of the city council. That meant that the city's police force was only as just as its mayor.

Corruption and Scandal in the Progressive Era

The MPD first rose to national infamy not in 2020, or even 2015, but 1903, under the city's most notoriously corrupt mayor, Albert Alonzo "Doc" Ames. Born in Illinois, Ames moved with his family near Fort Snelling when he was a child, joining a group of homesteaders in the territory. Ames enlisted as an army surgeon during the Dakota War, arriving just before the mass execution of thirty-eight Dakota warriors at Mankato. Leaving the service in 1865, Ames parlayed his war veteran status into political office, joining the Minnesota House of Representatives and later winning the mayoral race in the rapidly urbanizing Minneapolis in 1876.

As Ames shuttled in and out of office (serving 1876–1877, 1882–1884, 1886–1889, and 1901–1902), Minneapolis "with almost miraculous rapidity, developed from a village of a few thousands, to one of the leading cities of the west."[12] As the population boomed, informal social bonds in tight-knit communities were replaced with dislocated populations housed in tight urban quarters, policed by formal law enforcement agents. By 1890 the city numbered over 150,000 residents, patrolled by just under two hundred officers.[13] With each election, Ames seemed to move deeper into municipal graft; in the intervening terms, "reform" opponents would try to undo Ames's work, only to see him returned to power.[14]

In 1901 Ames appointed his brother, Fred W. Ames, as police chief. In addition to firing half the MPD, the Ames brothers installed famous underworld dealers in key positions throughout the force.[15] Using the heft of city hall, the Ames crew led an extortion racket that targeted gambling rooms, prostitution houses, opium dens, and "blind pigs" (unlicensed saloons) in the fledgling city—operations that landed Ames, and the city, on the cover of *McClure's Magazine* under the headline "The Shame of Minneapolis."[16] The exposé finally broke Ames's grip on the city, as the mayor faced criminal charges for corruption.

In the wake of the scandal, reformers again took control of city hall, but the legacy of corruption would linger for decades. This work unfolded in the context of burgeoning Progressive era reformism, a national movement to address social ills through good governance. Led by middle-class whites, including prominent women reformers, the Progressives argued that improved municipal services could solve the problems wrought by rapid urbanization, including crime and political corruption. Their solution was to develop and professionalize city agencies like sanitation, education, public health, housing, and police. Due to their efforts, cities developed more robust infrastructures, supporting the new immigrants from Europe who came across the ocean with little other than hope for a new life. As a result, these new arrivals were transformed into *white* Americans (rather than "Irish" or "Italians"), setting the stage for their children's prosperity.[17]

When it came to police, Progressive reformers sought to distance law enforcement from city leadership, converting these organizations and their workers from a political patronage model to regulated bureaucracies. Hiring would be based on merit and performance—not political favors—and the force would remain largely in place (with the exception of the chief) when a new mayor was elected. Policing would become a profession, with real training, impartial evaluation, and routinized discipline and promotion procedures.[18] As August Vollmer, the so-called father of modern policing, explained in the landmark 1931 Wickersham Report, the problem was that cities "take men of mediocre caliber without training or special ability and charge them with responsibility for solving ... vice, gambling, liquor, and narcotic problems of the most complex variety." The solution, he and other reformers insisted, was to hire men of talent and train them for the "complex" work of managing urban disorder.[19]

This wave of professionalization came alongside technological innovations, too. The first mass-produced automobiles (Ford's Model T) reached consumers in 1908. As an increasing share of the public moved to travel via automobile, officers began to patrol not on foot, but via police cruisers—fundamentally shifting the relationship between police and the public. In addition, managing traffic violations became a core part of police officers' job description, enabling pervasive stops (and searches) of American drivers and their vehicles and expanding the jurisdiction of police across the country.[20] Finally, changes in radio communication technologies allowed officers to work in closer coordination with precinct headquarters, where residents could go for help. Though it was a far cry from Americans' ability today to call 911 at any moment from their cell phone to summon a cruiser, radios paved the way for the start of citizen-directed policing.[21]

From Corruption to Strike-Breaking

The reforms of the Progressive era would coincidentally serve as a bookend to the city's run as an industrial titan. The economy had grown as Minneapolis became the flour-milling capital of the world, with factories lining the powerful Mississippi River churning out fortunes for landholding white settlers. The working poor at the time were still largely white, though a small number of Black residents had by then entered the city (often working, if employed, in the trains now crisscrossing the country), while the Indigenous peoples who survived the diseases and massacres were often pushed outside city limits and into reservations. By the 1920s, Minneapolis had a head start on deindustrialization, driven by the introduction of electric grain mills, which crushed the city's competitive edge.[22] The Great Depression, begun in 1929, thus reflected a doubly lean period in the city's history.

While reducing some forms of overt corruption, Progressive-era reforms had not ended the tight relationship between cities' police departments and their ruling class. Instead of collusion with vice operations, however, this era's police scandal centered on officers' roles in breaking up strikes. As a wave of labor militancy swept the country, law enforcement sided with business owners, working to reestablish the "order" that allowed owners to exploit workers. Minneapolis was no exception, with police and striking workers coming to blows in the 1934 Teamsters strike. In the run-up, union organizers had made inroads in Minneapolis, where their efforts were facilitated by the worsening economic conditions. This turn toward more populist, left-wing organizing was happening at the state level too, with the Farmer–Labor Party gaining strength. By 1934, for the first time in Minnesota, a Farmer–Labor politician was sitting in the governor's seat: Floyd B. Olson. Opposing the labor organizers in Minneapolis was the Citizens Alliance, a group of business elites who had controlled industry in Minneapolis since the turn of the twentieth century and virulently opposed unionization.

In May 1934, the city's bustling downtown streets were blocked by thousands of truck drivers on a week-long strike. By then, the number of MPD officers reached over five hundred, serving a city population of nearly 480,000.[23] This force, however, apparently wasn't enough; the Citizens Alliance mobilized an additional volunteer force of a thousand men (the "citizens' army") to help break the strike by assaulting the truck drivers.[24] The resulting melee left two of the strike-breakers dead, clubbed to death. The Battle of Deputies Run, however, turned out to be merely a prelude. After a brief return to work, in July workers authorized a return of the strike, stopping almost all mass transit of goods in the city. Mayor A. G. Bainbridge made it clear that he stood on the side of the Citizens Alliance, describing the union organizers as communists and "rabid opponents of all law and order."[25] The MPD chief, Michael Johannes, declared his force would break the strike, telling his men: "You have shotguns and you know how to use them."[26] On July 20, police opened fire on a truck of picketers in what became known as "Bloody Friday," leaving two strikers, including a noted union activist, dead and dozens injured. Order in the city would be restored only after a mobilization of the National Guard in Minneapolis by the governor, which would be followed by a historic win for the union, including union recognition and a minimum wage.

Bloody Friday represented a particularly extreme version of the role of police in the city's everyday life, but it highlighted a central challenge with police legitimacy: police take their orders from the elected officials who set policies and make the laws. And that means that police power will often reinforce, rather than challenge, systemic oppression. The police, in other words, might work to establish and maintain "order," but it is an *unequal order*. At the same time, however, it was also political elites

THE SHAME OF MINNEAPOLIS [27]

and the law that workers prevailed upon to ultimately win better protections, leaning on the state officials, including the progressive governor, to renegotiate the terms of their employment. This battle both against and through the law would foreshadow how activists in Minneapolis struggled to challenge the violence of the MPD in the decades to come.

Humphrey's Vision and
the Rise of the Officers Federation

By the close of World War II, Minneapolis was putting the lean years of the Great Depression behind it. American industry rallied, and a new wave of prosperity was building the much-mythologized (white) middle class of the mid-twentieth century. In 1950 Minneapolis hit an all-time population record of nearly 520,000 residents (earning it a spot among the twenty largest cities in the United States), while the MPD stood at 580 officers.[27] The city was still overwhelmingly white, with just 1 percent of the population identifying as Black or African American.[28] Even so, anti-racism and the civil rights movement would play a key role in the city's (and state's) politics, as Minneapolis sought to establish a new reputation as a liberal city.[29]

This period in Minneapolis politics is best remembered for its highest achieving mayor, Hubert Humphrey, who would go on to serve as a US senator and vice president, fighting for the landmark civil rights legislation of the late 1960s. In 1945, however, Humphrey was still a local political player—a new mayor trying to blaze a path in city politics, in part by cleaning house at the MPD. In his biography, Humphrey would reflect, "Minneapolis had been wide open," seized by the illicit industries of prostitution, gambling, and alcohol. As a result, he "made law enforcement the central issue of the campaign."[30] Humphrey's list of policing reforms included rooting out police corruption, improving the conditions for officers (e.g., raising officers' salaries and increasing the force size), and the first wave of police training reforms centered on "race relations."

Previously a professor of political science at a local college (Macalester), Humphrey was more explicitly race-conscious than many other political leaders in this era. At the 1948 Democratic National Convention, in fact, Humphrey's speech would decisively turn the party toward civil rights, building the modern democratic coalition (and pulling Humphrey away from Minneapolis).[31] Accordingly, as mayor, Humphrey understood racism (and anti-Semitism) as key challenges in Minneapolis, including for the MPD. Yet like most of his white contemporaries, Humphrey understood racism in policing not primarily as a structural problem, but one of individual bigotry. Through his handpicked chiefs, Humphrey sought to address the "minority problem" through educational efforts designed to root out explicit racism. In 1946, for example, the MPD was among the first departments to require officer training on the topic of "impartial" policing. In addition, the initiative (like many that would follow) attempted to connect police leadership and the rank-and-file with Black religious and civic leaders, who could serve as go-betweens for the police and the community to bolster the department's legitimacy.[32]

Mild as they now seem, the Humphrey-era reforms would also precipitate the first of many waves of officer resistance, empowering the Police Officers Federation of Minneapolis. While the federation was founded in 1917 (and would not gain union bargaining rights until the early 1970s), it took on a new role in *policing politics* during Humphrey's mayoral tenure. As historian Michael Lansing narrates, the federation came to see city leaders as threatening its officers' interests, and, in response, they moved into politics, campaigning for and against the mayoral and city council hopefuls who would set MPD policies and officers' wages.[33]

They also began lobbying for more positions. Arguing that the MPD was continually understaffed, given both population size and crime rates, in the mid-1950s the federation campaigned to write into the city charter a guaranteed minimum per capita number of officers that would put their staffing ratio more in line with peer cities.[34] By 1955 the city's police force numbered almost six hundred sworn officers, patrolling a city of just over 500,000 residents (representing the same 1.2 officers per 1,000 ratio of the city's earliest days). But in 1961 the federation would win via a ballot measure, enshrining in the city charter a *guaranteed minimum* of 1.7 police officers for every 1,000 city residents. The victory boosted a hiring wave, and though Minneapolis's population was already in decline by that point, the MPD continued to grow throughout the 1960s. The 1961 charter provision would also become the crux of the debate, sixty years later, about ending the MPD.

North Minneapolis Is Burning

By the time of the charter win, Minneapolis had experienced its first sizable influx of Black newcomers, part of the last wave of the Great Migration that brought Southerners north. From 1950 to 1970 the city's African American population increased fourfold.[35] These new residents found a city hostile to racial integration, blanketed by restrictive racial covenants on property deeds.[36] Together with redlining and federal home loan programs, these covenants enabled white families to build wealth through homeownership.[37] The state-sponsored white wealth-building was further aided by the Federal Aid Highway Act of 1956, which provided funding to construct massive highways through the city, connecting downtown to the booming suburbs, while tearing down thousands of homes in predominantly Black communities in the Twin Cities of Minneapolis and St. Paul.[38]

Often arriving via Midwestern gateway cities like Chicago, many of the Black migrants would come to settle in a set of neighborhoods in the northwestern corner of the city, known as North Minneapolis or "Northside." Far from the famous chain of lakes dotting the south side of the city, Northside was by then an established refuge for newcomers. Starting in the 1880s, a large Jewish population had established a socially and economically thriving community there in response to pervasive anti-Semitism and housing discrimination in other parts of the city. It was this predominantly Jewish neighborhood that many of the new Black migrants would move to, trying to escape the anti-Black racism pervasive in Minneapolis. A smaller cluster of Black migrants would also move to a set of blocks in South Minneapolis near what would, much later, become George Floyd Square. While these destinations provided a chance at a new life for Black Minnesotans, they were spatially and socially isolated from the rest of the city, locking them out of many opportunities.[39]

This toxic combination of racism and exclusion produced high exposure to victimization, including from the police. Throughout the 1950s and 1960s (and even earlier), instances of unjustified arrests and police violence against Black residents periodically made local headlines. The MPD's own statistics bore out systemic racial disparities, with Black residents substantially overrepresented in arrest statistics—inequities that would persist in the decades to follow.[40] Black residents were not the only minority group in the city to face the wrath of the police, however. Most notably, in this period, the MPD was infamously brutal toward the Native residents of South Minneapolis, who had come to the city in increasing numbers after serving in World War II.[41] Their shared exposure to violence would spark enduring connections between the Black and Native communities in Minneapolis, including in resistance tactics.

The simmering resentment produced by these inequalities came to a boil in May 1963, when police pulled over Raymond Wells, a former boxing champ and local legend. Running hot because of an incident earlier in the evening where another resident had shot and injured an officer, the police instigated a beating that left Wells severely injured and prompted a raucous melee between the crowd and MPD officers. In a precursor to later reports, the Minneapolis chapter of the NAACP responded by issuing a press release, declaring: "many policemen in Minneapolis treat Negroes and members of other minority groups as second-class citizens." Left unresolved, they warned, "tensions will continue to mount and someday the city of Minneapolis will reap the consequences."[42]

By 1963 the mayor was Arthur Naftalin, another political-scientist-turned-candidate and close collaborator of Humphrey's. The city's first Jewish mayor, Naftalin was elected as a liberal Democrat in 1961, the same year the officers federation won its charter amendment requiring a mandatory minimum number of officers. Like Humphrey, Mayor Naftalin attempted to both appease and reform the police force, and he shared similar blind spots when it came to the persistence of *structural* inequities in policing. After the Wells beating, for example, Naftalin suspended the officer, but released a statement that refused to critique the department more broadly. As the city's paper of record summarized in the headline: "Mayor Denies Any Serious Race Bias among Policemen."[43]

Not surprisingly, then, Naftalin's police reform efforts largely floundered. In 1963, for example, the city briefly attempted to establish a police review board for citizen oversight and accountability. The group folded almost immediately, however, when its members were advised that they could be sued for defamation.[44] The officers federation, in fact, made inroads instead. In an attempt to placate the group, Mayor Naftalin stopped enforcing the requirement that officers live in Minneapolis, formally ending the rule several years later. This allowed officers to join many of the city's white residents in fleeing the urban core for new suburbs. (In the decades that followed, citizens would continually call for reinstating the residency requirement, believing that if officers had to live in Minneapolis, perhaps they would treat its residents better.) By 1965 the Minnesota Advisory Committee to the United States Commission on Civil Rights issued the first (of several) reports on policing in the Twin Cities, arguing that "no antidote is provided to dispel the lack of confidence with which minority groups regard the police departments of Minneapolis and St. Paul that leads to hostility and provokes tensions on both sides which, in many instances, could be avoided."[45]

In 1967 racial justice activists' warnings proved prescient as the "Long Hot Summer" engulfed more than 150 American cities in riots.[46] In Minneapolis, the unrest was sparked on July 19, after the city's annual Aquatennial Parade (which celebrates its famed waterways). Tensions in the area were already high. By then, many of the Jewish families who could afford to do so had moved out of Northside, but they still owned and operated

FIGURE 1.1. Police in North Minneapolis, July 1967
Source: Mike Zerby, *Minneapolis Star Tribune,* courtesy of Minnesota
Historical Society.

businesses in the area, and there'd been an eruption of tension after an
altercation earlier in the summer. Accounts vary, but local activists told
reporters at the time that the incident began with a physical struggle
between police and a Black teenage girl at the celebration.[47] In response,
unrest erupted along Plymouth Avenue, as a crowd of outraged young
Black residents vandalized, looted, and torched local businesses, with some
chanting "Black Power!" As in other cities across the country, some of the
protesters squared off against firefighters and police, throwing rocks and
issuing provocations. In response, the MPD flooded Northside with hel-
meted officers, armed with nightsticks and shotguns, as shown in figure 1.1.

Mayor Naftalin, in consultation with Black community leaders,
stopped the MPD from conducting mass arrests on Plymouth Avenue,
preventing an escalation of violence. But the price of that restraint was
the arrival of hundreds of Minnesota National Guardsmen, called in to
restore order.[48] Community organizers stepped in as well, organizing a
public dance in Northside the same night the guardsmen arrived to diffuse tensions. Unlike the dozens of lives lost in Newark and Detroit, there
were no deaths in Minneapolis's unrest, and the scale of the property damage remained relatively isolated. The fires, however, poignantly marked
the end of Jewish-Black integration in Northside. And like the torching

of the MPD's 3rd Precinct that would follow, the Plymouth Avenue unrest would mark a moment of racial reckoning for the city.

The Lessons of Rebellion

The unrest of the summer of 1967 precipitated a national legitimacy crisis, spurring then-president Lyndon Johnson to convene a national commission on policing. Colloquially referred to as the Kerner Commission after its chair, former Illinois governor Otto Kerner Jr., the commission's members traveled to the cities that had burned, interviewing Black Americans to ask *why*. Shocking contemporary observers for its boldness, the Kerner Report concluded that the core of the problem was not the actions of "rioters," but instead what would come to be understood as structural racism:

> Violence and destruction must be ended—in the streets of the ghetto and in the lives of people.
>
> Segregation and poverty have created in the racial ghetto a destructive environment totally unknown to most white Americans.
>
> What white Americans have never fully understood—but what the Negro can never forget—is that white society is deeply implicated in the ghetto. White institutions created it, white institutions maintain it, and white society condones it.[49]

Put simply, "white racism" was ultimately responsible for the unrest throughout the nation.

The "choice," as framed by the report's writers, was whether to invest substantial federal time, effort, and money to remedy *structural* racial inequities. If no action was taken, they explained, the country would fracture into "two societies—one white, one black—separate and unequal."[50] At the same time, the Kerner Report continued, jurisdictions should work to improve the quality of policing through continued reform efforts. Suggesting the perennial favorites, the authors called for improving police-community relations, raising hiring standards, working to diversify the force, and building stronger training and accountability systems.[51]

The report became a best-seller, articulating the divide in American society just before Martin Luther King Jr. was assassinated, prompting another wave of unrest. Racial injustice, as historian Elizabeth Hinton argues in her book *America on Fire*, was a crisis, and what was called "riots" were instead *rebellion*, a political demand from the oppressed.[52] The lesson should have been that healing required massive federal intervention to alleviate poverty, suffering, and discrimination. Without it, America would continue to burn. Despite commissioning the report, however, President Johnson balked at the conclusions. From his perspective, the administration had already invested as much as it could into "root cause" approaches like the War on Poverty, to the detriment of Democrats' electoral chances. Republicans countered that these policies had failed and even backfired, emboldening the "criminal element." What the country needed instead was a return to "law and order," a racially coded dog whistle that linked Black protest with criminality. The quiet part of their message was that the civil rights movement had made America worse—what was needed was not just "order," but the return of the Jim Crow racial order.

Violence in cities, as measured by homicide rates, was in fact on the rise, helping to fuel alignment with Republican messaging. This growth in murder rates over the 1960s reflected, in part, the predictable consequences of trends in migration and the economy. A wave of Black migrants had arrived at Midwestern Rust Belt cities and Northeastern manufacturing powerhouses just as those employment opportunities bottomed out, with the predominantly white workforce zealously shutting out the new entrants. These employment barriers, together with pervasive housing discrimination, produced spatially segregated "ghettos" of concentrated disadvantage.[53] And it is these conditions of spatial isolation, social marginalization, and deep poverty that foster high rates of violence in *all* communities.[54] But as crime emerged as a national concern, commentators used the statistics not to highlight these social forces, but to further racist logics that ascribed the violence to biological differences between races.[55]

In the same year the Kerner Report was published, voters would choose presidential candidate Richard Nixon over Minnesota's own Hubert Humphrey. In terms of the popular vote, the race was close (though Nixon won in a landslide in the electoral contest). And while many may have voted for reasons separate from the urban rebellions (especially the contested war in Vietnam), Nixon's win cemented the symbolic power of "law and order" campaigns for the decades to come and began the turn of white Americans in the South toward the Republican Party. At the state and federal levels, Republicans largely won this ideological contest too, ushering in a starkly more punitive period of policy-making in the 1970s and onward. This rightward political shift meant that cities would *not* be getting that influx of federal dollars to address the crisis—and in fact would need to do more with less. The crises that were producing these separate and unequal societies would have to be solved using local tax coffers, a dwindling resource as white flight escalated. Lacking the political will or institutional structures to pursue redistributive policy on a mass scale, states and cities were instead left to fight violence on the cheap.

As scholars John Clegg and Adaner Usmani write, this meant that cities often turned to policing—one of the few resources under local control. Thus, the origins of our contemporary arrangements may be less about *over-investment* in policing and punishment than *under-investment* in redistributive policies.[56] The crises produced by that under-investment would continually prompt punitive responses, justifying more policing and punishment in a self-reinforcing cycle. In short, what followed the Long Hot Summer was a revolution in city, state, and federal policies and practices that made police contact, arrest, and imprisonment routine life experiences for much of Black America.[57] This expansion of the carceral state also, for a time, suppressed the dissent and revolutionary protest on display in urban communities in the 1960s—protests that would flare back with a vengeance in the 2010s.[58]

How a Cop Becomes Mayor

The cities that burned in 1967 got a front-row seat to this national drama. Even liberal Minneapolis would experience at least a decade of conservative local politics. Mayor Naftalin had attempted to thread the needle, supporting the police while also restraining their actions in the heat of unrest, a choice that produced substantial white resistance. Trying then to regain the narrative upper hand, he switched tacks, reinforcing white residents' understandings and declaring it "preposterous" that the riot was about police brutality—no, the mayor insisted, it had been the fault of "roving gangs of Black youth." An all-white Hennepin County grand jury similarly concluded in its "Minneapolis Riots" report that there had been "No Police Brutality" on Plymouth Avenue. Echoing the calls of some Black community leaders, the jury recommended that to "re-establish the rapport between the people and the authorities," the city should increase the size of the police force and deploy *more* street patrols in Northside.[59] Despite these concessions, however, the beleaguered Naftalin declined to run for reelection.

Meanwhile, as in cities across the country, MPD officers and their associations fought vigorously against calls for change.[60] In 1969, with the mayoral race open, the police federation in Minneapolis entered politics in an unprecedented way: the federation's president, Charles "Charlie" A. Stenvig, ran for office. Stenvig used the Plymouth Ave. riot as a wedge to garner the votes of white Minneapolis citizens, depicting the unrest as a product of devious "Black militants" who could only be restrained by an overwhelming display of force.[61] Paralleling Nixon's landmark presidential campaign, Stenvig's "law and order" campaign promised to "take the handcuffs off the police" and target "racial militants," criminals, and student protesters.[62] Yet instead of aligning with the Republican Party, Stenvig ran as an Independent, relying on the rank-and-file of the union to power his campaign. His strategy worked, winning him 62 percent of the vote.

Mayor Stenvig soon ran again for reelection, beating out civil rights icon W. Harry Davis, the city's first Black mayoral candidate, in 1971 with a whopping 71 percent of the vote—just months after local media printed a photo of two MPD officers dragging a young Black boy, Randy Samples, across the pavement by his ankles.[63] His parents' complaint against the police was ignored, a result in part of Stenvig weakening requirements that officers cooperate with civil rights hearings.[64] Pushed out of office in 1973 by Democrat Albert Hofstede, Stenvig reclaimed the mayor's office in 1976–1977 (losing again to Hofstede). The ambivalence of voters in these elections, as they parried between Stenvig and Hofstede, represented the last decade in which the city would be helmed by someone outside the Democratic–Farmer–Labor Party coalition built by Humphrey.

In addition to ushering in a temporary rightward shift in Minneapolis politics, however, the unrest of 1967 prompted a significant, if short-lived, attempt by both radicals and mainstream liberals to reorient the city toward racial justice. Black activists and Native leaders associated with the emergent American Indian Movement (AIM), for example, both developed community patrols, an ambitious effort to intervene between "potential law-breakers and law-enforcers."[65] And they attempted to spotlight the "war" police waged against the city's Black and Native residents. Northside leaders also called for reinvigorated efforts to address racism in the city more broadly, including addressing hiring and employment discrimination.[66] Activists would fight, too, for The Way, a Northside community center for Black Minneapolis youth that nurtured musical talents, including one Prince Rogers Nelson.[67]

These pathbreaking efforts, however, would largely fizzle out without changing the racism baked into city politics, facing political opposition and fading public interest in the 1970s.[68] After The Way shuttered its doors, in fact, its lot was repurposed as the site of a new MPD precinct building in North Minneapolis. Still, these alternative models of safety, and activists' efforts to challenge racism in the city, would be rediscovered in 2020 after the next fire in Minneapolis forced the city to again reckon with its legacy of violence.

Becoming Murderapolis

The 1970s also marked the end of Minneapolis's history as a growing, nearly all-white metropolis. As visualized in figure 1.2, the city's population decline corresponded with increasingly diverse newcomers. This time, it was not just Black migrants from the South, but immigrants from across the globe, including countries in Africa, Asia, and Latin America. The growing racial diversity of the city (and, as we'll see later, its police force), however, did not end its stark inequality.

The 1979 election of Mayor Donald Fraser represented the start of a four-decade (and running) period of Democratic control of Minneapolis. Fraser, a World War II veteran and graduate of the University of Minnesota Law School, was a champion on the left who served in the US House of Representatives (in what would become Ilhan Omar's seat) from 1963 to 1979. He left Congress for city hall, holding power continuously from 1980 to 1994. Like his liberal predecessors, Fraser promised to make the city safer *and* reform the MPD. In his bid to remake the police, Fraser brought in outside talent, appointing Anthony "Tony" Bouza, former assistant chief of the New York Police Department, to helm the troubled department. Bouza's professionalization campaign, however, looked a lot like earlier waves of reform, working to diversify the force, implement new policies and practices around use of force, and bolster oversight over officers' misconduct.

As Bouza later recounted, the department he inherited in 1980 was "damn brutal, a bunch of thumpers" who wanted to be "free to 'handle' assholes."[69] And though Bouza boasted that he did *not* allow his officers to "handle" assholes, when he left office there was little evidence that things had changed. According to historian Will Cooley, this failure reflected inherently contradictory demands:

> The chief was blamed both for not reining in the "thumpers" and for not doing enough to crack down on the city's expanding drug trade. Residents resented sluggish police response times and the MPD's inability to stop open-air drug dealing. Many African Americans felt they were getting "the cold shoulder" from the police department, a black city council member complained. He demanded that "every means possible" be used to eradicate these illegal activities.
>
> Fraser and Bouza were skeptical about street-level narcotics enforcement, but their hesitations were overwhelmed by citizen demands to "do something." The city's response unleashed the

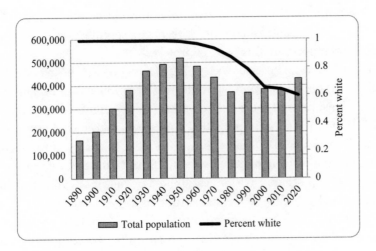

FIGURE 1.2. Minneapolis population and racial composition, 1890–2020
Source: US Census Bureau, Decennial Census of Population and Housing.

"thumpers" in militarized drug raids. After blowing open doors, cops screamed, "Police! Get your fucking asses down, down, you fuckers! Get the fuck down now! I want to see your hands behind your back, now, now, now!" After securing the inhabitants, the hunt for the spoils was on: freezers and food canisters emptied, garbage bags ripped open, furniture destroyed. An estimated 90 percent of the raids targeted African Americans, and officers poured salt into racial wounds, turning radios from rap to country stations and taunting suspects.[70]

These trends weren't just happening in Minneapolis: across the country, police were launching a newly energized War on Drugs to "crack down" on drugs and violence. And since it was a "war," the police increasingly got access to military-grade weapons, vehicles, and other equipment, often donated from the federal government.[71]

By 1989, under a new chief (John Laux), Minneapolis saw the strange fruit of this "war." It began when a police informant identified the Northside home of an elderly Black couple, Lloyd Smalley and Lillian Weiss, which they shared with others, as a drug den. The MPD sent a Special Weapons and Tactics (SWAT) team to the Smalley-Weiss home, which threw in a flashbang grenade, inadvertently sparking a fire. Police claimed they were informed that no one was in the residence, so they abandoned the blaze without a rescue attempt, leaving the couple to die from smoke inhalation.

Black activists in Northside were outraged. And the following year, an MPD officer shot and killed a Black teenager, seventeen-year-old Tycel Nelson, prompting another wave of protest.

This time, the MPD chief was willing to admit racism, telling reporters that "the whole society to different degrees has problems of racism." The answer, however, was more police reform: officers needed "more education."[72] The incident also propelled another push to introduce civilian oversight over the MPD. In 1988, at the end of Bouza's tenure, *not one* of the eighty-one complaints of excessive force against officers reviewed by the Internal Affairs Division was upheld by the city,[73] while the chief lamented publicly that he was hamstrung by union protections in firing "demonstrably unfit" or "even criminal" officers.[74] In January 1990 the Minneapolis City Council voted to establish the Minneapolis Civilian Police Review Authority (CRA).[75] Like the police review boards that preceded and followed, however, the new CRA walked a troubled path, tasked with "oversight" of the department's officers, yet given little power. And the review board rarely found evidence of wrongdoing by officers. Six years later, for example, only 10 percent of the 129 complaints against officers (nearly half of which were accusations of excessive force) were deemed of sufficient merit to have a hearing.[76]

By the time the CRA was written into law, the city's population had dropped to 368,000 residents, while the number of MPD uniformed officers climbed to over eight hundred (or 2.2 per 1,000 residents), as displayed in figure 1.3. Those officers were more diverse across race and gender than ever before, though 82 percent of sworn officers remained white men (just 11 percent of officers were women and 3 percent identified as non-Hispanic Black).[77] As Gleason Glover, then president of the Minneapolis Urban League, would tell investigators: "At best, they are moving too slowly to make a significant impact during a period of time when the police need positive representation in the minority communities . . . if they are going to try and overcome the negative image and distrust."[78]

Just three years after the Smalley-Weiss raid, police-community tensions spiked again. This time, the victim was a police officer. In 1992 Jerome "Jerry" Haaf, a white veteran of the MPD, was shot in the back during a morning coffee break. Haaf's "execution," as it was described at the time, came on the heels of the Los Angeles riots following the acquittal of the police officers who beat motorist Rodney King. It also came at a time of increased tension about police violence in North Minneapolis. Four young Black men, all associated with the Vice Lords gang, would eventually be prosecuted for the murder, which produced waves of panic

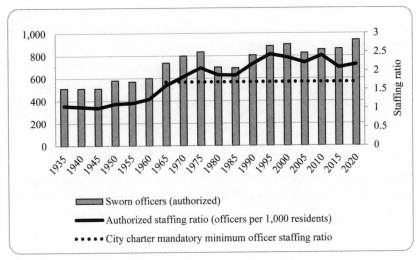

FIGURE 1.3. MPD sworn force size (authorized) and staffing ratio, 1935–2020
Sources: For 1935–1985, MPD staffing totals are compiled from Fossum, *History of Minneapolis Police*, 13. For 1990–2020, data are compiled from the Bureau of Justice Statistics, Law Enforcement Management and Administrative Statistics (LEMAS) series (1990, 1993, 1997, 2000, 2003, 2007, 2013, 2016, and 2020), https://www.icpsr.umich.edu/web/NACJD/series/92.
Notes: The authorized force is the number of full-time sworn officers the department is authorized to hire. Before 2020 the authorized force was usually equivalent to or slightly higher than the number on payroll. To estimate the rate for every five-year marker on off-years, I used the midpoint of surrounding years or the previous/following year, depending on which was closer. The estimate for 2020 represents the authorized force as of December 2019.

about the threat of gang violence and interrupted what in Minneapolis (as in L.A.) had been fledgling working relationships between youth intervention groups and gang-involved teens and adults working to staunch the bloodshed.[79]

Haaf's murder also served as a particularly grim marker of the city's newfound reputation as "Murderapolis."[80] In the six years between 1989 and 1995, the number of annual homicides recorded by the MPD nearly doubled, rising from forty-six to ninety-six (a peak rate of 26 homicides per 100,000 residents, which put Minneapolis on par with notoriously violent cities at a time when the national murder rate stood at 8 homicides per 100,000).[81] In the press, this spike in violence was often linked to the drug trade, producing more calls from residents to "crack down." The MPD again answered, rolling out the paramilitary drug squads, increasing "jump outs" on the streets (in which officers jump out of unmarked cars to swarm and search groups of young men), using confidential informants and undercover officers, and raiding supposed drug houses. Not surprisingly, the MPD staffing ratio surged during this decade, reaching a peak of 2.4 officers per 1,000 in 1997.[82] Seemingly unmoved by the lessons of the deaths of Smalley and Weiss, the MPD's SWAT team was by then conducting hundreds of drug raids every year.[83]

Policing in the Twenty-First Century

In 1994 Fraser handed the keys to the city over to Sharon Sayles Belton, a former city council member and the first—and so far only—Black mayor (and first woman). She entered office at the peak of the Murderapolis years, facing an uphill battle in governing the city. In 2001 she would lose the mayoral seat in a landslide to R. T. Rybak, a white man and former journalist who had gone on to run former MPD chief Bouza's failed bid for governor in 1994. Rybak would remain in office more than a decade, leaving in 2013 right before the start of the BLM protests.

Despite their differences, Rybak and Sayles Belton were aligned in wanting to fuel downtown development in the city in a bid to reverse the city's population drop. Building on earlier transformations, which demolished skid row with its seedy hotels, bookstores, strip clubs, and sex workers,[84] the mayors revived the city's population and economic fortunes by investing in downtown development. Fueling gentrification and new luxury buildings, however, these gains came at the cost of precipitating an affordable housing crisis and growing gulfs between the haves and have-nots. It also implicated the MPD, as the city turned to the police to manage public space in newly developed and gentrifying corridors.[85] As in previous generations, the new mayors' political fortunes were tied to the police chiefs they installed, as the city's Democratic leaders promised residents they would bring more safety and justice to the city.

Throughout these administrations, periodic police scandals rocked the city, prompting cycles of outrage and reform. Perhaps the most notable of these was a 2003 mediation agreement brokered by the Justice Department between the MPD and a group called the Unity Community Mediation Team. The agreement emerged after a series of cases involving police violence and community protest, including unrest in North Minneapolis after police shot and wounded a young boy during a drug raid in 2002. The agreement installed a thirty-member Police Community Relations Council to negotiate between police and the (Black) community, including community activist Spike Moss, one of the organizers behind The Way; Medaria Arradondo, who would go on to serve as the department's first Black chief; and John Delmonico, then head of the officers union. The agreement stipulated that the MPD implement new training on racially biased policing, use of force, and mental health issues; expand access to and use of "non-lethal" weapons; and increase the racial and gender diversity of the force. Echoing the failures of reform to come, however, the group was beset by infighting and routinely ignored by city and MPD officials, dissolving once the agreement expired despite persistent calls from some quarters to reinstate the council.[86]

Though individual cases of lethal police violence continued to be brushed off as isolated incidents, evidence was mounting that pervasive racial discrimination persisted in the MPD. Perhaps surprisingly, it was officers who most convincingly made the case. In 2007 the MPD was sued by a group of Black officers (the "Mill City 5," including later chief Arradondo) who argued that the department systematically discriminated with respect to discipline, pay, and promotion decisions in favor of white officers. One of the department brass named in the lawsuit was Lieutenant Robert "Bob" Kroll, who would later succeed Delmonico to become the president of the police federation, and who that year called US Congressman Keith Ellison (the first Muslim in Congress) a "terrorist." The city and officers initially reached a substantial settlement ($2 million in damages), and the city was required to start a unit on discrimination within the department, though these wins were scaled back in the year it took the city council to negotiate a final agreement.[87]

The special "vice" squad and militarized operations that expanded during the 1990s also came under scrutiny by the 2000s. For example, the Metro Gang Strike Force, a special cross-jurisdictional unit (including the MPD) organized to suppress gang activity, was shut down in 2009 after a series of scandals. The Strike Force was responsible for a massive number of stop-and-frisk searches, asset seizures, and allegations of unjustified police violence that disproportionately burdened Black and Brown boys and men. One of its members would also be responsible for the 2006 police shooting of nineteen-year-old Fong Lee, a Hmong American teen whose killing sparked local protests. Adding insult, officers were stealing (and sometimes selling) the property they confiscated. Though no criminal convictions followed against the officers, a class-action lawsuit by the victims eventually garnered nearly $1 million in payouts to those harmed by the Strike Force's "brutal, rogue" officers, the start of what would become an increasing number of settlements to victims.[88]

Hauntingly, this period also included a killing that, had its lessons been learned, might have prevented George Floyd's murder. In 2010 MPD officers killed David Smith, a twenty-eight-year-old Black man who died in a "prone restraint" position under the knee of an officer. The encounter began when officers were called to a downtown YMCA. Smith, who had long struggled with a cluster of challenges, including homelessness, substance dependence, and untreated mental illness, was in the throes of a mental health crisis that prompted an altercation with other gym visitors. Staff called 911. Video footage shows that the two officers, both appearing to be white men, encountered Smith on a basketball court and tased him repeatedly as Smith fought back, at one point punching one of the officers.[89] After tackling and handcuffing him, an officer pressed his knee into Smith's back for more than four minutes. Once they realized Smith was unconscious and had no pulse, officers initiated CPR as an ambulance was routed to the location. But the damage was already done; Smith died a week later in the hospital, never having regained consciousness.

Despite his family's heartbreak, this police killing provoked relatively little public outrage compared to the unrest that would explode in 2020. The medical examiner ruled the death a homicide caused by cardiac arrest with mechanical asphyxia as a major contributing factor, yet an internal force review panel (which included Janeé Harteau, who would soon become the MPD's chief) cleared the officers and blamed Smith for noncompliance, and a grand jury declined to indict the officers on criminal charges. Smith's family won a $3 million wrongful-death settlement, however, and the city committed to training officers on the dangers of positional asphyxiation.[90] And once again, the city overhauled its civilian oversight systems to little effect. What had previously been the Civilian Police Review Authority (CRA) would by 2012 become the Office of Police Conduct Review (OPCR), which would involve officers heavily in the misconduct review process.

One thing, at least, had changed. By the mid-2010s Minneapolis was no longer "Murderapolis," experiencing the great crime decline enjoyed by much of the country. In the City of Lakes, the overall number of homicides reported by the MPD now hovered around forty per year (or 10 per 100,000 residents), much lower than in years prior, though still disproportionately burdening poor communities of color.[91] By 2016 the police staffing ratio stood at 2.0, substantially above the mandatory minimum of 1.7 enshrined in the city charter but lower than the peak staffing rates of the 1990s. Those officers were more diverse than ever—white men now just 65 percent of the force, while 14 percent were female and nearly 9 percent identified as non-Hispanic Black.[92] It should have been clear, however, that the MPD was still struggling to root out the "thumpers"— and the culture, policies, and structures that enabled them.

The Long Shadow of Police Violence

Just before BLM protests would erupt in Ferguson and across the country, Mayor Betsy Hodges took office in Minneapolis. Hodges, a white Minnesotan who had earned her master's degree in sociology, previously served in several public-facing roles at city nonprofits and on the city council representing Ward 13 in the wealthy Southwest. Unlike the mayoral campaigns that would follow, Hodges's first election bid did not center on police misconduct. Once in office, Hodges retained the MPD chief selected by Rybak: Janeé Harteau, the first woman chief, first LGBT+ chief, and first chief of Native descent at the Minneapolis Police Department.

Like many of the men who preceded her, Harteau swept into office committed to changing the department's culture. Her signature reform was the "MPD 2.0" initiative, an attempted overhaul of the department's policies and practices to create more transparency and accountability. She would also continue attempts to reform disciplinary processes and models for community engagement.[93] But Harteau would run up against the limits of police reform that had blocked the efforts of her predecessors, including her own blinders about the scale of change needed, opposition from residents demanding the department *do something* about crime, and the resistance of the police federation. Harteau had only been in the position for a year before the May 2013 killing of Terrance "Mookie" Franklin, a twenty-two-year-old Black man who fled a traffic stop in South Minneapolis when officers tried to question him about a recent burglary and who was later shot by officers.[94] The chief's tenure would be book-ended on the other side by the 2017 killing of Justine Damond.

Thus, the shame of Minneapolis—its police force—would continue to haunt the city. The early 1900s concerns about mayoral racketeering and the 1930s strike-breaking had receded, but the department still operated under a haze of mistrust among the most marginalized members of the public. By the mid-2010s the spotlight would be brightly shone on the injustice of police violence (against Black men in particular) and on the city leadership's seeming inability to solve the crisis. Liberal city mayors and their police chiefs had fought to rein in the "thumpers" for generations as the city grew, implementing reforms that failed to hold police accountable while expanding the size and power of the department. Report after report came to the same conclusion: the Minneapolis Police Department was rife with racist, sexist, and homophobic officers who too often escalated violence when they responded to calls for help from residents.

In a *New York Times* op-ed penned after George Floyd's murder, Hodges would declare that this state of affairs persisted because white liberals blocked the kinds of large-scale structural changes in housing, education, and other arenas that would truly redress racial inequality. She knew, she wrote, because she had seen these same liberals fight tooth-and-nail against change. The police, she argued, knew this truth too:

> Whatever else you want to say about police officers, they know—whether they articulate it neatly or not—that we are asking them to step into a breach left by our bad policies. The creation of more-just systems won't guarantee the prevention of atrocities. But the status quo in cities, created by white liberals, invites brutal policing.[95]

The police, and police violence, Hodges understood, were as much a symptom as a cause of systemic inequities. But, as we've seen in this chapter, it was not simply liberals in the city who were to blame. Generations of leaders at the local, state, and federal levels had failed to address the problem, and the country's most vulnerable neighborhoods would continue to pay the price.

CHAPTER TWO

How Minneapolis Activists Fought to Make Black Lives Matter

A LITTLE AFTER midnight on November 15, 2015, the Minneapolis Police Department (MPD) was called to an altercation between a man, an ambulance crew, and an injured woman, RayAnn Hayes, in North Minneapolis. In the initial 911 call, Hayes told a dispatcher that she had sprained her ankle at a party after a man had slammed her to the ground. Paramedics responded. When they moved Hayes into the ambulance, however, Jamar Clark, a twenty-four-year-old Black man, attempted to get in, too, pounding on the ambulance doors. But Hayes had identified him as the man who had injured her. Unable to operate the ambulance without opening the back door, the EMT radioed for police help. MPD officers Mark Ringgenberg and Dustin Schwarze responded to the call; just one minute after their arrival, Ringgenberg had pinned Clark to the ground and Schwarze had fired his pistol, point blank, into Clark's head. Later, officers claimed that Clark had been resisting arrest, attempting to take Ringgenberg's gun. More surprisingly, they reported Clark had announced: "I'm ready to die." Among two dozen witnesses in the community, none could confirm Clark's uttered death wish (though they were farther back than the officers). Troublingly, some also believed they saw Clark handcuffed at the time he was shot. Clark died of his injuries the next day.[1]

Black Lives Matter protests emerged overnight, with activists coordinating a demonstration outside of the 4th Precinct station.[2] Those demonstrations grew into an occupation, ultimately blocking the building's entrance for eighteen days. Demonstrators also shut down a nearby freeway (leading to dozens of arrests) and marched to city hall. Protesters demanded the immediate release of the officers' dashcam footage and thorough investigations of the officers' conduct. The Minnesota Bureau of Criminal Apprehension began its work, and the Department of Justice opened a civil rights investigation. Four months later, Hennepin County Attorney Michael Freeman announced that no charges would be pursued against the officers. The federal investigation closed with the same result.[3]

The protests that erupted around Clark's death were a pivotal turning point in Black Lives Matter (BLM) activism in Minneapolis and the larger Twin Cities area. The response followed a playbook developed across the country in the initial years of demonstrations: protesters gathered, demanding the release of information and accountability, and authorities reviewed the evidence for misconduct and/or criminal offenses. The same happened in 2018, when two white MPD officers shot and killed Thurman Blevins Jr., a Black man sitting on a curb alongside a woman and a child in a stroller. Callers to 911 had reported a man shooting a gun in the air, so dispatchers sent a squad car over. Spotting a man on the curb with a gun in his pocket, officers jumped out, guns drawn, initiating a chase through the streets while shouting at Blevins: "I will fucking shoot you!" When he appeared to raise his gun toward officers in an alley, they followed through on the threat. And it would happen again later that same year, when MPD officers killed Travis Jordan, a multiracial Black and Asian American man, whose girlfriend had called 911 fearing Jordan might be suicidal. When police arrived, Jordan emerged from his home wielding a knife, advancing toward the officers until they shot him. Once again, city leadership said they were "listening" and held hearings while the state law enforcement investigated. Once again, little accountability followed.

Still, something new was happening, too: the same month Jordan was killed, activists with a new advocacy organization called Reclaim the Block flooded a city council hearing to demand that the city shift resources away from the MPD and "into alternatives that keep people safe." Providing public comments until after 10 P.M., the advocates pushed the city council to invest in better models of addressing community violence. And they scored a win: city leaders created the Office of Violence Prevention (OVP), designed to promote a public health approach to violence prevention. Though the $1 million of the city budget initially allocated to the OVP was a small fraction of the MPD's $185 million budget, its establishment marked a shift in city politics and activism.[4] Earlier that year, a city council member had also proposed a charter amendment that would shift control of the MPD, then under the sole purview of the mayor, to a shared governance model with more city council involvement. All three of these moves—attempts to pull funding from the MPD, build a public health model for public safety, and give the council more power over the police—would form the backbone of the contentious 2020 and 2021 Minneapolis city charter initiatives to "end" the MPD in the wake of the police murder of George Floyd.

This chapter maps this shift in the political struggle over policing in the initial years of BLM organizing in Minneapolis, drawing on interviews with activists and fieldwork in the anti-police-violence activism scene. It charts the rise of BLM in the mid-2010s, activists' early successes and failures, and the turn toward police abolition well before summer 2020.[5] I explain how police defunding and abolition emerged as viable strategies in Minneapolis because of the perceived failures of early BLM activism to meaningfully change the MPD. As losses from police violence continued to roil the city, state, and country, the procession of Black death retraumatized many organizers. Some burned out, some ran for office, some took up other activism and nonprofit work, and some began to fight for a new vision of safety: police defunding as a means toward abolition.

Yet not everyone in Minneapolis fighting against police violence would come to agree with abolitionists' diagnosis of the problem (and its solution). As we will see, some activists continued to fight for what I call *radical police reform*, arguing for more transformative shifts in the way police were trained, overseen, and held accountable. To them, reform had not failed; it had never been fully implemented. And even within groups who understood the ultimate goal of their efforts as police abolition, activists were split on how, exactly, to move toward the police-free future they envisioned. These fractures across activist coalitions in the late 2010s would, by 2020, rupture into canyons of distrust.

Movements in Context: Black Freedom Dreaming

The Black freedom fight has always been defined by visions of abolition, or the ending of previous modes of racial domination and the creation of new worlds. The primordial abolition struggle in the American context is the end of chattel slavery, an economic model predicated on the dehumanization and exploitation of Black bodies. The early white-led abolitionist movement attempted to challenge the law of the land while abiding by its rules, working through "moral suasion" and nonviolent resistance. As these techniques failed, however, and the number of enslaved African Americans rose, some abolitionists turned instead to resistance through strategic violence, including Black self-defense.[6] Ultimately, it would take the violence of the Civil War to legally end slavery. From the beginning, then, abolitionist struggle has been a story of violence—white supremacist violence, state violence, and (at times) the power of violent resistance.

Despite the early abolitionist victory of ending slavery, that pivotal win represented the start (rather than end) of struggles toward Black liberation. Rather than a simple narrative of linear progress, the period following emancipation is better understood as a complex and continuous struggle, marked by periods of more or less overt racial struggle and hope for change, periods of retrenchment, and the development of new forms of racial domination.[7]

For many Americans, the most salient historical period of racial struggle is the mobilization of the 1950s and 1960s, including the civil rights movement, which sparked a new understanding of the power of social movements to create change.[8] Their political demands were clear: equal rights and opportunities for Black Americans. Measured by national policy victories, the movement was an unrivaled success. In just a decade, movement leaders won a pivotal Supreme Court case (*Brown v. Board of Education* in 1954) and three landmark federal civil rights bills (the Civil Rights Act of 1964, Voting Rights Act of 1965, and Fair Housing Act of 1968).[9] Yet measured by lives and livelihoods, however, the victories of the period look less definitive, especially for the poorest Black Americans. While some racial gaps narrowed, stark racial inequities in education, housing, and wealth persisted. Policy, even landmark federal rights legislation, in other words, is not enough. When it comes to liberation, movement scholars conclude, periods of overt racial struggle are often too brief and divisive to propel and maintain the kinds of structural long-term shifts required.[10]

By the late 1960s, this slow pace of change, and the frustrations it induced, drove the disruptive, unruly, and sometimes violent urban rebellions that erupted in the Long Hot Summer of 1967 and continued well into the 1970s. Instead of a sign of movement decay, however, critical Black scholars argue this period was just as important as the canonical civil rights struggle.[11] Indeed, in the wake of the assassinations of Black liberation leaders Malcolm X (1965), Martin Luther King Jr. (1968), and Fred Hampton (1969), many Black-led organizations turned more radical. That Fred Hampton, the deputy chairman of the national Black Panther Party, was killed by police during a nighttime raid of his home made the connections between Black liberation and the police all too clear. These activists argued that in place of slavery, the police—and the law and "justice" system more generally— had become the primary mode of Black bondage in America. Rather than assimilate into the oppressive (white) state, Black Power activists and other more radical groups fought for independence and self-determination, including, for some, separatism and control of their own safety. The Black Panthers, for example, sent armed members to patrol neighborhoods, defending residents from police intrusion and white violence alike.[12]

State repression clamped down on this explosion of radical Black organizing, yet the core activists and those in the generation that followed continued to develop their goals and tactics.[13] By the start of the twenty-first century, as mass incarceration reached its zenith, organizers were increasingly certain that the proliferation of arrests, criminal records, and prison sentences clustered among Black Americans was evidence of the latest form of racial domination. In the infamous words of legal scholar Michelle Alexander, law and order was, in fact, the "New Jim Crow."[14] Accordingly, the new abolitionist struggle would involve the abolition of the "prison industrial complex" or the archipelago of state and private interests behind mass incarceration. Two decades later, this radical prison abolition organizing would inform demands for police abolition—and broader calls to abolish other forms of oppression, including family polic-ing (Child and Protective Services), Immigration and Customs Enforce-ment (ICE) agencies, and even the military, capitalism, and the state.[15]

But before we got to summer 2020, the country would elect its first Black president—Barack H. Obama—a win unimaginable to earlier gen-erations. Under a Black president, however, the persistent racial dispari-ties of the country grew more glaring, disrupting the narrative about a "post-racial" society. In recent years, Black Americans' unemployment rate has been, on average, roughly twice the rate for white Americans, a similar gap to what we see in homeownership and median household income, but far less than the nearly 6-to-1 disparity in imprisonment rates.[16]

Black teenager Trayvon Martin was killed by a vigilante in Florida in 2012. In 2014 another Black teen, Michael Brown, was shot and killed by Darren Wilson, a white officer with the Ferguson Police Department; less than a year later, Wilson had been cleared in both the state and federal investigations.[17] Driven by these three flashpoints, the Black Lives Matter rallying cry erupted, first as a hashtag on social media, then on the ground in Ferguson, and finally across the country. Its demonstrations were pro-pelled by grassroots collectives, including what would become local chap-ters of the Black Lives Matter Movement and members of the broader Movement for Black Lives coalition.

The movement's initial efforts focused on directing mass media atten-tion to police violence through social media channels and in-person protests. The organizers' goal was to challenge (white) America's aversion to thinking about racialized police violence, and thus contest the legitimacy of the police and the state more broadly.[18] Police violence, in this formulation, was not an aberrant or exceptional case in a "color-blind" society, but the routine and predictable outcome of anti-Blackness and pervasive racialized state violence.

Organizers explicitly drew on the work of Black feminist theorists, the intellectual lineage Robin Kelley argues has the most inclusive and radical *freedom dreams*.[19] And the work of the movement was to bring those dreams into waking life, making Black feminist thought a key piece of public discourse. Led by Black women, BLM organizers insisted that anti-Blackness was *intersectional*, with inequality shaped by the intersection of racial oppression with discrimination across gender, income, national origin, and other characteristics.[20] The movement thus centered those at the margins, including Black transgender and nonbinary people, Black queer youth, and Black immigrants. If *all* Black people were free, so too would be everyone else.[21]

BLM activists thus disrupted the "common sense" imbued in everyday American understandings of race and inequality, while drawing a new generation into politics. As political theorist Deva Woodly explains:

> The broad movement in defense of Black lives has contributed to a repoliticization of the public sphere and has been successful at gaining political acceptance. Through its efforts, the movement has changed the common ways we talk about race, inequality, policing, and well-being, and inserted a commonplace understanding of structural racism and anti-Blackness into mainstream American discourse. This incorporation of new concepts into the political lexicon has opened possibilities for redress that did not exist prior to the movement's work.[22]

Poll results evidence the successes of this work.[23] For example, between 2011 and 2015 the share of Americans who reported that race was a "big problem" in the country nearly doubled, from 28 percent to 50 percent. By 2020 that number would jump to 65 percent. These gains, however, were concentrated among Democrats (for whom the racial gap between Black and white attitudes on the persistence of racial discrimination has essentially closed), widening the partisan divide.[24]

But the movement also prompted an all-too-predictable backlash, beginning with "Blue Lives Matter" protests and conservative demagoguing. It was in this context that the belligerent Donald J. Trump was elected as the forty-fifth president in 2016, promising to "Make America Great Again," a not particularly subtle nod to returning to the white America of imagined yesteryear.[25] Perhaps not surprisingly then, during most of Trump's one term in office, BLM protests grew quieter as protest efforts shifted toward fighting the administration's reactionary politics, including draconian immigration policies. The movement, however, was poised to flare back, bigger than ever, in summer 2020. This time, the fire would start in Minneapolis.

Black Lives Matter in Minneapolis

As in many cities, the first BLM protests in Minneapolis emerged in solidarity with the summer 2014 protests in Ferguson, Missouri. BLM protesters marched through downtown, past city hall, and briefly blocked a major highway, staging a "die-in" to memorialize Michael Brown's death. And in December of that year, organizers orchestrated "Black Christmas" at the Mall of America. In the group's words, "Thousands of people stood together, refused to be intimidated, and disrupted business as usual on the busiest shopping day of the year at the biggest mall in the country. As long as innocent Black and brown lives are disrupted by police without consequence, we cannot go about business as usual."[26] Clearing out the scene by force, police arrested two dozen protesters.

Protesting police violence, however, had a much deeper history in Minneapolis, as we saw in chapter 1. The longest running of groups fighting against police violence was the Minneapolis NAACP, which had demanded justice in the wake of state violence and racial injustice in the City of Lakes for more than a century. During the BLM years, NAACP Minneapolis regularly shared membership and collaborated with BLM activists on direct actions. By the time of the Ferguson protests, the NAACP president was Nekima Levy-Pounds (later Levy Armstrong), a civil rights lawyer and organizer who would go on to run for mayor in 2017. She was among the BLM protesters arrested at the Mall of America in 2014 and served as a key spokesperson at the 4th Precinct occupation in 2015. As NAACP Minneapolis president she also would lead the fight—and win—to get the city council to repeal an antiquated ordinance that allowed police to arrest people for "lurking" or "spitting" in 2015. And she would be succeeded at the NAACP Minneapolis by Jason Sole, one of the Twin Cities abolitionists who would start an emergency hotline profiled in chapter 6.

Communities United Against Police Brutality (CUAPB) also had a history of mobilizing protest against police violence long before BLM became a rallying cry. The collective formed in 2000 after the police shooting of Charles "Abuka" Sanders, a Black man, by an MPD officer. In contrast to many of the BLM era activist groups that emerged in the city, CUAPB is led by white, now retirement-age organizers. Working with survivors and their families, who organizers often counsel in how to challenge their cases, the all-volunteer group staffs a twenty-four-hour police brutality hotline and holds awareness-raising public events. They also bring people out to protest. Much of CUAPB's work revolves around increasing the visibility of police violence, including by keeping an online archive of officers' reported misconduct and pushing for greater public transparency from the MPD and other law enforcement agencies in the state. As part of this work, they maintain a painstaking memorial of "stolen lives," with each victim of police violence recorded on a massive ribbon of paper unfurled at public events.

CUAPB's key spokesperson, Michelle Gross, herself a survivor of police brutality, has been an indefatigable presence in city politics, leading rallies, speaking to the media, and helping to file lawsuits against the city.[27] As the BLM protests erupted, CUAPB joined their calls in demanding that officers be held accountable for violence. During an interview with me in 2017, Gross interrupted a question about the biggest problem facing policing today, saying, "You don't even have to finish that question, I know what the answer is: accountability. Until we have some real accountability this stuff is not going to get better. Yeah, 'cause—I mean—you can make all the nice policies . . . but you don't enforce it." Instead of these "nice policies," CUAPB called for radical transformations in the power structure of policing—the sort that might truly end the reign of the "thumpers" and "killer cops." One of the group's signature initiatives, for example, was a police liability proposal they sought to get on the ballot in 2016 that would have required individual officers to self-insure for police malpractice, rather than having the city foot the bill.

With longtime organizers like Levy-Pounds and Gross sharing the mic with newer BLM activists, the 4th Precinct occupation in winter 2015 helped coalesce an anti-police-violence coalition in Minneapolis to fight for these kinds of structural changes. The bridges they built would serve organizers for years, generating a new sense of solidarity forged by resistance to the occupation by the MPD, counter-protesters, and even some older, more establishment Black civic and religious leaders who called for protesters to go home. The MPD, for its part, alternated between civil talks with protesters and sending out officers in riot gear. But repression did not come from the state alone. On November 23, five protesters were targeted, shot, and injured by white men who came to disrupt the occupation. Three days after the perpetrators were charged, police and municipal sanitation workers arrived in the pre-dawn hours, clearing the encampment. In response, protesters staged a march to city hall and, the following week, gathered hundreds of supporters at another Mall of America demonstration that ended with a dozen key activists again arrested.

Beginning a pattern that would repeat with many of the subsequent police killings in Minneapolis, Jamar Clark's death also spurred the formation of a new activist organization: the Twin Cities Coalition for Justice for Jamar (TCC4J). Developed by local Black activists, the coalition demanded the prosecution of the two officers responsible for Clark's death. More broadly, though, TCC4J was designed as a "vehicle that was independent and not accountable to grant makers, but to the community" that would respond to future "grave injustices."[28]

In their direct actions, BLM organizers and their allies drew a line from earlier Black liberation movements to their work, for example, bowing their heads under a Black Power salute and chanting Assata Shakur's words, "It is our duty to fight for our freedom. It is our duty to win."[29] Similarly, TCC4J called for a version of community control of the police that they traced back to the demands of the Black Panther Party. TCC4J envisioned the Civilian Police Accountability Council (CPAC) as a board of elected community representatives who would appoint the police chief and lead officer misconduct investigations and discipline. As a TCC4J organizer told me in 2018, the CPAC would mean that when officers "kill and it's not justified—and, well, they're never justified—but you could say, 'You don't get to keep your gun. You don't get to keep your badge. You're not going to get paid vacation until we investigate this case.'"

In 2016 Philando Castile, a beloved cafeteria supervisor at a local elementary school, was shot by an officer working for the St. Anthony Police Department, contracted by Falcon Heights, a suburb of St. Paul. After a brief back-and-forth during a traffic stop, in which Castile notified the officer he had a license to carry, Officer Jeronimo Yanez fired into Castile's car, fatally wounding him. Castile's girlfriend, Diamond Reynolds, live-streamed the immediate aftermath on Facebook, her four-year-old daughter looking on from her car seat in the back. This killing by police—like those that preceded and followed it—spurred Castile's loved ones and enraged onlookers to mobilize. It also continued to galvanize BLM protests in Minneapolis, pivotally turning protester attention toward state-level actors (for instance, through an occupation in front of the governor's mansion—an action that would prompt the formation of a state commission examining police violence in Minnesota).

Activists warned that Clark and Castile would not be the last victims of police violence—and they were right. Just weeks after former officer Yanez's trial, another person was shot and killed by the MPD. In an inversion of the typical pattern, however, this next victim was Justine (Ruszczyk) Damond, a white woman and yoga instructor, shot in a wealthy South Minneapolis neighborhood. The officer who killed her was a Black (Somali American) man, Mohamed Noor, who was relatively new to the force. Damond had called 911 just before midnight on July 15, 2017, unsure whether the sounds she heard in her alleyway were consensual sex, rape, or something else entirely. The responding officer team rolled down Damond's alley with their squad car's lights and sirens off. According to the officers, Damond appeared suddenly behind the vehicle, slapped the bumper, and walked up to the driver's side window. Both officers drew their weapons, but it was Noor, in the passenger's seat, who pointed his gun in front of his partner and shot Damond, hitting her in the abdomen. She would die minutes later as the officers desperately clutched her wound, body cameras still turned off. (At the trial, Noor's defense would focus less on the threat Damond herself posed and more on the hypothetical risk of ambush, citing the New York City police officer killed just ten days earlier.)

In the wake of Damond's killing, I started seeing bright orange street signs reading "WARNING: TWIN CITIES POLICE EASILY STARTLED," accompanied by a cartoon depiction of an officer with guns blazing. Though the city would remove the signs, they too would persist. As in Clark's death, family, community members, and activists publicly grieved the loss of life. Yet Damond's unique racial and gendered privilege changed the protest dynamics, with mourners, for example, leading a silent walk around Lake Harriet that some read as a critical commentary on the more disruptive and confrontational BLM protests organized for other victims. Damond's fiancé and her family (in Australia) seemed to take this tack too, pushing the local prosecutor to pursue a legal case and file a civil suit against the city, arguing that Damond's case was a uniquely unjustified example of police violence.

A group of Damond's friends and neighbors, who banded together under the name Justice for Justine, instead argued that her death was in fact emblematic of the problems plaguing the MPD. While Justice for Justine was led by white residents, they were deeply connected to the work of Black activists who had laid the groundwork and thoughtful about how Damond's race and gender gave their group unique public sympathy and political access. The problems in MPD that led to Damond's death, they argued, could be fixed, leading to less loss of life and dignity for Black residents. Describing their work in a 2018 interview with me, for example, one organizer rhetorically questioned why officers "were riding down the alley with their guns drawn, unholstered, no lights on, ready to go off on a moment's notice," answering: "That is absolutely what they're trained to do. That's because of their training that they do those things. And that's what led to Blevins' death, that's what led to Jamar Clark's death." For Justice for Justine organizers, what tied these cases together was poor training for officers. As a result, they aimed much of their work on ending the specialized "fear-based" or "warrior" training seminars they saw as contributing to this culture of violence, noting that many MPD officers, including Officer Noor, had attended such trainings before their fatal encounters.

In short, in the initial BLM protest years, groups like BLM Minneapolis, NAACP Minneapolis, CUAPB, TCC4J, and Justice for Justine all worked together to organize protests and push for policy change. The killings of Jamar Clark, Philando Castile, Justine Damond, and others activated an advocacy field fighting against police violence, bringing new voices and energy into the movement. In each of these cases, family, friends, neighbors, and strangers came together to demand internal affairs reviews, criminal investigations, and civil cases against the officers. Activists often framed these legal processes as a form of redress—or something that looked like justice—for the victims.

These groups wanted not just piecemeal reforms but transformative changes in the relationship between police and the public, an orientation I describe as *radical reform*. Yet these kinds of power shifts proved elusive. Both the liability insurance proposal and the CPAC initiative, for example, bumped up against state laws that insulated the police from those kinds of accountability. And, as we'll see, Justice for Justine's work to end "warrior" training ran up against the officers union. Even the more narrow redress of seeking justice for individual victims found few successes in the courts.

Seeking Justice: The Investigations, Lawsuits, and Criminal Cases

Despite the vigorous advocacy by local organizers, the officers responsible for Clark's death were never formally sanctioned. The local prosecutor, Michael Freeman, declined to indict, concluding that the evidence suggested that Clark had not been handcuffed at the time of his death and that officers faced a credible threat of violence (in particular, there was physical evidence consistent with the claim that Clark was touching one officer's gun).[30] An internal affairs investigation within MPD, which should be a lower bar to clear than a criminal case, similarly determined that neither officer had violated department policy. Indeed, the department went further, praising the officers' conduct. In a statement released after the investigation concluded, Police Chief Janeé Harteau announced: "I can say with absolute certainty that I fully support the actions of officers Ringgenberg and Schwarze. These officers did not dictate the outcome of this incident. This was an outcome that no one wanted."[31] When it was later released by the city, the officers' dashcam video showed only parts of the fatal encounter—and nothing that definitively confirmed or denied conflicting accounts.

After the 2016 police killing of Philando Castile across the river in Falcon Heights, political elites came closer to condemning the responsible officers. Minnesota governor Mark Dayton, for example, told the public that had Castile been white, he'd still be alive, concluding: "I am forced to confront, I think all of us in Minnesota are forced to confront, that this kind of racism exists."[32] Extensive media coverage reported on not just Castile's death but also the way police had "hunted" him for years, as he racked up dozens of traffic stops by police over the years with little cause.[33] Five months after the killing, Ramsey County prosecutor John Choi charged Yanez with second-degree manslaughter and dangerous discharge of a firearm. In the trial that year, however, Yanez was acquitted, touching off another round of protests in the Twin Cities. Federal charges were never filed. The City of St. Anthony, however, announced that Yanez had been asked not to return to the police force and, in wrongful death lawsuits, Castile's family and his girlfriend were ultimately awarded a combined settlement of $3.8 million.[34]

In contrast with these cases, Justine Damond's killing resulted in substantial punishment. Rather than commend the officers, Chief Harteau announced to the city that "Justine didn't have to die . . . I believe the actions in question go against who we are as a department."[35] Damond's killing also led to record-breaking legal and civil sanctions, with Noor in 2019 becoming the first on-duty officer in Minnesota to be convicted of murder. He was sentenced to twelve years in prison.[36] In her final statement on the case, Judge Kathryn Quaintance was damning, insisting that the MPD answer a series of questions raised by the case about how the department hired, trained, and supervised its officers. While the city never issued a public response, its payouts told a different story: in 2019, just days after the verdict, the city announced an unprecedented $20 million settlement with Damond's family.[37] It did not escape notice that the one case of lethal police violence to garner a substantial conviction and settlement involved a white victim and a Black officer.

Not Every Victim Gets a Headline

As these cases wound through the legal system, the MPD continued to use lethal force. Not all of these killings made it to the national headlines, however, and some were barely mentioned in the local newspaper. In between the deaths of Clark and Damond, for example, in 2016 MPD officers killed Raul Salvador Marquez-Heraldes, a fifty-year-old Hispanic man who was in the act of stabbing another man in an apartment when officers opened fire. As in Clark's case, Freeman announced that he would not press charges, but this time he went further, stating: "All of the police officers at the scene acted correctly and bravely," killing Marquez-Heraldes "to save a life."[38] In contrast to many activists' contention that all police killings are "murder," it appeared the legal system considered some heroic. That tension would continue to bedevil reform efforts.

Table 2.1 lists all the people killed by MPD officers in 2015–2019, as well as the outcomes of internal investigations, criminal cases, and civil settlements. In the two years after Damond's death (2018–2019), officers with the MPD shot and killed four men of color, all in North Minneapolis, including Thurman Blevins Jr. and Travis Jordan, whose deaths were described earlier. There was also Mario Philip Benjamin, killed in August 2019 just after he had shot a former girlfriend and mother of his two children in the chest. Police were tipped off not by a 911 call but by activations of ShotSpotter, an audio surveillance system that monitors for the sound of gunfire. When they arrived, Benjamin stood over the woman, who was bleeding out in the street with her four children nearby. After several unanswered commands to "Drop the gun!" Officer Jason Wolff shot Benjamin five times. And there was Chiasher Vue, a Hmong American man, whose son called 911 that winter day because Vue was drunk, armed, and had a history of domestic violence. His kids had made it outside, but Vue remained inside the house with his elderly mother, who used a wheelchair. Dispatchers sent several teams of officers (including Wolff and a Hmong officer who could speak in Vue's native tongue). Staged outside the man's home, however, officers shouted in English and trained their weapons. After coming to the door, Vue retreated, retrieved a rifle, and returned, at which point officers unleashed a torrent of gunfire. Vue died later that morning at the hospital.[39]

In two of these cases (Marquez-Heraldes and Benjamin), the circumstances of the police killings were overtly justified in such a way that little public outrage or media coverage ensued. The other deaths prompted somewhat louder calls from activists that the media, the police, and the

Table 2.1 People killed by the MPD (2015–2019)

Victim name	Victim race and gender	Month and year	Reason for police contact	Internal discipline	State or federal criminal charges	Civil settlement
Jamar Clark	Black man	Nov. 2015	EMT request for assistance	None	None	$200,000 awarded in 2019
Raul Marquez-Heraldes	Hispanic man	April 2016	911 call	None	None	None
Justine (Ruszczyk) Damond	White woman	July 2017	911 call (possible sexual assault)	Employment terminated	Third-degree murder and second-degree manslaughter conviction	$20 million awarded in 2019
Thurman Blevins Jr.	Black man	June 2018	911 call (man with a gun)	None	None	None
Travis Jordan	Asian and Black man	Nov. 2018	911 call (wellness check)	None	None	None
Mario Philip Benjamin	Black man	Aug. 2019	ShotSpotter activation	None	None	None
Chiasher Fong Vue	Asian man	Dec. 2019	911 call (domestic)	None	None	$700,000 awarded in 2023

Source: Minneapolis Star Tribune, "Every police-involved death in Minnesota since 2000," https://www.startribune.com/every-police-involved-death-in-minnesota-since-2000/502088871 (last updated January 12, 2023).
Note: This table includes only individuals killed during a physical confrontation with on-duty officers. Details about discipline, criminal charges, and settlement awards were last updated on September 14, 2023.

public "Say Their Names," though they did not lead to the kinds of wide-scale mobilization that attracted national media coverage to the city. No officers faced internal discipline or state or federal criminal charges (though in 2023 Vue's family was awarded a settlement of $700,000 in a suit related to both his death and his four children's treatment by police during and after the standoff).

Police Reform: The National Initiative

As outlined in chapter 1, in the years leading up to the BLM protests, MPD chief Janeé Harteau, appointed in 2012 as the city's first woman, Native American, and openly lesbian police chief, had pushed for "MPD 2.0," a culture shift in the department to (again) excise the "thumper" mentality among MPD officers and the rampant racism, sexism, and homophobia in the department culture. This home-grown leader was part of a national vanguard of progressive police chiefs who came together through groups like the Police Executive Research Forum and would collectively take the lead on "The President's Task Force on 21st Century Policing" report released in 2015 under President Obama.

That same year, the city successfully bid to be one of the pilot sites for the National Initiative for Building Community Trust and Justice, a project designed to turn the "21st Century Policing" reform pillars into action. A national demonstration project in six cities, the initiative was designed to respond to the concerns about police violence raised in the wake of the Ferguson Uprising. The Urban Institute, a nonprofit research consulting firm, was tasked with evaluating whether the reforms could "improve relationships and increase trust between police and community residents, particularly those living in neighborhoods with the most fraught relationships with law enforcement."[40] To achieve these goals, the initiative went through three sequential processes in each of the sites: officer trainings, reconciliation with impacted communities, and changing department policies and practices.

As tracked by the Urban Institute's team, the MPD implemented many of these efforts with fidelity, starting with officer training. For example, all of the MPD's nearly 850 sworn officers received twenty-four hours of specialized training on procedural justice and implicit bias, delivered by "credible messengers" within the department. Developed by legal scholars, this training is designed to encourage officers to give voice and respect to the people with whom they interact and to convey neutrality and trustworthiness in their decision-making. In turn, procedural justice proponents argue, the public will be more likely to perceive authorities as legitimate and therefore comply with their orders. Along with this high-level overview of procedural justice, officers completed a "tactical" curriculum that included simulations of real encounters to teach techniques consistent with the model. Finally, the program centered implicit bias training designed to improve police-public interactions, in this case by revealing to officers how their cognitive biases about certain groups (especially racial minorities) might impact their decision-making and lead to unlawful conduct.

The community engagement component of the National Initiative was delayed significantly, as Minneapolis and other pilot cities struggled to negotiate a new model of acknowledging the harms of policing, past and present. Building off the South African post-apartheid reconciliation model, these conversations were designed to provide opportunities for departments to learn and acknowledge the past harms of policing in their city, better understand continuing problems, and promise to make a set of changes to improve relationships. The MPD began "listening sessions" in summer 2016 (after the killing of Clark but before the killing of Damond), holding eight invitation-only meetings between Chief Harteau and stakeholders in specific communities, defined by race/ethnicity (African American, Latinx, Native American, and Somali), sexuality (LGBT+), and age (youth). Because these sessions were private, however, little about them or how they might have impacted the MPD's decision-making was conveyed to the broader public (or rank-and-file officers).

Third, the National Initiative work included department reforms to change use-of-force and misconduct policies. Most significant were two changes implemented in July 2016. The first amended the department's use-of-force rules to explicitly prioritize de-escalation in high-risk situations, molding the guidelines around a "sanctity of life" principle for both officers and residents. The second required that officers intervene when coworkers used excessive force. The MPD also promised to jump-start an early intervention system for officers at risk of more severe misconduct, a reform that had been promoted periodically over the years but never seemed to fully materialize. And in a move toward greater transparency, the department began more systematically recording the race and gender of people stopped by police and by 2017 was making this data public on an online dashboard that also reported on use of force.

Damond's death spurred another round of reform. For the first time, politicians were getting phone calls from their white constituents, worried they too might be harmed by police. As Linea Palmisano, the representative for Damond's ward, declared, "How do we make sure that this never, never

happens again?" The fact that Damond's death had not been caught on officers' body cameras (because they had not turned the devices on) exposed
the department's poor track record of enforcing its own rules. Instead of
turning on the cameras during every call, officers had been selectively acti-
vating the devices with little accountability. In a press conference following Damond's death, Mayor Betsy Hodges declared that officers' failure to
turn on their cameras was "unacceptable," concluding that "too much time,
money and effort" had been put into this technology "to have them fail us
when we needed them most."[41] In response, the MPD changed its policies,
announcing to much fanfare that it would now require officers to turn on
their body cameras any time they responded to calls for service (from the
moment they begin driving to the location, rather than when they exit the vehicle) or initiated traffic or pedestrian stops, and starting an audit program to
review officers' compliance. Failure to abide by these new policies, the chief
warned, could lead to discipline or potential loss of employment.

In some (limited) ways, this set of reforms worked, at least according
to the metrics used in the Urban Institute's 2019 evaluation reports. After
completing the training sessions, MPD officers increased their agreement
with procedural justice principles in evaluation surveys from an average
of 3.2 to 3.5 on a four-point scale from "strongly disagree" (1) to "strongly
agree" (4).[42] Comparisons of two samples of residents in the highest-crime
neighborhoods in Minneapolis before and after the reforms also suggested
small improvements over time. For example, on a five-point scale from
"strongly disagree" (1) to "strongly agree" (5), the average scores measuring
police legitimacy increased from 2.6 to 3.0 in these blocks, while average
scores on a scale meant to assess residents' perceptions of whether officers
engaged in procedurally just policing increased from 2.5 to 2.9 (for an
average rating of "neither agree nor disagree").[43] While residents thus still
reported a great deal of ambivalence and outright mistrust, the evaluators
concluded that things were trending in the right direction.

Results were more mixed, or even nonexistent, however, for changing police *practices*. During the main period of intervention, for example,
there was little change in the number of use-of-force reports filed and no
improvement in racial disparities in use of force or residents' exposure
to violent crime in Minneapolis.[44] And the key definition of success,
lethal encounters with police—particularly those where the victim was
unarmed or otherwise not posing an acute risk of lethal violence toward
others—showed little change during the intervention period. The MPD
continued to kill one to two people through direct lethal force each year
(though this was a lighter toll than seen in the previous decade).[45] The

"shame of Minneapolis" would continue to make headlines. This reality would become all too clear with the murder of George Floyd; as one of the Urban Institute's evaluators would lament: "It wasn't enough."[46] By 2023 all of these reform initiates would be rediscovered and reworked as state and federal investigators found that officers continued to use unjustified force, failed to intervene when witnessing other officers' abuse, and evaded reporting the race of the people they stopped (as we'll see in chapter 5). More of officers' violence was now caught on body cameras, however, which allowed investigators to call for audits of the footage, not just whether or not they had turned the cameras on.

Minneapolis, of course, is just one case. But there is little scholarly consensus on whether the BLM protests against police violence, and the reforms that followed, have reduced lethal violence in the United States. There is some preliminary evidence that cities with protests experienced fewer police killings in subsequent years (but perhaps more murders by community members).[47] Nationally, however, the number of people killed by police changed little in aggregate between 2014 and 2019. Only if you disaggregate by place can we see a potential effect: the number of killings in urban centers, especially of Black Americans, appears to be slowly declining, offset by an increase in white victims and killings in suburban and rural places.[48] Part of the explanation for these disappointing results, however, was not simply the failures of reformers but the resistance they encountered while trying to change policing.

The Union Pushes Back

As it had in the past, the police officers union, now headed by Robert "Bob" Kroll, became one of the major antagonists fighting police reform. Kroll, a department veteran and pugnacious union head, was one of the MPD brass listed on the lawsuit alleging that the MPD discriminated against officers of color in 2007 (in part because of his membership in "City Heat," a police motorcycle gang accused of being a white supremacist hate group). In 2019, after the city decreed that officers could not appear in uniform to endorse a political candidate, Kroll strode on stage to introduce the Republican president before a speech in Minneapolis clad in a red "COPS FOR TRUMP" T-shirt (which, incidentally, he was selling). By 2020 Kroll would make national and international headlines, calling those protesting after the murder of George Floyd "terrorists."

In Minneapolis, that kind of incendiary language had long come to be expected from Kroll, who routinely referred to BLM as a "terrorist organization."[49] After Castile's death in 2016, for example, Kroll and

Mayor Hodges had a public spat after officers refused to provide security for the Minnesota Lynx (a women's basketball team) after players emerged in BLM-themed warm-up gear. Speaking to the media, Kroll commended the officers for their wildcat strike, at which point the mayor wrote a public Facebook post deriding the federation head's "jackass remarks."[50] The following year, Kroll was overwhelmingly reelected to his federation post by the MPD's officers—who apparently believed he faithfully represented their interests. Soon thereafter, when an exposé came out about the high number of police officers who had been convicted of a criminal offense but never disciplined by the state police licensing board, Kroll belligerently replied to reporters: "Your SWAT guys, your heat seekers, your guys that lead in . . . arrests, guns recovered, shootouts . . . they're the ones where their personal life is a disaster . . . They drink too much. They cheat on their wives."[51] Officers' violence, on the job and in their personal lives, was precisely what made them good police, Kroll seemed to imply.

Having elected (and then reelected) Kroll as president, it's no surprise the officers union aggressively resisted management and city leaders' reform efforts. The federation, for example, objected to the "sanctity of life" policy, pushing to water it down so that officers had significantly more discretion to initiate violence. They fought the body camera policy, too, calling the reform "rushed and politically motivated" and arguing that officers' discussions with their partners needed to be off the record.[52] That particular battle they lost. But they won others, including defying a 2019 mayoral declaration that the city would no longer pay for officers to attend "warrior" style training. The week after the announcement, Kroll (on behalf of the federation) offered to pay for officers to complete the training, effectively negating the hard-won reform and making the Police Federation of Minneapolis briefly a cause célèbre among police unions.[53]

The resistance of the officers union to reform and its support of officers accused of misconduct (and even criminal violations) was starkly visible to reformers, who often framed the union as a powerful barrier to change. As a former city council member explained to me in 2017:

> The reason things have turned out the way they are is that the negotiations of contracts builds in so many insulations for cops that bad cops who are disciplined by the chief get rehired in the arbitration process . . . It's happened over and over again. Cops who have been disciplined, their discipline has been reduced because of that . . . They have to insure these cops and all of these things are built to insulate police officers from change and from correction and discipline, and so then why would they change?

The centrality of the police officers union in reform efforts eventually led the radical reformers to develop a new tactic: trying to break the control of the federation (and, by extension, the MPD's rank and file) over city politics.

By 2019 these groups—including CUAPB, Justice for Justine, and Nekima Levy Armstrong—consolidated into an umbrella coalition, "Minneapolis for a Better Police Contract" to fight for changes in the collective bargaining agreement negotiated between the city and its officers union. Their proposed reforms to the contract, the group declared, would "substantially reform the police contract to both improve the safety of our communities and increase accountability for our police force." The changes included capping overtime, adding routine mental health screenings after employment, and giving management more control over staffing assignments. At a minimum, they argued, these meetings should be open to the public so they could observe. The negotiations, however, would remain behind closed doors until after the next contract was approved.

Changing City Politics

Less than two weeks after Damond's killing in 2017, Chief Harteau resigned at the request of the mayor, the two having grown more distant after clashing on the 4th Precinct occupation.[54] In Harteau's place, Mayor Hodges appointed Medaria Arradondo, known locally as "Rondo," first as acting chief and then as the permanent department head. Arradondo was the MPD's first Black chief and, like Harteau, was home-grown (indeed, before his appointment, Rondo served directly under Harteau as her assistant chief). Rondo would continue to oversee implementation of the National Initiative and would be the person in charge when MPD officers murdered George Floyd. But he would do so under a new mayor and city council.

In addition to shaking up the MPD's brass, Damond's death happened at a pivotal moment in the run-up to the 2017 city election, which would seat a new mayor and city council. By that point in Minneapolis politics, public safety issues were beginning to compete for airtime with other critical issues like affordable housing and jobs. The incumbent mayor, Betsy Hodges, faced a bevy of challengers whose flyers bore messages like "Our city is in the news for all the wrong reasons."[55] Though policing was not yet at the forefront of mayoral campaigns in the way that it would be in 2021, Hodges and her top challengers all strove to present themselves as the ones who would rein in the police in the wake of Damond's death.

Ultimately, the election would go to Jacob Frey—a white man, former attorney, and relatively recent transplant to Minneapolis who had moved after running a local marathon. Prior to his mayoral campaign, he had served on the city council representing the downtown ward. He leaned into nostalgia for the days when a man was in charge of the state's largest city, declaring that he would bring "swagger" back to Minneapolis.[56] (He would also, years later, become an internet crush, compared to Canada's Justin Trudeau.[57]) On the campaign trail, Frey pledged that he would do more than Hodges to reform the MPD, while also increasing the number of officers. The goal, he argued, was to make people "feel comfortable calling 911." Hodges, in contrast, argued that Frey was running "on my right" and would "carry water" for police federation president Bob Kroll.[58] In the election run-up, Justine's grieving fiancé, Don Damond, endorsed Jacob Frey in a "letter to the editor" published in the *Star Tribune*, writing that he believed Frey could do a better job than the other candidates in reforming the MPD.

But it wasn't just Hodges and Frey in the mayor's race. A year to the day after Jamar Clark's killing, former NAACP Minneapolis president Nekima Levy-Pounds announced her own candidacy.[59] She, too, charged that Hodges had achieved too little change in the MPD, and that what was required instead was a "paradigm shift" in the city's police culture. Raymond Dehn, a white Minnesota state representative who had personally experienced addiction and recovery, added to the candidates' ideological diversity on the left, declaring that the city should disarm the police.

As these campaigns heated up, racial justice advocates in the city distributed a voter guide that reported on candidates' issue positions. One of the questions they asked candidates was: "Do you believe that we could ever have a city without police?"[60] Alongside seven candidates for city council, two mayoral candidates—Frey and Dehn—replied with a "yes." Levy-Pounds, however, was a no, previewing her later opposition to the charter amendment. After drawing heat from downtown business interests, the soon-to-be mayor, Jacob Frey, quickly equivocated to reporters that "getting rid of the police could only happen in a hypothetical world that doesn't exist." "This confusion," he continued, "arose when the questions were changed by those creating the survey."[61]

The final vote tallies in the 2017 mayoral race were an illuminating data point about both the depth and the limits of the city's progressive reputation. On a ranked-choice ballot with eighteen named contenders, the incumbent, Hodges, came in at third place in first-choice votes, behind Frey and moderate Tom Hoch, a white Democratic centrist known as the "Mayor of Hennepin Avenue" for his work in the downtown theater scene. But the more left-leaning candidates did well too, with Representative Dehn winning nearly as many first-round votes as Hodges (roughly eighteen thousand) and Levy-Pounds garnering nearly sixteen thousand votes (earning her the fifth spot). The ranked-choice reallocation process ended with Frey and Dehn as the two final competitors.[62]

The same election, however, ushered in a historically left-leaning city council, as key wards elected new, young progressives to office. Also answering "yes" on that survey question about a police-free future were five city council members who would go on to stand on the stage at South Minneapolis's Powderhorn Park, declaring their intention to end the MPD, in 2020. The first was Elizabeth Peterson "Lisa" Bender, a white former city planner who would be chosen by her colleagues to lead as city council president. Speaking in 2017, Bender noted that the idea of a police-free future was "aspirational," but the council had "a very long way to go before we would approach public safety without police."[63] Alondra Cano, who would be reelected to represent Ward 9 (one of the two wards intersecting at what would become George Floyd Square), similarly supported the idea of a police-free future, as did newcomer Jeremy Schroeder (Ward 11).

Also replying "yes" to this future were the two challengers about to win the Northside: Phillipe Cunningham (Ward 4) and Jeremiah Ellison (Ward 5). Both were young, progressive, Black, and won against more moderate opponents. Ellison (the son of the first Muslim congressperson and later Minnesota attorney general, Keith Ellison) was a local artist who had participated in the demonstrations at the 4th Precinct. A photo of him, with hands raised up as an MPD officer pointed a rifle at him, became one of the iconic images of the occupation. Cunningham was the first openly transgender man of color elected to local office in the United States. He pushed out a more conservative white incumbent, Barbara "Barb" Johnson, who had been in office for two decades (notably, she was the lone "no" on the 2015 vote repealing the lurking and spitting ordinance, arguing that it would fuel crime).[64] Though winning by a narrow margin, Cunningham's election in particular decisively shifted the influence of the Northside on the city council.[65] Once in office, Cunningham became critical to building up violence interruption programs, and after 2020 Ellison would become the council's key spokesperson for abolitionist approaches.

Yet, previewing the struggles to come, Andrea Jenkins, the winner of the Ward 8 contest (which included three corners of 38th and Chicago), a local poet and the first Black, openly transgender woman to be elected to public office, replied "no" to the police-free future question. She elaborated: "I would try to get rid of all the guns, everyone has guns. Men beat their wives and girlfriends, we don't need to get rid of police, we need to end white supremacy, patriarchy and racism." Once in office, Jenkins was frequently the swing vote on public safety issues on the council, standing between her more leftist colleagues and the more moderate voices on council. She would later ascend the stage at Powderhorn Park and eventually the dais as council president.

In sum, while activists seemed to make little headway on transformational reform in the early BLM years, the growing anti-police-violence movement indelibly shaped the 2017 city elections, bringing into power a particularly left-leaning city council. Soon, this new team of public officials would become disillusioned with their lack of power over the police—moving to gain more direct oversight over the MPD, beginning to pilot more transformational changes to public safety, and inspiring an even more left-leaning set of challengers in the next wave of elections four years later.

The Rise of Abolition

During the early BLM years, abolitionist visions for policing began to percolate in Minneapolis as in leftist organizing spaces across the country.[66] As I continued to interview local activists between 2017 and 2019, I increasingly heard calls for "transformation" and the "abolition" of police, not simply reform—changes that led me to shift my interview questions. Police reform, they argued, had failed; what was needed was something new. In response, activists fighting for abolition, as summarized in table 2.2, would build a new model for understanding both the "problem" in policing as well as its solution.

One of the early movers in this space was Neighborhoods Organizing for Change, a racial and economic justice nonprofit, which organized a series of community meetings and policy advocacy in the wake of Clark's killing. One of the ideas it began to promote was an early version of police defunding, asking the city to divert funds spent on "tasers and guns and fortifying precincts" and instead spend "on community centers, on counselors, on social workers, on mental health response teams."[67]

By 2017 the organization was defunct, fueled in part by staff outrage after the director called in police to resolve an altercation at an event. By that point, the BLM Minneapolis group was also largely disbanded, as activists experienced burnout and moved into government, nonprofit, and other local activist arenas. Others, including Kandace Montgomery and Miski Noor, both queer Black women organizers, went to work for the Black Lives Matter Global Network, building their organizing skills for several years before returning to organizing in Minneapolis. Many became radicalized as the movement scene reshuffled.

The organizers in this space were largely Black, often queer and/or transgender, and young, drawn into BLM during their formative teen and early adulthood years. And they had been through hell. They had cried. They had protested. They had demanded change and faced repression. Yet, the police continued to kill Black people. As Montgomery later recalled to a reporter about when Philando Castile was killed, she was "feeling like I can't even cry. I'm so exhausted from this."[68] The procession of racist violence they had witnessed, and the lack of accountability that followed, created deep trauma for activists—and pushed them to demand something else.[69] As one abolitionist organizer described to me in a 2018 interview:

> We were traumatized and doing direct actions to try to force some sort of change. But there wasn't a deep . . . solution-oriented systemic analysis at that point. We were asking for the same things that we've always been asking for, which is prosecution of the individual officers, which is additional constraints on police behavior, which is harsher union contracts, crisis intervention training, and others like that. But it was, I think after the Philando Castile shooting, really, where a lot of us started becoming very disillusioned with that sort of change methodology. And we were realizing that a lot of us burned out. A lot of us had been beaten up by cops, maced . . . and fundamentally nothing, none of the pieces on the board had been moved in any deep and meaningful way . . . I think people have started to radicalize themselves around that, in some ways becoming aware of the fact that reforms that we are traditionally handed don't work, and they don't change the underlying structures that are leading to the problems that we're seeing.

The answer, these activists came to believe, was working to end policing and start anew.

Organizers in Minneapolis fighting for police abolition in this new "post-BLM" context would eventually form a trio of groups: MPD150, Reclaim the Block, and Black Visions.[70] Though their members overlapped significantly, each carved out a unique niche. MPD150 went public first, named after the group's first publication—a report on MPD released on its 150th anniversary in 2017. The report, entitled "Enough Is Enough: A 150-Year Performance Review of the Minneapolis Police Department," outlined the long history of police violence in Minneapolis. As the report concluded, "Our analysis locates the roots of police brutality, corruption and racism in its history and founding mission."[71] The problem was policing, not just

Table 2.2 Visions of change for Minneapolis

	21st century police reform	Radical police reform	Police abolition
Defining the problem in policing	Poor police-community relationships	Too much power granted to police and their unions and too little police accountability and community oversight	Policing is a form of racial oppression that benefits the powerful and enacts state violence on the poor
Paths toward a solution	Hiring, training, accountability, and transparency reforms	Liability insurance for officers, community control, public input on union contracts, prosecution of "killer cops"	Police defunding, building alternative models of safety, mutual aid, cop watching
Representative actors and groups	National Initiative for Building Community Trust and Justice Mayor and MPD leadership	Communities United Against Police Brutality (CUAPB) Twin Cities Coalition for Justice for Jamar (TCC4J) Justice for Justine	MPD150 Reclaim the Block Black Visions

"bad" cops. And no kind of "reform" could ever change that. As the activist who described the new change methodology behind abolition summarized: "The underlying problem is you have officers who are armed and are trained to kill people, and you have a socially ingrained fear of Black men. There is no way, without changing one of those two things in the equation, that you can prevent police murders of Black people from happening."

Drawing a line from slavery to policing, the report argued that police abolition was "the only way forward."[72] It was time "to take the idea of police-free communities out of the realm of fantasy and place it firmly in the public agenda as a practical necessity."[73] To begin seeding the ground for this future, MPD150 worked to expand the imaginations of both community members and city leaders. They were a "narrative change organization," working to challenge commonsense understandings of police. Indeed, it was one member of the MPD150 collective, Ashley Fairbanks, who spearheaded the 2017 voter guide that asked candidates their belief in the possibility of a police-free Minneapolis. The group then included the candidates' responses in the MPD150 report, using the nine "yes" responses to show the momentum for police abolition. Minneapolis, they argued, was already taking the initial steps toward the imagined police-free future.

Seeding the Ground

As MPD150 worked to create narrative change, Reclaim the Block began work on policy steps toward abolition while Black Visions worked initially behind the scenes to build the movement. As an organizer told me in 2018, MPD150 was important for "fertilizing the soil . . . shifting narratives around policing," but activists also needed "people in action to make that effective." One of the lead Black Visions organizers was Kandace Montgomery, one of the BLM activists arrested at the 2014 Mall of America protest. Speaking to a reporter in summer 2020, Montgomery described how her approach had shifted: "In 2015, I think that we were very righteously angry, and we were clear about the problem. Now, we are clear about the solution. I think that's the distinction. Now in 2020, we know that justice is not just arresting the officers. Justice goes so much further."[74]

Back in 2018 the abolitionist trio was already beginning to shift the terrain toward justice. Most notably, throughout the city budget negotiations in 2018 and 2019, Reclaim the Block pushed the city council to divert funding from the MPD to "communities, not cops" and support initiatives that would provide real safety for the community. As a Black Visions activist argued in a 2018 interview with me, "in terms of reducing violence especially, the biggest step that can be taken at a policy level is taking money away from this armed militia and actually investing it in the services that people need to live their fullest lives and to prevent crime in the first place."

The group staged disruptive protests at city hall meetings, issued press releases, and mobilized supporters to participate in public hearings. In negotiations over the 2019 city budget, Reclaim the Block and its allies also successfully pressured city council members to reduce Mayor Frey's proposed increase for the MPD's budget, ultimately redirecting $1.1 million. That funding, in turn, helped build the Office of Violence Prevention, championed by Councilmember Cunningham, which adopted a public health model for responding to and preventing violence.[75] The next year, the groups again urged the city to reduce MPD funding, working alongside TCC4J to pack public budget hearings with supporters[76] and ultimately helping to increase alternative public safety funding.[77] These budget transfers represented a tiny fraction of the MPD's overall spending, but were nonetheless meaningful early wins.

Organizers were also seeding the ground for what would become the struggle to change the city charter to replace the MPD and its governance structure. Beyond the creation of the OVP's public health approach, which would eventually form the backbone of the 2020 effort, the city's BLM activism had pushed a new slate of city council members into office who were fighting for more power over the MPD. By 2019 the fault lines between the council's most left-leaning members and Mayor Frey had grown clearer. One result of this growing tension was a proposal for a charter amendment that would shift direct supervision of the MPD from the mayor to shared control between the council and mayor. The council also began to consider proposals to challenge another aspect of the city charter: eliminating the mandatory minimum number of officers, a provision won by the officers federation in 1961. While neither of these proposals ultimately moved forward, they were early forays into the council's increasing desire for more direct oversight of the MPD and its officers.

The new narrative undergirding police abolition, however, did not go uncontested, even among other anti-police-violence activists. In a 2018 interview, for example, when I asked a TCC4J organizer to describe the current moment in policing, she replied that there was now a "division" within "people who are anti-police." The dividing line was not just (or even primarily) about abolitionists versus non-abolitionists, but also about differing strategies about how to best end "policing as we know it." Describing the pushback TCC4J had received from abolitionist organizers on the CPAC model, she said other activists believed "we should be calling for total abolition" rather than community control. The TCC4J organizer agreed, partially: "I agree with abolition, but . . . community control can be that step towards it. It's not like a reform, like there's some insignificant group . . . rubber stamping stuff. This is actually people saying, 'This is how . . . we want our communities to be policed! This is how we want our communities to feel safe!'"[78]

Other organizers in the radical reform camp were more ambivalent about abolition, grappling with its implications. An organizer with Justice for Justine, for example, noted in a 2018 interview:

It's something that I'm trying to continue to educate myself on because on the face of it sounds . . . it sounds crazy that you would do away with police. At the same time, the current system is untenable and needs to be fixed. And I don't know if it can be fixed in a way that fully addresses all the issues that our community has. So I'm receptive to the idea. I'd like to know what the end state looks like and how you handle various situations. Like, I don't know what that looks like. It's a very long-term kind of process. I guess what I would say is, I'm focused on finding the kind of things we can do right now to make the situation [better], while continuing to support people working for complete structural changes to the system that would alleviate all of the major problems.

This kind of ambivalence about police abolition and what exactly "complete structural change" might look like would, by 2020, foster an enormous distrust across radical reformers and the abolitionist trio, even as many of the reformers embraced the idea of abolition. And it previewed Minneapolis residents' eventual ambivalence about the charter amendment to end the MPD.

Taking Stock

Through several years of BLM protests, including the 4th Precinct occupation in 2015, activists successfully raised the salience of police violence in Minneapolis, changing the common sense about the MPD and helping to elect city council members willing to consider deeper shifts in policing. Yet there was no slowing in the pace of lethal police violence (nor the protests that followed) in the City of Lakes. By 2017 this perceived failure of reform led some activists to begin to fight for something new: police defunding as a route to abolition. Abolitionist activists and their allies quickly got to work, building the public imagination and desire for a police-free city. Though no one knew what the future held, they were seeding the ground for more radical transformations that would take root in unexpected ways by 2020.

Of course, not everyone was on board with this framing of the problem of police violence or their preferred solutions. As explicitly abolitionist groups like MPD150, Reclaim the Block, and Black Visions gained traction, other activists and organizers pushed back, arguing that reform had not failed; we had just never solved the accountability problems plaguing the MPD. Others argued that there were better routes to abolition, including community control of the police. As a result, while some activists in Minneapolis pushed forward bigger and bolder defunding initiatives, building eventually to the 2020 and 2021 charter initiatives, others continued to fight for *radical reform*, including challenging the power of the police officers federation. Perhaps unexpectedly, the radical reformers would be joined in opposition to the charter initiative by a seemingly unlikely set of allies—including downtown business elites and some of the violence interruption groups working to deescalate conflicts in the community who are profiled in chapter 6. And all of these groups would work to claim that their group best represented the interests of the city residents most exposed to both police and community violence.

CHAPTER THREE

The Residents Left Out

*(with Amber Joy Powell and
Christopher E. Robertson)*

IT'S THE EVENING of November 16, 2018. Gathered inside a room at
the University of Minnesota's Urban Research and Outreach-Engagement
Center, situated right next door to the 4th Precinct station of the Minneapolis Police Department (MPD), is a multiracial and mixed-age crowd of
Northsiders in conversation with their council member, Jeremiah Ellison.
As we saw in chapter 2, Ellison was a young Black progressive, local artist,
and key figure in the 2015 occupation of the 4th Precinct, elected to office
in 2017 in part through promises of challenging police power. Forums like
this one, held so that Ellison could hear his constituents' dreams for their
neighborhood, gauge their policy priorities, and build community, were
happening across the city. Many focused specifically on public safety: How
did residents want the new slate of council members to address police
violence?

As Ellison's constituents gathered around tables laden with markers and
poster board, the event was disrupted. Activists, predominantly young and
Black, interrupted the meeting, taking turns on a bullhorn to castigate
Ellison (another "dirty politician"), the audience ("white faces . . . looking at us in disgust"), and the event (a "nice little meeting" where people
would "sit here and talk about nothing, for a whole 'nother year").[1] This,
too, was happening throughout the city: as residents and city leaders gathered, activists often disrupted them, castigating the forums as a waste of
time and energy, nothing more than an attempt to pacify the public without making real change.

But this night was special. This community forum was held a year into the new council members' tenure and three years, to the day, since Jamar Clark died. Ellison's team had scheduled it on the same day as a major commemorative rally organized by Twin Cities Coalition for Justice for Jamar (TCC4J). This lack of recognition looked to activists like a failure and a sign of deeper rot in the city. These kinds of events, and the politicians who led them, they argued, would never make change. What would? As one of the key TCC4J organizers, Sam Martinez, declared to Ellison's constituents: "Our feet—the people's feet—in the streets . . . these are the people who brought you a better Minneapolis, none of these fucking politicians." The "true makers of history," Martinez continued, were the people whose sacrifices had changed the city.

At first glance, it might seem strange to shut down a community meeting—ostensibly a people's forum—to shout at an elected official for not listening to "the people" or "the community." Not surprisingly, Ellison took this tack, telling the activists that those in the audience were "Northsiders" and "your neighbors." But to the activists this was *not* their community. As Nekima Levy Armstrong, the former president of NAACP Minneapolis and a 2017 mayoral contender, toddler on her hip, replied: "Not a single one of you," she said, was "in sight" when "the people" came to the streets and saw "Jamar's blood was still on the ground!" Her neighbors were the people who were with her across those eighteen days of the occupation. Another protester added, "These are not our neighbors if they not standing with us . . . My neighbors are the ones who stand with me!" Addressing Ellison, they declared: "If you're not standing with the community, you're standing against the community, and the community will stand against you." For the protesters at the event, *the community* was not the residents of the neighborhood, but instead what sociologist Andrea Boyles describes as the protest community, or people who are part of the movement.[2]

Ellison and the city council, which had recently failed to push forward a charter amendment to gain control over the MPD from the mayor, the demonstrators argued, had failed the protest community. They demanded that the investigations against the officers who killed Clark be reopened because "no one deserves to be killed by the police." Most importantly, they argued that only with community control of the police—through the Civilian Police Accountability Council (CPAC)—could the city end the terror of "killer cops." Those changes would happen not in the city council but rather through the work of the people, including the Minneapolis residents they envisioned as being elected to serve on the council. Importantly, TCC4J insisted that CPAC would be run not by a new set of politicians but by people who had real experience with police violence, either as defenders of vulnerable groups or as survivors. Those were *the people* and *the community* who would be able to finally rein in the "cold-blooded murderers."

This confrontation was a particularly sharp example of the tensions emerging between different visions of *what* should be done about MPD and *who* should direct that process. As sociologist Jeremy Levine argues, these kinds of community forums often make clear that "there is no such thing as a single, cohesive community voice."[3] Instead, the bounds and voice of the "community" are an active site of political struggle as activists, community leaders, and elected officials strive to define the community's interests and position themselves as its *authentic* representatives.[4] The jockeying would only intensify in Minneapolis after 2020.

In this chapter, I press pause on the unfolding story of political struggle over the MPD in Minneapolis to better understand how everyday residents worked to make sense of this new scrutiny on police violence and imagine potential solutions—as well as the ways these attitudes were shaped by people's racial identities and experiences with police. To understand these divides, we spoke directly with Northsiders; between 2017 and 2019 our research team interviewed more than one hundred residents, interviewing people who responded to recruitment flyers and wanted to share their experiences.[5] A few of these participants had been active in demonstrations or other public-facing events, but many were unlikely to show up at either protests or community forums. They represented not necessarily the average resident, but instead, a diverse range of voices in Northside's neighborhoods, people who were often left out of the public conversation about policing despite elected officials' and activists' invocations of community. It was through this diversity that our team came to better understand the complex politics of policing that would define the city's ambivalent response to the murder of George Floyd.[6]

North Minneapolis in the Black Lives Matter Era

Recall from chapter 1 that North Minneapolis has a long history of acute police-citizen conflict. The area was a destination for Black migrants during the Great Migration, and it was Northside's Plymouth Avenue that erupted in flames in the Long Hot Summer of 1967. Thus, it was no surprise that some of the largest early Black Lives Matter (BLM) demonstrations in the city emerged there. And that was what led our team to focus on Northside as we turned to listen to residents' voices.

Table 3.1 Demographics of interview participants by race

	Residents of color		White residents	
	%	N	%	N
Race/ethnicity				
White	—	—	100	24
Black, African American	74	65	—	—
Native, American Indian	7	6	—	—
Latino, Hispanic	1	1	—	—
Asian, Asian American	1	1	—	—
Multiracial or Other Race	17	15	—	—
Sex/gender				
Male	57	50	33	8
Female	42	37	63	15
Nonbinary	1	1	4	1
Age				
18–30 years	32	26	17	4
31–50 years	34	28	38	9
51+ years	34	28	46	11
Educational attainment				
Less than high school	12	10	0	0
High school graduate	32	27	4	1
Some college	47	40	50	12
Bachelor's degree or higher	9	8	46	11
Total N		88		24

Note: Data are from participants' responses to a self-administered survey completed prior to the interview. Some respondents did not answer all questions; percentages are only for non-missing responses. Percentages may not sum to 100 due to rounding.

These interviews, conducted by a team of undergraduate and graduate students of color, began in 2017, two years after the killing of Jamar Clark and right before Justine (Ruszczyk) Damond was shot and killed. Recruiting through flyers and word-of-mouth referrals, we ended the formal interviews in 2019, having witnessed the stories of 112 Northside residents.[7] As summarized in table 3.1, we talked to fifty-eight men, fifty-two women, and two non-binary adults, ranging in age from eighteen to seventy-six (with a median age of forty-three years). The majority identified as people of color, with nearly 60 percent of our respondents identifying as Black or African American.

Unlike the better-studied poor communities of color along the densely populated East Coast, or even in nearby Chicago, where the emblematic image of the neighborhood is a dilapidated high-rise, in North Minneapolis the most common building type is a single-family home. That visual difference does little, however, to alleviate the stark poverty, environmental risks, or spatial and economic isolation of the area. But it does mean that there are more white residents living in North Minneapolis than in many other hyper-segregated low-income neighborhoods in urban centers across the country. As table 3.1 documents, these white residents in Northside occupied a different socio-economic stratum. The white residents we spoke with benefited from substantially higher incomes, educational attainment, and homeownership rates. Thus, while white participants and participants of color shared social proximity in Northside, they also occupied distinct socio-economic worlds—divergences that shaped their attitudes toward police as we show later in the chapter.

Black America's Legal Estrangement

When our team published a public report on these interviews in 2020, we titled it "Over-Policed and Under-Protected," reflecting the key theme— and tension—at the heart of the project.[8] As we will show, most residents of color detailed pervasive negative encounters with law enforcement, or what the Minnesota Department of Human Rights would later describe as "race-based policing," including frequent police stops and abusive treatment. And each time the police killed someone, in Minneapolis or elsewhere, it reinforced residents' sense that they too could be the next victim. But they also perceived a great deal of disorder and violence in their neighborhoods committed by other residents, which left them exposed to unacceptably high victimization risks. This feeling of exposure resonated with a broader sense of being excluded from the benefits of policing services, including delayed responses to 911 calls, apathy or outright hostility from officers when they did respond, and the MPD's seeming indifference to well-known problem spots in the neighborhood. They described, in other words, feeling over-policed and under-protected.

This result was, in some ways, unsurprising. As sociologist and legal scholar Monica Bell argues, this dual reality of over-policing and under-protection has defined many low-income Black Americans' relationship with the police, not just in Minneapolis but across the country and stretching back generations.[9] The result is what Bell describes as *legal estrangement*, or "the intuition among many people in poor communities of color that the law operates to exclude them from society."[10] Importantly, in this account, inadequate protection is fueled not simply by the failures of law enforcement (i.e., "under-policing") but also by the many other government agencies and services, from education to welfare and health care, that reflect, reproduce, and sometimes exacerbate racial and economic inequality. Together, these overlapping layers of exclusion stratify life outcomes by race, positioning police as simply the most visible face of state oppression.[11]

That means that the answer cannot simply be trying to change policing in Black communities to look like it does in white communities, because the problem is not simply under-policing but everything else that makes those neighborhoods look and feel different. And it was residents' explanations of this intuition that in the end were the most unexpected and illuminating. We were witnessing not just the oft-repeated problems in policing, but residents' ideas about what it might take to "make everyone feel safe." As our interviewees explained, the problem was not simply "police violence" but instead racism in America. Yet residents' deep legal estrangement also prompted a guarded kind of realism about whether and how much change was even possible. If true redress was unlikely to come, some concluded that their only option was to turn to the police and hope for the best. These tensions would later become central to the contestation over the charter amendment to "end" the MPD, as city leaders, organizers, and residents debated which option would best protect North Minneapolis.

Confronting Crime, Seeking Protection

Concerns about disorder and violence in the community were often front and center as our interviews began and we attempted to understand how residents felt about their neighborhood's safety. Our participants often conveyed significant worries about crime, including gun violence, open-air drug markets and the opioid crisis, prostitution, teenage loitering and public fights, domestic disputes, and high-speed traffic. And many went to great lengths to ensure their personal safety, adapting creatively to persistent disorder and danger—including frequent gunshots and sirens.

We often heard variations of "I take care of myself," as residents assured us that they avoided neighborhood violence by staying home and keeping a low profile. Denise, a Black woman in her late thirties, for example, told us that she felt safe in her neighborhood because she knew how to navigate the streets.[12] But she continued: "I mean, you hear gunshots . . . people getting robbed . . . [people getting] beat up." The two nights before our interview, Denise had heard gunshots while in her home. Many other Northsiders described similar disconnects between their thoughts on community violence and their own security. But they were also often boosters of the community, proud of what they, their families, and their neighbors had built in Northside—including strong community bonds, racial and ethnic diversity, and locally owned businesses and other amenities.

The persistently high exposure to potential violence shaped how our participants thought about police. Many concluded that law enforcement did not "serve and protect" Northside. Police were too slow to respond to visible disorder, criminal activity, and violence in their neighborhood. Tyrone, a Black man in his mid-fifties, recounted his frustration, saying the police would drive past scenes like "guys hanging out at the bus stops, selling drugs, and doing what they wanna do." He questioned, "After you done passed by six times, see the same guy out there, wouldn't you stop him? Fifteen, twenty minutes you been out there . . . Ain't called the boss, you know. So what are you doing out here? That's one of the things. The Northside is a very dangerous side."

Local "hot spots" for crime, long known to both residents and the police, served as particular sore subjects for residents like Tyrone. They pointed to certain bus stops and businesses, including a Cub Foods grocery store (which would be looted in 2020) as well as a gas station known to residents as "Murder Station." This strip of Northside was often full of disorder, from trash in the streets to a large number of unhoused and mentally ill people and young men milling about with seemingly little to do. If the city knew these blocks were frequently used as open-air drug markets and sites of violence, why was so little done to address the problem? Police seemed ever-present in this area and yet wholly uninterested or unable to respond effectively. For a few residents, the conclusion was obvious: the MPD allowed crime to fester in North Minneapolis to punish residents.

This perception of neglect was fueled by *how* police entered these spaces. When asked how they typically interacted with police, many described officers speeding by in their cars (often with sirens blaring), sitting around in parking lots, or doing off-duty security work for local businesses. On some blocks, officers would drive up and down "five to ten times a day." And when officers looked at them, it wasn't with a smile but with a scowl, mean-mugging residents as they flew by in SUVs. Our interviewees rarely witnessed police officers getting out of their cars, walking the "beat" to get to know residents, or otherwise positively interacting with the community. All of this made officers seem more like an occupying force there to punish and control rather than agents of the state there to serve and protect residents.

When police did appear in situations where they were needed, residents often saw them as under-delivering on the promise of protection. Residents described interactions where officers showed up but were unwilling to render aid, failed to provide adequate levels of attention and concern, or responded to the needs of respondents with derision. For example, Kayla, a Black woman in her mid-thirties, recapped an incident where her car ran out of gas as she was driving home late with her young son:

> I seen the police. I flagged 'em down. They did a U-turn. I said, "Oh, that's some relief," because I don't like being out here in these streets late at night. And when they pulled up I was like, "I ran out of gas and I'm trying to get to the gas station. I just don't have a gas can but I've got money." You know what they told me? They told me they couldn't help me . . . So, you know, me and my son was left to walk from Plymouth [Avenue] all the way to our place.

Kayla lodged a complaint, but she never heard back from the department.

More frequently, residents experienced police contact through vehicle and pedestrian stops—encounters fraught with risk. Many of these stops were what scholars call pretextual: officers use low-level violations (e.g., expired vehicle tags or jaywalking) to stop "suspicious" adults walking or driving in the community. These kinds of investigatory stops are one of the most common forms of police-citizen contact across the country, producing powerful signifiers of who is included or excluded in our society. Such stops disproportionately target people of color, particularly young men, who conclude from the experience that they must live under a kind of "second-class" citizenship, enduring intrusive stops and demeaning treatment to which white Americans are rarely exposed.[13]

Such stories were common in our interviews, especially among young men of color. DeJuan, a Black man in his early twenties, shared:

> Some people on my block used to sell drugs and stuff. So my block would be watched heavily . . . One time, I'm coming home from a friend's house . . . and this police officer followed me . . . never turned on his lights, and then as soon as I was about to park, he flashed his lights and then didn't even come out of the car. He pulls up to the side of my car and then with his gun pointed out, he's like, "What are you doing?" And I'm like, "What do you mean what am I doing? I'm going home." And you know, that also builds that mistrust, because now, you

won't even get out and identify yourself. You're just going to point a gun at me out your window? And then when I ask, like, "What's your badge number?" you throw a ticket at me . . . I don't really have really good experiences with police, especially being a dreadhead. I'm automatically assumed a threat or like someone to watch and keep an eye on.

For DeJuan, his hairstyle, together with his age, race, gender, and area of residence, meant that he was stereotyped as one of the "usual suspects" rather than as a law-abiding resident.

The aggressive policing of everyday behaviors galled many respondents. Instead of dealing with crime, they saw police as busying themselves by harassing residents. As Darnell, a Black man in his early twenties, summarized: "Any other day they'll show up just to harass you and racially profile you. But when there's actually a murder, like of a kid . . . he got shot and killed in his own house, and they still haven't found who did that. So, you know, I don't really—I don't know if they're there to protect and serve or—not us!" Ricky, a Black man in his early fifties, was more direct: police "like to fuck with [people of] color. That's what they do." Residents, in other words, largely did not simply want "more" policing, knowing all too well the harms of over-policing. What these quotes express is a desire instead for policing that was responsive and reflected the dignity of neighborhood residents, rather than control-oriented policing aimed at community suppression.

The Trauma of Police Violence

Residents' sense of legal estrangement was fueled not just by this everyday harassment and failure to protect, but also by their experiences of police violence, and those of their friends, family, and neighbors. For residents of color, racialized police violence was visceral and personal. For some, it began with formative encounters in early life, or what political scientist Vesla Weaver describes as "state baptism,"[14] which continued to haunt them for decades. For others, the experiences were quite recent. Together, three-quarters of the Black, Hispanic, Native, and multiracial men in our study described some kind of direct maltreatment from officers (ranging from verbal abuse to assault). People recalled slurs, shouted threats, being shoved and choked, invasive pat-downs and body searches, tight handcuffs, and more in their encounters with police officers.

Thomas, a fifty-something Black veteran, described a harrowing story of getting stopped in his car late at night by two young white officers:

It was about 2:00 in the morning. The police stopped us and they said, "What you niggers doing out here? Were you up stealing something?" And we said, "We're veterans." You know, they called us niggers. So they took [us] out, put our hands on the car, and they took everything out of our pockets except the money. So seeing all our items—phones, keys—on the car, we're like, "Where's our money?" And one of the police officers said, "Nigger, we don't have your money." The money's in our pocket but we don't see the money on the car. So the police officer said, "Well, you want to check your pockets?" Then, all of a sudden, you're thinking about checking your pocket, he unloosens his weapon. So if you go in your pocket, he's gon' say you're reaching for a weapon. So we were like, "Fuck it. Keep the money." So he gave us up, but the money was in our pocket. Still, though, he didn't put the money on the car. He was provoking us, you know, enticing us to go in your pocket so he's got a reason to shoot us. And that was a setup.

This traumatic incident piled up multiple police abuses, from the stop without cause, to not being seen or recognized as an honorable citizen (and veteran—"C'mon, We served this country"), to the racial epithet, to the lethal threat posed by officers with their weapons out. Although the missing money was in Thomas's pocket, it is notable that his default assumption was that the officers could and would steal with impunity—or, worse, that it was a "setup" for murdering him.

These negative encounters were reinforced by police killings of Black Americans, locally and across the country, especially those that went "viral" after public pressure and BLM activism.[15] These deaths of people who looked like them reminded participants that their life was on the line too, and were a deep source of trauma for many.[16] Ending his interview by invoking the names of several recent victims of lethal police violence, Thomas concluded: "I hate what they [police] do. Like, oh my God, man. And all of them getting away with murder." Thomas's experience of facing an officer's gun was not unusual. Several men we spoke to recounted vivid memories of having their life "flash before their eyes" as they stared down the barrel. David, a Hispanic man in his late twenties, similarly had many negative encounters with police, including being arrested after calling 911 to report that his fiancée had endangered their infant and other "fucked up shit." David recalled watching the video of "the whole Jamar Clark thing" and concluding that police "hate . . . people of color" and "don't like dealing with us . . . It's just like, 'Fuck you! Shut up! Get in the car! You're going to jail!'"

These cases weren't just media stories; they were *personal* to some of our participants who knew the victims. Timothy, a Black man in his mid-twenties, had known Jamar Clark growing up and described the way his friend was killed as "worse than torture," reflecting that afterward, he was "really fearin' for my own life." Another one of our participants, Marlon, a Black man in his mid-forties, was among the crowd that witnessed officers shoot and kill Clark. When asked whether "witnessing that horrific event . . . change[d] the way" he thought about police, Marlon replied that instead it "solidified" his beliefs about police violence, adding that "we've been hearing about police shooting for some years," tracing this history back to Amadou Diallo's killing in 1990s New York. But cell phone recordings and social media had made these recent cases even more visible. From these experiences, Marlon concluded, "Police . . . view us as disposable. I think they just don't care."

As a result, these men (to varying degrees) worked to avoid the police, with a few participants describing police nearly exclusively as a threat. "I do not feel safe with the police, period," said Teddy, a man in his mid-thirties:

> Because I've been targeted too much by the police, you know, jump-ing out on me, violating my rights, putting my life in danger while they point guns at me for no apparent reason just to stop me, detain me . . . The people I feel most scared about is the police in the Black neighborhood. I'm more scared of walking by the police officer or being harmed by a police officer in my neighborhood more than I fear a gang banger . . . They can be the hardest guy in the hood, I'll walk right by him. But if the police down that way, I'm not going that way.

Ronnie, a young Native and Black man, agreed: "They're crooked just like regular street people. And that's just my honesty. They just as bad. They're a gang, too."[17] DeJuan, the Black twenty-something profiled for his dreads, said similarly that police "don't stoke a sense of security or a sense of protection. They're more like that bully you don't want to see in the hallway, 'cause you don't ever know what their day is like. So you don't want to walk by and then get punched in the face."

Though less frequent, women of color also experienced police violence directly—as well as through threats to their children and partners. Of the thirty-eight Black, Native, Asian, and multiracial women interviewees, over half described experiencing threatening behavior from police toward themselves and/or their loved ones. Cameron, a multiracial person in their twenties, described one of their earliest experiences with police. An officer called in to mediate a dispute between Cameron (who identified as non-binary, but described themself then as "a very tiny woman")[18] and two other people turned quickly to violence. Cameron narrated that the officer:

> slammed me on the police car and continued to search me . . . And not only did he do that, his body was completely pressing up against my body and I could feel his genitalia on me. And so it's like not only do you not treat me like a human being, like a person, you don't even speak to me. The first thing you do is put your hands on me . . . And then I got arrested . . . and I got left in a car. For about 15, 20 minutes, and it was 95 degrees. So you can imagine. I felt like I was about to die inside this car. And I remember being terrified not knowing what was next. Not knowing if they would pull around the corner, if they would go in the alley, if they would beat me, if they would rape me. I didn't know what was next. I don't put anything past these people because they beat people. They rape people. They rob people. They kill people. I just remember being terrified. That's my first run-in with the police.

This experience, and ones like it that Cameron heard from friends and relatives, deeply shaped their attitudes about police. And as in Thomas's narrative, it wasn't just because of what officers did, but also what the cops *could* have done. Cameron's awareness of those threats turned the encounter from painful to terrifying.

Women also experienced vicarious criminalization as they attempted to mitigate the threat officers posed to their partners and children. This distress was most acute among Black women with teenage sons.[19] Donna, a Black mother in her mid-forties, talked at length about how the police viewed her son and how that impacted her:

> I know he's feared . . . I know that he's . . . America's most wanted, and not America's most gifted . . . that's the reality for us . . . We don't know . . . if we gon' see them when they come home! God forbid if they wanna have some dreads! . . . Because then they gon' be really profiled! You know, so it's like you have that . . . you have that fear when you bringing up boys.

Similar accounts came from younger women with romantic partners who they feared would be exposed to police violence. Dee Dee, a Black woman in her twenties, described the vicarious trauma of witnessing police abuse. In one of several instances she told us about, police accosted the father of her child in a parking lot after he had gone to grab something from a car. As she witnessed the interaction, he shouted at her to "Record them!" She did, thinking about the video of Philando Castile dying after being shot by police, filmed by his girlfriend. While this specific confrontation ended without further violence, knowing what could have happened haunted her.

These very real concerns about police violence made some women hesitant to turn to police when they experienced gender-based violence, including sexual assault, stalking, and domestic violence.[20] In addition, involving the police carried a risk that the person reaching out for help could also be criminalized. Detailing her attempt to enlist law enforcement for help after a sexual assault, Imani, a multiracial woman in her late thirties, told us:

> I called them [police] one specific time when I had got raped . . . and what I remember about that is let's just say . . . [he] was a friend, but evidently, he wasn't too much of a friend to slip a [drug] in my drink at the bar. But I remember leaving from the bar disoriented and [with] blurred vision and blacking out. When I woke up, I was somewhere else that I don't remember getting there and everything, but I was raped. And I called the police and they treated me like I was a disease. Like I was the suspect. I'm the one, literally like I'm defending myself and just . . . How you think—you think I just ran out here in the middle of the street with hair, barely half-dressed with no shoes or something on?

Imani's account reveals the frustration victims of sexual violence often encounter when enlisting the help of law enforcement. Instead of listening to her story and trying to help her remove her items from the perpetrator's house, they treated her like a "disease" and a "suspect." This treatment, in turn, reinforced her lack of trust in police.

As with the men of color, some of the women of color concluded that they would *never* want to call the police for help. Cameron, for example, who described their experience of being locked in a police car, told the interviewer:

> If I am in trouble, if I have a situation, I'm wrapping my brain on who is it that's actually going to come to my rescue. And unfortunately, I have never ever thought that the police was a good idea to call . . . You have to ask yourself every single time when you pick up the phone, "What is this phone call going to transpire to?" Because people that look like me . . . have to ask ourselves: Are they going to make the situation worse? And unfortunately, it hurts to say, but a lot of times they do make the situation worse.

Cameron concluded that help would have to come from somewhere else. While not everyone was this adamant about not calling the police, the underlying fear of police violence was pervasive among Black respondents. And it was not just in Minneapolis; by 2020 national polling found that half of Black Americans would rather be robbed or burglarized than be stopped by police.[21]

The Exceptions That Prove the Rule: Positive Experiences

Our participants' experiences with police were not uniformly negative. Indeed, among Black respondents, two-thirds reported that they had experienced a positive interaction with an officer.[22] These positive experiences included getting assistance, help, or information; prompt response times and polite interactions; and police going beyond their obligations to help. In many cases, these stories reflected the inverse of the procedural injustice described earlier—for example, we heard about officers providing assistance when residents were locked out of their cars, responding after a tornado, calmly breaking up potentially violent situations, and choosing to let people go with a warning rather than a ticket.

But in many cases, these stories represented low expectations for what constituted a positive interaction rather than protective and responsive policing. For instance, asked if she was satisfied with the police response to a violent altercation, Porsha, a Black woman in her mid-twenties, reported, "Yeah, I was. You know, they didn't come in with no hostility, like, 'Oh you guys are out here trying to fight, we're gonna just take you both to jail.' No, they tried to find other ways to get a solution." Similarly, another Black resident described that after getting pulled over with a friend for a broken taillight, "the cops was pretty nice." He continued: "It wasn't an ugly incident . . . I didn't get disrespected." Similarly, Marsha, a Black woman in her late forties, described how officers responded promptly when she called to report her daughter as a missing person. When her daughter came home shortly thereafter, police stopped back to check up on the incident and talked to the girl, showing what Marsha read as real concern. For many Northside residents, interactions were positive when they were resolved without verbal or physical aggression, unnecessary arrests, or apathy.

Other residents—even sometimes the same people who'd had negative interactions with police in the past—described how police had protected them. Imani, who described how she felt police treated her like a "disease" after a sexual assault, also told us another instance where, "If it wasn't for the police that day, I would be dead . . . I really needed 'em right then and there, and they couldn't have come no sooner." These mixed experiences left Imani deeply ambivalent about police. Similarly, Timothy, the family friend of Jamar Clark, described how an officer had been called to respond to a domestic violence incident where he was being abused by a female partner. His partner had told observers to call the police and identified Timothy as the instigator. Police arrived and roughed up Timothy. Yet, he said, "They looked into it and seen both sides of the situation." Seeing the injuries on Timothy (which had been documented in previous altercations), the police asked Timothy if he wanted to press charges. For Timothy, even a situation where he was *physically assaulted* could be perceived through the lens of a positive experience—because at least police were "fair" in their eventual response.

The last kind of positive experiences were interactions with police at community events, often through community policing initiatives. Though less common than the one-on-one encounters noted previously, these kinds of events sometimes came up in conversation as examples of positive interactions. Several participants, for example, noted the programs police ran for youth, including rehabbing bikes, giving out certificates for McDonalds, and appearing at events like National Night Out. These events were often the kinds of get-to-know-you opportunities many residents expressed a desire for police to attend.

Yet participants would often note that these interactions were disconnected from everyday policing (often involving different officers) and did little to allay broader concerns about law enforcement. Dee Dee, who earlier described filming the police while they interacted with her partner, told us about another time her younger relative had received a bicycle from the police through one of these outreach programs. When asked if that experience would "increase the trust" or give her "hope about police relations," Dee Dee replied: "It don't do that much. Because the bad outweighs the good. We see that one lil' good thing, rarely, but you always hearing something negative or bad. And it's not just North Minneapolis police. It's not just Minnesota police. It's police US-wide." Rudy, a Black woman in her late thirties, was even more critical. Describing the National Night Out event, she argued: "It's just something they can check off on their list of 'We did something cool in an under-served community. Um, don't be mad at us when we shoot your children.'"

As Rudy and Dee Dee's comments suggest, positive experiences with law enforcement were often drowned out by the procession of negative ones they experienced personally and vicariously through their friends, families, and media. Or as Marcel, a Black man in his late fifties, summarized, "I seen them do good things, you know. I seen some good cops. I'll put it like this—I've seen twice as many bad as I've seen good." In that context, community outreach was sometimes construed as clumsy propaganda rather than a real sign of change or commitment to care.[23] Yet while the existence of "good" officers did not negate the pervasive experiences of discrimination and abuse so many residents experienced, it did fuel residents' cautious hope that when they might have to call 911, maybe it would not go so badly. This continual promise of the law's potential to provide help also shaped attitudes about police reform.[24]

The Possibilities and Limits of Police Reform

In some ways, what residents wanted from the police was deceptively simple. As Kel, a Black man in his early fifties, succinctly put it: "Stop killing Black folks!" Yet for many respondents the "problem" was not just police violence, but racism more broadly, which impacted their lives through multiple and overlapping institutions of exclusion.[25] Thus, while residents of color often supported police reform, many saw it as woefully inadequate to address the under-protection and over-policing of Northside. And they were *right*: police reform through decades of city history had largely failed to stop racialized police violence in Minneapolis (a headline that would ricochet across the world after George Floyd was murdered). Reactions to this reality varied—from disengaging with the process, to settling for reform despite its limits, to promoting more radical changes in public safety.

When asked about police reform directly, the Northside residents we spoke with largely supported the kinds of initiatives pursued during the BLM era in Minneapolis and other cities, including diversifying recruitment, eliminating racial profiling, and ending aggressive "quality of life" policing (which residents felt—and scholars have argued—led to racial profiling).[26] Training on mental health issues, racial disparities, and cultural differences, and more uses of alternatives to lethal force, were also popular ideas. And residents desperately wanted more oversight and accountability for police violence. Many of our interviewees directly connected these reforms to specific instances of lethal police violence that might have been prevented, concluding that officers "need more training" or that if officers lived in the neighborhoods they policed, they might be more compassionate toward their neighbors.

Support for reform quickly turned critical, however, in discussions about how much could really change in policing. This was perhaps clearest in discussions of body cameras, the reform effort best known to residents at the time. Our interviewees were largely supportive of requiring officers to wear body cameras, hoping that they would improve accountability.[27] For example, Rhonda, a Black woman in her fifties interviewed alongside her husband Phil, commented: "I think that that would help . . . [to] see exactly what's transpired." But Phil interjected, "After something done happened and you need the body camera . . . they holds back on it." Rhonda reluctantly agreed, noting that body cameras would not increase accountability if cameras were turned off, leadership hid the footage, or police "made excuses." AJ, a Black man in his twenties, similarly reflected, "Body cameras are trash because most of them don't wear 'em . . . They turn 'em off."

Residents did not have to turn to hypothetical examples to make the case that body cameras were no panacea—the reality of that was all over the news. Teddy, who described his deep fear of police, for example, commented on a police shooting in a Southern state where a female officer (likely Betty Shelby of Tulsa, Oklahoma) "killed a man on camera." He concluded, "I mean, man got his hands up and everything! . . . In front of the whole world, she kills him and she didn't serve no time . . . Why even record it? . . . Why even say bring a body cam, dash camera, anything. What use is it?" Teddy expressed that each time a new case made the news, he would think, "Ah, here it go again. They trying to cover up . . . They don't want to hold they officers responsible . . . It's just a joke." Police violence, and the lack of accountability that followed, seemed an unbreakable cycle, each instance of police aggression invalidating the possibility of reform. "It hasn't worked then," concluded Kenneth, a Black man in his early sixties, "and I doubt it's going to work now."

Just like the activists profiled in chapter 2, residents were distressed by this continued pace of lethal police violence throughout the early BLM years, which fueled perceptions of a "crooked" system. As Dee Dee decried, "We have body, you know, body cameras or innocent bystanders' footage saying you got this on camera and you STILL don't have no justice . . . No! . . . This is manslaughter!" Dee Dee continued that justice would be: "You need to be ripped of your badge and you need to go to jail." Similarly, Marcel, who noted that he'd seen twice as many bad cops as good, argued: "The laws should matter all the time for police officers, for civilians, for everybody," but instead there were three "standards": "your standards for whites, your standards for people of color, and then there is police standards." Police, he continued, "violate every one of their standards, but they're never held accountable for it."

Repeatedly experiencing this trauma reinforced for many residents the reality of racism and anti-Blackness, which was unlikely to be reformed away. As Donna, the mother who described her fear for her son, told us: "We have to be real about it. We have to talk about the institutionalized racism. We gotta talk about the systemic racism." Ms. Lenora, a multiracial woman in her sixties who was interviewed with Donna, added: "They [police] think of [us as] animals and dogs . . . So until that changes, which ain't going to happen no time soon, it's just another day, another time . . . because [they] fear our Black faces, hate our Black faces." Racism, not policing, was the root of the problem.

Or as David, the man who argued that police "hate us," concluded, "I mean it's fucked up, but, uh, you know, we live in America." And in America, not only was racism alive and well, but police had power. And that power blocked change. As Kayla, the woman who had to walk home after running out of gas, described, BLM organizers could bring people together "when the police are not right." But, she continued, "They only can do what they can do, and that's protest . . . fill up the courtrooms in support . . . But at the end of the day, it's still they word against the police." Or as Kel, who cried out for cops to stop killing Black people, put it with a rueful laugh: "[Reform] is not gonna happen because there's always going to be "more white cops . . . in charge."

Damned If You Do, Damned If You Don't

These quotes show how residents powerfully voiced what Derrick Bell, one of the founders of critical race theory, understood as the *permanence* of racism in the United States.[28] But that did not stop them from yearning for, and striving toward, something better. Like the activists discussed in chapter 2, some Minneapolis residents were shifting in these years toward a more radical approach. Rudy, the woman who described her distrust of National Night Out events, was perhaps most forceful:

> We're still dying quicker than we can effect change . . . I don't wanna be dead before I experience a neighborhood where I feel safe when the police are around . . . We all deserve to feel safe in our homes and . . . our neighborhoods. We all deserve to have policing in our communities, or ways of managing things in our communities that are, like, helpful and positive . . . that build rather than tear down and destroy.

Rudy's powerful call exemplifies how residents were beginning to envision broader horizons for change beyond the police. In this vein, a handful of participants connected Northside's long history of racial segregation—including a lack of affordable housing, failing schools, environmental concerns, and limited economic opportunities—to today's disorder and crime. Solving these issues far beyond policing, they implied, was another way to build a safer Northside.

Roughly one in every six residents of color we interviewed had started to explore these kinds of bold transformations, and a few espoused explicit support for police abolition. Evoking Black nationalist discourses, for example, one interviewee described how the community should retreat from the (white) state, "build[ing] our community back up" and "policing our own," instead of "rely[ing] on government and the system."[29] Cameron, one of the strongest voices for abolition among our participants, argued that police will "continue to murder people and . . . make the situation worse" because they "are not here to serve and protect people with pigment in their skin. Period." Instead of policing, the community needed a new blueprint. Cameron had such a clear picture, in part, because they were among the few interviewees who were active in the local protest scene. As a result, they had thought a lot about the imagined future activists were striving toward.

More commonly, however, residents described a future in which police officers still played a role in maintaining order—but in a form unrecognizable to today's residents. Pam, a sixty-one-year-old Black woman, advised: "Get rid of 'em all and go from scratch!" Why? Because if "you keep one bad apple in that bundle, the rest of them apples gon' get bad too!" Pam dismissed the MPD's supposed reforms: "I don't pay no attention to that—'cause they gon' do what they wanna do anyway." Similarly, Teddy wanted to get "all the crooks, all the racists, all the—yeah, you just have to clean it all out . . . from the chief on down to the patrol." For these residents, only starting from "scratch" could produce a police force that would really protect and serve the community.

Despite these radical dreams, however, the most pervasive narrative we heard was doubt that elected officials would either invest in Northside or rein in the police. As Pam concluded after describing how the police should start over: "That's what I think, though it don't matter." In this realism, Minneapolis's Black residents were again giving voice to what pollsters would later see in national trends. In the heat of 2020's racial reckoning, for example, half of Black Americans told researchers that they thought the moment would *not* lead to major policy changes to address racial inequality. By 2021, 65 percent reported that they had not seen these changes happen in the intervening year.[30]

Black Northsiders' hesitation to believe in the possibility of change away from policing as we know it was also connected to their concerns about violence in the community. As noted at the start of the chapter, residents did face serious safety concerns, including high rates of gun violence. For many, this meant that police would have to be part of the equation, especially for situations involving violence. Rudy, for example, spoke of going to the community (using social media) to help resolve things like interpersonal disputes or open drug dealing, but noted that she would call 911 if she saw someone with a gun, a frequent occurrence in her neighborhood.[31]

Black women, who bear the brunt of both racism and sexism, most frequently relayed this beleaguered and resigned ambivalence on police. As Tanya, a Black woman in her fifties and longtime survivor of intimate partner violence, put it, "Sometimes—I'ma say this even though I don't like 'em [police]—I like to see them because if anything happen to me, they around. But I see 'em a lot. I see 'em a lot."[32] Tanya's deep ambivalence about the police, with her repetition of "I see 'em a lot," was a stark reminder of both the need for transforming public safety and the challenges advocates would face in trying to accomplish it. Kamela, a Black woman in her early forties, similarly described her bind: "I don't have faith in them [police] at all . . . But then at the same time, you gotta call them if you need 'em. You know what I mean? And then when they come and you need 'em, they shittin' on you. So it's like, you damned if you do, you damned if you don't."

Who's to Blame for Violence?

Residents were not only frustrated with the police. Indeed, many understood that police didn't call all the shots—they were responding, in part, to the decisions of elected officials, activists and community leaders, and everyday residents. As a result, residents often expressed frustration not only with police, but with city leaders who made bad policy, activists they saw as out of step with the community, and the community members wreaking damage on the streets.

Sometimes their frustration was with us, as a team of researchers with the University of Minnesota. This was never clearer than in a 2019 public forum we held in Northside to present early results from this study. As described in more detail in the author's note that follows this book's conclusion, we held the forum to report back to the community and to gather additional ideas for policy recommendations. But, like Ellison's forum, we collided with the divisions within the community and ideas about what would really create lasting change for Northside. At the end of the forum, one of the audience members criticized us for "wasting people's time"—why, they asked, had we spent so many resources just to lecture residents on what they already knew? Those resources, they argued, would have been better directed to the community, who already understood the racism of the MPD. (Similar concerns would be raised in the wake of the state and federal reports on the MPD, which largely redocumented and reiterated long-standing grievances against the department.)

Why had we convened, in other words, another *nice little meeting*? It wasn't just that activists and city leaders (and researchers) had failed to rein in police violence. It was also, for many residents, that these actors and groups had simplified the problem by trying to address violence in the community *or* police violence against residents—but rarely both at once. And no one, not city leaders, or reform proponents, or researchers, seemed to be moving with the speed and urgency the situation demanded. One audience member pointedly asked our team what we were going to do to stop their "babies from being killed" on the streets. Young Black boys and men, another audience member added, were an "endangered species."

This pushback echoed what we'd heard from some residents during our interviews, especially from the small share of residents of color who were predominantly *supportive* of the police. In defending the men (and women) in blue, these residents would often foreground concerns about community violence, at times invoking the "Black-on-Black crime" terminology to disparage the BLM movement and activists. For example, Denise, who earlier in the chapter described hearing gunshots from her home at night, located the problem not in law enforcement but in "people out in the street that don't wanna follow those rules." Protest organizers, by extension, were focusing on the wrong problem(s). As Wayne, a thirty-year-old Black man, told us: "Black people kill Black people all the time. So Black Lives Matter, it's them, too."

This ambivalence among Black Northsiders about whether (and which) activists and city leaders represented their real interests—including what the problem(s) were facing the community, how to fix them, and even whether change was possible—would come to form the crux of the debates over the charter amendment to end the MPD. Because the police represented a potential source of protection, challenging police power was often met with stark resistance, not just from the city's elite but sometimes also within those communities most at risk of police violence. And when there was no one, singular "voice" for the community, its elected officials would struggle to make change in their name.

White Residents on the Police

As noted previously, Northside has a substantial share of white residents, who benefit (on average) from higher incomes and other class privileges than their neighbors of color. We interviewed some of these residents as well, conversations that allowed us to trace the attitudes about policing, police violence, and police reform among white Minneapolis residents. Like their neighbors, white Northsiders provided a diverse set of perspectives on policing and police reform in the city that would soon become an epicenter of "anti-racism" efforts.[33]

In contrast to residents of color, the white participants in our sample were largely shielded from routine experiences of criminalization and police abuse. Their experiences with police were typically positive, and they often saw police as a community resource rather than a threat. In just a handful of cases, white residents spoke about the extra police scrutiny or disrespect they garnered by living in North Minneapolis (i.e., being "out of place" in a Black neighborhood). Yet these experiences largely did not translate into experiences of abuse. Only one white respondent—Vic, a man in his early thirties who was a friend of Jamar Clark and had a history of police contact due to illicit substance use—described a personal fear of police violence. Similarly, two white women described negative interactions with police, though both attributed these encounters to their substance use problems rather than officers' misconduct. Each concluded that police were just "doing their job," a theme that appeared much more frequently in white residents' accounts.

To varying degrees, white residents were thoughtful about their racial privilege in police interactions.[34] Indeed, most of our white respondents "somewhat" or "strongly" agreed that "Police officers will judge you based on your race/ethnicity." Josh, a white man in his thirties, described how he interacted with police at neighborhood watch meetings. Whiteness, for Josh, meant that police assumed that you were their "allies" in the neighborhood. It also gave you the power to direct police attention toward people and properties white residents deemed "concerning," a power Josh felt weaponized whiteness.[35] He also shared examples of times he had directly witnessed police treat Black teens unfairly and explicitly noted the privilege he had in those interactions. Others wryly joked about these dynamics. Kerrie, a white woman in her mid-forties, for example, joked: "I'm not driving while Black, so I'll be okay."

Unlike Black residents, for whom police violence was often deeply visceral and intimate, white residents' reflections on police violence often emerged only in discussions of high-profile police killings, surfaced in mainstream consciousness by disruptive protests. Digital recordings and BLM activism allowed white residents to witness these events more directly.[36] As Rebecca, a middle-aged white woman, reflected, activists were "bringing what has been happening for a long time to the public's attention—which is . . . police murdering Black people." And it prompted many of them to develop what political scientist Jennifer Chudy terms "racial sympathy" or "distress over black suffering."[37] Three-quarters of white interviewees brought up recent high-profile cases of police violence, often noting them as inflection points in their attitudes about law enforcement. Sheila, a white woman in her forties, described a shift: "I'm much less trusting than I was before, especially with, you know, a mile away Philando Castile having been shot. I think it's changed a lot of people's thinking, mine included." Lucile, in her late sixties, similarly described how watching video footage from Clark's killing showed that "the racism in our society ends up being a big problem . . . Those kinds of incidents are usually the culmination of multiple mistakes along the way." Had Clark been white, she concluded, the paramedics or officers would have de-escalated and "the whole thing wouldn't have happened."

For some white residents, the death of Justine (Ruszczyk) Damond, a white woman, cemented concerns about out-of-control lethal police violence. Cindy, who told us earlier in her interview that seeing her Black son-in-law's experiences with police had shifted her attitudes, shared this about Damond's killing:

> I had a hard time understanding what Philando Castile did to deserve to be shot and killed. But this one this weekend is really over the top for me. I can't even imagine a scenario that would even explain it and absolutely not justify it. It's unbelievable to me. And I think that my skepticism has been growing.

Cindy did not explicitly name Damond's race, class status, or gender, though her emphasis that this case was "over the top" signaled how residents perceived the case as unique. Yet unlike the deaths of Jamar Clark and Philando Castile, which were deeply resonant with Black residents' personal experiences and lives, white residents interviewed in the wake of Damond's death did not describe her killing as a personal loss or one that echoed their own experiences and fears. For white participants, specific instances of police violence were experienced as isolated events, rather than a collective racial wound.

Given their rising awareness of lethal police violence, some of our most "woke" white participants described what felt to them like a new awareness of the "ethical dilemmas" in calling 911. Sheila, who earlier described her shift after Castile's killing, recounted a recent domestic violence incident that she witnessed: "I realized the cop is white and this woman is Black, and then I felt nervous . . . Have I really helped her by calling the police, or is there a chance I've just put her in harm's way?" Calling the police, Sheila concluded, "is maybe not the solution." Similarly, Samantha, a white North-side schoolteacher, reflected that she would call the police when needed, but recognized that her "best friend . . . who's a woman of color" or "her students . . . [and] their parents" did not have that same privilege. Josh, the neighborhood watch meeting attendee, reported that he would have to do "a lot of analysis" before deciding to call the police, because "it's a flawed system, 'cause you don't know who's gonna show up and how they're gonna interact . . . and we've got, you know, a Jamar Clark, a Philando Castile."

But even among the majority of white residents who saw police violence as a serious problem, their conviction about the depth of the problem—and means of redress—often wavered. Many white interviewees acknowledged problems in policing but believed that MPD officers were largely effective and professional. Police killings were not a sign of systemic rot, but the work of individual "bad apple" officers. Carol, a sixty-something white woman who questioned why officers were "pulling guns really quickly," nonetheless concluded that most were "doing the best that they can at this point" with a uniquely "tough job."

Correspondingly, the majority of white Northsiders supported modest reform interventions. As with residents of color, their suggestions included de-escalation and crisis intervention training, recruiting officers from the city, increasing officer accountability and punishment for misconduct, and, more broadly, changing the culture of policing. Departing from their neighbors, however, white residents rarely critiqued the insufficiency of reforms or called for structural transformations. The few who did push further described policing as a "complicated" policy conundrum, rather than a direct threat to their lives. Whereas Kel demanded simply that police "Stop killing Black folks," Sheila dithered:

> So, I still think it's worth throwing as much money at that [implicit bias training] as we possibly can. [But] I don't know that it has a huge

impact ... We have to diversify police ... But I know that people have stereotypes against their own race and other races also, so that's not necessarily a fix. So, I don't know, I guess I see it's complicated. It's worth any effort we can to have reform. I do think we have to hold people more accountable in the judicial system when things go wrong, and police officers who do make bad decisions, holding them accountable. That's not happening in society currently, so I think we have to change our laws, sort of the standard against which people are held accountable. I think that has to change. Then, I get the whole thing of we're going to have fewer people applying to be police officers, and blah blah blah. I get it. It's super complicated.

Each time Sheila brought up a reform, she immediately negated its potential impact or feasibility, ultimately concluding that it was all "super complicated."

Perhaps the closest any of the white respondents came to abolition was Samantha, the schoolteacher, who noted that even "good" officers could serve as tools of oppression and wondered aloud, "If the roots are rotten, can something better come from that? I don't really know." Similarly, Josh described what would become the logic of the defund demand: "I think if we focus on, like, 'OK, let's continue to fund our police department at, you know, many millions of dollars and then just trying to get them to be less, you know, racist or biased or whatever,' like that might not be the best approach." Instead, Josh suggested, "Let's actually take a chunk of this and invest in our young people so that there's ... more opportunity for them to be successful." Still, these respondents expressed abolitionist ideas as hesitant questions rather than forceful conviction.

On the other end of the spectrum were white residents whose perspectives on policing were resolutely positive, even with a media spotlight on police violence. Roughly a quarter of our white respondents denied *any* serious problems in policing. They backed the blue. Many of these residents thought the media portrayed a skewed perspective on policing, only showing the worst examples. As Janet, a woman in her mid-thirties, summarized, "There are some [officers] out there that are genuine and good," and so if the media were "gonna show the bad," they ought to "show the good too." Similarly, Sebastian, a man in his thirties, thought most officers were well-intentioned and said firmly, "I don't have a problem [calling 911]. I don't feel uncomfortable reporting something."

White residents who rejected the frame of racialized police violence would also deploy their own positive experiences with police to advance color-blind discourses.[38] For example, George, a white man in his seventies, referred to the MPD as a "fine bunch of people" doing "a good job." When pressed on how he knew this, George added, "I have no personal experience with them not doing a good job, so I have to say that they're doing a good job." When the interviewer asked if police treat all people fairly, George took the same tack: "I have not observed them treating anybody unfairly, so I have to say yes." George was resolute, in other words, that he only wanted to understand policing through his own experiences, not those of people who were perceived quite differently by the police.

Among these residents who aggressively defended the police, attitudes toward BLM activists were quite negative. Some called the movement "divisive," or made "All Lives Matter" style arguments that accused activists of sowing racial division.[39] By focusing so centrally on race, these residents argued, activists were *creating* the divisions they claimed to be fighting. Kerrie, a white woman in her forties who had generally positive attitudes toward the MPD, was one of the more outspoken voices on this topic: "I think Black Lives Matter is a pot-stirrer . . . We're all in the same place; it would be nice if everybody could kind of pull together and not have this black versus white thing all the time." Other white respondents expressed similar attitudes, albeit veiled in a layer of "Minnesota nice" (the state's polite version of passive aggression) that made their views more difficult to parse.

Like the (less common) vocal defenders of the MPD among Black residents, some white interviewees pushed back loudly against activists' efforts to challenge the MPD, focusing instead on crime in the community. Will, a white man in his twenties, called himself "extremely supportive of the work that the police are doing" and castigated activists "trying to . . . villainize the police" rather than attack "those who are committing the violence." This viewpoint required residents to construct their own justifications for police violence. Jane, a white woman in her early fifties, denied the existence of racial disparities in officer use of force, then cited a seemingly hypothetical case that was starkly reminiscent of the fatal police stop of Philando Castile:

> Do I think those people need some force from the police? Damn right—
> if they're caught. And if they're pulling someone over when a robbery
> just happened and the dude looks like the suspect that the description
> was given of? Is that fucking racial? No. They're pulling over someone
> who was just near that area, you know, has a gun and whatever, and
> their car is filled with dope, or smoke of marijuana . . . What I have
> seen is police are just doing a job.[40]

For Jane, even fatal use of force was legitimate (and not "racial") in the context of a suspected robbery and the presence of a gun. For these residents, no amount of media coverage of police violence, or protest, would change their minds.

Police Violence in Black and White

Living side by side, white residents and residents of color in Northside experienced separate social realities. Across both racial groups, many of our participants were moved by BLM organizing, but in qualitatively different ways. Most Black residents described how their own negative experiences with police and collective trauma were reinforced by the repeated examples of police killings and the lack of justice that followed. This cycle often resulted in a *realist* perspective on police violence, which understood police killings as an endemic, perhaps permanent, social problem produced by racism and the persistent dehumanization of Black people.[41]

With pervasive anti-Blackness, stark residential segregation, a lack of economic and political power in Black communities, and majority white police departments, police unions, and courtrooms, residents of color questioned how much police reform—even propelled by dedicated activists and happening under the city's first Black police chief—could stop the violence. The reforms the MPD had implemented in 2015–2019 were too little, too late, continually invalidated by police violence across the country. As a result, residents were critical of the ability of city residents and activists (and researchers) to change their reality. Simultaneously, however, many of them desperately wanted more safety in Northside, even at times when that meant relying on the abusive police force.

White participants, in contrast, typically described being newly conscious of racialized police violence. Many expressed increased racial sympathy toward their Black neighbors, raising issues of racial profiling, police harassment, and the threat of police violence—all victories of BLM protests, activists, and organizations. Yet many white interviewees continued to minimize the harm of police violence as the work of a "few bad apples" rather than systematic oppression. Being at "arms-length" from police violence also changed the tenor of interviews, with white residents questioning the role of the police as an abstract dilemma, not a direct threat to their lives and their loved ones. As a result, white residents more often shied away from the deeper, more transformative visions of what needed to change in policing and society.

All of these themes would come to shape the city's response to the murder of George Floyd. The palpable distress of residents at the lack of change through several years of BLM protests undergirded much of the rage on the streets of Minneapolis in summer 2020. So too did Black residents' support for more transformational change help to explain how and why demands to "end" the MPD emerged and gained traction. Yet the problem was not simply police violence but the continued bind of violent *over-policing* and negligent *under-protection*. Powerful visions of the promise of policing persisted even as residents saw the failures of the current system baked into their daily lives, which bolstered charter opposition across racial divisions. So too would the lack of trust in city leaders, as well as white resistance to challenging police power, come to serve as bulwarks against change. Ultimately, resistance from both Black and white Minneapolis would come to haunt efforts to end the MPD. And in its wake, Northsiders would once again be left out, experiencing an unprecedented rise in violence on their streets.

PART II

In the Wake of Rebellion

CHAPTER FOUR

George Floyd Is Still Dead

As far as I'm concerned, they could burn this bitch to the ground. And it
still wouldn't be enough. And they are lucky that what Black people are
looking for is equality and not revenge.

—AUTHOR, ACTIVIST, AND FILMMAKER,
KIMBERLY LATRICE JONES[1]

IN JUNE 2020, for a moment, anything seemed possible in Minneapolis.
In the midst of a deadly global pandemic, much of the country had gone
on "lockdown," radically reorienting work, family, and community life. We
had witnessed a horrific murder committed by a police officer, filmed by a
teenager and broadcast to the world. The largest protests in the country's
recorded history erupted, spreading the Black Lives Matter (BLM) rallying cry across the globe.[2] The Minneapolis Police Department (MPD) had
tried to implement the police reform playbook, and yet, George Floyd was
still dead, the city still burned.[3] If the department could not be reformed,
perhaps then it must be reimagined. In the wake of the rebellion, nine
city council members took to the stage at Powderhorn Park, festooned
with giant letters that read "DEFUND POLICE." Standing next to activists fighting for police abolition, the elected officials pledged to "begin the
process of ending the Minneapolis Police Department," developing "a new
transformative model for cultivating safety." Media headlines across the
country blared that the city was poised to "end," "dismantle," or "abolish"
its police force.

That process of dismantling, however, would quickly become a tedious,
contentious, and years-long political struggle over amending the Minneapolis city charter to change the section on the MPD, a protected department
in the city's governing document. Advocates would argue for striking out

all of the text on the MPD (including the provisions about a mandatory minimum number of officers and the mayor's executive control), replacing it with a description of a new department oriented around holistic public safety (which *could* include the police). And, because of the mayor's opposition, to pass this charter amendment the council members would need the support of a majority of city voters.

This proposal to "end" the MPD faced the expected opposition, as downtown business interests sided with the mayor, police chief, and officers union in deriding the "radical" proposal. But it was not simply the mayor's bloc opposing the charter initiative. Indeed, on this particular issue, downtown business leaders, the police union, and some Black community leaders, including a few prominent radical anti-police-violence activists, agreed: the charter amendment to end the MPD was a dangerous path for Minneapolis. As a *Star Tribune* article in July 2020 blared: "Egregious, grotesque, absurd, crazy, ridiculous. These are a handful of the words that some local African American leaders are using to rebuke the Minneapolis City Council's moves toward dismantling the Police Department, even as they demand an overhaul of law enforcement."[4]

Though these groups' critiques of the proposal varied, a core throughline was the idea that city council members had been led astray by abolitionist activists, who did not represent the interests of many (Black) city residents or their ideas about safety in the City of Lakes. These critics included Nekima Levy Armstrong, former president of the Minneapolis NAACP and arguably the most high-profile organizer associated with BLM in the city, whose interruption of the Northside community forum opened chapter 3. After the vote on the charter amendment in 2021, Levy Armstrong would pen a castigating *New York Times* op-ed, concluding: "We expected a well-thought-out, evidence-based, comprehensive plan to remake our police department. Instead, what we got was progressive posturing." Echoing the findings reported in the previous chapter, Levy Armstrong explained that police violence and community violence had to be addressed together: "Black lives need to be valued not just when unjustly taken by the police, but when we are alive and demanding our right to be heard, to breathe, to live in safe neighborhoods and to enjoy the full benefits of our status as American citizens."[5] They needed, in other words, responsive police protection.

To understand how and why such disparate groups came to share opposition to the charter amendment, in this chapter we finally return to the murder of George Floyd and its aftermath, culminating in the historic election of November 2021. As we'll see, the divide across activist coalitions, and between activists, city leaders, and residents, witnessed in earlier years had by 2020 ruptured, producing starkly different ideas about safety. As a result, while the fires that blazed a path through the city reshaped Minneapolis politics, much stood unchanged in the ashes of rebellion.

The Murder of George Floyd

Heading into May 2020, Minneapolis was weeks into a "lockdown" designed to slow the spread of the new COVID-19 pandemic. In Minnesota, as across the country, Black Americans faced higher viral exposure in the workplace and mortality rates.[6] These statistics prompted a flood of media stories about the burdens of structural racism and Black Americans' disproportionate exposure to premature death. And as spring turned to summer, a new slate of racist violence across the country reignited the BLM movement that had flagged during the Trump presidency, in part because many Americans were increasingly glued to their screens while stuck at home. In early May, video emerged of some of the last moments of Ahmaud Arbery's life, murdered by three white men who saw him jogging in Georgia. Early on May 25, a white woman called the cops on birdwatcher Christian Cooper in New York's Central Park. By that night, George Floyd had been murdered. And the unrest his murder prompted would spotlight media attention toward the fatal police shooting of Breonna Taylor in Louisville, Kentucky, two months earlier. Together, these cases precipitated a national reckoning about race in America.

George Perry Floyd Jr. was a forty-six-year-old Black man with a life story that all too clearly illustrated the toxic combination of racism and poverty in America. Floyd grew up poor in Houston's Third Ward projects. Entering high school tall and broad-shouldered, Floyd excelled at both basketball and football, eventually landing a college scholarship. But he struggled with the academics, ill-equipped to succeed off the field, and was eventually pushed out without a diploma. Floyd turned to side hustles and a budding rap career under the stage name "Big Floyd." But by then, he had begun a disastrous relationship with illicit substances, eventually spending more than a decade moving in and out of jails and prisons as his addiction ebbed and flowed and the legal system found reasons to stop, search, and punish men who looked like him.[7]

In 2014 he moved to Minneapolis, part of an effort to "get right" for his young daughter back in Houston. Here, he worked a series of jobs, including as a truck driver and club bouncer,[8] but the COVID-19 pandemic disrupted what little stability he'd found. On Memorial Day, 2020, Floyd was spending time with a friend who dealt drugs. Both were using that day, getting high and running errands before a barbeque. Just before dusk, they stopped by Cup Foods, a small convenience store at the corner of 38th and Chicago that Floyd visited often, where his friend was picking up a computer tablet (the store was known for selling cheap used electronics, as well as a site for drug deals). Cup Foods sat at the intersection of several multiracial neighborhoods in South Minneapolis, some more gentrified than others. Though neighbors knew that the block was part of the local Bloods gang's territory, by 2020 the same corner boasted an art gallery and an upscale coffee shop I often visited.

Floyd went into Cup Foods to buy cigarettes as his friend talked to the staff about the tablet. And that's where the day turned. The teenage cashier, a recent immigrant from West Africa, noticed the $20 bill that Floyd had used looked counterfeit. After checking with the store manager, he was instructed to go out with a coworker to ask Floyd, now in a parked car across the street, to return the cigarettes. But by then, Floyd was starting to nod off, and he was unresponsive to the clerk's request. Instructed to call 911, the teen told the call-taker that Floyd seemed "awfully drunk" and had used a counterfeit bill. Police were dispatched. Two rookie officers, both less than a week out of their on-the-job training period, arrived first: Thomas Lane, a thirty-seven-year-old white man, and J. Alexander Kueng, a twenty-six-year-old biracial man.[9] Both had been hired under the promise of a "guardian" model of policing, holding bachelor's degrees in sociology and later telling reporters that they had joined the force to help people.[10] As shown on officers' body camera footage, by the time they arrived, Floyd was sitting in the driver's seat of the car. After tapping on the window with his baton and not getting an immediate response to see Floyd's hands, Lane drew his weapon. Floyd put his hands up, though, and Lane reholstered his gun to pull Floyd out of the vehicle. The officers then cuffed Floyd, moving him to the sidewalk in front of the store for questioning.

Instead of resolving the conflict there, perhaps asking him to return the cigarettes or provide other funds and have someone sober drive the car home, the officers decided to arrest him for the attempted forgery. That meant getting him in their squad car. But Floyd was scared and claustrophobic, in part from his earlier stints behind bars. As officers attempted to shove him into the backseat, Floyd flailed and begged. It was during this tussle that Officer Derek Chauvin—a white man, nineteen-year veteran of the department, and Kueng's recent field training officer—arrived on the scene with Officer Tou Thao, a thirty-four-year-old Hmong American man. Chauvin pulled the struggling Floyd out of the squad car, bringing him to the ground and pinning him down with the weight of his body. As Floyd repeatedly called out—"I can't breathe!" "Mama!" "Don't kill me!"— Chauvin held him firmly on the pavement, face-down. Soon, Floyd lost consciousness, and Lane twice asked whether they should roll him to his side (a far safer position for breathing). But Chauvin resisted, telling the rookie that they were waiting for the ambulance. By the time that ambulance arrived, Chauvin's knee had been on top of Floyd for more than nine minutes, causing irreparable fatal damage.

As officers pinned him for those nine minutes, an increasingly distraught crowd gathered. The witnesses started filming and shouting at officers, with Officer Thao holding them at a distance and issuing derisive dismissals ("Don't do drugs, kids"). A teenage girl named Darnella Frazier captured the indelible cell phone footage that shook the world. In it, plain as day, was a white police officer, seemingly indifferent, kneeling on the neck of a Black man as he lay dying. As Floyd stopped breathing, witnesses demanded officers look for a pulse. An off-duty firefighter pleaded with officers to let her assist the clearly dying man. A martial arts expert who saw in Chauvin's actions a "blood choke" told the officer he was "trapping" Floyd's breathing. "Get off of his fucking neck," he yelled. But their pleas seemed not to register with officers, even after they tried and failed to find Floyd's pulse. Chauvin remained in place, kneeling on Floyd, until paramedics arrived and made him move so they could load the man onto a stretcher and into their rig. Unresponsive, Floyd was declared dead at the hospital.

In the overnight hours between May 25 and May 26, two different reports of what happened at 38th and Chicago were released online. On the one hand was the MPD's press release, which reported that Floyd's death was the result of an unspecified "medical incident." And on the other, Frazier's video, which would by morning go viral, its visual evidence directly contradicting the MPD's account. By then, the name George Floyd had begun to take on a new life. No longer just a man who had moved to Minneapolis to turn his life around and unabashedly declared "I love you!" to friends and family, Floyd was now a local, national, and international symbol of the horrors of structural racism and the urgent need for change.

The Minneapolis Uprising

What followed was an intense week of mass mobilization in Minneapolis and across the country. The volume of attention paid to the city felt like nothing I had ever experienced, before or since. It was summer, and many of us who could afford to do so had spent weeks at home as a result of the pandemic. There was, it seemed, nowhere else to look. And what we saw was *horrifying*. The video of Floyd's torturous nine-minute-long murder sent shockwaves across the globe, inspiring the largest protests in recorded US history. On June 6, crowd counters clocked the protests reached an all-time high, with more than 500,000 demonstrators coming out to the streets across more than five hundred cities and towns. By mid-June, estimates suggested that roughly twenty million people in America, or 6–10 percent of the country's adult population, had gone to at least one demonstration honoring George Floyd—a shocking total to movement scholars. Half of those protesting on the streets told pollsters it was their first time doing so.[11]

In addition to the first-timers, those numbers included dramatically more white protesters than in previous waves of mobilization for racial justice as protests erupted across small towns and big cities alike—prompting commentators to suggest that perhaps white America was finally "waking up." More so than even in the most intense days of the Ferguson protests, it seemed like everyone, everywhere, was talking about police violence and racism. Across the country, newspapers, TV news, and social media feeds were dominated by coverage of the murder, including the officers' histories and each of the pivotal moments in the fatal encounter, and the protests sweeping the nation. Op-eds by activists and scholars, and book sales for anti-racism tomes, surged. It was a *racial reckoning*. As one of the most influential social movements scholars, Douglas McAdam, concluded to a *New York Times* reporter: "It looks, for all the world, like these protests are achieving what very few do: setting in motion a period of significant, sustained, and widespread social, political change."[12]

And Minneapolis was its epicenter. In the city, waves of protest became a new normal. All day and well into the night, crowds gathered at 38th and Chicago, which would quickly become the semi-autonomous George Floyd Square, producing an outpouring of protest art that commemorated the loss of George Floyd and others killed by police. Artists created a giant cemetery nearby too, commemorating George Floyd and others whose lives were cut short by police violence. Organizers also planned marches to the homes of political leaders, including rallies at the governor's mansion and protests outside the home of the county prosecutor. Protesters marched en masse downtown, beseeching city hall. Minneapolis was showing up to fight for what was right. And nowhere was this mobilization clearer than outside the 3rd Precinct building, home base for the officers involved in Floyd's murder and only a short drive from where

Floyd died. In addition to the mass mobilization on the streets, city leaders, community representatives, activists, scholars, and everyday residents alike shared their voices on social media spaces like Twitter, tweeting and retweeting to call out the violence of the MPD.

As in previous social movement struggles for racial justice, however, attention to the precipitating event—the murder of George Floyd—proved hard to sustain as public attention quickly turned to violence, both in the form of unrest (or "rioting") and the violence meted out by law enforcement. Both types of violence held important lessons, which commentators would struggle to define for the public. Though nearly all of the demonstrations when the sun was overhead were peaceful, the situation grew more tense after dark. Conflict between protesters and law enforcement began as early as dusk on the first day of protest, as demonstrators and officers squared off in front of the 3rd Precinct. As protesters threw rocks and water bottles at officers and slashed tires on their cars, police in riot gear appeared on the streets and the roof of the precinct. Ignoring policy, officers sprayed tear gas and rubber bullets indiscriminately into the crowd without calling dispersal orders.[13]

Some council members, most vocally Northside's Jeremiah Ellison, demanded the city's police stand down, arguing their presence simply inflamed the situation. Police stayed, and the two following nights, conflict escalated. In addition to skirmishes outside the 3rd Precinct, arson and looting hit nearby AutoZone and Target stores, a housing complex under construction across the street, and a small business corridor nearby on Lake Street. By Thursday, fires had spread to blocks in St. Paul and seemingly random neighborhoods across Minneapolis (including far from the 3rd Precinct in North Minneapolis). That morning, Mayor Jacob Frey had ordered police to prepare to evacuate the precinct building in preparation for retreat, moving files and equipment to other locations. That night, with the precinct again under siege, the mayor made the call: *People over property*. The remaining officers, who had been preparing to deploy tear gas, fled the precinct on foot and in squad cars, to an eruption of cheers and threats from the crowd and the explosion of fireworks overhead. In the wake of the officers' departure, the predominantly young, ebullient crowd torched the building, live-streaming videos with the feel of a raucous block party.[14]

The country's most left-leaning voices framed what was happening in the city as a righteous uprising driven by police violence. Protesters had seized the cops' house, in what was a *logical* response to the horror of George Floyd's murder.[15] As Atlanta-based writer Kimberly Latrice Jones would declare in a viral video explaining racism as a rigged game of Monopoly, the fires erupting across the country were not just about Derek Chauvin and the rest—they were a fight against white supremacy and for equality.[16] Some anarchist groups, too, hailed the siege of the 3rd Precinct, with one site publishing a detailed first-person narrative of how exactly the radicals laid siege to police headquarters.[17]

But it wasn't just radical leftists, racial justice activists, and anarchists joining the fray; the Boogaloo Bois and other far-right white militants had come to Minneapolis, too, bringing their tactical gear and AK-47s with them. These extremist groups were here to capitalize on the protests and incite violence as part of their broader efforts to attack what they understood as government oppression and, perhaps, foment a race war. Regardless of precisely who was setting which fires, the night after the 3rd Precinct burned, a post office station and a Wells Fargo bank location on Lake Street were torched, as looters also targeted pharmacies across the Twin Cities. Contentious late-night protests also coalesced around some of the remaining precinct buildings, now fortified with fences and barbed wire.

By then, though, there was a new force in town. The night South Minneapolis's flagship Target store had been looted, with police confronting protesters outside the 3rd Precinct, Mayor Frey called Governor Tim Walz to request assistance from the state's National Guard. But the troops arrived too late, just hours after the precinct went up in flames—a delay that the mayor and governor would each blame on the other in the following days. When they arrived, hundreds of soldiers took to the streets, alongside law enforcement brought in from across the region, deployed to key assets and sites of protest. In addition, Mayor Frey initiated an 8 P.M. curfew, turning protest after dark into an offense.

The curfew implicitly authorized law enforcement to "take back" the streets. At demonstrations all over Minneapolis, officers deployed aggressive crowd-control techniques, including tear gas, flash-bang grenades, and "less lethal" munitions, often without warning or sufficient cause.[18] Hospital records would later reveal that police injured at least eighty-nine people in Minnesota so severely that they required medical attention; several would lose eyes or suffer serious head injuries from "non-lethal" rounds shot directly at the crowd.[19] An MPD SWAT team would later be revealed to have driven down Lake Street in an unmarked van at night, with orders to "Fuck 'em up, gas 'em." The "first fuckers we see," their sergeant declared, should be "hammered" with rubber bullets. One of the men they would "hammer" was Jaleel K. Stallings, a twenty-nine-year-old Black army veteran. Thinking that he was under (real) fire from white supremacists, Stallings shot back, his bullets piercing the officers' van. Though

Stallings surrendered as soon as he realized they were law enforcement, he was beaten in retaliation.[20]

As in decades past, this violence of the police worked, in part, to further demonstrate the message of the protesters: police were a threat. Residents and activists worked to spotlight this reality, as images of abuses of power by law enforcement spread rapidly on social media, including a video of law enforcement shooting marking rounds at people on their porch and several MPD officers indiscriminately spraying tear gas into protesters' faces. Journalists worked to broadcast these messages further, often radicalized when they themselves became the targets of police violence (despite the legal protections for media). And these images from Minneapolis joined those coming in from protests around the country, with one headline announcing: "The Police Are Rioting."[21]

Yet during this dystopian military occupation of the city and wave of state violence, there were also vibrant protests continuing during the daytime across the metro area. Neighbors came out together to clean up each morning from the night before and contribute to pop-up mutual aid centers helping others. A group of organizers even created a shelter for some of the city's vulnerable unhoused population, temporarily taking over an empty hotel.[22] People also began to reach out to their neighbors, developing networks of care and protection. Some of these experiments would later take root in communities long after the fires went out, including in the space that would become George Floyd Square (as we'll return to in chapter 6).

Responding to Rebellion

During the week immediately following Floyd's murder, city and state officials made a series of public announcements, attempting to pacify the volatile eruptions across the city.[23] In an unprecedented move, on May 26, 2020, Chief Medaria Arradondo swiftly fired all four officers. This time, the department would not wait months for the results of an investigation into the officers' conduct. He also visited George Floyd Square to pay his respects and meet with the crowd. Mayor Frey backed the chief, saying the video we had all seen showed an incident that was "wrong on every level." However, in a precursor to the criminal trials, Frey also began to distance the department (and its reform efforts) from the behavior of these four officers: "This does not reflect the values that Chief Arradondo has worked tirelessly to instill. It does not represent the training we've invested in or the measures we've taken to ensure accountability."[24]

Other key political players, however, further inflamed protests with their initial statements. These comments included Hennepin County prosecutor Michael Freeman's first announcement that he was not yet filing charges because "there is other evidence that does not support a criminal charge."[25] (Days later, he would announce charges against Chauvin, and later the three other officers, as detailed in chapter 5.) The pugnacious police union head, Lieutenant Robert "Bob" Kroll, who had long antagonized BLM activists in the city, entered the fray too. Insinuating a potential defense of the involved officers, Kroll released an incendiary public letter that castigated city leaders and charged: "What is not being told is the violent criminal history of George Floyd."[26] Perhaps most egregiously, President Trump intervened to threaten military violence. Unlike Kroll, the Republican president did not denigrate the victim—he criminalized the protesters, tweeting: "Those THUGS are dishonoring the memory of George Floyd, and I won't let that happen. Just spoke to Governor Tim Walz and told him that the Military is with him all the way. Any difficulty and we will assume control but, when the looting starts, the shooting starts." In response, Mayor Frey and Governor Walz tried to distance themselves from the president, whose message was censored by Twitter for "glorifying violence."[27]

Local and state officials also attempted to shift the blame of the unrest on "outside agitators" who had come to Minneapolis to wreak havoc, symbolically separating residents' righteous protest with illegitimate violence by outsiders. Residents were instructed by their neighborhood associations to watch out for "suspicious" persons and vehicles, to bring in any outdoor furniture that could be used as projectiles, and to sweep the alleyways for incendiary devices. Some developed their own nighttime patrols or hired private police. While we would soon learn that most of the people arrested during those days of protest were from within the state, at least some of the destruction was in fact initiated by (white) outsiders. For example, according to videos taken by protesters, the first fire set on Lake Street at the AutoZone appeared to be committed by a white man in a gas mask. Some of the protesters had tried to stop him.[28] And at least one white man from out of state and affiliated with the Boogaloo Bois would later plead guilty for shooting up the 3rd Precinct.[29]

Regardless of the degree of real threat, this rhetoric about outside agitators, white supremacists, and a potential race war succeeded in shifting attention. On Sunday, May 31st, the mass-scale protests of this week came to a tumultuous end after a near-miss. Protesters had gathered in the afternoon to block I-35W, a major highway that cuts across Minneapolis. Right at dusk, a gas tanker semi-truck came barreling down the otherwise empty highway, careening toward a line of kneeling protesters. People fled, and thankfully the driver was able to come to a stop before causing any fatalities, but rumors spread that the truck had been coordinated as a right-wing assault on the protests (a claim that later seemed to be unfounded). The scare on the highway, however, would come to serve as a traumatic closure point for the more contentious public demonstrations that had marked a historic week in Minneapolis. Protests, and as we'll see soon, activists' demands on the city, however, persisted.

As the fires burned out, commentators attempted to take stock of the scale of the unrest in Minneapolis. One measure was mass arrests; the Minnesota Department of Public Safety reported that police made more than six hundred arrests in the Twin Cities alone.[30] Unlike the rebellions in Watts in 1965, Detroit in 1967, or Los Angeles in 1992, however, there were not mass casualties.[31] But at least two people died during the unrest in the city, with one body found in the rubble of a burned-down pawn shop and another man shot in front of a different pawn shop by its owner. A third man died later from injuries sustained from a "less-lethal" projectile shot by law enforcement that left him with fatal brain damage. So too did commentators tally the damage to property. While less destructive than the record-breaking Los Angeles riots in 1992, there was an estimated $500 million in damages across fifteen hundred properties in the Twin Cities (with less than half covered by insurance). The worst of it was concentrated in a corridor of Lake Street near the 3rd Precinct, home to many small minority-owned businesses. Some of those buildings would remain closed more than two years later, the scorched former 3rd Precinct building still ensconced in razor wire.[32]

Yet there was a sense of hope on the streets, too. Minneapolis had come together to protest, defend itself, and rebuild. City residents were traumatized, yes, but the food banks, mutual aid and community-defense networks, and clean-up drives had shown that the city could care for its own. Change was in the air.

Do "Riots" Work?

Scholars have vigorously debated the benefits and costs of various kinds of disruptive tactics, like protest marches to block highways, that movements can deploy.[33] Rather than lean on moral suasion alone, disruption works by forcing the public and elected officials to pay attention to problems they are otherwise motivated to ignore.[34] Indeed, analyses of the early years of BLM protests found that they not only helped raise public concern over the persistence of racism in the country but also helped Democrats in electoral contests in the 2010s.[35] And to the extent that peaceful protests garner brutal repression from law enforcement, that state violence on display can also further activists' message and shape legislative agendas.[36]

Riots, the extreme end of disruptive tactics, however, have a more complex political history. These include not just protests, but setting fires, property damage and looting, and (in some cases) armed resistance. As historian Elizabeth Hinton argues, what Americans call "riots" in the context of urban unrest are better conceptualized as *rebellions*, or powerful cries against injustice from the voice of the oppressed. They are not simply "senseless" destruction, but instead a distinctly political claims-making process.[37] And, sometimes, they "work," at least in part. In Los Angeles, for example, the 1992 riots that erupted after the acquittal of the four officers who brutally beat motorist Rodney King were followed by a liberal shift in the next election.[38] Riots can also provide a direct attack on predatory institutions and businesses that extract resources from poor communities.[39]

Yet violent resistance also carries a high risk of political blowback, potentially hardening public opinion *against* activists and their campaigns. The canonical example is the unrest that followed the civil rights movement, especially the rebellions of the "Long Hot Summer" of 1967, which helped to propel Richard Nixon (against Minnesota's own Hubert Humphrey) into the White House.[40] In other words, rebellion can prompt an intensification of state repression, potentially thwarting the movement's ultimate aims. As a result, within radical movements, there are often vigorous debates on the benefits and costs of such tactics.[41] Would this kind of active resistance bring about the revolution, or spur another rightward political turn?

These complex historical lessons were top-of-mind for political observers during summer 2020, as pundits debated whether the unrest would help or harm the chances for Democrats retaking the White House from President Trump and the broader socio-economic transformations protesters demanded. And, in Minneapolis, the question was whether the rebellion would spell the beginning of the end of the city, paralleling the post-1960s decline of cities like Detroit, Michigan, or the beginning of a radical new transformation in public safety.

The Pledge to End the MPD

Regardless of the longer-term implications of the uprising, the immediate consequence was clear: Minneapolis residents had called for something to change. Abolitionists were there to answer, including the trio introduced in chapter 2: MPD150, Reclaim the Block, and Black Visions. Drawing on the strength of the protests, on May 29 Black Visions and Reclaim the Block circulated a petition, demanding Minneapolis city council members defund the MPD by $45 million, invest in "community-led health and safety strategies," commit to never again increasing police funding, and work to end police violence against community members. "Our city is on fire, our people are hurting, and Black communities are crying out for health and safety in the midst of pandemic," they concluded. It was time for real solutions—ones that would get the city closer to the "police-free future" activists had been dreaming of for years.

And they had help. With the national media spotlight trained on the city, donations poured into Minneapolis. After the Minnesota Freedom Fund, a community bail fund, was overwhelmed with contributions, they directed donors to Reclaim the Block and Black Visions, which garnered an overwhelming $30 million (and, accompanying the funds, new community scrutiny about how that money would be spent).[42] This funding would transform what was previously the trio of local police abolitionist groups—MPD150, Black Visions, and Reclaim the Block—from a small, local coalition to high-profile national leaders in a newly powerful demand to defund, and ultimately abolish, policing as we know it. Black Visions, led by young, Black, and largely queer organizers, took center stage, eventually leading the campaign to change the city charter. In addition, national organizers who saw Minneapolis as a possible test-case for more radical transformations in public safety, began conversations with both activists and city leaders about what to do next.

Activists were also bolstered by a series of public condemnations of the MPD. In the initial week of unrest, the Minnesota Department of Human Rights opened an investigation into the MPD's pattern of rights violations. University of Minnesota president Joan Gabel announced that the university would cut (some) ties with the MPD, including no longer contracting with the department for event security. The Minneapolis Public Schools system distanced itself from the politically toxic department, too, ending its use of MPD's uniformed staff as school resource officers. Even the Minneapolis Park and Recreation Board (an important body responsible for the city's large parks system) and prominent downtown businesses made statements denouncing and seeking to end contracts with the MPD. The politics of policing in Minneapolis were shifting, creating an opening for change.

As the large public marches wound down, activists undertook more targeted demonstrations outside the homes of city council members, demanding that the city's elected representatives come outside and answer for their complicity in the murder. On June 6, less than two weeks after the murder, activists with Black Visions amassed a crowd of thousands to confront Mayor Frey, the final demonstration in a series of planned events that afternoon, including a march and "die in." Organizer Kandace Montgomery held a mic to Frey's face, demanding he give a yes/no answer to their demand to defund the MPD.[43] Clad in an "I Can't Breathe" face mask, Mayor Frey declared that he did not support abolishing the police. He then walked away, to the cheers of protesters shouting: "Go home, Jacob!" Narrating the viral videos, the *New York Times* described the scene as "humiliation . . . reminiscent of the excruciating walk of shame from 'Game of Thrones.'"[44]

At the same time as they were pressuring the mayor, activists worked both publicly and behind the scenes to cajole the city council, including staging mock cemeteries on their lawns. It worked. The day after the crowd booed the mayor, nine of the thirteen council members joined abolitionist organizers at Powderhorn Park, just a mile away from where George Floyd was killed, to make a public declaration. It was a veto-proof majority, including the representatives for the two wards that intersected at 38th and Chicago (Alondra Cano and Andrea Jenkins), both Northside representatives (Phillipe Cunningham and Jeremiah Ellison), and council president Lisa Bender. Every person of color on the city council was on stage. Reading the pledge printed on a giant poster board and held aloft by organizers, the Powderhorn Nine declared their intention to begin to end the MPD.[45]

In a surprising show of unity, the city council quickly approved a unanimous resolution, signed by the mayor, promising "a transformative new model for cultivating safety in our city." While not quite as bold as the Powderhorn Pledge, the resolution was stunning. It declared that "police violence and the use of excessive force have led to community destabilization, a decrease in public safety, and the exacerbation of racial inequities in Minneapolis" and concluded: "No amount of reforms will prevent lethal violence and abuse by some members of the Police Department." Instead, the city would "commence a year long process" to "engage with every willing community member" and "identify what safety looks like for everyone."[46]

Defund the Police?

Almost as quickly as Minneapolis came to dominate the national conversation about police violence and calls to reform, defund, or abolish the police, Americans on the political left began to fracture over the meaning of these calls to action. Some imagined "defund" as a kind of transformational reform: invest more in alternatives to police (including alternative first responders) and "root causes" (e.g., housing, poverty, and health-care initiatives) while also reforming police departments—especially their use of force and oversight policies. Others, like the abolitionist organizers in Minneapolis, saw defunding as a path to full police abolition, a leftist vision of "starve the beast." Still others, including presidential candidate Joseph "Joe" Biden, called for investing more money into policing while also supporting reform and alternatives to the police. Debate raged over the meaning of the defund slogan and whether it mobilized or alienated voters, a conversation that would continue among pundits, the public, and academics for years.

Often lost in this political discourse, however, was that the call to defund the police was never meant to be politically palatable. As traced in chapter 2, the campaign came out of *radical* organizing work. It wasn't meant to reflect public opinion, but to *change it*, disrupting the public's assumption that police (and the broader legal system) provided safety. By this metric, the movement succeeded wildly, at least for a time. Outrage over George Floyd's death, and the protests sparked across the world, propelled police abolitionists into the mainstream conversation, radicalizing the public and generating unprecedented visibility for the idea of a police-free future.

In a landmark *New York Times* op-ed published on June 12, 2020, longtime organizer Mariame Kaba declared: "Yes, We Mean Literally Abolish the Police."[47] Tracing the long history of failed police reforms (including in Minneapolis), Kaba concluded that police reform "won't happen" because "when you see a police officer pressing his knee into a black man's neck until he dies, that's the logical result of policing in America." Under that understanding, the only *real* solution to police violence was to reduce the scale and power of police departments. Kaba's op-ed was just one of hundreds in centrist and left-leaning outlets that began to take the idea of police abolition seriously (or at least serious enough to engage in critique).[48]

The Powderhorn Pledge is hard to imagine without the years of movement-building that seeded the ground. Indeed, it was the work of these activists that made the statement possible—including, in a literal sense, the words city council members read, which reproduced nearly verbatim some of the opening lines from MPD150's 2017 report described in chapter 2. The support activists had built in the community also mattered, as they turned to their networks to mobilize large-scale protests in those pivotal days. The question, with the world watching, was what would become of these new seeds for change in Minneapolis and elsewhere.

#ChangeTheCharter

By summer 2020, the Minneapolis city council seemed poised to "dismantle" the MPD and "transform" public safety in the city. Yet the council members faced a significant set of barriers. For one, the political risk of this plan, even in Minneapolis, was plain—and they already knew as much. As Councilmember Andrea Jenkins, a Black trans woman and representative for one of the wards that converged at what became George Floyd Square, speaking to the crowd on the day of the pledge, summarized: "There are 431,000 people in this city that call this city home. Everyone has to have a voice in this conversation. This is a very beautiful, very gorgeous crowd out here right now, but this is not the entirety of Minneapolis." The entirety of Minneapolis, Jenkins implied, were not police abolitionists. Asked why she nevertheless supported the pledge, Jenkins replied to a reporter: "Because nothing has worked. We've got to change this. It's possible to be conflicted and know what the right thing to do is."[49]

In addition, council members should have known the day of the pledge that the city council had little power to directly "end" or "dismantle" the MPD alone. The Minneapolis city charter, which, like a city constitution, outlines the organization and powers of Minneapolis's government, is unequivocal: "The Mayor has complete power over the establishment, maintenance, and command of the police department. The Mayor may make all rules and regulations and may promulgate and enforce general and special orders necessary to operating the police department."[50] Common in other cities, such stipulations typically mean the mayor is able to hire (and fire) the police chief as well as set department policies. City lawyers in Minneapolis further interpreted this language to mean that the city council could not legislate *any* MPD policy. The council's power was instead the *purse*, responsible for negotiating the city's budget with the mayor. Yet the scale of the MPD's budget (like many agencies) is primarily determined by the number of staff, with the number of uniformed offers constrained by the charter as a minimum of 1.7 sworn officers per every 1,000 residents (a provision that officers fought to have included back in 1961).[51]

That meant that to "end" the MPD or even radically change its budget or staffing levels, the city council would need to change the city charter. Some of the Powderhorn Nine had even fought in the past to introduce this exact kind of amendment, which can be made in two ways: through a unanimous vote of both the city council and the mayor or through a ballot question decided by Minneapolis voters. In either case, a move to change the city's charter had to be reviewed by the charter commission, a fifteen-member volunteer group appointed by the chief judge of the Hennepin County District Court and tasked with providing recommendations. While the city council is empowered to override their recommendation, commission members are entitled to 150 days to review proposals before the ballot printing deadline in August. This meant that all charter amendments should have been sent to the commission in the spring, to be safe. And it was already June.

Coordinating with local and national organizers, five council members (led by Northside representative Jeremiah Ellison) pushed forward what would become the first proposal to "end" the MPD: an initiative to amend the city charter to strike out all of the text on MPD and instead write-in a Department of Community Safety and Violence Prevention. Since the mayor was *not* in favor of police defunding, it would have to go through the ballot. Consistent with its name, the proposed new department would be helmed not by a police chief but by a director with "non-law enforcement experience in community safety services, including but not limited to public health and/or restorative justice approaches." And by striking out all of the language in the old MPD section of the charter, this initiative would delete the charter provisions about a mandatory minimum number of sworn officers and the mayor's exclusive control.[52]

While the proposal would "dismantle" the MPD, insofar as it would delete the MPD as a protected department in the charter and replace it with a new one, the council members stipulated that the new department "may" include a "division of law enforcement services, composed of licensed peace officers," language the abolitionists initially fought to exclude. (As in other states, police have long been referred to as "peace officers" in Minnesota statutes—this language, however, in the ballot initiatives led some to believe, incorrectly, that the city would be developing a new model based on "peace" officers rather than "police" officers.) That division could have a police chief, but they would report to the new department commissioner. Exactly what a "public health" approach would constitute was left undefined, later becoming a source of political debate. But the theory behind it was to create a more holistic approach to public safety modeled off the Office of Violence Prevention (OVP), then housed among the city's public health work. The new Department of Community Safety and Violence Prevention would, the logic went, subordinate police underneath this broader public health mandate, marking a true departure from policing as we knew it in Minneapolis. And it would, in theory, create a better structure for building out the kinds of supportive alternative models of public safety some abolitionists envisioned.

Crucially, though the charter initiative was framed as a "defunding" initiative in much of the press coverage (or even abolishment of the police among both its most ardent supporters and detractors alike), the measure actually said nothing about funding for law enforcement. Instead of dictating the shape or scope of the new department, the charter amendment changed the *terrain of the political struggle*—opening up the possibility of radical defunding (or even full abolition) by eliminating the mandatory minimum and shifting power away from the mayor, who (at the time) was positioned to the ideological right of the council. In addition, some council members argued that the proposal would make policing more democratic, by bringing the discussion of the MPD's policies and practices out from behind the closed doors of the mayor's office and into the public arena of city council hearings. If the measure passed, the devil would be in the details: as written, the proposal could have led to almost no changes in policing in Minneapolis other than an administrative restructuring and renaming, or a radical downsizing of the police force, or something else entirely. The outcome would depend on politics, or, more specifically, *who* was empowered to implement the changes after the vote.

And those politics were messy, even among the Powderhorn Nine. As Northside's Phillipe Cunningham, the council's primary architect for the OVP, would later tell a reporter, the meaning of the pledge to "end" the MPD was "up for interpretation," and "it was very clear that most of us had interpreted that language differently."[53] The most left-leaning council members envisioned the charter amendment as a meaningful step toward a police-free future. But many of the other council members envisioned something more moderate, and vocally supported Chief Arradondo, arguing that he should be involved in all efforts to reimagine public safety— even ones that meant ending the department he helmed. Some of the council members also envisioned "ending" the MPD by disbanding and rebuilding a new police force, much in the way Camden, New Jersey, had reconstituted its police department, in part to break the power of the officers union.[54]

It was unclear if that was even legal in Minnesota. As sharp-eyed legal observers pointed out, a 2019 Minnesota Supreme Court decision involving a five-member fire department in Brainerd suggested that disbanding and reconstituting city forces to break a union violated the Public Employment Labor Relations Act.[55] This meant that using the charter amendment to end the federation's hold on city politics could expose the city to a disastrous lawsuit. It would only be just before the November 2021 vote that the city finally made public whether officers would have to reapply for their jobs if the measure passed. The waters were muddy, to say the least, as the political struggle over the charter amendment began in earnest.

Strange Bedfellows and the Pangs of Violence

The loudest opposition bloc to the 2020 charter amendment proposal initially was the city elites aligned with Mayor Frey, including downtown business executives. The group argued that what would provide *real* safety was more (and better) police reform, insisting that the council members' "radical" proposal would send businesses and tourists fleeing an ever-more crime-ridden city. As Steve Cramer, the chief executive officer of the Downtown Council, told a reporter: "Without a clear understanding that policing services will [be] reinvented but not eliminated . . . we can anticipate the desirability of Minneapolis as a community to live, visit, invest and create and maintain jobs will diminish."[56] Banding together under several coalitions, these same allies began to argue for bringing more police to the streets of Minneapolis (and, soon, for the reelection of Mayor Frey), drawing public attention to crime and disorder. This group also coordinated with Chief Arradondo, strategically deploying the first Black police chief's opposition to the charter amendment to bolster their cause.[57] By then, public opinion polling showed that Arradondo was more popular than either the mayor or the city council.[58]

Meanwhile, city council members' ambiguity about the proposal at times hurt their cause. For example, Lisa Bender, council president and representative for a central Minneapolis ward, gave a live television interview with CNN in which the reporter posited that the language of "dismantle" made some people "nervous." She raised a hypothetical in which an intruder entered her home, asking Bender, "Who do I call?" Bender's response was not to outline how the new system would work to ensure residents' safety through holistic support, but instead to reply that the impulse to call the police "comes from a place of privilege." Reckoning with that privilege, Bender seemed to imply to the correspondent, had to come first.[59] This seeming indifference to safety concerns was then used as a wedge by those fighting against the proposal, who argued that the council wanted radical, reckless change and had little regard for individuals' or the community's collective safety.

The police union, predictably, went further still, explicitly stoking fears that a "police-free" Minneapolis would lead to anarchy and mayhem. Led by Lieutenant Kroll, who himself had long been accused of racist behavior (including a claim lodged by Chief Arradondo a decade prior), representatives of the officers union sat down on June 23, 2020, with a reporter from Minnesota Public Radio to make clear their stance on the proposal.[60] Building on the letter he penned during the unrest, Kroll and his team declared that they had "no" confidence in the city's chain of command; officer morale was at an all-time low. The lone Black officer in the room, Rich Walker, argued that Arradondo was in a "tough spot" after being "compromised by the overreach of our City Council," including the city's failure to approve the chief's 2019 request to add four hundred officers by 2025 to build the "resources the department needs." The union's ire extended to the mayor, too, who had ordered the evacuation of the precinct even as he steadfastly pushed back against the city council.

It wasn't the violent practices of the MPD, the union charged, but the failures of city leadership that were responsible for the unrest in Minneapolis—and for what the union characterized as a disastrous rise in crime. In fact, while various kinds of criminal offenses were trending in different directions during the pandemic in Minneapolis, as across the country, *homicides*, the most feared and costly form of crime, were indeed rising precipitously. During summer 2020, homicides were nearly twice as high as the previous summer (with thirty-nine homicides from May 25 to August 25, compared to nineteen in the same period in 2019),[61] representing the start of a distressing surge in violence.

At the same time, the MPD's force size was also shrinking rapidly. The MPD had not been defunded or dismantled, yet officers were deciding to retire early or leave on disability claims, largely for post-traumatic stress disorder (PTSD) from the unrest. Authorized to have a sworn officer count of roughly nine hundred officers, by mid-July 2020 the MPD had nearly two hundred officers out and filing for disability—a "staggering" level of claims that the city (not the police) would have to pay in the following months and years.[62] Fueling the problem, the remaining officers appeared to be retaliating against city leaders and residents. In a series of media reports, both residents and officers themselves told reporters that the police, as a way of voicing their frustration at the city, were slowing responses or not responding at all to calls for service in certain neighborhoods—in essence, withholding services out of spite.[63] It turned out defunding and dismantling didn't just have to happen through the budget; it could happen through a war of attrition and a suspicious outbreak of the "blue flu."

Calling the city a "warzone," Kroll insisted that things were only going to get worse: "The crime that you're seeing . . . is a preview of what you would see if they actually go forward with this 'defund the police,' this is a snapshot." Sitting next to Kroll was federation vice president Sergeant

Sherral Schmidt, a white woman (positioned to become the union's president after Kroll was pushed to retire in 2021). Schmidt argued that officers didn't have the support they needed for the "proactive" stops that would get "guns off the street," fueling the violence. The "failed politicians" had made it so that people would continue to shoot their guns at one another because everyone knew that officers' hands were tied. The failures of politicians (not police), the union argued, had caused the city to burn, making community members "fearful" and "furious." Those law-abiding residents *wanted* the police, the union representatives claimed.

The "community" that wanted the police, according to the union, was not just downtown elites or wealthy white residents in million-dollar homes along the chain of lakes, but also Black residents and business owners. And no one had to look hard to find these spokespersons. Indeed, by June 2020 many of the more establishment civic and religious Black community leaders, especially in North Minneapolis, were publicly deriding the city council for declaring the "end" of the MPD just as a spate of murders wracked the city and its poorest blocks. Reporters were eager to print this seemingly contrarian take on the city council's proposals, while white elites capitalized on this Black opposition to rebut charges that opposition to the charter amendment was racist.[64] As a result, Black residents who wanted more police presence in their neighborhoods became the public face of the opposition to the charter change.

The Black community leaders opposing the charter amendment were often middle-aged or older, representing a *generational* divide with the younger activists who preferred more radical changes. They also carried more social and economic status than many of the radical activists, enmeshed (at least in part) with the city's power structure. But, as we saw in chapter 3, such voices did in fact represent an important set of perspectives and preferences in Northside. They were not simply "out of touch" elite Black spokespersons but rather a representation of the real divides within the community on what to do about the scourge of both police and community violence.

In August, frustration about the rise in violence would lead a group of eight North Minneapolis residents (the "Minneapolis 8") to initiate a lawsuit against the city for inadequate protection, using the fact that the department was now well below the mandatory minimum staffing numbers to sue. This group's public face was a highly influential Black power couple, Don Samuels, a former member of the city council and Minneapolis Public Schools board, and Sondra Samuels, the CEO of a large nonprofit (the Northside Achievement Zone). In August 2020 the couple published an op-ed in the *Star Tribune* decrying the rise of crime in Northside. On their block alone, they wrote: "A mother's car was shot up with eight bullets, with her infant on board." As a result, "Neighbors are leaving their Northside homes to stay with relatives to keep their children safe." This violence, they argued, was a direct result of the wave of officer departures at the MPD—flight from what they characterized as "hostile working conditions" created by city leaders.[65] Casting the charter amendment proposal as a source of public safety problems rather than a solution, they called for transformative reforms that would create a city where "all citizens are treated as fully human by all cops."[66] And real reform, they argued, could only happen with the MPD at adequate staffing levels—an approach they described as "both/and" rather than "either/or," language that became a catchphrase in the unfolding political struggle.

Adding insult to injury was the fact that this historic move was happening after the appointment of the city's *first* Black police chief—who, they argued, was already working toward police reform and better police-community relationships. Pushing out the chief was not a victory for racial justice, they said, but instead a way to disempower Black voices in the city. Steven Belton, president and CEO of the Urban League Twin Cities, for example, told a reporter: "Why now, when you have an African American chief who is highly regarded and trusted in the Black community? This strikes me as being passive-aggressive Minnesota Nice on steroids. This is a hit on Chief Arradondo."[67] As a result of their support for the chief, this collection of Black community leaders would go on to back not only the MPD but also Mayor Frey, who had positioned himself as an ally willing to battle city council on behalf of the department and its chief.

These concerns were shared even by some BLM activists, including Nekima Levy Armstrong, whose op-ed opened this chapter. Levy Armstrong and many of the Black organizers she collaborated with understood themselves as radicals, tracing their political lineage back to the Black Panther Party. Their opposition to the charter amendment, however, was not primarily about its perceived attack on the chief. Instead, their worries were around the potential exacerbation of the accountability failures under the charter change. Recall from chapter 2 that Levy Armstrong and the other radical reform activists (groups like Communities United Against Police Brutality [CUAPB], Twin Cities Coalition for Justice for Jamar [TCC4J], Justice for Justine, and BLM Global Network chapters [Twin Cities Metro Area and BLM Minnesota]) believed that police reform had *not* failed. It was instead that the reforms enacted so far were "phony," unable to address the root of the problem. As a result, these groups called for transformative accountability reforms that would create meaningful change, including requiring officers to hold personal liability insurance, creating community control of the police department, and community input in union negotiations.[68]

The charter amendment proposal did none of these things. Instead, it put more power in the hands of the same city council members who had continually failed to rein in the police. The "hastily drafted" amendment, they argued, would in fact *reduce* accountability, by diffusing supervision over the department and leaving it ambiguous as to who was ultimately responsible for the department.[69] In addition, despite some of the radical reformers envisioning police abolition as the final end-point of their ideal reforms, the coalition sharply critiqued language that said the department "may" include law enforcement officers, which they argued in the short term opened the door to contracted police forces in Minneapolis (which would be less democratically accountable than a city police force). Even for those in this coalition who desired a police-free future, in other words, the charter amendment as a whole seemed a poor vehicle for change.

Again, the devil was in the details—would the proposal reduce the city's reliance on police, or simply shift policing work to different agencies and an ambiguous chain-of-command? At best, the radical reformers argued, the amendment was nothing more than a rebranding of the same violent department. At worst, it was a dangerous proposal that would expose people to more violence and less accountability.

Who Speaks for the People?

Amid all this jockeying by activists, elected officials, and community leaders to define the terms of debate, everyday residents' actual voices were often left out. What would make all residents, especially Black Northsiders, "feel safe"? As described in chapter 3, there was no singular voice of residents across any racial group. This was as true in Northside as it was in other kinds of neighborhoods scattered across the city. And that meant there could be no one answer. Inadvertently, the city confirmed this after administering an online survey about public safety preferences as part of their community engagement process. Dryly, city staffers summarized the results at a city council meeting: "Some residents want more police; some residents want less police."[70] Indeed, as we'd heard in our earlier interviews, city residents largely agreed that police violence was an issue. But they were divided both across and within racial categories when it came to how to best move forward, torn between the threat of police violence and the promise of state protection.

A summer 2020 poll conducted by local media similarly showed that city voters were roughly split on whether Minneapolis "should or should not reduce the size of its police force," with 40 percent in favor of reductions and 44 percent opposed. Black voters' *opposition* to staffing reductions was even slightly higher than for all voters (with 50 percent selecting "should not"). These attitudes sat awkwardly alongside quite negative perceptions of the MPD among white and Black voters and everyone else. The issue, again, was not support for this police department but instead the role of police in public safety. Yet fully 73 percent of those polled (and 76 percent of Black voters) supported redirecting "some funding from police to social services, such as mental health, drug treatment or violence prevention programs."[71] These results were in line with national data that showed stronger support for questions that asked about redirecting spending toward emergency response mental health professionals and other alternatives to police contact rather than invoking the "defund" slogan explicitly.[72]

Importantly, however, public opinion was not simply out there, ready to be measured by pollsters, but instead actively constructed by the political struggle. Activists, civic and political leaders, and the police department were all fighting for the hearts and minds of the public, or at least their votes.

Blocked from the Ballot in 2020

Before the first charter amendment proposal could make it to a vote, it had to make it through the city's charter commission, which was entitled to a 150-day review period. This volunteer group of appointees had, like much of the city, erupted in debate over the ballot question. Some thought the amendment should move forward. Others believed its vague wording wouldn't pass legal muster or that the different changes it proposed should be broken up into individual ballot questions. In the end, the commission could not come to a consensus, instead deciding to take its full review period, which effectively meant blocking the question from the 2020 ballot—cooling, if not killing, its chances altogether. When the charter commission later issued a recommendation to the city council, it was to reject the charter amendment.

The idea of a charter amendment to "end" the MPD, however, was not so easily squashed. Over the next year, supporters of a new department pushed forward two initiatives to get the question on the 2021 ballot. First, as in 2020, a set of council members worked on drafting a new council-led proposal, taking in the feedback from the failed first initiative. Second, because ballot questions can be put forward by citizen petition, organizers set out to gather signatures. By April 2021 the charter campaign led by abolitionist activists in the city (including Black Vision's Kandace Montgomery, who had pressed Frey for a yes or no answer on defunding the MPD) had gathered over fourteen thousand verified registered voter signatures—more than enough to guarantee that the question would appear on the ballot. In response, the city council members supportive of the change pulled their version of the proposal. The vote to #ChangeTheCharter would use abolitionists' language, from the people for the people.

The year in between the two charter amendment proposals could have given activists time to organize, plan, and build support for a new model of public safety—especially among the other anti-police-violence activists who would seem natural allies. Perhaps the new proposal might include some of the reforms suggested by the other coalition or otherwise address their concerns about accountability. But that coming together never happened.

Nor did much change between the two iterations of the charter amendment, now slated as "City Question 2" on the November ballot. The 2021 version would again strike out all language related to the MPD (including mayoral control and the mandatory staffing minimum) in the city charter, replacing it with a new department oriented around a public health approach. The name had changed, however, now the Department of Public Safety, language that allowed charter supporters to argue that *they* were the ones who took the "safety" of Minneapolis seriously. While rhetorically powerful, the name also held ambiguous connotations since most existing public safety departments (including the State of Minnesota's) were heavily oriented toward law enforcement. Yet the 2021 proposal was even more ambivalent about the role of police than its previous iteration—rather than saying the new department *may* include a law enforcement division, it stated that the department *could* include licensed peace officers "if necessary" to serve its functions.[73]

Further complicating matters, another yes-or-no charter proposal would also appear on the ballot above the question on the MPD. "City Question 1," if approved by voters, would give the mayor *more* power over city operations, essentially extending the executive power they held over the MPD to all other city departments. This kind of "strong mayor" system had for generations been a goal of Minneapolis politicos (including Humphrey in the 1940s), with supporters arguing that the prevailing "weak mayor" system led to dysfunction in city hall—especially when the city council and mayor were at odds. Notably, however, the 2021 version of this initiative was authored by the chair of the charter commission, the same group that had blocked the first attempt to end the MPD. While its supporters sold Question 1 as a question of administrative efficiency (ending the so-called "14-boss problem"), the proposal was also a clear rebuke to the city council members who had fought for greater control over the MPD.

Thus, at the same time that Question 2 would decide the fate of the MPD, voters would also decide whether to reelect or replace the mayor, choose how much power to give that mayor with Question 1, and select a new slate of city council members.

Defining Safety in 2021

Violence, like the rain and snow, follows a seasonal pattern in Minneapolis. And as winter turned to spring, tensions again flared, both on the streets and in city hall. It turned out the violence of summer 2020 was just a prelude. By the end of 2021 the city would lose nearly one hundred victims to homicide, an annual tally on par with the worst year of the "Murderapolis" era and more than double the typical number of annual homicides across the 2010s.[74] Though the city had grown slightly since then, the homicide rate was still an appalling 22 homicides per 100,000 residents, nearly reaching the 1990s peak. Further, the speed at which homicides had spiked was unprecedented, both nationally and in Minneapolis.[75] Similarly, as carjackings—a relatively unnoticed crime across the city in earlier years—rose, so too did the headlines and public fear.

At the same time, the number of uniformed police at the MPD was still dropping, both in terms of payroll totals and the actual number of officers not on leave and available to respond to calls for service. While the MPD reported 900 active sworn officers in May 2020, by the end of 2021, that number had dwindled to roughly 640 (and was still dropping).[76] The last time the department had been that small was the early 1960s. Opponents of the charter initiative would continually link these trends, blaming the rising crime on declining officer capacity. While the research on whether hiring more police officers reduces crime is surprisingly fraught (in part because of the challenges of both defining and measuring crime), there is compelling causal evidence that adding officers to a force can reduce homicides (though those gains come with both fiscal and social costs).[77] That research, however, had limited capacity to explain what would happen if a police department suddenly lost nearly a third of its effective force, in the context of the most widely protested instance of lethal police violence in American history.

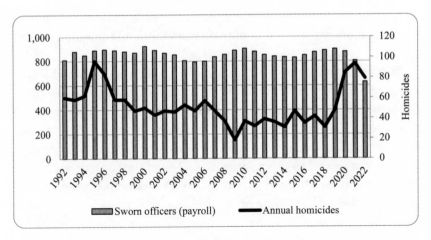

FIGURE 4.1. MPD sworn force size (payroll) and annual homicides, 1992–2022
Sources: Data on payroll staffing totals for the MPD in 1992–1996 from Kevin
Diaz, "Council Takes Up Police Staffing," *Minneapolis Star Tribune*, October 12,
1996. Data for 1997 are from the Bureau of Justice Statistics, Law Enforcement
Management and Administrative Statistics (LEMAS), 1997. Staff totals for 1998
and 1999 were estimated through linear interpolation. Data for 2000–2020
are from the Minneapolis Police Department, Public Information Office, and
represent payroll totals as of January 1 for each year (received July 14, 2023;
on file with author). Homicide totals for 1992–2018 generated from the Federal
Bureau of Investigation, Crime Data Explorer, available at https://cde.ucr
.cjis.gov (v. 23.4.1). Homicide totals for 2019–2022 collected from the City of
Minneapolis, Crime in Minneapolis Dashboard, NIBRS Crime Offenses (last
accessed June 26, 2023).

But the police weren't necessarily the only, or even the primary, driver
of the rise in violence. Indeed, if we look at trends in the MPD's size and
homicide rates in the city over the past three decades, there is little corre-
lation between force size and homicides. As figure 4.1 shows, while murder
rose and fell over three decades, the MPD's uniformed force size stayed
relatively constant until 2020. That's because many other social forces
beyond the number of police shape homicide rates. Most important for
understanding the rise in 2020 and 2021 was the COVID-19 pandemic,
which led to mass unemployment, closed schools, and precipitated a wave
of fear and grief. Looking to the pandemic, which began just before Floyd's
murder, also better explains why homicide rose across the country, not just
in left-leaning cities or places where police power was challenged.[78] (And
it better matched what would happen in 2022 in Minneapolis, when officer payroll numbers continued to fall even as the homicide wave receded.)

This kind of academic research and its nuance, however, was not top-
of-mind for the amendment's opponents. Whether or not it was true,

charges that the Powderhorn Pledge was responsible for the uptick in violence, and predictions that it would only intensify should Question 2 pass, became a powerful bludgeon against change.

The rise in crime became not just families' tragedy, but a political disaster that played out on the front page of the news. Though some would blame the media for sensationalizing violent crime in the city, they were not simply manufacturing a crisis. This coverage, and the city's grief, was most intense after three young Black children were caught in Northside's crossfire over several weeks in spring 2021. Two of the children would die from their injuries. On April 30, ten-year-old Ladavionne Garrett Jr. was shot in the head while riding in the backseat of a car with his parents. (Remarkably, he would survive after spending six months hospitalized.) Two weeks after that shooting, nine-year-old Trinity Ottoson-Smith was shot, also in the head, while jumping on a trampoline at her best friend's birthday party just as a young man drove past intent on murdering another man sitting on the side porch of the house. Twelve days later, she would die at North Memorial Hospital. And Aniya Allen, just six years old, was shot while strapped into a car seat in her mother's vehicle, waiting at a McDonald's drive-through. Aniya languished in critical condition for two days before dying of her injuries at the same hospital. In a small-city coincidence, Aniya's grandfather was K. G. Wilson, a prominent and tireless peace activist in North Minneapolis. (Three years later, only the person who killed Trinity would be identified, arrested, and convicted, even with a large reward offered for tips.[79])

In the days following the third shooting, Mayor Frey and Northside's council members, Jeremiah Ellison and Phillipe Cunningham, held dueling press conferences—inadvertently spotlighting the political dysfunction of the city's response to violence. At the mayor's conference, he was flanked by a majority-Black crew of victims' family members, Chief Arradondo, and community leaders who supported his public safety plans. While there were some council members in attendance, notably missing were Northside's actual representatives. Salting the injury, Mayor Frey announced a new safety plan (unsubtly doubling as a campaign brochure) that highlighted the need for the kind of violence prevention programs long championed by Cunningham.[80]

In front of a crowd of reporters, the mayor declared that stopping the bloodshed would mean enacting police reform, building sustainable alternative approaches to violence prevention, *and* expanding the size of the MPD. Contrasting his approach with the council members' fight for police defunding, Frey claimed his was a "data-driven approach to community safety" that "listened to community"—implicitly coded as the Black community.[81] The answer, according to the mayor, was (at least in part) more police. As Chief Arradondo would argue the next month, after a three-year-old was injured in another shooting: "The biggest threat to public safety in our city, and particularly to our African-American community, is not the police." Instead, the problem lay in gun violence by residents: "We have an epidemic right now of unequivocal gun violence particularly in our African-American communities. And that must stop."[82]

The day after Frey's event, Councilmembers Ellison and Cunningham offered a different diagnosis in their own press conference. Violence in the community was spiking, they argued, because the "status quo" in policing remained. Northside remained unsafe because of the failures of the city's leadership. What Minneapolis—and, more precisely, the Black residents of Northside—needed was a reimagining of public safety. Noting that they supported "parts" of the mayor's plan, they argued: "We deserve a more comprehensive plan than simply adding more police or focusing on police reforms." And they, too, invoked "data," arguing for a holistic approach to addressing violence that would combine "data-driven street outreach, engagement and social services with highly targeted law enforcement for individuals who remain violent."[83] The mayor and police chief, they argued, were not solving the problem, but instead had stalled the kinds of changes Northsiders desperately needed.

Despite their differences, the two press conferences shared a key outcome: both were interrupted by frustrated residents demanding more than grandstanding politicians. Residents were tired of the turf wars at city hall that, like beefs on the street, were exacerbating the violence.[84] They wanted city leaders to get "together on the same stage" and figure out a plan for the city as a whole.[85] The problem was, of course, that no one could quite agree on what that plan ought to look like exactly, with both sides dug in on what ailed Minneapolis.

Changing Hearts and Minds

As spring turned to summer in Minneapolis, campaigning for the 2021 election began in earnest. By then, advocates and opposition for Question 2 had solidified into two opposing camps: "Yes for Minneapolis" (the campaign for the amendment) and "All of Minneapolis" (the coalition against the amendment). Each group attempted to garner the votes it needed to win, blanketing the city in flyers and teams of door-knockers. They also debated one another in public forums across the city and media outlets.

Both sides had regrouped the now-familiar players: on the "pro" side of the ledger were abolitionist activists and their allies, and on the "con" side were the same set of defenders of the mayor and the chief of police who had been fighting the defund initiatives since 2020.

Whereas in most political fights the "establishment" side is expected to have more financial resources, heading into the charter amendment debate it was actually the abolitionists who had garnered the most dollars in fundraising, both through grassroots donations from summer 2020 and the support of national progressive groups.[86] This funding allowed the "Yes" team to build out significant infrastructure, hiring canvasser teams, for example, rather than relying on the labor of organizers and protesters who also had to hold down day jobs. And it was the establishment trying to catch up—using their internal resources and political heft to make up for their weaker ground support of activist labor.

In flyers blanketing the city, "Yes for Minneapolis" argued that a holistic public-health approach would minimize the chances of police violence, particularly for Black, Indigenous, Latinx, and other marginalized residents, by reducing the number of armed police interacting with residents, replacing them with social workers, mental health professionals, addiction counselors, housing specialists, and more. When residents called 911, they promised, the city would send the *right* response. And the result would be stronger public safety for everyone—with some flyers suggesting that if this new department had been in place before 2020, George Floyd would not have been killed by police.

The campaign was evasive (or perhaps strategically ambiguous) about how many law enforcement personnel would remain in the new department. On the stylized cartoons depicting multiple first responders, for example, the campaign noted that some incidents (involving violence) would require the response of "armed police." Yet the flyers shied away from explicit promises about police, likely attempting to keep radical leftists onboard while not losing their more moderate liberal supporters. In campaign materials and at public events, spokespeople for the campaign took pains to clarify that a yes on Question 2 did *not* mean the immediate end of police in Minneapolis (or even "defunding"). Instead, the new Department of Public Safety would increase resources for public safety *and* go beyond the current "police-only" approach.[87] Other organizers with the campaign, however, would tell reporters that they were working toward "total abolition" of police on a five-to-ten-year time horizon.[88]

The argument from the opposition was simple: replacing the police department in the charter would lead to more disorder and violence on the streets of Minneapolis. Not only would Question 2 imperil public safety, but the city's mayor was already taking the lead on police reform—efforts that would be derailed by the end of the MPD. Amendment opponents particularly highlighted the "lack of a plan" for implementing the initiative—and spurred fear of what would follow. For example, reason number 1 in "Top Ten Reasons to Vote NO on Question 2" on an early "All of Minneapolis" flyer told residents that the amendment "would **remove** the police department 30 days after the election with no timeline or plan for its replacement." That meant, opponents charged, that there was no guidance as to how many officers would remain in the department, what new staffers might be brought in, and what the organizational structure of this new department would look like exactly. As Chief Arradondo would quip about the lack of planning: "At this point, quite frankly, I would take a drawing on a napkin."[89]

In truth, there was no detailed plan for the proposal's implementation—by the city's design. Back when the charter amendment proposal was proceeding through the council-led process, Phillipe Cunningham had been interrupted mid-presentation by the city's ethics officer, who announced that actively planning for the passage of the ballot question would constitute a violation of campaign ethics (because of a prohibition on using city resources to promote ballot questions). Instead, all of the city ordinances that would flesh out the new department's operations, giving residents the details they were clamoring for, would need to be designed *after* the vote. And by then, we would have a new city council, too.

These struggles between the two dueling campaigns spotlighted how complex and contradictory this moment was for Minneapolis's politics of policing. From the name of the group to their calls for more alternative responders, "All of Minneapolis" continually mimicked the language of the charter supporters in their materials, just as Mayor Frey had folded Council Member Cunningham's violence prevention initiatives into his safety plan.[90] After George Floyd, you could not simply be pro-police in Minneapolis—but you could support increasing funding to the police for *reform*. After months of each campaign working to position themselves as the *real* locals and *authentic* spokespeople for Minneapolis's residents,[91] it was finally time to let voters pick a side.

A Historic Election

The public safety amendment dominated the 2021 election, turning the mayoral and city council elections into proxy fights for Question 2 on creating the Department of Public Safety (and, by extension, Question 1's provocation to extend mayoral authority). The centrist editorial board of the *Star Tribune*, for example, recommended a "yes" on Question 1 and a "no" on Question 2, nearly uniformly endorsing the candidates who opposed Question 2.[92] In contrast, more progressive and left-leaning outlets pushed for those candidates who supported the new Department of Public Safety, telling voters to select "no" on 1 and "yes" on 2.[93]

Key to leftists' strategy was electing a mayor who would support police defunding, putting the unwritten goals of Question 2 into practice. Mayor Jacob Frey faced a slate of contenders, but only two consistently garnered substantial support: Sheila Nezhad and Kate Knuth. Nezhad was an organizer, one of the coauthors of the MPD150 report, and a street medic, committed to becoming the city's first queer woman of color mayor. Nezhad was among the Reclaim the Block organizers who pushed city leaders to envision a police-free future, arguing in 2020 that the abolitionist groups had "primed" the council members to accept the idea that "reform won't work," moving instead toward a new plan: "We are going to abolish the police."[94] Instead of police, Nezhad envisioned a robust set of holistic violence prevention resources, leading with "healing, not fear" and creating a "safe Minneapolis" through "stable housing, inclusive mental health care, accessible food and livable wages."[95] Her campaign—which ran under the slogan "Sheila for the People"—continually garnered national headlines declaring that an abolitionist might become mayor of Minneapolis.[96]

Kate Knuth, a white woman and three-term Minnesota House Democratic–Farmer–Labor Party representative whose career had focused on environmental justice, positioned herself between Nezhad and Frey— providing a more progressive alternative to the incumbent without quite as radical a stance on the MPD as Nezhad. Knuth argued that the city needed to "unbundle and transform" (not abolish) the police, shifting away from a "policing first" approach so that the MPD could more effectively "respond to violent crime."[97] She also promised to promote police accountability measures—something Nezhad framed as reforms that don't work. Despite their ideological differences, Knuth and Nezhad formed a coalition against Frey, attempting to coordinate the city's ranked-choice voting by telling voters #DontRankFrey. Perhaps surprisingly, there were no viable challengers to Frey's political right—meaning that the contest was largely between the incumbent mayor and two more progressive women.

Many of the city council races were deeply contested as well—with city hall contenders staking out their positions on the possibility of a police-free future. Cunningham, for example, fought against a more moderate challenger, LaTrisha Vetaw, a Black woman and vocal opponent of the charter initiative who ran while serving on the Minneapolis Park and Recreation Board. Jeremiah Ellison, the other Northside representative, similarly battled a number of more moderate challengers, including one of the neighbors who were suing the city over inadequate police protection. And Steve Fletcher, the representative for downtown and Northeast Minneapolis and another of the Powderhorn Nine, squared off against Michael Rainville, an older white man whose family had been influential in Minneapolis politics for generations[98] and who stood to become the council's most conservative representative. These races were closely watched as proxy contests for Question 2: Would the council members be rewarded or punished for their association with the "defund" slogan?

Let the People Decide

The final weeks leading up to election day were chaotic. The Samuels and their allies filed a last-minute lawsuit to block the ballot question altogether, resulting in a tense back-and-forth right up to the printing deadline between the mayor and the city council over the wording of Question 2. Key to this struggle was exactly how much detail about the deleted text on the MPD, and what the new department might look like, should be included in an "explanatory note" attached to the ballot question. In the end, the two sides compromised on an explanatory note nearly as long as the question itself, as displayed in figure 4.2.

As absentee ballots began rolling in, endorsements and statements of opposition from prominent Democrats flooded the headlines, paralleling national consternation over the police. Chief Arradondo reiterated his opposition in the final days, too, holding a press conference in his dress blues to denigrate the charter initiative (later deemed an ethics violation). Just days before the vote, the city seemed to resolve the most pressing union question—in a memo sent to city employees and leaked to the press, city administrators wrote that officers would *not* have to reapply to their jobs. The police would be automatically transferred to the new department should the ballot question pass. The implication was that the charter would not be used to break the federation's grip on Minneapolis politics.[99]

In the end, voters ultimately rejected Question 2, with 56 percent voting "no" to 44 percent "yes." Alongside the "no" on Question 2, city residents said "yes" to Question 1, the "strong mayor" proposal (with 52 percent in favor) and reelected Mayor Frey.[100] The mayoral ranked-choice vote tallying process was relatively quick, lasting only one round of elimination.

> **City Question #2**
> **Department of Public Safety**
>
> Shall the Minneapolis City Charter be amended to remove the Police
> Department and replace it with a Department of Public Safety that
> employs a comprehensive public health approach to the delivery of
> functions by the Department of Public Safety, with those specific
> functions to be determined by the Mayor and City Council by
> ordinance; which will not be subject to exclusive mayoral power over
> its establishment, maintenance, and command; and which could
> include licensed peace officers (police officers), if necessary, to fulfill
> its responsibilities for public safety, with the general nature of the
> amendments being briefly indicated in the explanatory note below,
> which is made a part of this ballot?
>
> Explanatory Note: This amendment would create a Department of
> Public Safety combining public safety functions through a
> comprehensive public health approach to be determined by the Mayor
> and Council. The department would be led by a Commissioner
> nominated by the Mayor and appointed by the Council. The Police
> Department, and its chief, would be removed from the City Charter.
> The Public Safety Department could include police officers, but the
> minimum funding requirement would be eliminated.

FIGURE 4.2. Charter amendment question on the November 2021 ballot

Tallies showed Frey led in the number of first-choice votes (with 61,620 votes), with Nezhad in second place (with 30,368 first-choice votes) and Knuth a close third (26,468). That Nezhad won roughly a quarter of the first-choice votes (far less than the amendment's 44 percent support) suggested that Minneapolis's most fervent abolitionist voting bloc was large, but still far from a majority in the city. Voting strategically, many of Nezhad's voters ranked Knuth second, catapulting Knuth to become Frey's final challenger. In that second round, Frey won with 56 percent of the vote, while Knuth trailed with 44 percent.[101]

While keeping Frey in place (and handing him more power), voters reshuffled the city council. In contrast to the 2017 elections, the council did not swing left. The progressive side of the council lost some of its champions. Rainville beat out Fletcher, and Cunningham lost in a landslide to Vetaw, who would now serve as the chair of the Public Health and Safety Committee. But Jeremiah Ellison held onto his Ward 5 seat in a very close race, while others of the Powderhorn Nine were reelected on wider margins, including Andrea Jenkins, whose challenger barely registered as real opposition. And in the three wards where pledge supporters declined to run for reelection, they were replaced by a younger and farther left cohort, as voters elected a record-breaking three candidates endorsed by the Democratic Socialists of America, including Robin Wonsley (then Wonsley Worlobah), to represent the ward that encompassed the University of Minnesota and its young, left-leaning voters. Of the three council members who declined to take the Powderhorn Pledge, two remained in office and one was replaced by a council member who vocally supported Question 2. In short, the council's center of gravity remained roughly the same as it had been—but both of its edges had pulled farther apart.

Defunding the police, it turned out, was *both* a powerful rallying call and, for some council members, a liability. Yet, in a testament to the power of the BLM movement, for the first time, the city had a majority BIPOC council—there were more people of color on the dais than white elected officials. Importantly, for all the reading of the tea leaves in these results, some of the races were tantalizingly close (leaning on just dozens of votes), meaning that how they ultimately fell is best understood as a matter of chance. Had just a few voters chosen differently, skipped the polls that year, or decided to vote rather than stay home, it would have produced a substantially different Minneapolis city council. What we saw were voters, in the aftermath of the murder of George Floyd, as conflicted toward the city council as they were toward the charter amendment. With Frey in charge as a strong mayor, however, the council's policing politics mattered even less now.

It's important to note here too that only *half* of all registered voters decided these pivotal races. Had the charter amendment question been on the 2020 ballot, it would have coincided with a presidential election. Voter turnout that year reached an all-time high of 81 percent of registered voters in Minneapolis. (And, had the vote been in 2020, the Powderhorn Nine and other city council members would have been in office another year to implement the plan afterward.) Instead, in November 2021, only 54 percent of voters went to the polls—a record-breaking turnout for a municipal election in Minneapolis, but far less than the turnout for presidential elections.[102] We cannot know how these residents might have voted, but low turnout was another consequence of the delay. So too was uncertainty about the other races (for the mayor's seat and city council) that would shape the initiative's implementation.

After the election, people wanted to know not just whether police defunding had won or lost in Minneapolis—but *who* was responsible. As Levy Armstrong declared in her derisive *New York Times* op-ed, were the "white progressives" who had supported the ill-fated proposal to blame?[103] On this question, she and the mayor were aligned. As Frey often repeated to reporters: "I'd walk down the street and I'd hear from White people, 'Defund the police! Defund the police!' And then I'd hear from a Black person a half block later, 'Hey, we really need to have some additional help.'" Supporters of the charter amendment would rebut this narrative, spotlighting the BIPOC activists at the helm of the charter initiatives. As Sheila Nezhad replied to a reporter: "I'm not White. So when Jacob Frey talks about only White people want to defund or whatever . . . I think that he is perhaps shaping the narrative to benefit his political goals."[104] Making things more complicated to parse, supporters of the charter amendment often insisted it was white (and wealthy) voters who had *blocked* the initiative.

The truth, however, resisted a simple narrative. While individual-level voting data are not public, we can look at precinct-level vote counts, displayed in figure 4.3. These results show that voters in the precincts in North Minneapolis, home to the greatest share of Black residents in the city, on average narrowly rejected the ballot initiative (although these neighborhoods also saw some of the lowest turnout rates). But the staunchest opposition to Question 2 (and highest voter turnout) came from the southwest precincts—predominantly wealthy white neighborhoods. Support for the charter amendment, in contrast, was highest in the multiracial communities around George Floyd Square in South Minneapolis, where residents had been radicalized in the wake of the murder, and in areas with younger voters, including near the University of Minnesota.

Public opinion polls launched just before the election generally confirmed these spatial patterns. In a September 2021 poll, just under half (49 percent) replied that they supported the initiative to replace the MPD with a new Department of Public Safety,[105] several points higher than the share of voters who would say "yes" two months later at the polling booth. Racial differences on the charter amendment question were small, but white voters were slightly *more* in favor of the proposal on average (51 vs. 42 percent). The data suggested that anyone arguing that *only* white progressives were supporting the amendment or that *only* white voters were driving opposition to the amendment was wrong. In contrast to the muted divides across race, gaps in attitudes across age in the poll results were striking, with 57 percent of voters under age thirty-four years in support, compared to 39 percent among those age sixty-five and up.[106] The charter amendment, it turned out, was propelled by *young* voters and blocked by their more conservative elders.[107] There was a clear demographic divide, but it was across *generations*, not race.

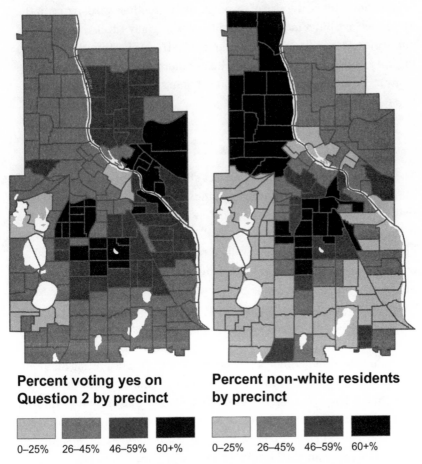

Percent voting yes on Question 2 by precinct

0–25% 26–45% 46–59% 60+%

Percent non-white residents by precinct

0–25% 26–45% 46–59% 60+%

FIGURE 4.3. Precinct-level voting results for question 2 and racial demographics
Sources: Office of the Minnesota Secretary of State, Election Results, City Question 2 (Minneapolis), Reports by Reporting District (last updated November 8, 2021); US Census Bureau, 2020 Census Redistricting Data (P.L. 94-171) - Table P1, Race (Washington, DC: US Department of Commerce, 2021).

Yet these poll results also reveal how much city residents struggled to understand what exactly a "yes" vote on Question 2 meant, and whether or not it would bring them more safety. As in the 2020 polls, registered voters in September 2021 continued to report a largely unfavorable opinion of the MPD, with just 28 percent of Black voters and 34 percent of white voters describing their opinion of the MPD as "favorable." Yet despite this lack of support, just over half (55 percent) of polled voters— and a full 75 percent of Black respondents—reported that the department "should not" reduce the size of its police force. In other words, trust in the MPD was low, but a majority of residents (especially Black residents) did *not* want fewer police patrolling the city's streets. Putting those results together implies that even among Black voters who wanted more police, many still decided "yes" on Question 2, hoping it would bring them a better system of public safety.

Lessons Learned

The fires that torched the 3rd Precinct after the murder of George Floyd unsettled local politics, prompting nine city council members to pledge that they would begin the process of "ending" the MPD. Yet, in the wake of the November 2021 election, the MPD stood intact, with an even larger budget. In short, when the swell of progressive mobilization crashed against the politics of policing, the radical vision for change in Minneapolis faltered. Blocking challengers' attempts to wrest power over the MPD were a series of legal and regulatory barriers that slowed down the process of change. These too were part of the politics of policing, erected by city leaders (and state legislators) to bulwark police power in earlier eras.

In the intervening time, homicides in the city spiked, shifting attention from violence by *police* to violence by *residents*. And, in the meantime, the department had lost nearly a third of its effective force. As the editorial board of the *Star Tribune* summarized in their election guide, the proposal to include police in the new department only *if necessary* had "an ominous ring in a city with an already understaffed police force and a crime wave in progress."[108] As the tide turned back again, many of the groups that had cut ties with the MPD (including my own university) quietly reestablished those connections, reaching to the city's police force for the promise of protection. Even anti-police-violence activists known for their blistering critiques of the department came to the defense of the MPD, arguing that the charter amendment would take the city in the wrong direction. The mayor, his allies, and the police union went a step farther, directly blaming the Powderhorn Pledge for emboldening criminals and prompting the mass exodus of officers that left the city with rampant "lawlessness." The factual basis for some of these claims may have been weak, but they were powerful rhetorical weapons. Together, this odd coalition of opponents convinced enough voters to select "no" on the ballot, dashing abolitionist activists' hope of eliminating the charter's mandatory minimum number of officers.

The same national news outlets that had blared that Minneapolis was "abolishing" its police department in summer 2020 now pivoted to headlines about failure. "Defund the police," pundits gloated, was a flop as a political slogan. Yet the reality on the ground in Minneapolis was more nuanced. Indeed, that 44 percent of the public supported a measure associated with police abolition, in the context of a significant homicide spike, was a victory of sorts. And to the extent that 44 percent constituted a "win," it didn't come just from the fires of summer 2020, but from the years of organizing that had worked to unsettle residents' assumptions about the police. The results of this groundswell of support for police abolition would be felt in the years to come, sometimes in surprising ways. And the abolitionists weren't going anywhere.

CHAPTER FIVE

Seeking Justice

ACCOUNTABILITY FOR "KILLER COPS"

IN THE HEAT of the unrest, Minneapolis residents and activists demanded "Justice for George." The murderous "killer cops," activists declared, needed to be held accountable. And the justice system, seemingly for the first time when the victim was Black, appeared to listen. Following pleas from George Floyd's family, activists, and residents distrustful of Hennepin County attorney Michael Freeman's handling of the case, Minnesota attorney general Keith Ellison joined the prosecution team, escalating the charges against Derek Chauvin to second-degree murder and indicting the other three officers (J. Alexander Kueng, Thomas Lane, and Tou Thao) for aiding and abetting murder. The family also filed a wrongful death lawsuit against the city, while federal prosecutors would bring civil rights charges against all four officers. As the jury was being selected for the state criminal case against Chauvin in 2021, the city agreed to pay a record-breaking $27 million civil settlement to the Floyd family (dollars that would be pulled from the general city fund, not the police budget). With the world watching, in April 2021 the court announced the first criminal conviction: the killing was legally declared a murder, with Chauvin found guilty on all three charges and later sentenced to an unprecedented 22.5 years. Federal courts followed suit, and by February 2022 Chauvin, Kueng, Lane, and Thao were all convicted of violating Floyd's civil rights.

These convictions were a historic set of legal punishments imposed on officers, hailed as an important win in the struggle for justice for victims of police violence. After the Chauvin verdict, celebrations erupted outside of the courtroom, in George Floyd Square, and around the world as people cheered, embraced, and cried, releasing years of exhaustion and struggle. Yet not everyone saw these outcomes as a victory. Some of the abolitionist activists introduced in chapter 2, for example, argued that these trials were a form of image repair for the police department, allowing the Minneapolis Police Department (MPD) to criminalize Chauvin as a "bad apple" while valorizing its policies, practices, and leadership, many of whom testified in court against the "rogue" officer. Real justice, abolitionists argued, would be a world in which George Floyd was still alive. The next best outcome would be a future in which it was impossible for the MPD to murder someone again—because the department (and armed police) no longer existed.

As activists, residents, and city leaders struggled over the meaning of justice, the department faced its own trials. In the midst of the Floyd protests in summer 2020, the Minnesota Department of Human Rights (MDHR) announced a civil rights investigation into the embattled department. After President Donald J. Trump lost his bid for reelection that fall, Democrat Joseph "Joe" R. Biden Jr. took office, installing leadership at the Department of Justice (DOJ) who supported federal investigations of local police departments (or "pattern and practice" investigations). And in April 2021 the DOJ announced the launch of an investigation of systematic bias and constitutional violations in the MPD's operations. These two investigations proceeded alongside the battles over charter amendments to end the MPD, the city budget, and—at the city, state, and national levels—police reform legislation. This chapter takes stock of these unsettled efforts to secure "Justice for George." As we'll see, just as there was no one understanding of what "safety" looked like to everyone, so too were there many interpretations of what "justice" or "accountability" might mean after the murder of George Floyd.

The Structure of Police Accountability

American policing, like much of our criminal justice system, is highly decentralized. Most policing policy (and funding) is set at the local level—diffused across nearly 18,000 police departments. Further, in Minneapolis (as in many other cities), there are *multiple* police departments, including not just the city police, but transit police, park police, and university police. These local police departments are embedded in a complex legal and regulatory maze shaped by local, state, and federal politics. This structures the ways individual officers can (or cannot) be held accountable in the wake of misconduct as well as the opportunities and barriers to changing department-level policies and practices. In short, an array of rules at

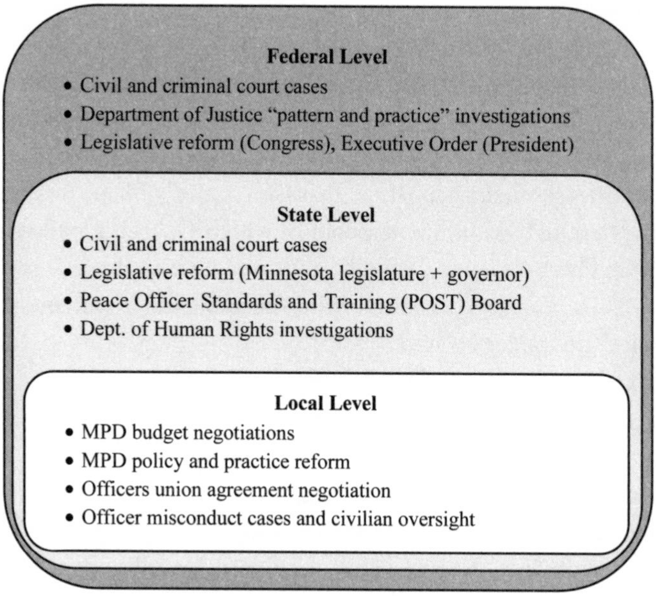

FIGURE 5.1. Routes toward police accountability

various levels of government both enable and constrain political leaders and challengers in their efforts to change policing.

Under the umbrella of "accountability," in this chapter I include all of the proposals pushed forward by activists, civic leaders, and elected officials to respond to George Floyd's murder, specifically, and changes to the MPD and American policing, more broadly. These accountability mechanisms, summarized in figure 5.1, vary across several dimensions. First, while some accountability mechanisms focus on the conduct of individual officers (e.g., criminal trials and internal misconduct investigations), others center on the department (e.g., the charter amendment) or even all police in a state or country (e.g., legislation or court decisions). Second, the type of entity driving the changes varies, from elected officials and MPD leadership, to activists, judges, and union negotiators. Finally, the locus of control for these mechanisms varies—while some are driven by local politics, others happen at the state (e.g., Minnesota Board of Peace Officer Standards and Training, which licenses officers and training programs) or federal level (e.g., DOJ pattern and practice investigations).

These layers of law and regulation over policing can be mutually reinforcing or in opposition. For example, while Supreme Court decisions and state criminal statutes set a legal minimum standard for officers' use of force, individual departments can choose to impose more stringent guidelines, imposing discipline (up to termination) for behavior that does not meet that standard. In that instance, internal department policy and misconduct review processes operate to reaffirm and extend the civil rights protections built into state and federal law and court rulings. But these same processes can also block accountability, thwarting activists' efforts to fight the police. For example, state laws that require a licensed police officer to respond to certain kinds of 911 calls limit the scope of budding police alternatives, while other legislation limits the role of civilian oversight in officer discipline. State-level union protections and arbitration regulations can also allow officers to petition for reinstatement after discipline and enable the union to fight back against policing reforms.

All of this complexity means that trying to change policing practices can be a maddening "whack-a-mole" game mired in technicalities and years of debate and litigation. Abolitionists argue that this failure is *by design*—the legal system is structured to protect police power.[1] And indeed, the law often did protect the police in Minneapolis. Yet activists also seized on these tools, as they had in decades past, using whatever they could grasp to leverage change. Law and policy, in other words, both constrain and enable efforts to challenge policing. Neither was a fixed structure, but instead, an active target of struggle as advocates worked to change the laws, policies, and regulations around policing. That meant that not only did activists and city leaders trying to change public safety have to win public support, but they also needed to develop the expertise to target the right linchpins of local, state, or federal policies and practices. By 2020 they would have help; as Minneapolis emerged at the center of a national (and international) mobilization against police violence, outside experts and advocates flooded into the city to force change.

As each set of activists, organizers, everyday residents, and city leaders developed its own account of what was wrong with policing (whether that be inadequate protection, failures to punish police for violence, or too much funding for the police) and a vision toward accountability, each pursued its own legal and political struggles, sometimes pushing the city in contradictory directions. And few of these processes would be swift—the court cases, for example, would stretch on for years, by which point public attention and outcry had shifted away from police violence and toward violence in the community.

The Trials

In the wake of the murder, Floyd's family sought financial recompense from the city for their loss. Not only would this civil suit change the lives of his family, but it would force the city to acknowledge the scale of the harm their police had caused. On March 12, 2021, the city agreed to pay a record-high $27 million in the wrongful death settlement, a small piece of which would provide support for the square through the George Floyd Global Memorial organization, which linked Floyd's kin to 38th and Chicago. Because the city was self-insured for police misconduct claims, city taxpayers would ultimately pay for this settlement, a fact activists continually spotlighted as an injustice.[2] It also meant that the MPD budget was in fact even larger than listed in the city's records because it *excluded* these costs, which continued to grow as the city settled lawsuits stemming from the explosion of police misconduct during the unrest.[3]

News of the civil settlement was broadcast publicly during the jury selection for Chauvin's criminal case, the first of several departures from business-as-usual in the court. In addition, the jury seated for Chauvin's trial in Hennepin County was *more* racially diverse than the population; of the twelve final jurors, four were Black and two were multiracial. Ranging in age from their twenties to sixties, most of the jurors explicitly supported the Black Lives Matter (BLM) movement and had seen the videos of Floyd's death, though they asserted that they could make a fair assessment of the facts of the case. (In a screening questionnaire, three-quarters of potential jurors disagreed with the statement that police treat people of different races/ethnicities equally—a testament to the growing impact of the BLM movement.[4]) Also unusual was that the entire trial proceedings were broadcast online (due to the combination of public interest and the ongoing pandemic), as viewers across the world watched Judge Peter A. Cahill preside over a historic trial in real time. This meant that the witnesses' testimony, too, would rapidly circulate in news and social media.

Broadcast to the public, Chauvin's criminal trial was also a disorienting inversion of the typical courtroom drama. In most criminal cases, the prosecutor and police are aligned, with the prosecutor relying on evidence collected by police and, often, testimony provided by officers. In this trial, of course, the defendant *was* a police officer. While Chauvin never took the stand, a slew of officers in uniforms and suits addressed the court—including MPD training officers, supervisors, and Chief Arradondo himself. Rather than defend their brother in blue, these representatives of the MPD sought to distance the department from Chauvin, arguing that holding his knee on

Floyd's neck and back for nine minutes was against department training and policy. "In our custody is in our care," the chief declared from the stand, a directive they maintained Chauvin had ignored in disregard for Floyd's life.

The prosecutors took pains to assert this narrative, making it clear that neither policing nor the MPD was on trial—only Derek Chauvin. Good policing, they argued, was essential to the city's well-being. What the city (and world) saw on Memorial Day, they argued, was not good policing. It was a crime. As special prosecutor Jerry Blackwell concluded, in his searing closing statement: "You were told, for example, that Mr. Floyd died because his heart was too big . . . The truth of the matter is that the reason George Floyd is dead is because Mr. Chauvin's heart was too small."[5]

The weeks of the trial were tense in the city. Fearing another period of unrest should the jury fail to convict, the city and state brought together local law enforcement and the National Guard to blanket the city and fortify the downtown building where the trial took place, an effort dubbed "Operation Safety Net." Then, the week before closing arguments, another high-profile police killing would erupt in nearby Brooklyn Center, a relatively affordable and racially diverse first-ring suburb just north of the city. The victim was twenty-year-old Daunte Wright, born to a white mother and Black father. Pulled over for a traffic stop after officers spotted an expired registration tag, Wright had outstanding warrants. When officers attempted to arrest him, Wright sat down in the driver's seat of his car (which was still running), appearing ready to escape. In response, officers struggled unsuccessfully from both sides to pull Wright out of the vehicle. Pulling out her service revolver, veteran police officer (and field training officer) Kimberly Potter shouted "Taser!" as she shot and killed Wright in the front seat.

Protests over Wright's killing spread rapidly across the Twin Cities metro area, including at times violent clashes between the Brooklyn Center and Operation Safety Net police and protesters. Replaying the early days of the 3rd Precinct siege in Minneapolis, protesters gathered in front of the Brooklyn Center Police Department, chanting peacefully during the day and turning more confrontational at night. As a handful of people in the crowd lobbed water bottles and other small items toward the officers in riot gear, Brooklyn Center police and their defenders responded with escalating force, using so much tear gas and flash-bang grenades that residents of a nearby apartment complex were forced out of their homes, choking on the air. As in the summer 2020 protests, police at times deliberately targeted members of the press and often incited violence without provocation or warning. Attempting to avoid the scale of the unrest after Floyd's murder, Brooklyn Center mayor Mike Elliott—the city's first Black mayor—quickly fired the city manager (who managed the police department) and pushed the police chief to resign.[6] And, as we'll see in chapter 6, he called in violence interruption workers.

Just as the Brooklyn Center protests began to burn out, the Chauvin jury was sequestered to deliberate. Once Chauvin's conviction had been secured, the state criminal trial began against the other three officers— J. Alexander Kueng, Thomas Lane, and Tou Thao. By that point, Chauvin had pled guilty to federal charges that he had deprived George Floyd of his civil rights (alongside violations stemming from *another* instance of violence, that time against a minor) and been sentenced to twenty-one years in prison, time which would be served concurrently with his state sentence. For the other officers, the federal trial would precede the state's case. All three were charged with violating Floyd's civil rights for failing to provide appropriate medical care. Tou Thao and J. Alexander Kueng were also charged with an additional civil rights violation for failing to intervene when an officer used unreasonable force (a charge not levied at Lane, who did intervene to ask Chauvin if they should reposition Floyd).

In January, another jury was seated for these criminal cases. Many of the same witnesses and experts from the Chauvin trial again took the stand. Interestingly, while fewer viewers were tuning in, in this trial the MPD seemed to come under more direct scrutiny, in part a result of the officers' attempts to shift blame onto Chauvin and, by extension, the department. Much of their testimony focused on what they claimed was the paramilitary culture of the MPD, which dictated that rookie officers never contradict a senior officer. This time, Chauvin was again positioned as a "bad apple," but now as the sort that had already "spoiled the bunch"—in part through his elevation to field training officer. It was an indictment of the department's training, but, as a legal defense strategy, it failed. In February 2022, all three officers were found guilty and later sentenced; the state criminal cases followed the next year, with Keung and Lane pleading guilty and Thao found guilty in trial. All three are now expected to spend two to five years in prison.

Punishment or Justice?

When the verdict against Derek Chauvin was announced, crowds outside the courthouse and across George Floyd Square cheered. The activist groups that had helped plan demonstrations in support of the prosecution celebrated what seemed like the first real victory against racist police violence in the courtroom. Finally, activists' perceptions of the severity of state harm were in alignment with the seriousness of the legal sanction. Justice, some argued, had been served. Floyd's family released a statement, transmitted by their attorney and civil rights champion Benjamin Crump, that described the verdict as a step toward a world in which holding a police officer account-able for wrongly taking the life of a Black man was no longer "exceptional."[7] Similar cheers emerged following the guilty convictions against the other officers, though responses were more critical in respect to their much shorter sentences. As Floyd's uncle, Selwyn Jones, would tell a reporter: "Once again, our judicial system favored people that should be locked up forever."[8]

Chauvin and his colleagues' convictions were exceptional. Almost none of the officers responsible for the more than one thousand victims of lethal police force every year wind up behind bars. Between 2005 and summer 2019, for example, a total of just 104 local and state police officers were arrested and charged with murder or manslaughter. Only thirty-five were convicted, often on lesser charges through plea bargains.[9]

Much of this lack of response to police killings is because such deaths are never coded as a crime by the legal system in the first place, due to officers' wide discretion to use lethal force. Replicating the language of precedent-setting Supreme Court decisions about lethal police interac-tions, especially 1989's *Graham v. Connor*, most states authorize deadly force in situations in which a "reasonable officer" would perceive an imme-diate threat to themself or others.[10] Each of those words has been closely scrutinized in legislative hearings and courts: Who constitutes a "reason-able" officer? How "immediate" must the "threat" be?

Beyond the letter of the law, both prosecutors and juries have histori-cally been hesitant to convict police. As noted earlier, there is a mutual dependence between police and prosecutors that helps to shield officers from accountability following misconduct.[11] Prosecutors rely on police to do their job in the courtrooms, with police collecting the evidence that makes a case and often testifying as a witness for the prosecution in trials. In addition, juries have historically been hesitant to convict police officers even when prosecutors attempt to make the case, worried about punish-ing officers for "just doing their job." In addition, the ambiguity of the reasonable force standards makes it more difficult for juries to come to a "guilty" verdict in trials, especially when officers testify that they feared for their lives. All of this helps to explain the decisions noted in chap-ter 2—moments when the Hennepin County Prosecutor's Office chose not to indict MPD officers who had used lethal force.

After the murder of Floyd, however, there have been some indications that this is (slowly) changing. In 2021 a record twenty-one officers were charged with murder or manslaughter.[12] And back in Minnesota, former

officer Potter, the woman who shot and killed Daunte Wright, would follow Chauvin to prison in 2022, convicted of first-degree manslaughter.
Unlike Chauvin's lengthy sentence, however, she was released after just
over a year behind bars.

These limits of the legal system to regulate officers' violence were one of
the reasons abolitionist groups in Minneapolis had a more muted response
to Chauvin's conviction. Throughout the trial, they had balanced their
public messaging, both supporting the idea that Floyd's family and others
might want to see a conviction and pushing back against the framing
that a guilty verdict would mean justice was served. Justice was instead
a world where an officer kneeling on the neck and back of a man prone
in the street and not resisting for nine minutes would be unfathomable—in
no small part because police as we know them had been abolished. Real
justice would be a world in which "George was still here with his family,
loved ones, and community."[13]

For many organizers in local groups like Black Visions and Reclaim the
Block, and in police abolitionist circles across the country, this trial was
a moment to showcase not activists' victory but the limits of looking to
the state for redress. Abolitionist activists noted how much time, energy,
and money had gone into the prosecution—all to legally determine what
should have been immediately apparent: officers murdered George Floyd.
Turning to a racist legal system to adjudicate whether this was in fact murder and (at best) get a conviction, which could and would be challenged on
appeal, was a fool's errand. Further, the end result of that conviction was
(again, at best) incarceration, another form of state violence. Punishment,
they argued, was not justice.

The state had gone to great lengths to convict Chauvin, abolitionists
argued, not to pursue justice but to distract and pacify the public, showing
that the system was doing *something* about police violence without changing any of the real "pieces on the board."[14] Worse, such convictions neu-
tralized anti-police-violence protests by scapegoating Chauvin and thereby
recuperating the MPD's image. Invoking Audre Lorde's "the master's tools
will never dismantle the master's house," abolitionists argued that what
was needed instead were new tools.

Put Your Money Where Your Mouth Is

One of those new tools was police defunding. In Minneapolis, activists
had for years fought against proposed *increases* in police funding. In the
heat of the unrest, activists demanded that the city instead substantially

defund the MPD as a means of redress for the department's wrongs. As debates over the charter amendment ebbed and flowed, activists continued to push the city council members who took to the stage at Powderhorn Park to make good on their promise of taking "immediate steps" to dismantle the MPD and fight for accountability through the budget.

In the years immediately preceding Floyd's killing, spending on the MPD had crept up, from $146 million in 2014 to $181 million by 2019.[15] By then, Minneapolis was under fire from abolitionist groups for spending a third of the city's general funds, or the dollars earmarked for unrestricted city spending, on the MPD. It was substantially more than the city spent on the health department ($26 million) or housing policy and development ($46 million).

This seemingly massive police spending, however, was in part a fiscal illusion, driven by all of the spending cities do *outside* of general funds (i.e., spending that is earmarked for specific categories). If we look instead at the city's entire budget, funds devoted to the MPD comprised just 8 percent of the city's expenditures in 2019. Another way to measure it was that the city spent roughly $420 per year on policing for each of its 430,000 residents (roughly equivalent to the median per capita spending among the seventy-two largest cities in the United States).[16] We can also benchmark spending on the MPD to other categories in the budget. Again looking at all spending, the largest share of Minneapolis's operating budget went not to police but to the public works department (17 percent), followed by nondepartmental expenses, capital improvements, and the city coordinator's office.[17] Minneapolis is not unique in this respect, either—across the country in 2017 an average of roughly 13 percent of municipal governments' typical annual expenditures went to the police.[18]

Not only does money that goes toward police constitute a minority of all city spending, but many of the kinds of "life-sustaining" interventions abolitionists call for are funded outside of city budgets. For example, the Minneapolis city budget excludes the Minneapolis Public Schools, which operated in 2019 on an annual budget of $620 million, with funding levels determined by a state allocation formula based on the number of enrolled students.[19] So too does it exclude the Minneapolis Park and Recreation system, which spent $84 million in 2019 and includes its own police force and elected board of commissioners.[20] Looking at state-level spending makes this even clearer. In 2017, for example, state and local governments across the country spent a total of $115 billion on law enforcement or less than 4 percent of all expenditures—a share of spending that has remained relatively constant since the late 1970s (though the overall spending has increased). Local and state governments spend another 3 percent on their corrections systems (jails, prisons, etc.). In contrast, spending on public welfare (including Medicaid and cash assistance programs) and education comprises just over 50 percent of all state and local spending. Spending on health and hospitals, and highways and roads, both also exceed state and local funding for the police.[21]

Cities spend on the police in part because it's the "cheap" solution under the control of local policymakers to address the persistent holes in the social welfare net and the crises it produces.[22] That does not mean that spending on law enforcement is equivalent to social spending in terms of its meaning or outcomes—indeed, while much of social spending can be read as supporting thriving communities, police spending implies repression and control. In fact, in recent decades police spending increased the most in cities with a growing share of Black residents, driven in part by federal aid for law enforcement, giving evidence to the argument that policing represents federally funded *racial* repression.[23]

But it does mean that the scale of spending on policing is smaller, in relative terms, than it seems at first glance. There is less to invest-divest, in other words, than it sometimes seems. The $181 million spent on the MPD in 2019 (plus the $20 million settlement to Justine Damond's family that year, paid out of other city funds) was certainly not paltry—it could have funded any number of other kinds of community initiatives. But the sum was unlikely to alone meet the scale of need required to truly address poverty, education, housing, and health care systematically. Activists in Minneapolis were committed, however, to redirecting what they could.

Their point of leverage was the budget negotiation process. Every year, the mayor first sets the terms of the initial budget proposal, which is revised and approved by the city council. The mayor then has veto power over the council's changes, which can force the revised budget back to the council (though a two-thirds vote can overturn the mayor's veto). In September 2020 Mayor Jacob Frey proposed a 2021 city budget with $179 million earmarked for the MPD. One way of looking at it was that Frey—who had told protesters at his door that he did *not* support defunding the police—had, in fact, just proposed *reducing* the MPD's budget compared to 2019's total (by $2 million). But the budget was overall slimmer, as the city had responded in 2020 to the economic impacts of the COVID-19 pandemic, and so the new figure represented an *increase* in the share of city spending allocated to its police department. He'd spared the MPD, in other words, more than other departments in the cuts.

Activists stoked outrage at Frey's proposal—the mayor was reward-ing the police for their violence. Instead, they argued, the MPD's budget should be slashed. *The People's Budget*, an initiative organized by aboli-tionist activists at Reclaim the Block and their allies, demanded that more than $80 million from the budget be moved to programs that would "put health first," "fund prevention, not punishment," and "prioritize people over profit." To do this, the collective outlined both where they would cut the MPD budget *and* where they would invest those dollars. The largest share of the redirected funds would go toward expanding the city's invest-ments in affordable housing, addressing a crisis they argued was at the root of many criminal offenses.[24]

While the city council did not take up this call directly, a group of council members agreed that (small) cuts to the MPD's budget should go toward alternatives to police, part of the transformative new model of public safety they had promised at Powderhorn Park. There was especially strong support for creating a new mobile mental health crisis response team, an initiative that had garnered consensus support from the city's diverse interest groups, including business owners and anti-police-violence activists alike. Proposing a "Safety for All" amendment to the mayor's proposed budget, city council president Lisa Bender called for moving $8 million out of the MPD's proposed 2021 allotment and into non-police mental health crisis response teams and the work of the Office of Violence Prevention.

Controversially, the budget amendment would also reduce the depart-ment's authorized staffing levels from 888 to 750 officers. This debate was largely theoretical; the MPD's force size by that point was substantially below 750 officers anyhow and the department would continue to lose officers. But the lower authorized force size would mean the mayor would need council approval to go above 750 in the future (if the department could find officers to hire). Seizing on this amendment as an opportu-nity to distance himself from the "activist" council, the mayor threatened to veto the budget. In a late-breaking compromise, the council agreed to remove the authorized staffing reduction from its proposal and set aside an additional $5 million in reserve funding for the MPD, effectively negat-ing the small budget cut.[25] By the end of 2021 the city budget would list the real spending on the MPD as just under $170 million, capped there only because the department had struggled to find enough staff to actually spend down its full budget even with all the overtime pay. The following year, the mayor would push through a budget that increased the depart-ment's funding to above its pre-pandemic levels, though the department ultimately spent just $180 million. And by 2023 the proposed budget would reach a new high, at almost $206 million, just under 10 percent of all city spending.[26]

While the literal defunding of police was piecemeal and short-lived in Minneapolis, the diverted funds for alternative safety approaches represented the city's most substantial move to shift away from the MPD, or what activists described as the city's "police-only response." Like other changes in Minneapolis, this incremental progress was the hard-won victory of years of organizing. And these new teams of violence interrupters and crisis interventionists, the subject of chapter 6, would represent the real start of a new model of public safety, though built on a shoestring budget.

Reforming the MPD

After the blockage of the first charter amendment in 2020 and the struggles over the 2021 city budget, attention turned to Mayor Frey and Chief Arradondo: How would they make good on promises to reform the police department? Frey, who had resisted calls to defund the department, had staked his credibility on the promise of reforming—and holding accountable—the beleaguered department. And residents' trust in the mayor would soon be tested with the November 2021 election, where voters could select a new mayor and city council. As campaign season warmed up, Frey gave a long-form interview to a reporter with the local *Sahan Journal*, boasting that he had done more to change policing policies than any other mayor in the city's storied history.[27]

On the misconduct front, Frey pointed to MPD policy changes that prohibited officers from reviewing body camera footage or speaking with union officials after critical incidents, enhanced documentation requirements for use of force and de-escalation, banned shooting at moving vehicles, and limited the use of projectiles as crowd control. The city attorney's office had also gained a seat at the table during officer disciplinary procedures. In addition to the stronger policies around officers' duty to intervene when they witnessed unreasonable use of force (required by the initial court order under the MDHR investigation), the city was investing in a training system that promised to turn officers into "active bystanders." Neck restraints and choke holds were now barred in cadets' training. In addition to these changes in policies and practices, the department had redoubled its efforts to recruit officers from diverse backgrounds, Frey noted, including people with work histories in social services, and overhauled the field training officer program to provide new oversight of both mentors and mentees. These changes, the mayor argued, were "data-driven"—his pushback to what he framed as the ideologically driven declarations of the council. And, he promised, there was "more to come" on the police reform front.

While these policies sounded good on paper, their impacts were harder to substantiate. And, like the murder of George Floyd, a police killing soon fractured any sense that the MPD had been successfully reformed. In campaign materials, Mayor Frey boasted that he had "banned no-knock raids," changing the MPD policies to require officers in most circumstances to announce their presence before entry (in a nod to demands following the police killing of Breonna Taylor in March 2020). Yet in February 2022, Amir Locke, a twenty-two-year-old Black man, was shot and killed in downtown Minneapolis by one of the MPD's SWAT teams during a no-knock raid. The raid was at the request of the St. Paul Police Department, though it was the MPD that insisted on it being no-knock.[28] As officers loudly stormed the apartment where Locke lay asleep on the couch under a blanket, he groggily awoke and began to rise with a gun in his hand. The officer facing Locke opened fire, killing the young man less than ten seconds after entering the apartment. While the MPD would describe Locke initially in its statement as a "suspect," he was not named on the arrest warrant. St. Paul's police were in fact looking for Locke's cousin, who was wanted as a suspect in a homicide. Locke's parents would later tell reporters that their son's gun was registered as a licensed concealed carry, purchased to defend himself against potential carjackers during his work as a delivery driver. Tragically, Locke was in the process of moving out of the city, headed to Texas to embark on a potential career in music.

It turned out that the "landmark" new policy the mayor and police chief had heralded on no-knock warrants in fact offered officers broad leeway to use the controversial tactic. The new policy did not even put a dent in the number of no-knock warrants submitted to the courts, which totaled ninety requests in the nine months after the policy reform.[29] Facing an ethics violation on activists' charges that "Frey lied, Amir died,"[30] the mayor replied to criticism on this point by saying that on the campaign trail, language around a ban "became more casual," a passive construction of the facts that fell far short of an apology.[31] In response to Locke's death, Frey would later revamp the MPD's no-knock policies once again, arguing that no-knock raids would *now* only be used in truly exceptional circumstances. The new (new) policy, however, kept a carve-out for situations in which the MPD deemed a no-knock raid necessary, leaving open the possibility of "exigent circumstances."

Amir Locke was not even the first Black man shot and killed after the murder of George Floyd by MPD officers. He was the second.[32] The first, Dolal Idd, had been killed in a shootout at a local gas station in December 2020 just a mile away from George Floyd Square. While the interaction was prompted by police (initiating a gun-sale sting operation), Idd appears to have fired the first shot. The killings of Idd and Locke were later deemed legally "justified" by authorities, but they suggested that the MPD's practices of violence against Black men continued despite the stark drop in the number of officers on the street. Even as the number of contacts with residents continued to decline, the MPD's internal data similarly showed no major declines in use-of-force incidents in the year after Floyd's murder.[33] And while the rate of discretionary vehicle stops in the city declined in this period, racial disparities in those stops did not.[34] Finally, as we'll see later, both the MDHR and DOJ investigations would ultimately report that officers' racially biased misconduct and failure to intervene when they witnessed misconduct continued through 2021 and 2022, sometimes even right in front of investigators doing ride-alongs.

In short, the policy reforms were, again, not enough, repeating many of the failures of the "MPD 2.0" and National Initiative reforms described in chapter 2. As with their predecessors, the reforms were marred by a crushingly steady rate of police killings as well as routine surveillance and harassment of communities of color. They failed in part because there was no one theory of what, exactly, was driving police violence in the city, or what kind of police violence should be the focus of reform, and what to do about it. As the department and city responded to specific high-profile instances of police violence, they attempted to change specific policies thought to be at the heart of each case (e.g., responding to mental health crises, officers' failure to intervene, no-knock raids, high-speed vehicle pursuits, etc.). None of these attempts, however, seemed to solve the underlying problem. The "thumpers" remained, with some of the old guard now in positions of authority.

Union Contract Negotiations

One reason the "thumpers" remained, and were at times promoted, was because of the wins of the police officers federation, which negotiated to ensure that officer seniority drove officer placement and promotion. In summer 2020, both Mayor Frey and council members continually identified the terms of the union contract as a key barrier to change. Even the police chief, Medaria Arradondo, agreed, telling reporters in 2020 that the police officers association, led by Robert "Bob" Kroll, would need to "come to a reckoning that either they are going to be on the right side of history or they're gonna be on the wrong side of history . . . [and] they will be left behind."[35] The charter amendment *might* have been able to break the union, though it would have likely embroiled the city in a costly lawsuit. In the wake of the amendment's failure, however, it was up to the council and mayor to negotiate a union contract that served the city better.

Back in 2017, the last agreement between the city and the Police Officers Federation of Minneapolis had been approved, set to expire in December 2019. As described in chapter 2, by then, the radical reform activist groups had formed a new coalition—Minneapolis for a Better Police Contract—to attempt to insert community voice into the city's negotiation process with the federation. In addition to pushing Frey for more access to that process, the coalition leaned on city council members for support. Activists also attempted to sit in on the negotiation sessions, arguing that these sessions should, under Minnesota's open meeting law, be available to the public. In response, the city and union moved the negotiations to mediation—taking them outside of the public's purview.

The murder of George Floyd, at first, seemed to regalvanize attempts to use the union negotiation process as a vehicle for change. In the aftermath of the rebellion, Chief Arradondo announced that the city would withdraw temporarily from negotiations, concluding that the department would need sweeping changes—especially to the discipline and arbitration rules that the chief argued allowed officers to win back their jobs after being fired.[36] Indeed, reporting in the wake of the murder showed that roughly half of officers who had been fired from the MPD in recent years had won their jobs back through arbitration.[37] It was unclear at the time, however, how stepping back from negotiations would help the city; some legal observers worried it would put the city in breach of state bargaining rules. By 2021 the city had resumed negotiations, still thwarting the activists' coalition from attending, which in turn prompted the group to sue the city, arguing that blocking them from observing the negotiations was a violation of state law.[38]

In March 2022, with the lawsuit on the open meetings still in process and Frey reelected, city residents would finally see the results of the city's negotiations. In the revised union contract, the accountability clauses Mayor Frey promised reporters in 2021 were nowhere to be found. In public comments, the mayor and his staff vacillated between blaming state laws for limiting the bargaining process to promising reporters that the city had added "layers of accountability" into the misconduct review process in department policy, which was more flexible than the union contract.[39]

Adding insult, the new contract included a $7,000 bonus for officers who stayed with the department, an inducement meant to respond to the continued labor shortage. None of the recommendations of the Minneapolis for a Better Police Contract coalition were adopted—a failure activists called on city council members to rectify by voting "no" on the contract. With a warning from Mayor Frey that if the council failed to approve the new contract it would go into arbitration, potentially giving the union an even stronger hand, the council voted to approve.

City council members vowed to start negotiations afresh the next cycle. Changing the MPD via union contract negotiations was once again the work of the future, promises that papered over the failures of elected officials to rein in the federation's power over city politics.

Civilian Oversight

As the city council, mayor, and activists struggled over funding and reforming the MPD, another mechanism that was ideally positioned to be the public's voice on police accountability was sidelined: civilian review. As described in chapter 1, Minneapolis had a long history of failed efforts at civilian oversight of the police. In 2012 the city had adopted a bifurcated process that created two bodies for civilian review. First, the Minneapolis Department of Civil Rights housed the Office of Police Conduct Review (OPCR), a misconduct investigation unit outside of the MPD that included officer and civilian investigators who investigated the evidence on each case under their jurisdiction. The investigators' summaries were then reviewed by the civilian director of the OPCR and the sworn officer heading Internal Affairs. After several review panels, the case would ultimately go to the police chief, who would take into account the OPCR's nonbinding recommendations and ultimately impose discipline (or not). This process, the MDHR would later conclude, meant that the city did not provide "meaningful independent review" of officers' misconduct, since each case was "assessed or guided by sworn MPD officers."[40]

Second, the city formed the Police Conduct Oversight Commission (PCOC), a volunteer-based citizen advisory committee appointed by the city council. Unlike the OPCR, which was formally integrated into the MPD and city governance structure, working in tandem with both the MPD's Internal Affairs and the city's civil rights unit, the PCOC was an island unto itself. Instead of reviewing specific allegations of misconduct, the commission's role was to audit trends (including through summaries of misconduct investigations) and provide community feedback to the department on specific issues (e.g., body camera policies) or concerns raised by the public (e.g., officers telling EMTs to inject people with ketamine during fraught police encounters). But the MPD, city council, and mayor were not required to take the PCOC's advice under formal consideration.[41]

Critics of Minneapolis's system of civilian "oversight" had long argued that both of these groups failed to hold officers accountable—ultimately enabling someone like Derek Chauvin to evade discipline despite a slew of misconduct allegations. For the OPCR, critics argued that investigations rarely led to officer discipline, even when the complaints were sustained (or supported by the available evidence). According to OPCR's public reports, for example, of the roughly six hundred complaints filed in 2019, only eight cases ended in discipline (one letter of reprimand, six suspensions, and one termination).[42] Part of the issue was that the most common outcome for cases that made it past the first phase of review was coaching, a form of intervention requiring a conversation between an officer and their supervisor, but not officially considered "discipline," which allowed the department not to release those records publicly.

The dysfunction of the PCOC looked different but produced the same outcome: little meaningful public oversight. While political leaders would periodically point to PCOC as an important external review board, painting the MPD with a veneer of legitimacy, in practice the group was almost entirely sidelined. Its members worked for no pay, volunteering for the city out of civic goodwill, and the group's reports and briefings were routinely ignored by the mayor and city council, even during moments where the city was gathering public "input" on policing. Back in 2016, for example, the chair of the PCOC responded to a reporter: "My goal, at this point, is to have the MPD reading our reports."[43] The following year, after Justine Damond was shot and killed by an MPD officer who had not activated his body camera, the PCOC would point to its (ignored) report on best practices with regard to body camera policy. Only after Damond's death would the department and city leadership take seriously officers' camera deployment, asking the OPCR to begin conducting compliance audits.

In the wake of Floyd's murder, attention to both the OPCR and PCOC exploded. Not only did it seem like these processes had failed to stop Chauvin; so too did officer misconduct during the unrest appear to go unchecked. By the end of 2020, the MPD's disciplinary records did not show a single officer disciplined for violence during the week following Floyd's death—not even in the cases for which the city was in the process of settling million-dollar civil cases (e.g., police violence that blinded several protesters and at least one journalist).[44] The officers who beat Jaleel

Stallings, the Black veteran who shot at a police van, had not yet been disciplined. The case became a public scandal only when officers' camera footage was revealed in a criminal case *against Stallings* (who was soon acquitted). In some cases, this lack of discipline was because officers left before they could be punished. Indeed, two of the officers in the SWAT unit involved in the Stallings case left the department on disability claims and a third retired. But the chief publicly defended these officers' conduct, arguing that "context is important and that the officers had just been through four days of rioting, looting, arson and the burning of the 3rd Precinct" in comments to the press.[45] (Stallings sued the department for violating his constitutional rights, naming nineteen officers, including two SWAT team officers who would go on to be involved in the fatal raid in 2022 that killed Amir Locke. The city settled the suit, awarding $1.5 million to Stallings.[46])

In many other cases, the issue was how long the OPCR process took to resolve. The group had been overwhelmed with disciplinary complaints in the wake of the uprising, slowing what was already a tedious and long process. Released in 2022, an after-action report on the unrest would confirm that the MPD failed to expand capacity to adjudicate these disciplinary cases.[47] In the second quarter of 2020 alone, the OPCR hit its usual annual total, with nearly six hundred complaints filed. In 2022 the city reported that of the 1,341 complaints filed with the OPCR in 2020 and 2021, forty-eight had ended in a disciplinary decision from the chief, a substantial increase from 2019's discipline rate, but still less than 5 percent of cases. By that point, the OPCR had doubled its number of staff (to nine full-time positions) and was trying to hire a new director.[48] But the average time it took a case to go from complaint to the chief's decision was still nearly two years.[49] This delayed investigation process thus precluded swift discipline for officer misconduct.

The review process, however, was not so slow for officers who spoke out against the department. Indeed, the discipline cases related to the unrest that made it to front-page news in 2021 were not about police violence, but officers critical of the MPD. One of those officers was Colleen Ryan, an MPD officer who spoke anonymously to a reporter about the workplace harassment she had faced as a lesbian woman and outspoken Democrat among officers enamored of President Trump.[50] The other was Art Knight, a Black twenty-eight-year-veteran of the department who had served as coordinator of the National Initiatives reform and was, at the time, the deputy chief. Talking to the *Star Tribune*, Knight asserted that the department could not keep using the same recruitment strategies, or else it would continue to "get the same old white boys." Those white boys complained, loudly, successfully pushing Chief Arradondo to demote Knight in a rebuke for supposed racial discrimination toward white men.[51] (Knight and Ryan would both go on to sue the city for discrimination, winning a $70,000 and $134,000 settlement, respectively.[52]) The punishment of officers who spoke out against the department, while seemingly turning a blind eye toward violence meted out against protesters, further inflamed public distrust of the MPD.

Scrutiny fell on the PCOC too as the mayor and city council played tug-of-war over public safety. In response to Floyd's killing, and as city leaders positioned the PCOC as a key part of this new phase of police reform, city residents eagerly applied to serve on the board. Yet for months, as the city debated the first charter amendment, seats on the commission sat empty. Meetings were canceled because they lacked a quorum—there simply weren't enough commission members to hold a meeting. Despite their calls for "community input," no one at city hall seemed to be very interested in empowering even this admittedly weak form of civilian over-sight. And once the commission was fully staffed, the department and city continued to stall its progress, making it difficult for commissioners to find information and even harder to have the PCOC's recommendations taken seriously.

In late 2020, for example, the new commissioners, led by Abigail Cerra, a former public defender, and Cynthia Jackson, a social worker, called on the mayor and MPD leadership to reclassify coaching as discipline, which would open those disciplinary records to public review. The commission argued that the department's policies deliberately tried to work around open records laws, alternating between treating coaching as discipline and not discipline in its guidelines. In response, Frey and Arradondo updated the manual, making it more explicit that coaching was *not* discipline (despite an ongoing lawsuit by the Minnesota ACLU challenging this logic).[53]

By spring 2022, after a series of resignations, the commission meetings were again canceled due to lack of a quorum. The body, city leaders replied, would be put on pause until it could be redesigned. Only well into 2023 would they start to stand up a new civilian oversight group, now called the Community Commission on Police Oversight. This new model would involve the civilian group more directly in the OPCR's misconduct review process. As a policy mechanism, however, the commission was still volunteer-run with little formal mandate. It could make requests for information, analyze complaint patterns, and issue recommendations, but the city was still not obliged to listen.

Where's the State in State Violence?

These attempts to rein in the MPD were largely situated within city politics. But as described earlier, the legal and regulatory structure at the state
level matters too. So did state (and national) politics. Just as law could be
wielded as an axe or shield, state and federal laws and regulations created
both opportunities and barriers to change.

One of the most salient pieces of state law is legislation regulating officers' roles, responsibilities, and limits. State legislatures write the criminal
statutes that describe the legitimate (or legally sanctioned) uses of lethal
force by police officers, as well as what kind of conduct among the public
is criminal and thus subject to law enforcement's domain. State law also
outlines which law-enforcement-related activities must be carried out by
licensed police officers (which, in Minnesota, includes criminal arrests
and traffic stops). These were the statutes the radical reform activists cited
when arguing that the charter amendment would lead not to abolition of
the MPD, but police-for-hire, as described in chapter 4. States further control the licensing boards responsible for setting training standards, certi-
fying officers, and, when necessary, revoking licenses or imposing other
sanctions. In Minnesota, this body is the Board of Peace Officer Standards
and Training (POST).

In addition to setting officers' standards, the state can also enable or
constrain cities' attempts to respond to police misconduct. Most important
in Minnesota was the state's Police Officers Bill of Rights, legislation first
written into law in 1991, which mandated a set of protections officers were
entitled to during misconduct investigatory and disciplinary processes.[54]
According to Campaign Zero, Minnesota has three of the five common
protections in state law that shield officers from accountability: restricting or delaying interrogations, giving officers access to investigatory information, and limiting oversight of the police.[55] The last one—a statutory
provision that a "civilian review board, commission, or other oversight
body shall not have the authority to make a finding of fact or determina-
tion regarding a complaint against an officer or impose discipline on an
officer"—undergirded many of the failures of civilian oversight described
in the past few pages.[56]

State-level laws and regulations regarding public-sector unions also
influence policing politics. While Republicans have in recent decades
aligned themselves most closely with law enforcement groups in legislative
maneuvers, union protections have often been championed by Democrats
(often with other types of union workers in mind). For example, officers

who were disciplined by the department were granted the power to grieve those decisions in arbitration, sometimes allowing them to win back their jobs, salaries, and promotions—especially if they could show the department had not disciplined other officers similarly for the same conduct in the past (a serious barrier when the problem is a historical lack of consistent discipline). Recent changes in protections for unionized government workers also gave MPD officers wider latitude to file disability claims for post-traumatic stress disorder (PTSD) after the unrest, effectively allowing early retirement via disability with very little burden of proof or attempt at treatment.

After Floyd's murder, Democrats in the legislature, led by the Minnesota People of Color and Indigenous Caucus, introduced a series of police reform and accountability measures designed to use the power of the state to reduce police violence. These included legal pathways for greater community oversight and more restrictive use-of-force laws. In 2020, however, Democrats only controlled the state House, not the Senate. Republicans, who controlled the Minnesota Senate, largely blocked the measures. What did pass eventually was a watered-down consensus bill that (largely ineffectively) reworded the state law defining officers' use of deadly force,[57] banned chokeholds under most circumstances, expanded state-wide data collection on police violence, restricted "warrior-style" police training, and mandated crisis intervention and mental illness training for officers.[58]

While mostly ignoring the proposed officer accountability reforms that activists had demanded, the bill did strengthen the POST Board, by then helmed by a reform-oriented chair. These changes included creating a new fifteen-member advisory council, with six spots reserved for community members, to guide the board's work in licensing police officers and training programs. By 2022 this group of advocates successfully pushed forward new guidelines that would allow the POST Board to revoke the licenses of officers who violate conduct guidelines, a move that was previously limited to officers who had been convicted of serious criminal offenses. As John Laux, a former MPD chief, told a reporter, the new rule would finally give the board some "teeth," letting the state play a stronger role in maintaining officer conduct standards instead of relying on local departments to police their own.[59]

The legislative stagnation in 2020 on police reform measures was due largely to the vigorous opposition of law enforcement associations and their Republican defenders.[60] Yet rather than a simple left-right debate, this conflict saw internal divisions among Democrats, too. Was the goal to rein in police violence through state policy-making, or simply build in modest guardrails on appropriate police conduct? Was Chauvin a single "bad apple," or an indication that there was deeper systemic rot? Many of the representatives from outside the Twin Cities metro area, whose constituents were primarily moderate suburban and rural white voters, balked at the more systemic changes called for by their metro area colleagues, defending "their" police as a force for good. Further intensifying the conflict, these debates took place in the context of the 2020 presidential election, as Republicans denigrated Democratic challengers as part of the "radical left" that had attempted to abolish the police in Minneapolis.

Despite these attempts to paint the Democrats as "soft on crime," in the November 2020 election they would pick up one seat in the Senate, which left the Republicans narrowly in control. Operating with this disadvantage, in 2021 Democrats tried again to move forward police reform, pushing a new package of bills that most radically would block most pretextual vehicle stops by police and require the state licensing board to regulate officers' support for white supremacist groups. Neither proposal passed the Republican-controlled Senate, with Minnesota legislators compromising on a bill much narrower than that imagined by reform champions, weakly limiting no-knock warrants (and requiring data collection on them) and creating an option for the courts to issue "sign and release warrants" for lower-level offenses that meant law enforcement did *not* have to arrest motorists found with an open warrant for a missed court date (motivated by the death of Daunte Wright).

Another legal change championed by activists that did make it through the legislature in 2021 was Travis' Law. Named after Travis Jordan, a man shot and killed by MPD officers in 2018 during a mental health crisis, the law required that 911 call-takers dispatch mental health crisis response teams (where and when available) to respond to calls for wellness checks and other mental health issues. The law left open the option for 911 call centers to dispatch police (who, in some cases, would need to respond first to ensure the scene was "safe" for other first responders) and did not require jurisdictions to develop mobile mental health crisis response teams. But it helped to recognize and move forward the work already happening to develop alternative first responders.

Democrats' surprise victory in the November 2022 election finally gave the party control of the Senate in Minnesota, opening opportunities for deeper state-level reform. And in May 2023, nearly three years after George Floyd's murder, the Minnesota legislature passed a sweeping public safety bill (without any Republican support). The legislation included bold criminal justice reforms that activists had worked on for years to reduce imprisonment rates. But unlike the transformative policing measures proposed in the summer of unrest, the reforms related to policing in the 2023 bill were relatively mild, including additional limits on no-knock warrants (in response to the killing of Amir Locke) and restrictions on officers' ability to join or support extremist hate groups. Reflecting the new focus on gun violence in the community, the bill also tightened gun control laws and increased funding for crime prevention programs.[61] Even this compromise measure was too much for Republicans, who complained to the press that "this is a bad bill that actually coddles criminals . . . [and] infringes on the rights of law-abiding gun owners."[62]

These same political struggles and gridlocks played out at the federal level, largely producing the same (in)action. In 2020 Democrats in the US House of Representatives began work on the George Floyd Justice in Policing Act. In contrast to the BREATHE Act proposed by the Movement for Black Lives and their legislative allies, which called for divestment from police and prisons across the country, the George Floyd Act was squarely reformist. The proposal introduced new federal requirements and statutes, including creating a federal registry of officers' misconduct, restricting qualified immunity, and limiting the transfer of military equipment to law enforcement. The bill also used the power of the purse to incentivize local departments to adopt body cameras and state legislatures to ban chokeholds and no-knock warrants for drug investigations, as well as stipulate in law that deadly force was legal only when used as a last resort. Finally, the bill would have provided grants to state prosecutors to investigate excessive force. Even these reform measures, which would have increased police funding, were too radical for the Senate, especially the provisions about police accountability. The bill failed to make it to a vote in 2020.

In 2021, with Democrats holding a slim majority in the Senate, the revived act was blocked by a filibuster. Like President Trump before him, President Biden would push forward policing reform through executive actions rather than legislative victories. In an order signed two years after Floyd's murder, Biden's pen strokes would force through the bare minimum: improving data collection, banning chokeholds, and restricting no-knock warrants for federal law enforcement agencies. But it did little to change policing by city agencies across the country. By 2023 President Biden was making headlines not for police reform but for signing a bill that overturned recent criminal justice reform legislation in Washington, DC, bolstering his "law and order" credentials in the run-up to the 2024 presidential election.[63]

While it is easy to view these legislative failures through the lens of craven politicians, afraid to confront police unions and take back power for the people, the story of inaction in the wake of Floyd's murder in Minneapolis, Minnesota, and America is also one of deep public ambivalence and divided attention. Are police producers of violence, who need to be reined in through every possible lever and mechanism? Or are they society's protectors, who run toward the sound of gunfire? And what, exactly, did we need to do to expand public safety?

The ambivalence of voters on these questions fueled the political gridlock. Democrats, even once in the majority, did not have the votes for more transformative reforms, worried about backlash if they got out too far in front of public opinion. What good was it to enact change, if you would be voted out of office before those laws made a difference? It was this majority of *voters* activists had to convince, not just political elites, to make lasting change. Minneapolis, the famously liberal city, after all, had reelected Jacob Frey. As Minneapolis mayors throughout the city's history knew all too well, the liberal police dilemma persisted: How could elected officials reduce police violence while also assuring voters that their police would address violence in the community?

Using the Courts to Force Police Reform

While local, state, and federal-level police reform legislative processes largely came up empty-handed, investigators with both the state and federal government were meticulously cataloging the department's failures, past and present. On June 1, 2020, the Minnesota Department of Human Rights opened an investigation into the city for civil rights violations by the MPD. The following week, the city agreed to a court order that banned chokeholds and added a "duty to intervene" requirement for officers.[64] It also expanded the OPCR's power to audit officers' body camera footage and initiate complaints against officers. Yet aside from posting a website with a list of reports on the MPD, in the two years that followed the court order the MDHR investigation in Minnesota largely went quiet, proceeding outside the glare of media coverage and the contested 2021 city elections.

Under President Trump's tenure, it was clear that "the feds" were not going to come to investigate in Minneapolis (which was why the MDHR had stepped in so quickly). After the inauguration of President Biden in 2021, however, the winds turned and the DOJ opened a "pattern and practice" investigation of the MPD. These kinds of investigations were first authorized as part of the Violent Crime Control and Law Enforcement

Act of 1994 and have continued to be used to assert federal control over local police departments—often following high-profile cases of police violence. The investigations move beyond specific instances of police violence to examine broader patterns of legal and regulatory violations by departments. And they give federal investigators the leverage to take cities and their police departments to court, using the threat of litigation to incentivize negotiations over police reform measures, often written into a legally binding consent decree. In many cities, such settlements have led to yearslong review of departments by appointed court monitors, lifted only when the court decides the city has adequately remediated the law and policy violations.[65]

In Minneapolis, radical reform activists largely cheered this development, hoping the investigation would lead to a consent decree for the troubled department. Indeed, Communities United Against Police Brutality (CUAPB) helped the DOJ investigators directly, organizing forums for residents to describe past abuses by the MPD and directing a team of community canvassers to register complaints. The group helped generate one thousand complaints against the MPD to hand to DOJ investigators, including complaints of officers harassing their canvassers. Importantly, those complaints were not simply about officers' use of force. Residents also wanted better *protection*; more than a third of the complaints were about lack of service by the department. When residents called for help, they wanted responsive and respectful policing. They wanted policing that worked.[66]

Abolitionist organizers, in contrast, expressed skepticism at the DOJ investigation, framing it as a public "distraction" that would not provide a path to justice. As Reclaim the Block organizer D. A. Bullock told reporters: "Minneapolis' violent and murderous police department is built on the Obama Justice Department model of 21st century policing. We don't expect real change to come out of the DOJ."[67] Advocates for the new charter amendment to replace the MPD also worried that a consent decree with the DOJ might require the city to invest *more* in policing (including more resources for officer hiring, retention, and training) rather than developing the new transformational approach promised by the city council. If Question 2 passed in 2021, the legal status of a potential consent decree with the former department was unclear. Would a new department be held to the consent decree of its prior incarnation?

In April 2022, following the failure of the Department of Public Safety initiative, the MDHR released its report, confirming what much of the city already knew: the MPD used more severe force against Black people than white people, even in similar circumstances, in a persistent pattern of civil rights violations.[68] The report outlined a series of inequities and injustices, from inappropriate use of neck restraints and chemical irritants to illegitimate traffic stops and vehicle searches, racial disparities in arrests and citations, and a pervasive culture of misogyny and racism. Perhaps the most politically explosive claim was that officers had been using covert social media accounts to surveil and harass Black community members, elected leaders, and organizations alike. But the report did not stop at the MPD's rank-and-file. Instead, it placed blame on poor training and oversight, from the department brass all the way to city leadership, who had allowed the toxic culture of the MPD to fester through their inaction. Further, the investigation charged that all these problems, from police targeting people of color to violence and the lack of oversight and accountability, had continued well into 2022. The result, investigators wrote, was a persistent regime of "race-based policing."

Once the report was released, the MDHR began months of deeply contentious negotiations with the city over potential reforms. While these negotiations happened between phalanxes of lawyers arguing behind closed doors, investigators contracted with the Minnesota Justice Research Center to hold a series of listening sessions with community members, especially those most impacted by policing, to inform their strategy. Echoing what my team found in chapter 3, the report concluded that while most residents were deeply unsatisfied with the status quo, there were a lot of different and contradictory ideas about how to best move forward. The researchers summarized these diverse sets of voices through three key recommendations: moving away from a "culture of violence," including by regulating use of force and building more expansive visions of public safety; building better relationships with residents, including through MPD trainings on the history of the department and MPD officials accurately describing critical incidents to the public; and creating stronger accountability for officers who committed misconduct, including through an effective court monitoring team.[69]

Nearly a year after the MDHR's investigatory report, in March 2023, the news finally arrived: the MPD was set to enter a court-enforced agreement, or consent decree, with the MDHR (though it would take until July for the court to approve the agreement). By then, the department was under a new chief, Brian O'Hara, after Chief Arradondo, having helped defeat the charter amendment, retired. The first outsider to lead the department in two decades, Chief O'Hara came to the city from Newark, New Jersey, where he had risen through the ranks to oversee the implementation of a federal consent decree. This chief, the mayor promised, would finally bring change to the MPD. And while there was some resistance to replacing the city's first Black chief of police with a white man, initial reports of O'Hara's engagement in the community were largely positive. Chief O'Hara had a new boss, too. After the 2021 election, Mayor Frey followed through on a late-breaking campaign promise to create the Office of Community Safety, a new initiative that now organized the MPD alongside other emergency response departments (including the 911 call system and the Fire Department) and the violence prevention programs. To helm the new office, the city appointed Cedric Alexander, a Black law enforcement veteran and one of the members of President Obama's Task Force on 21st Century Policing.

The department now had a new organizational structure, and the agreement with the MDHR represented the first time the state's courts would be involved in ensuring that reform proceeded as promised in Minneapolis. The goal was to end "race-based" policing, replacing it with "nondiscriminatory and impartial" policing.[70] But could the department end race-based policing in a racially unequal city (and country)?

For the negotiators, moving the MPD forward came down to key policy levers designed to change the department's culture. The carefully worded consent decree, in part, extended the 21st Century Policing reforms of earlier years, requiring more de-escalation, limiting officers' authorized use of force, and strengthening pieces of the misconduct review. In a more structural reform, MDHR lawyers negotiated restrictions on certain kinds of pretext stops and banned searches based on the smell of cannabis, both of which have the promise to reduce racial disparities in stops and searches. Perhaps most importantly, the agreement will put in place a court monitor charged with evaluating whether city officials' lofty promises accurately reflected what was really happening inside the department and in the community. But, in a limitation decried by some activist groups, the consent decree would not intervene in officers' collective bargaining process, making it clear that changes to misconduct review and promotion processes would only be implemented insofar as they were consistent with the union's labor agreement.

In June 2023 the results of the DOJ investigation were released, joining the MDHR in its condemnation of the department.[71] The MPD, investigators concluded, used "unreasonable" force, including deadly force, failed to intervene in fellow officers' misconduct, and denied aid to people in custody—all constitutional violations. Black residents were not the only disproportionately impacted group; the report also noted the high rate at which Native

American residents in the city experienced police stops and police violence. The report also noted the department's violations of protesters' First Amendment rights, largely drawing on the summer 2020 unrest.

As in the MDHR report, the problem according to investigators was not simply rank-and-file officers' misconduct but the ways unconstitutional policing had been tacitly sanctioned in the department (and city) by its inadequate training, supervision, and accountability systems—problems that all persisted after 2020. For example, DOJ investigators reported that officers continued to use "chokeholds" and neck restraints after the MDHR-imposed ban, in part because department leadership provided little guidance after adopting the new rules. The department never sanctioned officers for failing in their duty to intervene in fellow officers' misconduct. Instead, officers accused of serious misconduct were sometimes appointed as field training officers. And some excessive force occurred literally in front of investigators as they conducted ride-alongs with officers.

The final finding DOJ investigators presented was the MPD's systematic violations of the rights of people with behavioral health disabilities, a protected group under the Americans with Disabilities Act. They found that the police often responded to behavioral-health-related calls where there was no threat of violence and too often inflicted harm on vulnerable members of the public. In a turn from earlier DOJ reports, which emphasized training police officers on behavioral health and developing co-responder models (which pair officers and mental health professionals) in response to such concerns, this report also included an enthusiastic review of the city's new Behavioral Crisis Response team, which sends out mental health professionals to respond to certain 911 calls. As I outline in the next chapter, this program represents one of the most promising alternatives to police for mental health crises that developed in Minneapolis in the wake of Floyd's murder, though, as investigators noted, questions and implementation challenges persist.

As of this writing, the city is in negotiations with the DOJ over a likely second consent decree, which in theory will bolster the struggles of MDHR lawyers to force the city to revamp its training, policies, and misconduct review processes. Perhaps it will include requirements too that the city adequately fund and support alternative first responders. But, as the abolitionists noted, the DOJ is unlikely to fundamentally push the city to move away from policing. Instead, its goal is to reform the police, which will likely funnel more resources into the department.

It is too soon to know what impact the agreement and court monitoring processes will have on policing in Minneapolis. We can learn, however, from what has happened in other places facing consent decrees in the wake of high-profile cases of police misconduct. In cities across the country, protracted federal interventions have sometimes, often slowly, reduced rates of officer brutality and civil rights violations. The work is painstaking, requiring enormous amounts of time, negotiation, and money to implement and sustain. In the best-case scenario, the process is used to strengthen the role of community members in shaping acceptable policing practices and responses to injustice.[72] Yet in some of the cities where such consent decrees have proved successful, the gains were vulnerable to back-sliding when the consent decrees resolved and the court monitor left.[73] And it's unclear whether such monitoring processes improve or worsen crime, and thus their effect on community safety more holistically.[74]

In short, research suggests that a consent decree might push forward meaningful police reform, if the effort is implemented well and given sustained attention. Yet it is unlikely to resolve the core tensions of policing in the City of Lakes, produced by the structural barriers to change that largely remain in place—from state laws protecting police, to the power of the federation, to the inability of cities to meaningfully increase access to life-sustaining services at scale, and a deeply ambivalent public.

Three Years Later

In the three years following George Floyd's murder, everything and nothing seemed to change with the MPD. This chapter asked how the MPD was (not) held accountable for its violence. The answer, in short, was that even as the mobilization of summer 2020 produced a groundswell of support for radical changes in public safety, it was not ultimately enough to dismantle the police department. The first challenge was that there was no one voice across city leaders, activists, community leaders, and residents as to what "Justice for George," or *real* accountability, should or could mean. Instead of a fixed meaning, "justice" was as contested as it was elusive. Was the punishment of individual officers accountability, or did redressing the historic harms of the MPD require the end of the police as we knew them in Minneapolis?

As advocacy groups pushed for their conflicting calls for change—including the charter amendment, police defunding, hiring more police, revising the police union contract, and changing state and federal law to make police more accountable—efforts to transform the system largely floundered. Police reform at the Minnesota State Capitol and Washington, DC, broadly speaking, failed. The charter amendment failed at the ballot.

And the MPD was never defunded, even as the number of active duty officers continued to fall in 2023. As time has marched on, the chance of radical change has seemed to grow slimmer as public attention fades. In Minneapolis, that deflation of radical goals was accelerated by the hard swing in public attention away from police violence to community violence, fueled by both real shifts in victimization and the politics of policing.

Change, however, will continue to come to Minneapolis—and we should think about the real time horizon for change as taking years not weeks. Indeed, some of the interventions with the most "teeth," including the state and DOJ investigations, inevitably take months and years to grind through the legal, bureaucratic, and political systems. Though these kinds of state-led initiatives are unlikely to end policing, they do hold the promise of making some incremental improvements in how often police abuse their authority and the consequences for doing so. Beyond these investigations, change continues on the streets of Minneapolis, driven by everyday residents and policymakers alike. Perhaps most important were the new initiatives to expand public safety, including the mental health first responders and violence interrupters given more funding through fights over the city budget. As the MPD continued to struggle to hire and retain officers, and violence spiked, these programs would attempt to take up a growing share of the city's public safety work at a fraction of the cost.

CHAPTER SIX

Safety without Police?

IN JUNE 2021, as street violence and the fight over the ballot initiative to replace the Minneapolis Police Department (MPD) heated up, Whittier Cop Watch, a neighborhood abolitionist group on the city's south side, released a zine. Its "Field Guide to Twin Cities Collaborators" identified a set of violence interruption groups that had received funding from the city, including MAD DADS, We Push for Peace, the Minnesota Freedom Fighters, and the Agape Movement.[1] These groups, which often hired formerly gang-involved men, were designed to diffuse tensions and mediate conflict in high-crime blocks as an alternative approach to addressing violence. But the field guide had a different perspective: such groups were "snitches. mercenaries. peace police. do-gooders. bootlickers. state agents" and a strategy for "defeating rebellious movements such as the George Floyd Uprising." Rather than real alternatives to police, they were "cops in t-shirts" who gave the city a path to "recuperation," or the appearance of aligning with radicals while in truth resisting and pacifying demands for change.

Many of the violence interruption groups listed on the zine had by then received funding from the city, as grants flowed from the Office of Violence Prevention (OVP), an agency tasked with developing public health approaches to violence prevention. As described in earlier chapters, the OVP had actually grown out of protest mobilization and early "defund" demands, and in the summer of racial reckoning, the OVP's approach was prepared to take center stage in the city's new *transformative model* of public safety. As a result, in 2020 and early 2021, funding to the OVP grew exponentially, in the process increasing the coordination between violence prevention groups and city leadership.

Before the new Department of Public Safety even went up for a vote in November 2021, however, some abolitionist groups had already soured on the OVP. As you will see in this chapter, this rift emerged in part because the city had begun sending in violence interrupters to mediate between police and activists at BLM protests—a practice the office would disavow the following year. But, more fundamentally, the critique was of the city's interpretation of "violence prevention":

> The name of the department is a misnomer because while it funds programs it believes will help prevent interpersonal violence and violence from those with little power directed toward those with much power (for example, looting), it does not seek to address structural violence (like evictions) nor violence from those with much power directed toward those with little power (such as police killings or mass incarceration).

In a nod to the "All Cops Are Bastards" (ACAB) slogan, the group invited feedback at the email address AllCollaboratorsAreBastards@ protonmail.com.

This final empirical chapter examines alternatives to policing that emerged in Minneapolis to better understand how the mobilization from George Floyd's murder reshaped public safety even after the failure of the charter amendment. What we will see is that it was no longer enough in Minneapolis to support simply moving money away from policing and toward other programs. Scrutiny now turned to the programs receiving funding from the city, and the fledgling alternatives to the police got hit from all sides—from conservatives who "backed the blue" and scoffed at what they called "hug a thug" programs as well as radicals who increasingly understood violence prevention programs as simply a veiled form of state repression. Violence prevention that focused on the actions of the marginalized rather than those in power, they argued, would never be a truly radical approach to public safety.

Operating on a shoestring budget, these experiments in new approaches to safety carried the weight of a traumatized city. Could community-based violence interruption groups and other innovations serve as a blueprint for a form of community control of public safety, or were they simply cops by another name, held to even fewer mechanisms of accountability?

To answer these questions, we will look across three case studies: the violence interrupters and OVP, a mobile behavioral crisis response team launched by the city, and an abolitionist hotline. Rather than formally evaluate these pilot programs, I draw on interviews with violence prevention workers and fieldwork conducted in 2022 to explore the possibilities these models open for the future and their vulnerabilities. Perhaps not surprisingly, as each effort sought to reimagine public safety, they faced challenges reminiscent of both the history of policing (e.g., struggles over uniforms and standardization) and its present-day critiques (e.g., questions of accountability for violence). But they also offered a glimmer of hope for challenging police power while responding to community violence.

Violence Interruption Groups in Minneapolis

In the early Black Lives Matter (BLM) protest years, commentators would ask pointedly (and often in bad faith) why activists organized against *police* violence but not interpersonal or community violence. Didn't those victims—those Black lives—matter, too? But, in fact, throughout American history, Black communities have organized against both community and state violence. And throughout the early BLM protest years Black residents and community leaders have fought to keep people safe, whether through everyday acts like caretaking for vulnerable community members or cookouts to cool "hot" corners, or direct actions and policy advocacy.[2] Even in the initial Ferguson, Missouri, protests, activists and on-the-ground organizers took to the streets to demand safety from *both* community violence *and* state violence. The skewed perception was in fact media bias: protests against police violence drew media coverage whereas the day-to-day grind of building safer communities did not.[3]

In Minneapolis, these two groups of activists—those fighting against community violence and police violence—were largely separate (though at times overlapping) groups, which is why "peace" activists were largely left out of the story of BLM mobilization told in chapter 2. But the work of these other activists was vitally important on the ground. And some of these groups had been struggling for *decades* to quell violence. Minneapolis's MAD DADS (which stood for Men Against Destruction—Defending Against Drugs and Social Disorder), a local chapter of a group founded in 1989 by African American fathers in Omaha, Nebraska, had, for instance, worked to combat the violence associated with gang wars over the drug trade since 1998.[4] Founded by VJ Smith, a North Minneapolis minister who had tangled with crime in his younger days, the MAD DADS staff and volunteers attempted to intervene positively in young people's lives to quell violence in the city's toughest neighborhoods. By the mid-2010s the group was involved in crime prevention and intervention (perhaps most notably serving as "peace" forces on city buses when teens were traveling across the city to and from school) and offered youth and family development programs.

A Mother's Love Initiative was founded in 2014 by Lisa Clemons, one of the few Black women to spend more than a decade in uniform with the MPD. After retiring from the force, she brought together mothers who had lost children to gun violence to help steer young people away from perpetrating such violence. The initiative provided life skills and tutoring programs, domestic violence interventions, and other services for community members.[5] Clemons also followed the example of her own mother—a woman who would confront gang members in the streets of Chicago with tough love—to intervene directly in brewing conflicts in North Minneapolis.[6] The team's volunteers also surveilled police radio chatter, often showing up at the scene of shootings to support the family members and diffuse the cycle of retaliatory violence that often followed.

Such groups' work often looked like what sociologist Nikki Jones describes as "bridging" and "buffering." They bridged the space between young adults and positive community ties and resources, and they buffered against violence by mediating and mitigating conflicts between youth.[7] They also buffered between youth and the police, trying to prevent police contact for community members. Peace workers were looked to for the sort of community interventions that police so often failed at, VJ Smith explained to me in a 2017 interview:

> You can't just lock everybody up, and you can't handcuff everybody. The way we handcuff people is with love and support and resources. And so that's something that the police really don't specialize in. We do. We're able to go into a situation, defuse it, and give people resources they need and help them go in a direction they need to go to.

Smith elaborated that the police were there to solve homicides once they happened, but MAD DADS was there to "prevent things from turning into a homicide."[8] As a result, MPD's leadership often described groups like A Mother's Love Initiative and MAD DADS as their allies, sometimes directly calling them to scenes in the community.

This relationship with the police, however, grew more fraught in the context of the Black Lives Matter protests, as a younger wave of Black community leaders emerged with a new vision for change. Some of these new voices, like NAACP Minneapolis's Jason Sole, would work to both take up the bullhorn at BLM protests and intervene on the streets to stop beefs. Eventually, this would lead him and other organizers to build a new abolitionist model of community safety (described later in the chapter). In contrast, the older Black anti-violence organizers who came of age in the city's "Murderapolis" years envisioned a future world with more responsive and just policing and saw their work as building a bridge between the community and the MPD. As a result, the groups helmed by retirement-age organizers sometimes kept a bit of distance from BLM activism. As VJ Smith told me, "We think it's important to protest and fight for what you feel is right . . . [but] our goal is to save our men and to save our families and save our community, and we do that by building better men in our community. This is what we do. Protesting is not what we do, but we'll support that."

By 2020 some of these more established violence prevention workers would become vociferous opponents of the charter amendment, part of the wave of Black resistance to Question 2 described in chapter 4. Lisa Clemons, for instance, told a reporter, "Black hating Blue—that sells. But you can't 'reimagine Minneapolis' with crime gone." The answer, she insisted, was supporting both the police and groups like A Mother's Love Initiative.[9]

These divides were not just *generational* but also tied to organizers' gender and sexuality. While most of the violence interruption programs were led by middle-aged cis-gender Black community leaders, often men, and hired mostly cis-gendered young Black men, the abolitionist coalitions tended to be led by young organizers and included many women and transgender, non-binary, and/or queer organizers. Echoing the charter amendment voting patterns, divides across these groups were also *spatial*, with many of the long-running violence prevention groups based in North Minneapolis, which faced the most devastating rates of lethal street violence, while the abolitionist organizing would take deepest root in relatively safer central and southeast corridors of the city.

After summer 2020, new neighborhood-based violence prevention and interruption groups proliferated across the city, often growing out of the self-defense networks that emerged organically during the unrest. For example, Agape (named for the spirit of unconditional love) emerged in the nascent George Floyd Square (GFS). Co-founder Alfonzo Williams was a self-described ex-gang member active in the World Wide Outreach for Christ, a Black church located at the corner of 38th and Chicago, kitty-corner from Cup Foods. After Floyd's murder, the collective formed to "transform street energy into community energy," working to connect the "young brothers" with the services, resources, and assistance they needed to "turn their life around." The explicitly spiritual group put this mission into practice, hiring these young men and bringing them into the organization to "bridge the gap between the community and law enforcement."[10] They also saw themselves as a buffer, patrolling the square and responding to some of its daily low-level nuisances to keep the peace without police.[11]

The Minnesota Freedom Fighters were perhaps the most visually arresting of these new groups, often posing for social media posts while wearing bullet-proof vests and displaying AR-15 rifles. Formed during the unrest in response to the NAACP's calls to protect Northside's businesses from white supremacists, the Freedom Fighters explicitly positioned themselves not as a violence interruption group but rather an "elite security unit" made up of Black men (and a few Black women), armed and ready to defend their community. Drawing on the history (and iconography) of armed Black resistance, including the Black Panther Party,[12] the Freedom Fighters argued that Black communities' armed self-defense was necessary and righteous. The group went on to collect security contracts, including taking city payments to keep the peace (unarmed) at protests and to provide a visibly armed security detail at community events with a high risk of retaliatory violence, including funerals for young men killed in gang conflicts. Like Agape, the Freedom Fighters explicitly described themselves as a "bridge" between police and the Black community, attempting to diffuse the threat of violence between the two.[13]

Thus, by the close of 2020 Minneapolis had a complex and diverse group of violence interruption groups cropping up across the city, each with a complex set of politics. City leaders would try to harness this community energy and fashion it into a coordinated, responsive, city-led violence prevention strategy.

The Office of Violence Prevention

As described in chapter 2, early efforts by police abolition activists to shift money away from the MPD and toward "things that keep us safe" helped create the OVP in 2018, championed by Northside representative Phillipe Cunningham. In 2020, the OVP was thrust into the public spotlight, with Councilmember Cunningham and his allies arguing that the public health model of violence prevention was *the* way out of the city's continual cycle of outrage (and reform) over police violence *and* the crime plaguing the city. Yet just as violence interruption work represented a tenuous bind between community-led safety strategies and the police, the OVP functioned as an even more precarious bridge and buffer between police, community-led safety, the city's leadership, and the public.

From its inception until 2022, the OVP was helmed by Sasha Cotton, a criminal justice and ethnic studies double-major in college with experience working in corrections and social services for victims of violence. From this dual vantage point, and as a Black woman, Cotton often straddled the divide of people calling for system transformation, or abolition, and reform from the inside. Housed among the city's public health initiatives (not the MPD), the OVP's initial efforts involved expanding earlier pilot projects like a hospital-based intervention with gun violence victims. The OVP also began developing an anti-violence initiative modeled on the "Cure Violence" program, using one-on-one mentorship between current and former gang members and access to city services to support people in their efforts toward desistance from criminal activities.[14] Similar to other violence prevention work, the mentors would attempt both to intervene in at-risk teen and young adults' lives and to more broadly change the social norms that enabled gun violence.[15]

As homicides rose in Minneapolis, advocates argued that the city should double-down on these more preventative approaches. As a result, the OVP's budget rapidly expanded, growing to $11 million by 2021 (though it would ultimately spend closer to $8 million).[16] Much of this funding was contracted out to community groups through the "MinneapolUS" initiative, which provided funding to formalize community-based volunteer efforts into city-funded contracts, paying interrupters $30 an hour.[17] The A Mother's Love Initiative gained first-round funding, as did a number of other small community-based organizations. By early 2022 Director Cotton would report that nearly 150 city-funded violence interrupters were now positioned in key corridors throughout the city. In the second half of 2021, the OVP-funded teams reported de-escalating 1,500 conflicts and making nearly 9,000 contacts with people at high risk of being a victim or perpetrator of violent crime.[18]

One of the OVP's key challenges in this period was attempting to organize multiple, sometimes mutually antagonistic, community-based groups into a coordinated city effort with a clear strategy and chain of command. That meant figuring out a coordinated uniform (a branded T-shirt and sweater that took months for the city to procure), as well as how to train, deploy, and provide oversight over a fleet of violence interruption contractors, some of whom had been doing this work informally for decades and others who were newly returned from prison (and everyone in between). It also meant balancing contradictory logics, defending the interruption groups as both evidence-based *and* deeply specialized or hyperlocal to meet the need in the community. But how could you standardize a program connected to the charisma and reputation of individual outreach workers on specific blocks who were largely left to run their programs independently? And how could the community evaluate the groups' impact, when so much of the relationship-building happened without visible outcomes? When there were public shoot-outs, people began to ask not just "Where were the police?" but "Where were the violence interrupters?" But the OVP's spending represented just 5 percent of the MPD's, and its violence interruption programs were never designed to be a 24/7 presence or emergency response.

These growing pains were also connected to ambiguity about what precisely violence interrupters were supposed to accomplish in communities. Research by sociologist Patrick Sharkey and colleagues shows that as the number of a city's nonprofits devoted to violence prevention and community-building increases, violent crimes reported to the police decline.[19] They posit that such nonprofits reduce violence by building up neighborhoods' informal social control—or the mechanisms that allow residents and community leaders to prevent crime without the coercive apparatus of the law. Yet getting more detail about how such programs work (or should work) has proved more difficult.

As a recent review of the implementation of the Cure Violence model in several cities concluded, there is substantial variation in how different programs implement the model (what researchers call "fidelity"). Is the goal to be a visible deterrent of crime? To intervene in specific cycles of retaliatory violence with individuals or to more broadly challenge a culture of violence? Or to provide a job and services to the most at-risk youth? It is just as hard to set benchmarks for measuring the programs' success. Is the outcome the number of contacts programs make, their influence on young people's attitudes, or crime reduction? In some sites, program evaluations have shown that violence interruption programs moved aggregate social norms or reduced violence, while others reveal few of these macro-level impacts.[20] (It's worth repeating from chapter 4 that the research base on policing strategies, while larger, is no less contested. As newer programs, however, they were more vulnerable to threat from such mixed evidence.)

There were also questions around coordination and cooperation with law enforcement.[21] On the one hand, violence interrupters generally try to keep a certain distance from police to maintain "street cred," avoid a "snitch" reputation, and have the "juice" to work effectively in the community. Workers could only be successful if they were already known and respected by residents and seen as unaffiliated with law enforcement. That meant, in part, that some of the violence interruption workers brokering truces were not simply formerly gang-involved, but sometimes still actively participating. And it meant that the staff had often had many negative experiences with police. All of that sets up many anti-violence workers to be potentially suspicious of law enforcement. For their part, police are often equally suspicious of violence prevention workers, struggling to step out of the mindset that equates a person's gang involvement (however long ago) with life-long dangerousness.

On the other hand, as sometimes complementary public safety approaches, there are points of cooperation, mutual respect, and shared experience between police and violence interrupters. For one, you want police to recognize (and not, as happened at some protests, arrest) violence interrupters when they're patrolling the block. There are also times when violence interrupters may want to convey a general message to law enforcement (e.g., a "hot corner") or encourage a perpetrator to confess to police. And through the OVP, violence interrupters, like the MPD, ultimately reported to city leadership. Finally, both groups also shared occupational trauma, exposed to both direct violence and its bloody aftermath.[22] The challenge then was how to coordinate a public safety response that joined together these disjointed approaches.

Another question was how the OVP (and violence prevention programs not funded by the city) would ensure accountability. What would happen if these contractors enacted violence themselves? Where could residents file a complaint, and how would that disciplinary process work? These questions were not hypothetical. Consider, for example, the OVP-funded group We Push for Peace, a job-training program that connected young people with services, training, and employment. Replacing off-duty police officers, the group also won a contract to provide security to the large Cub Foods grocery chain (not to be confused with Cup Foods at 38th and Chicago), which its members argued would allow them to provide services to people found shoplifting. Echoing abolitionist rhetoric, the group's founder, Trahern Pollard, told a reporter in May 2021 that this approach represented the "community taking care of the community."[23]

But in August 2021 a We Push for Peace worker illustrated that the community could also brutally enforce the unequal social order. A staffer outside a St. Paul Cub Foods was caught on film beating a man who appeared to be unhoused and panhandling outside the store. Critics like CUAPB who had long decried the MPD for a lack of accountability began to argue that the groups funded by the OVP and private businesses were nothing but a cover for the city "to violate people's rights by proxy and without consequence."[24] At least police, they argued, had *some* training, legal and policy standards, and disciplinary processes in place.[25] In this case, the publicity around the beating was substantial, and the worker, absent a law enforcement officers union protections or legal deference to a "reasonable" officer's perception of risk, was swiftly fired. Something that looked like justice—the firing—was seemingly easier to come by when the source of the violence wasn't a cop (and when, unlike police, workers did not carry guns on their hips).

In the wake of the incident, however, it remained unclear who should receive reports of misconduct, what constituted misconduct for these workers, and who would investigate and discipline these now publicly funded private security forces. These questions would grow more urgent as street outreach workers stepped up their role at protests.

Interrupting Violence or Interrupting Protest?

By spring 2021 the main point of friction between violence interrupters, city leadership, activists, and residents was at protests against police violence, which would ultimately sour some abolitionists on the OVP. The clearing of George Floyd Square was perhaps the most visible example of this tension. In the wake of the murder, the square had become a vibrant revolutionary space. There were large-scale murals, a community garden, mourning art, and an iconic Black Power fist sculpture, as shown in figure 6.1.[26] The former Speedway gas station had been remade into "The People's Way," the new sign scrawled in red text. What used to be a bus stop was now a free, community-run clothing and supplies closet, while an independent medic system provided health care in the square (named 612 MASH for the city's area code and "Minneapolis All Shall Heal"). Organizers also built their own security force, complete with guard posts at the four entry points to monitor the potential threat posed by outsiders.

As GFS evolved as an experiment in "autonomous" space, it became an acute point of conflict between city leaders and activists.[27] As early as August 2020, less than three months after the murder, the city declared its intention to start a phased reopening of the square, planning to remove some of the barricades installed immediately after the murder. That same month, the Cup Foods store on the corner reopened. In the weeks that followed, calls to reopen the square grew louder from some residents, including, most vocally, a group of Black small business owners whose storefronts were inside or near the square's boundaries and who argued that the traffic blockages were harming their businesses.[28] The square also sat along the 38th Street corridor, a vital city artery that connected east to west. Reopening the square would allow the city to resume normal city services, city leaders argued, including regular trash collection and bus routes for residents.

FIGURE 6.1. George Floyd Square in 2021
Source: Author's photo collection.

Protesters at the square, meanwhile, refused to "cede these streets" until they saw justice. They issued a set of twenty-four demands to the city's leaders. These included recalling County Attorney Freeman, firing several state employees at the Bureau of Criminal Apprehension, ending qualified immunity for officers, investing in the neighborhood, and keeping the square barricaded until all four officers' trials were over.[29] The coalition also demanded space for the Agape Movement. Yard signs supporting activists' demands with the slogan "No Justice, No Streets" appeared across the city. And Marcia Howard, a neighborhood resident and key organizer at GFS, patrolled in a bullet-proof vest, declaring to reporters that the square would be opened "over my dead body."[30] Though many of the demands were ultimately not met (with some well outside of the city's scope), Minneapolis did invest in the square, memorializing it as "George Perry Floyd Jr. Place" and providing forgivable loans for small businesses nearby. The area around 38th and Chicago was designated a key cultural district to promote economic growth alongside racial equity, an initiative long championed by Councilmember Andrea Jenkins.

As the city and protesters squared off about opening GFS to traffic, the debate became enmeshed with a broader concern about public safety in and near the square. On paper, the MPD still controlled the territory, but it was largely the square's own security forces that visitors encountered. And those forces, at times, seemed to be intimidating visitors, including media personnel. In May 2021, for example, a photojournalist covering the one-year anniversary of the murder was questioned by protectors at George Floyd Square who seized his camera drone and told him never to come back.[31] And gun violence was escalating, belying these forces' provision of safety. On the same day the photojournalist's equipment was seized, live broadcasts of the memorial event were interrupted by a barrage of gunfire that left one person injured and journalists ducking for cover on-air.[32] Agape even lost one of its own, thirty-year-old Imez Wright, to a shooting in the square, right outside Cup Foods, where he bled out before help could reach him.[33]

The mayor and police chief announced they would open GFS to vehicular traffic after the conclusion of the trial against former officer Derek Chauvin. Behind closed doors, Mayor Frey deputized the Agape Movement to lead the action, using his pandemic emergency powers to fund the contract without seeking city council approval.[34] Agape chose 4:00 A.M. on June 3, 2021, to stage the reopening, descending on the square with city sanitation crews to dismantle makeshift barricades and open it to traffic while preserving much of the protest art. While Agape, hoping to avoid confrontations, loudly announced that no officers were involved, MPD officers were stationed blocks away in riot gear, a physical reminder of the ties between community anti-violence groups and the police. Though there were some minor skirmishes in the following hours and weeks as activists tried to replace the barricades, traffic was regularly open in the square again. Critics decried this collusion with the city, while Agape's leadership defended their work as *protecting* the community. Opening the square, they argued, would bring more safety to the neighborhood's residents: it was community-led public safety in action.

As with the charter amendment, each side in the dispute claimed itself to be the *authentic* representative of the "community."[35] To negotiate between these claims, the city fielded two online surveys to gauge public opinion. But, ruling out the possibility of permanent closure, the city instead asked residents a much narrower question: which of two memorial designs—keeping the fist sculpture at the center of a traffic circle, or relocating it closer to the spot where Floyd was killed—did residents prefer? The first survey in 2020, available in multiple languages, garnered nearly a thousand responses; 65 percent picked one of the two design options. But the rest refused the forced choice, often writing in that they wanted justice demands addressed before reopening. When the survey was repeated in spring 2021, 81 percent of respondents selected one of the two design options, but others still refused to choose. Some wrote in "Justice" instead.[36]

GFS protest organizers decried both the "weaponized" survey and the plan to reopen the square to traffic. They spoke of betrayal and heartbreak that their Black allies in the square would be the ones to force the city's will. As lead caretaker at George Floyd's memorial, Jeanelle Austin, summarized: "They're desecrating something—people's pain, people's hope." Marcia Howard, the public face of the occupation, was quoted in the same article telling reporters that the Agape deal was a payoff: "The reality is, it's cheaper to pay somebody a contract than it is to actually give something that looks like justice to our four-corners community."[37]

The Politics of Violence Prevention

The role of Agape in conflict over reopening GFS was not new, but, rather, an escalation of the new role for violence prevention workers at protests, including the April 2021 protests in Brooklyn Center after the police killing of Daunte Wright (see chapter 5). Law enforcement, mobilized for the conclusion of the Chauvin trial, defended the Brooklyn Center station with vigor. But so too did the city summon violence interrupters, including the Freedom Fighters. As at the clearing of the square, activists claimed that these staffers instigated violence *against* them rather than preventing it, including hurling transphobic slurs.

It happened again in June 2021, just after Agape reopened GFS, when a US Marshals Service task force shot and killed thirty-two-year-old

Winston Boogie Smith Jr. in the Uptown neighborhood of Minneapolis. Following the new playbook, protesters gathered, claiming space to build a memorial and mourning site. This time it was We Push for Peace staff who announced to protesters, in the pre-dawn hours, that they had minutes to gather their things and leave before police forcibly cleared the area. Protesters claimed the workers threatened them and physically assaulted one member. Adding to the dizzying array of "alternatives" to the police now present in the city, private security, run by ex-military and paid for by the local businesses, had threatened protesters too.[38]

It was in this context that the Whittier Cop Watch released its field guide, revealing a telling tension in violence interruption programs: Was their goal to keep the peace, or to produce justice? Could they do either in an unjust world? Spokespersons with the violence interruption groups argued that by sending in their violence interruption teams, everyone could "win"—protesters would have a safe space to express their grief and outrage with some state protection and less threat of arrest, tear-gas deployment, or lethal police violence. Yet in working not only with the leadership of the city but also police, violence interrupters were coercing the crowd into complying with law enforcement's directives—implicitly using the threat of police violence to justify their actions and thwart further rebellion.[39]

Rather than sort through these murky politics, the OVP retreated. Violence interruption teams, they concluded, should no longer be deployed as protest mediators. As Phillipe Cunningham declared in a city council meeting, it was not the role of the OVP and its violence interruption teams to take on the MPD's dirty work. The city should no longer ask these groups to "behave as cops."[40] While this response quieted public resistance to the violence prevention programs run by the OVP, it did little to address the broader structural critiques of what it meant to try to address community violence through individual-level interventions rather than structural transformations or attacks on powerful institutions.

Tensions, as a result, linger as these violence prevention groups continue to work across Minneapolis, whether city-funded or not. As described earlier, these conflicts are in part a *political* divide—not between the left and the right, but largely among people on the political left, liberals and radicals and everyone in between. And, as with the charter amendment, these debates sometimes inverted the stereotypical racial divides on policing. In many of these conflicts, the abolitionists, for example, had more white comrades on their side—prompting sometimes uncomfortable encounters between white leftists and the Black organizers they were critiquing.

For example, in early summer 2022, a reporter was trailing an Agape crew when a "20-something white man" with "big earrings and baggy pants" hassled their group, calling out: "How can you be part of the liberation when you take money from the police?" Marquis Bowie, one of the Agape leads, replied that his group wasn't the police, they were "the alternative," and rhetorically challenged the young man's critique of his group: "You're a white dude, telling us about freedom," Bowie said. "How's that sound?"[41]

In addition to revealing the complex racial politics around public safety in left-leaning cities, these debates over the OVP and its role in "violence" remain a poignant case study of the challenges of putting abolitionist goals into everyday city policy—and a reminder of why some see the only path forward as programs operating *outside* the violence of the state.[42] It also shows, in parallel to chapter 4, how the persistence of violence in communities complicates attempts to move away from policing. In this way, the goal of the OVP to address community violence was not separate from confronting police violence, but instead intimately connected. As many anti-violence workers argued, if their work could slow the bloodshed, that would not only save lives, but prevent police-citizen contact and also create more political space to reimagine public safety.

In this way, the OVP represents one of the most promising seeds of a different public safety approach in Minneapolis. Even if violence interrupters are sometimes "cops in t-shirts," the fact that they are unarmed community members is a move toward harm reduction in public safety. And that harm reduction work requires a real coalition to support such programs. The field guide, and the divided opinion among abolitionists it represented, threatened to unravel the fragile political consensus behind the public health approach just before the pivotal charter amendment vote. This fracturing among would-be allies made the work exhausting. As one organizer confided to me, whatever the path toward liberation, "this ain't it."

Calling 911 for Help:
The Behavioral Crisis Response Teams

While violence interruption work has been the focus of the chapter thus far, it wasn't the only game in town trying to reimagine public safety. As described in chapter 5, one of the major victories of the city council in 2020 was wresting a small amount of funding away from the MPD to invest in the OVP *and* a new model for responding to mental and behavioral health crises. The project was led by the city's Office of Performance and Innovation, the unit tasked with researching alternative public safety responses back in 2018. Designed in the wake of the police killings of Jamar Clark and Justine Damond, under the newly progressive city council elected in 2017, this work group was tasked with developing unarmed alternative responses to 911 calls to reduce the number of officer-citizen contacts across the city.

Advocates pointed out that these programs would not only promote public safety but also save law enforcement resources for the kind of violent and/or serious criminal offenses police were best trained to handle. Indeed, research shows that most police officers' time is spent responding to 911 calls from community members that have little to do with the threat of violence. Looking at three departments' data on the time use for a typical on-duty beat cop, the *New York Times* reported in summer 2020 that only 4 percent of officers' time was spent responding to violent crimes, compared to more than 30 percent on noncriminal calls and nearly 20 percent on traffic enforcement.[43] Similarly, a staffing study of the MPD's patrol division found that officers spent less time on the kinds of emergencies that require a police response (including violent crimes in progress) than on other kinds of service response. They estimated that fully a quarter of 911 calls dispatched to the MPD in 2020 might have instead been routed to alternative responders, including the nearly 10 percent of all 911 calls that evaluators categorized as behavioral health issues.[44] Many prominent social scientists and lawyers across the country came to similar conclusions, calling for "unbundling" what now falls under policing services.[45]

Yet the answer of what to replace police with, exactly, is less obvious. As foundational policing scholar Egon Bittner pithily summarizes, the police do not have a clearly delineated role but instead are called in to respond to infinite permutations of *"something-that-ought-not-to-be-happening-and-about-which-someone-had-better-do-something-now!"*[46] Police are called in to such situations, in part, because they are one of the few state-provided services that run 24/7, dispatched in response to residents' 911 pleas for help.[47] Second, police are called in because they alone are endowed with the power of legitimate state violence, allowing them to coerce compliance more than other agencies or professionals. So the question is not just how many calls today could be rerouted to other first responders, but also, how many could be rerouted in the future if we developed effective alternatives, and what would be the costs and benefits of sending armed police versus these alternatives?

By 2021 the team tasked with developing alternative response models in Minneapolis had successfully implemented some of their proposals, including shifting some nonurgent 911 calls (e.g., reporting recent property theft and parking-related complaints) to the city's 311 line, civilian staff, and online reports. The most consequential pilot that emerged was a new approach to people experiencing mental and behavioral health crises in the city.[48] Rather than a co-responder model, which pairs police with a mental health professional (and had been piloted by both the city and county in previous years), this new team would deploy *only* mental health professionals in response to 911 calls for behavioral crises.[49]

Advocates argued that other cities had already proved that this approach could work. In particular, they pointed to CAHOOTS ("Crisis Assistance Helping Out On The Streets"), an alternative crisis response team in Eugene, Oregon, that captured national attention in 2020. The program pairs a medic and a crisis responder with mental health-care training in a mobile response van dispatched by 911 call-takers, thus providing an alternative to police responders.[50] At the same time, like violence interruption, CAHOOTS works in part through organizational coordination with the police, who in fact manage the 911 emergency response dispatch in that city. Further, sometimes individual officers request the CAHOOTS team after responding, and CAHOOTS has the police to call as backup should the situation require it. The same interorganizational dependency (albeit with an independent emergency call center) would emerge in Minneapolis as the city worked to stand up its own behavioral crisis team.

As in Oregon, the city decided it would contract out this work to a mental health provider rather than building capacity in-house. It took the better part of 2021 for the city to develop the call for proposals, select a vendor, and launch the response team program. The contract went to Canopy Mental Health and Consulting, a Black-owned business from nearby Richfield, Minnesota, that provided community-based mental health services and would develop their Canopy Roots program to build a new model of crisis response. The Behavioral Crisis Response (BCR) teams initially consisted of two mobile units (each staffed by two responders), operating from 7:30 A.M. to midnight, Monday through Friday, throughout the city of Minneapolis. Soon, they expanded to twenty-four-hour weekday operation, adding partial weekend coverage by summer 2022.

Even with a nearly full-time schedule, the BCR was tiny in scale compared to the MPD. By mid-2022 the Canopy team would employ just twenty BCR staff. But the goal of the pilot was to demonstrate its safety and utility, something that could be done on a small scale (and still have a big impact). Like the city's OVP-funded contractors, BCR crews wore official city gear—with blue hats, shirts, and jackets identifying them as the "BEHAVIORAL CRISIS RESPONSE." Their vans, which would be a struggle to source and maintain, were also marked as property of the City of Minneapolis and Canopy Roots. The vans did not, however, have bright lights or sirens, a choice meant to avoid escalating situations (with the built-in limit of slowing response times). The program chose vans because they were large enough to transport someone to another location if the person requested it (e.g., their home, the hospital, or a treatment center). The vehicles also carried water, snacks, and other small supplies that could be provided to people in need.

To get a BCR response, callers need only dial 911—but a dispatcher would need to determine that BCR was the best response team, and one of the BCR vans had to be in service and available. City council members eagerly spread the word in their newsletters to residents, though it was still unclear what exactly constituted a behavioral crisis that would summon the BCR and what kinds of services or referrals the emergency responders would be able to offer people in crisis beyond the initial response. What was clear from the first brochures was that the BCR team was *not* to be dispatched to any call involving a firearm or "violent behavior" (a limitation tied to state law) and that, should a weapon and/or threat of violence emerge during a BCR call, the responders would call in for police backup.[51] Behind the scenes, the city's emergency response staff worked to distinguish what would be deemed a "medical" issue, which would get routed to emergency medical services staff in ambulances (who were paid to transport people to the hospital by insurance providers), in contrast to a "behavioral health" concern, which would go to the BCR teams in vans (who were entirely funded by the city)—another murky distinction that would cause some initial conflict and confusion.[52]

In spring 2022 I reached out to the Office of Performance and Innovation and Canopy Roots to learn how the pilot was going. Candace Hanson, Canopy's owner, reported that the teams were up and running. A typical call was a welfare check request from a loved one or neighbor, though some people in crisis called in themselves. Roughly half of the calls, she estimated, involved people who were unhoused. And most calls involved counseling people on the resources available to them and, in some cases, transporting people to care. This description lined up with my experience on a ride-along with the BCR staff in June 2022. Over an eight-hour shift, the team covered five back-to-back person-in-crisis calls, including a woman who seemed to be in a manic episode and was acting erratically and walking into traffic, a man convinced that he smelled a fire in the building even after the building was cleared by the fire department, and a teenage boy whose father called due to worries about his son self-harming.

In the first case, BCR responders spent nearly two hours convincing the woman to go to the hospital for help, ultimately enlisting her family and an ambulance crew to succeed; in the others, they calmed the person in the moment and provided information on longer-term resources.

The response from the MPD's officers was, perhaps surprisingly, very enthusiastic. The police were *happy* to be able to divert some calls and to summon the BCR when they needed a softer touch. On my ride-along, a BCR responder referred to officers as "our biggest fans," noting that officers understood and respected the BCR team's ability to more effectively de-escalate and address behavioral crises. Hanson also reported that her team members had not been pressured to criminalize behavior in the community—other than imminent threat of bodily harm, there was no push to call in law enforcement. Low-level legal violations, like open alcohol or drug use, trespassing, and the like, were not the concern of BCR responders. That meant people they encountered would not be arrested or jailed for such offenses.

Despite their professional camaraderie, the BCR staff were not cops. Most critically, while the public is required to obey officers' commands (or face the consequences), communication with the BCR team is entirely voluntary. As a result, BCR staff approach situations without officers' need for control, allowing them to calm and de-escalate tensions more effectively. This power difference was conveyed visually, too, with the BCR's more casual uniform and lack of a bulky duty belt with weapons, as well as the demographics of the staff; unlike the majority white men on the police force, the majority of the BCR's trained staff are people of color and/or women, non-binary, or transgender. The limit of the BCR's consensual person-centered approach, however, is that BCR staff have little power beyond persuasion to compel behavior, which meant that they sometimes left situations without any redress and in other cases had to call in police.

In April 2022 the Office of Performance and Innovation presented at the Public Health and Safety Committee, sharing the early results of its pilot to an eager group of city council members.[53] The team reported that in just over three months of operation, BCR staff had responded to roughly one hundred calls per week. This tally was already outpacing the number of person-in-crisis calls that were being dispatched to the MPD. Roughly one in ten of the calls the BCR responded to originated with the MPD requesting their assistance. Given the small scale of the pilot, these data were an encouraging sign that the BCR teams could handle an even higher call volume if given more resources. Indeed, city staff reported that 911 operators sometimes dispatched MPD officers when the BCR vans were offline, tied up, or too far away. With a van in each of the city's five precincts, staff argued, the BCR could more effectively handle a higher call volume with better results. Operating at scale, and with more assurance that callers would get a BCR response, there was hope that more callers might lean on 911 to get more proactive mental health assistance in moments of crisis, too.

Gina Obiri, a program manager for the city, summarized: "Our city is reimagining public safety, not just in theory, but practice," while a BCR staffer lauded, "Every city needs it." Simply responding to these calls with mental health professionals instead of police is a victory; it reduces police-citizen contact, minimizing the risk of citation or arrest for low-level offenses and thus improving public safety.[54] And it can reduce the routine forms of police surveillance, harassment, and use of force that people with behavioral health issues all too often confront. The shift to the BCR also creates the potential for people to get professional mental health care right on the street from a professional. That help is mostly triage, of course, but the hope is that people connected to resources through the BCR will be more likely to access long-term care than those whose crises are triaged by police (though it is too soon to evaluate these longer-term impacts).

What is less clear is whether or how much the BCR program (even if substantially expanded) can reduce lethal police violence, the original impetus for the pilot. The need for interventions for people in a mental health crisis is clear—estimates suggest that roughly a quarter of people killed by police across the country have a history of mental illness. Yet in the vast majority of these cases, persons both with and without a history of mental illness were armed with some kind of weapon.[55] Under the current BCR guidelines (and Minnesota state law), these calls would thus be ineligible for a BCR-first response. The worrying implication is that changing the first responders will not reduce lethal police violence if they are prevented from responding to calls involving weapons or the threat of violence—the sort that are most likely to end in death and that police are arguably better equipped to handle.

Consider whether any of the calls that prompted the interactions in which MPD officers killed civilians during the BLM protest years could have been avoided had the BCR existed. Jamar Clark came into contact with police because an ambulance crew asked for police backup. Raul Marquez-Heraldes, Thurman Blevins Jr., Mario Philip Benjamin, and Chiasher Vue all had guns. Justine Damond called 911 concerned about a possible sexual assault, or a violent crime potentially in progress, another call that would still go to police. And, unless 911 dispatchers interpreted the call from a Cup Foods employee as a welfare check for someone under the influence rather than a possible forgery, it is unlikely that a BCR team would have been called to respond to 38th and Chicago.

The best fit would be the 911 call requesting a wellness check for Travis Jordan, the victim who inspired Travis' Law, which instructed 911 call-takers to dispatch mental health providers (when available) to such calls. Indeed, in the Department of Justice's 2023 report on the MPD, Jordan's death was listed as one of several reasons to expand non-police responses to behavioral crisis calls, arguing that this loss might have been prevented. But since the caller (Jordan's girlfriend) was worried about the imminent threat of suicide and was unsure about the presence of weapons, it is not clear whether it would (or could) be dispatched to the BCR team. When police arrived, they found an agitated man who yelled at them through a window. As police demanded he come out, Jordan emerged holding a knife and advancing toward officers, even as they shouted "Drop the knife," "Do not come outside," and "I do not want to do this!" By the time Jordan was killed minutes later, his girlfriend had dialed 911 again, telling the operator that Jordan had a knife.[56]

Perhaps, as the DOJ investigators wrote, people with mental health expertise might have been better positioned to de-escalate, perhaps allowing Jordan to stay inside his home, had they been called to respond. So too might Jordan have not perceived them as a route to self-harm since they came unarmed, thus prompting an automatic de-escalation. But, if he had still come out with a knife, the BCR would have retreated and called for immediate police backup. Indeed, the week before my ride-along, BCR workers told me that they had encountered a woman who had just stabbed her sister. As trained, the mental health professionals *ran away* when the woman opened the door with a knife, alerting the MPD they needed urgent help.[57] And so it was police who ultimately resolved this call, with one sister (whose wounds had been staunched by the BCR staffer in the meantime) transported to the hospital and the other to jail.

Thus, in the end, my best guess is that the BCR will prove to be a critically important solution to social problems, including the criminalization of poverty and the more frequent less-lethal forms of police violence like "take-downs" of people with behavioral health issues. It also might improve mental health care for the most vulnerable members of the public. But the BCR, and this category of intervention more broadly, seem less likely to substantially reduce the number of people killed by police every year on their own.

Community Keeps Us Safe?

While the OVP was growing its violence interruption teams and the Office of Performance and Innovation was launching the BCR, other experimental safety strategies were being tested *outside* the confines of city government. Building off the success of mutual aid networks developed in summer 2020, abolitionists argued that it was *community* that could keep Minneapolis safe. And while the idea of community-based safety for organizers comes out of a long tradition of Black liberation struggles, there is also contemporary social science research that supports the model. For example, sociologist Robert Sampson's work shows that in communities where collective efficacy is higher, that is to say places where residents believe they can work together to reduce crime and disorder, rates of reported crime are lower, even amid high poverty rates.[58]

We know less, however, about *how* communities—especially ones facing multiple layers of marginalization and exploitation—create these feelings of solidarity and safety, and still less about what this might look like in the absence of police. Scholarly studies of collective efficacy almost always measure the impact of this social cohesion in the context of a visible police presence and the frayed social safety net of this country. In other words, most of our social science knowledge is based on the premises of the world as we know it—not what radical imagination might envision for a liberatory future.[59] Interestingly, this has meant that activists seeking to build new futures have often looked instead to the past—going back to times and places where there was no formal law enforcement administered by the state but, instead, more informal means of social control. These examples include the practices of Indigenous communities and the radical self-determination models that came out of leftist organizing in the 1960s.

In the heat of summer 2020's unrest, such alternative visions of safety became temporarily dominant as neighborhoods began to experiment with community-led safety by necessity. Some of these grassroots groups would seek city funding from the OVP in following years, but others would remain independent. One such model was an abolitionist collective that developed a radical emergency hotline.

Their work began during the uprising, as long-time local organizers Jason Sole and Signe Harriday started responding to the urgent demands for help coming from community members. As noted in chapter 2, Sole was the president of the Minneapolis NAACP chapter in the early BLM years and had launched a successful national campaign selling black hoodies with the logo "Humanize My Hoodie" in memory of Trayvon Martin. As described in his memoir, Sole went from being incarcerated in Minnesota state prisons to earning his PhD and becoming an educator and activist-organizer.[60] Harriday had a similarly long organizing history, grounded in creative arts and arts education as a path to social change, and together they pooled their resources, connections, and expertise.

The "new normal" following the unrest saw many mutual aid projects fizzle out, but Sole and Harriday's work instead expanded. Growing their core team,[61] the new collective became REP, or Relationships Evolving Possibilities, an abolitionist experiment to build an "interconnected eco-system of projects and resources that build the conditions for safety, free-dom, and dignity in our communities" outside of the violence of racial capitalism. The project had several components, each with the acronym "REP," including the "radical ecosystem pods," or community groups that built neighborhood capacity by working and training together, and "revo-lutionary emergency partners," a hotline designed to "provide emergency care to community members" by trained volunteers.[62]

Unlike many staff-run programs, REP was designed to rely on ordi-nary residents and build community networks of solidarity. The experi-ment had some paid project managers, but the people who responded to calls were not "on the job"—they were community members responding to their neighbors to provide mutual aid, or loving care. REP used donations and foundation grants to provide stipends for these volunteers' training, which involved completing seven ten-hour training sessions, which REP describes as "studios." Led by their five core team members, the studios cover the daily work of the hotline—including training and scenario role-playing on mental health first-aid, de-escalation tactics, cop watching, and use of the team's technology systems—as well as the history and philoso-phy of REP and legal guidance on the bounds of its work in community.

Any funding for REP, its organizers promised, would have to come without strings; REP would not be caged by city money or city agencies. Operating independently allowed the REP hotline to eschew all contact with the police, unlike the violence interruption programs organized through the OVP. REP could stand true to its abolitionist principles, pro-viding emergency response with no risk of police involvement. As Harri-day described in a March 2022 podcast, calling a "system [that] does not see us as people" was not the answer. Instead, REP would allow people to call "each other, other abolitionists"[63] and engage in "radical consent," meaning that the caller would decide what kind of response from REP (or other services) they wanted. As Sole described to me in a 2022 interview, he and his co-organizers formed this model with their own experience in mind. Having attempted to build alternative models of safety within the confines of the city (both in Minneapolis and St. Paul), they decided that only an independent model could avoid co-optation.

As they built the model, the organizers worked to spread the word about the hotline, posting on their website social media platforms to inform community about the days and hours they would be open. The hotline went active in summer 2021, initially responding to calls on Friday evenings (7 P.M. to midnight). Though the first call they answered was in North Minneapolis, the project had no firm geographical boundaries, and it took calls from across the Twin Cities. REP directs community members to call the hotline for things like noise complaints, mental health crises, neighbor disputes, and conflict de-escalation, but not acute medical crises or in-progress theft or violence (though REP envisioned these as potential growth areas after the pilot phase). The hotline response teams consist of three REP members: a community resourcer—the call-taker who handles the emergency response line, linking people to resources and (where appropriate) dispatching a response—and the response team, consisting of a driver and a CARER ("Community Aid, Resourcing, and Emergency Response") who takes the lead at the scene.

Building REP has been enormously hard work, requiring coordinating a large team of volunteers to run an ambitious experiment in safety. To staff the line, REP had, by spring 2022, in addition to the five core team members, several project managers and roughly twenty trained CARERs. But the scale of aid directly provided by the hotline was still limited, operating on Friday and Saturday evenings, with periodic pauses to regroup and build capacity. During an interview in April 2022, Sole told me that over a recent weekend, the line received five or six calls, with half dispatched to an on-site team. The kinds of calls REP received were varied, including medical crises where community members wanted someone on the line with them while they waited for an ambulance; disputes among friends, partners, and neighbors; and mental health crises.

This phase was just a pilot though, with the REP core team setting a goal of training a thousand people to respond to their community's needs. How the program might evolve was left flexible—they would just keep trying to provide "deep love" for (and by) the community, promising a ten-year commitment. And as they built out the model, "riding the bike as we build it," REP's team worked to deepen their connections to other local groups experimenting with community-led solutions. Importantly, too, the REP hotline was just one part of its broader work. REP's leadership was also building the "radical ecosystem pods," strengthening community mutual aid networks, and training community members in how to administer Narcan and diffuse conflicts.

REP's goal was not to take over all 911 calls in the city (or region) single-handedly, but to propel forward that broader ecosystem of radical organizers and organizations through its trainings, the pods, and a political education campaign on the promises of abolition. As Harriday described in a March 2022 podcast, REP's greatest achievement wasn't to be measured in the number of calls answered but by its contributions to radical imagination: "We're not trying to abolish emergency response. We're trying to create new imaginations of what that looks like."[64] The goal, as Sole told a *Vice* reporter in winter 2021, was to see "more groups showing up in a REP kind of way" to provide safety for their own communities.[65] Both pushed back against putting REP in a box or on a pedestal—REP wasn't "the" answer to the problem, because there was no one right answer. Instead, REP was one of hopefully many attempts to put Black liberation philosophy into practice, sparking further radical possibilities for real safety.

Reimagining Public Safety?

Policy scholar David Thacher contends that shrinking the footprint of the police is a fraught endeavor because police provide a *residual* service, stepping in where informal community structures and other state services have failed. In other words, police are often called to respond precisely because no other agency exists to do something about the problem at hand or has the authority to coerce compliance.[66] As a result, he argues, perhaps part of the answer to scaling back policing lies in working with law enforcement to identify the failures they're seeing on the street, ultimately building capacity to better prevent 911 calls to police in the first place. While none of the three models described in this chapter took quite this tack, each in their own way is attempting to imagine better models for interrupting violence and responding to emergencies. And by growing radical imagination, moving the public away from the deeply entrenched belief that police should be the catch-all managers of public safety, all three have the potential to reduce police power and expand public safety.

Yet, as we have seen throughout the chapter, many of these new models of safety face some of the very same challenges as police departments past and present, including difficulties around hiring, training, misconduct, and accountability. Who should be in these roles, and how might cities recruit, train, and review them? In addition, assuming such programs can get to scale, how will we hold such alternatives accountable for any violence and harm they cause in the community? Put differently, developing alternative models reveals there's no simple "fix" to the problem of policing; each attempt instead prompts a whole new set of questions about how to ensure that these new agencies and services can fulfill their promises to communities in need.

An update on the BCR is instructive on some of these implementation challenges. By spring 2023, as documented in the DOJ report, the contracted team had taken twelve thousand calls (with zero reports of violence toward residents), but was still not operating 24/7 because of challenges staffing overnight weekend shifts as well as mechanical problems with the vans.[67] Worse, city politics had left the program under-resourced and isolated. In a *Star Tribune* article published in July, the BCR team's lead, Candace Hanson, reported that Canopy did not know whether their contract would even be extended after the summer and that she had been unable to even meet with Commissioner Cedric Alexander, appointed less than a year earlier by Mayor Frey to helm the city's new Office of Community Safety.[68] Shortly thereafter, though the BCR contract had since been extended—with the initiative now housed under the "Neighborhood Safety" department, or what used to be the OVP, in order to facilitate contact with the new office—Alexander had announced his intention to retire from the position. In short, it is worth remembering that these are pilot programs, vulnerable to political and bureaucratic challenges as they work to scale up.

It is also important to be clear-eyed that these kinds of initiatives have the potential to reproduce and reinforce the political status quo even as they move the city away from police. It wasn't police clearing out the barricades at George Floyd Square, but Mayor Frey still led the action, quietly deputizing Agape to deploy force. Changing the types of city-led services that enact such preferences is unlikely to change the existing power structures, even when programs claim the mantle of "community." Nor does it resolve the fundamental tension of governing in diverse cities, where a kaleidoscopic range of opinions exists on the path forward. Proponents of more "democratic" or participatory styles of governance (in contrast to top-down, or technocratic, approaches) often argue that a devolution of power to the community will lead to less punitive policies and practices.[69]

Yet simply shifting the locus of power without changing public opinion or the broader social structure may simply empower the loudest community voices, not bring more justice.[70] Survey research confirms that many members of communities, even those beset by high crime rates, often have quite punitive (though nuanced and context-dependent) attitudes about policing and the broader criminal justice system.[71] "Power to the People!"

is a powerful call—but it can't produce outcomes that are better for the working class, people of color, LGBT+ communities, and other marginalized groups absent mass support for the goals and tactics of those fighting for revolutionary change.

Many abolitionists understand these dynamics, recognizing that their work is politically unpopular, in part because of "copaganda," or the ways in which police define the terms of the safety debate in popular consciousness. Instead of simple invocations of the "community" then, abolitionist theory tells us to center the multiply marginalized, and to direct attention on actions that will make policing and prisons *obsolete*.[72] Of the three case studies in this chapter, the REP hotline provides the clearest example of trying to put this set of ideas into practice, operating (not coincidentally) outside the confines of city governance. Yet by operating independently, REP necessarily limited its scale and scope. Only people who knew about the hotline—largely because they followed REP on social media or were otherwise connected to abolitionist organizing—would know to call. While such internal movement work can be a powerful seed for change, it remains to be seen how such efforts can diffuse and scale up untouched by mainstream political institutions, especially as the immediacy of the rebellion continues to fade.

Perhaps more fundamentally, if the problem of police violence goes so much deeper than policing—to the foundational race and class cleavages in America—then so too must its solution go beyond changing first responders' uniforms or the number folks call when they need help. Simply changing *who* responds might reduce the harms of violence, but it will not resolve the underlying structural tensions. Sending mental health professionals in response to 911 calls about persons in distress or violence interrupters to violence-plagued corners, for example, does little to address the underlying causes of those social problems. For example, violence interruption, while it can provide important paths to stability and meaning-making for street workers, is unlikely to "cure" violence as long as young people continue to enter schools where most students drop out, job markets with few options for dignified work, and neighborhoods plagued with environmental hazards.[73] Similarly, BCR responders might connect people to social workers, but those workers can't place people in permanent affordable housing if units aren't available.[74] As Candace Hanson summarized in our April 2022 conversation: "I do think that my responders are, more often than not, still expressing that there's not enough resources out there, particularly related to housing." To build deeper changes then, Minneapolis will need *structural* solutions to what are clearly structural problems.

Conclusion

ON JULY 14, 2022, officers with the Minneapolis Police Department (MPD) killed twenty-year-old Andrew "Tekle" Sundberg. Initial reporting described a late-night standoff between police and a man in a mental health crisis who had fired a gun inside his apartment. Hours later, after the building had been evacuated and the full force of the MPD mobilized outside, snipers shot and killed Sundberg through the window of his third-floor apartment. Heartbreakingly, his parents were at the scene, too, having been summoned by police to encourage the son to surrender. In the days that followed, the mayor and police chief *thanked* the officers involved in the "incident," though they were vague about what exactly had immediately precipitated the shots that killed Sundberg—deferring, they said, to state investigators. Later, publicly released video would document that in the seconds before the fatal shooting, Sundberg had appeared in his open window, holding what officers below the apartment believed was a gun in his hand. The snipers said the word "gun" and shot.[1]

Before these details were released to the public, activists staged a Black Lives Matter (BLM) protest outside the apartment complex. They were interrupted by an unexpected guest: the potential victim of Sundberg's gunfire. Under other circumstances, Arabella Foss-Yarbrough, a woman of color with pink hair and a neck adorned with tattoos, would have looked like any other protester. That day, however, she was there to demand that activists stand down. Sundberg, her neighbor, she told the crowd, had stalked and attempted to murder her. She had called 911, seeking help after bullets sailed through her walls. Haunting body camera footage later corroborated this account, showing her and her two young children (one a toddler clad only in a diaper) running toward officers in SWAT gear (who themselves had been fired upon by Sundberg in the stairwell). Confronting the distrustful crowd, Foss-Yarbrough insisted: "This is not a George Floyd situation. George Floyd was unarmed. This is not OK."[2]

This tense interaction—in which protesters yelled at Foss-Yarbrough and she volleyed back in grief and outrage—ignited conservative media commentators eager to expose the "hypocrisy" of a movement that claimed to value Black lives while ignoring crime victims. Invoking the all-too-familiar "Black-on-Black crime" trope, they argued that Black communities understood better than anyone why the country needs police. Activists calling for police defunding and police abolition, by extension, were misrepresenting the *real* demands of the community, they argued. As Foss-Yarbrough acknowledged implicitly in comparing Sundberg's killing to Floyd's, and others would say much more explicitly, Sundberg was not an "innocent" victim. His killing was not an example of unjustified, illegitimate, or murderous police violence—it was *good* policing in action. It was protection. In this version of the story, police were not the villains but the brave heroes who ran toward gunshots, spent six hours attempting negotiation, and protected a woman and children from deadly violence. The nascent protests soon fizzled, remaining mostly a local issue rather than a national or international story.

Conflicts over the meaning of these kinds of less clear-cut, but more common, lethal police interactions speak to the core tension of *The Minneapolis Reckoning*, which is that police represent both the *promise* of state protection and the *threat* of state violence, sometimes all at once.[3] And it is not simply that police protect some, while threatening others, but rather that the people and communities most in need of state protection experience the brunt of state force. Further, the force deployed by law enforcement is not just lethal violence, a rare and yet all too frequent event, but also the broader spectrum of state coercion. Even routine police actions can be a form of state violence.[4] Picture, for example, the maltreatment from police described by Northsiders in chapter 3, including frequent police harassment, being locked in a broiling police car, threats of lethal violence, and being treated like a "criminal" when seeking help after sexual assault. Or all the harms that come from low-level arrests for the crimes of poverty, including sweeps of housing encampments, prosecution for shoplifting infant formula, and more. This capacity for, and threat of, violence—from the demand to comply with officers' orders, to the force of an involuntary arrest, and finally to fatal encounters—lies at the heart of the police role.[5]

That means violence is baked into the institution of policing. But it is not simply a threat. It is also a response. It is the police, not social workers or community members, who can compel people to leave a corner or home, who can force individuals into the squad car and jail, and who decide whether or not to draw their service weapons and fire. Thus, when community members have few resources for managing the problems that accompany stark inequality—including housing instability, substance use and mental health disorders, domestic violence, gang violence, and more—they turn (in part) to the police. And they turn to guns, fueling threats and retaliatory violence in a quest for dignity and protection.[6] This is the context into which our cities send police. As Rosa Brooks, a law professor who became a reserve officer in Washington, DC, summarizes: "Police officers have an impossible job: we expect them to be warriors, disciplinarians, protectors, mediators, social workers, educators, medics, and mentors all at once, and we blame them for enforcing laws they didn't make in a social context they have little power to alter."[7]

None of this means that community members in such neighborhoods *want* police occupying their streets and homes. Instead, as we've seen throughout this book, marginalized residents in our cities often experience both a deeply visceral fear of police harassment and violence *and* a beleaguered and ambivalent dependence on law enforcement to manage the social problems that accompany poverty. Foss-Yarbrough, like many of the women of color my team interviewed in North Minneapolis, knew intuitively that she faced an impossible bind, exposed to both gender-based violence *and* the worry that calling the police could contribute to the criminalization (or even death) of Black men.[8] Recall Northsider Kamela from chapter 3, who said of police: "I don't have faith in them at all . . . But then at the same time, you gotta call them if you need 'em. You know what I mean? And then when they come and you need 'em, they shittin' on you. So it's like, you damned if you do, you damned if you don't."

This ambivalence—damned either way—in turn fuels the complex and contradictory racial politics of policing seen in Minneapolis and elsewhere. Ultimately, what I take from all of this tragedy is that the debate between whether Black communities want *more* or *less* or *better* policing is tackling the wrong question. (So, too, is the inverse fight over whether white Americans are clueless progressives supporting police defunding out of misguided racial guilt or violent defenders of the racist status quo.) When you look deeper, the truth on the ground and in our hearts and minds is messier. The roots of calls to defund and abolish the police are often grounded in Black Americans' experiences with brutal police maltreatment.[9] At the same time, many also desire better policing to help solve predicaments they see on the streets today, even as they desire more holistic approaches for community thriving in the long term. No racial group, in other words, is a monolith. More importantly, if there is a "silent majority" among Black Americans, as some argue,[10] it is a deeply *ambivalent* majority with varied and conflicting attitudes and preferences about how to get from here to a place where everyone might feel safe.

The better question to ask is what these contradictions tell us about race and policing in America—and how to get past the tug-of-war between public attention paid to police versus community violence. Both the vision of police as protectors and the vision of police as a source of violence, I argue, hold important truths for envisioning what it might take to create a more just world.

Reformers, for instance, must reckon with the reality that police are inextricably linked to violence—there has never been and never will be a perfect police force that only uses the "right" level of violence against the "right" targets in the "right" moments. (If there was, we wouldn't have seen BLM protests erupt across the world—even in the Scandinavian countries American liberals often envision as a benchmark for progressive criminal justice policy.[11]) The best you can hope for is to get closer to a policing ideal that values the sanctity of human life and uses force sparingly within tightly regulated boundaries. The parallel is that those fighting for police abolition, to the extent they want to win key policy debates, will need to grapple with vulnerable communities' ambivalent reliance on police. For me, the most promising avenues for real justice then are to be found at the messy intersection of these visions of change, where police abolition and police reform collide.[12] To create real change, we all will need to do the hard, complicated work of building (and rebuilding) lasting and effective responses to prevent and respond to harm inside and outside of the bounds of the state.[13] And ultimately, the problem, as we saw in chapter 3, is not just how to solve unjust police violence, but how to redress racism in America.

What Happened in Minneapolis?

This story began in Minneapolis at 38th and Chicago in May 2020. Wracked by a generation-defining police murder, city leaders promised to build a "transformative" new model of public safety. *The Minneapolis Reckoning* has sought to understand how we made it to that day as well as what—if anything—changed in the months and years that followed. To understand the present, we began in the past, examining earlier eras in Minneapolis's history and the long struggle over police reform, up to the explosion of BLM protests in the mid-2010s. Through this lens, the

Powderhorn Pledge (and charter amendment that followed) were not simply a spontaneous response to just the murder of George Floyd, but the
hard-won victories of generations of activists in Minneapolis.

As a precinct building went up in flames, the answers about the "why"
of police violence that police abolitionists had been honing for years suddenly better matched the public's rage. The time for mere police reform, it
seemed, had ended. In this way, the mass protests and unrest provided a
critical opening for radicals, shifting the terrain of political struggle. And
yet—while the four officers were all eventually incarcerated, the family
awarded an unprecedented settlement, and both state and federal investigators sent to Minneapolis—deeper transformative changes to policing in
Minneapolis have proved elusive.

In the end, the MPD was never "ended," "defunded," or "dismantled,"
though its size shrank considerably as officers departed and the department struggled to hire new police. In part, these struggles were tied to
political and bureaucratic barriers that slowed change. As the fires and
public pressure died down, public (and media) attention turned toward
the rise in violent crime by residents rather than officers, making radical calls less resonant. But the charter amendment also struggled under
strategic ambiguity: Was it a path toward abolition on a ten-year time
horizon, a transformational reform, or nothing more than a name (and
reputation) change? Seeking a broader coalition while retaining their radical roots, organizers for the charter amendment attempted to position
the new department as an approach to public safety that could somehow
include police *and* serve as a direct route to abolition.[14] That ambiguity
made the proposal confusing to residents and more vulnerable to critique
and misinterpretation.

As a thought experiment, though, what if the charter amendment had
garnered the necessary 51 percent of the vote? That would have made radical reductions in the number of officers policing Minneapolis *possible*, but
it would not have forced change. Indeed, with a newly empowered Mayor
Jacob Frey in office, further reductions in the police department's budget
would have been unlikely. Nor was the charter change needed to create a
new department for a more holistic model of public safety. Indeed, after
the November election, the mayor created an Office of Community Safety,
housing the MPD, the fire department, emergency services, and the Office
of Violence Prevention (now named the Department of Neighborhood
Safety) together. (And, this time, it was the leftists on the council in opposition, arguing that the MPD's culture of violence might pollute the other
initiatives.)

In addition, while international headlines blared the failures of "defund" efforts, behind the scenes, the city and its residents were continuing to build out the kinds of alternative responses and initiatives made more urgent by the racial reckoning. A new behavioral crisis response unit changed responses to 911 calls, while violence interruption programs funded by the city worked to reduce conflict on the street. As they grew, these programs inevitably diverged from some visions of abolition—including through their collaboration with police—precipitating the searing critique that opened chapter 6. Yet they also provided tangible wins toward a new model of public safety in which both police and other first responders and prevention programs are adequately funded, staffed, and supported.

In short, while a "yes" on Question 2 would have been a profound symbolic victory for innovative approaches to public safety, in practice, perhaps the only thing different between the city now and that potential alternative future might have been the elimination of the charter provision establishing a mandatory minimum number of officers with the MPD. And the department's number of uniformed officers remains substantially below the minimum anyhow, due to ongoing staffing challenges.

Most important, change is still coming to the City of Lakes. It will take years to build, as the MPD emerges on the other side of the consent decrees and alternatives flounder and flourish. Just as movement actions in the early BLM protest years laid the groundwork for what would emerge in summer 2020, so too does this latest period of mobilization hold the potential for all kinds of impacts, some that might be hard to envision from where we sit today. The activists, organizations, community members, and elected officials who lived through the summer of rebellion, when police abolition made it to the op-ed section of the *New York Times*, have been changed.[15] Yet all the forces that entrench police power—residents, advocates, business interests, as well as local, state, and federal political dynamics—coexist with the myriad visions of justice. Each will continue to fight for their respective positions, taking advantage of political openings, rearranging coalitions, and witnessing the arrival of new players on the scene.

The World Is Watching

In sociology, we are constantly asking of qualitative research projects: *What is this a case of?*[16] That is, how should we make sense of data collected in a given time and place in order to generalize from these experiences to broader theoretical claims? And so I heard that question a lot as I worked on this book: *What is this—Minneapolis's moment of reckoning—a case of?* In some ways, what happened in Minneapolis is simply its own story. No other place faced the same intensity of mobilization, grief, and national scrutiny after George Floyd's killing. The world, as a piece of graffiti in downtown declared, was watching. And yet, my core claim is that what happened in Minneapolis has lessons that can and should travel far beyond its borders.

My working title for this project when I began in 2016 was "Policing the Progressive City." Minneapolis, as I understood it then, was a case of the boundaries of liberal police reform in the BLM era. In other words, I wanted to see what we could learn by studying places that might be considered a *best-case scenario* for police reform in diverse cities, places where elected officials at least agreed in principle that Black lives mattered, even as vast economic and racial disparities separated the city's Black and white residents. I wanted to know how the sanctity-of-life policies, the use-of-force trainings, the diversity initiatives, police violence watchdog groups, and other initiatives described in chapter 2 were (or were not) changing policing, including in the attitudes of everyday residents. The answers to those questions then could inform what kinds of change strategies to pursue.

By 2020, it was clear that Minneapolis was anything but a model of police reform. It was, however, an illuminating model of the stark limits of such reform. And it is not just Minneapolis that seems unable to resolve the fundamental liberal contradictions in policing. Indeed, in recent years, left-leaning cities across the county, both majority Black and majority white, on the coasts and in the midlands, have struggled with how to move forward with transforming public safety.

Consider, for example, New York City, home to the country's largest police force. In 2021 city voters chose Eric Adams, a Black former police captain, as mayor over several more progressive challengers. Adams ran on a liberal law-and-order platform and, in office, he has sought to roll back many of the criminal justice reforms his predecessor put in place.[17] Just down the Eastern Seaboard in Philadelphia, a third of the city's new civilian oversight board recently resigned, calling out the "toxic dysfunction" that would be familiar to anyone who knew about Minneapolis's Police Conduct Oversight Commission.[18] Closer to home in the Midwest, in Chicago, Illinois, Mayor Lori Elaine Lightfoot, the city's first Black lesbian mayor, was pushed out of office in part due to her handling of several tragic incidents of police violence, including the fatal shooting of thirteen-year-old Adam Toledo in March 2021, alongside rising homicide rates in the city. Brandon Johnson, a Black former county commissioner, won the 2023 mayoral race in Chicago, in part by running to the left of Lightfoot and others. Yet even Johnson has promised to "get tough" on gun crime in the city, championing policies that have historically locked up disproportionate numbers of Black men.[19]

If we zoom to left-leaning cities in the South, the same ambivalence reigns. In Austin, Texas, activists successfully pushed in 2020 to cut the city police department's $434 million budget by *one-third*. Yet by 2022, in the context of the homicide spike and aggressive threats to the city's budget from the Texas state legislature, the city council had restored and even increased the department's funding (though voters rejected a proposition that would require Austin to have a mandatory minimum of 2 officers per 1,000 residents, just slightly higher than Minneapolis's required 1.7 to 1,000 ratio).[20] In Atlanta, Georgia, as I write, police abolitionist activists are being arrested over protests against the new police training complex, "Cop City," for which the city council approved $31 million in funding for construction.[21]

Perhaps the most surprising post-2020 reform victory happened in the small college town of Ithaca, New York. In a plan similar to Question 2 in Minneapolis, Ithaca's mayor proposed reorganizing the police as a division under a new Department of Community Safety, requiring in this case that officers reapply for their jobs. Vigorous officers association resistance to the plan and legal bureaucratic challenges about its implementation, however, led to uncertainty and slowed progress. Three years later, the national media long since decamped, the Ithaca Police Department remains in place.[22] Minneapolis perhaps then is not so unique.

Finally, I've focused here on so-called progressive cities. But those are not the only places where police kill with impunity. Indeed, while media coverage can give the impression that police violence is largely an issue in liberal mega-cities, the truth is the opposite. Indeed, by 2019, there were nearly twice as many police killings in suburban zip codes, as compared to urban locales (a gap that has widened since 2014).[23] While most of the country's largest cities lean liberal, in the six cities with over 250,000 residents that reliably lean conservative,[24] four have seen more police killings than Minneapolis in recent years. For example, police in Oklahoma City, Oklahoma, which has a population of roughly 532,600, killed fifty-eight people in 2013–2021, compared to ten in Minneapolis with its population of 435,000.[25] And red states have higher per capita homicide rates than blue states—both for intra-community and police violence.[26] Yet police killings in these places rarely make the news. What makes places like Minneapolis stand out then to a national audience is not just the city's police, but its residents and the well-organized anti-police-violence activist groups, local journalists, and others who force a public conversation about the legitimacy of police violence.

Lessons for the Future

Many sociological books, full of rich analysis and complexity, end by arguing that the kinds of entrenched structural (or "wicked") problems we study will never be solved without fundamental transformations of the racial and economic order. And they're right. We can't expect crises produced over generations to be solved through quick fixes. But the inevitable critique is just as right: Why has the author studied this topic for years, only to have nothing to say about *what we do now*? And so, after resolving the need for an end to capitalism, sexism, and racism, sociologists too often rush to offer short-term policy ideas that might be worth considering. Sometimes, these suggestions turn out to be unsuccessful or even in contradiction with the book's core claims. So let me be clear at the outset: I do not believe that truly addressing the crisis of racialized police violence is work that can be accomplished in a five-to-ten-year time horizon. It is probably not work that can be accomplished in just one lifetime, and it is not as though a single policy victory will allow us to declare mission accomplished.[27]

Yet change is not just possible, it is inevitable. After the Civil War, the system of chattel slavery—which undergirded America's political, economic, and racial order—was abolished. Mass incarceration did not always exist; it grew over a four-decade period of rapid policy innovation and diffusion. So too have the ways in which police appear in residents' lives looked dramatically different over time, as we saw in chapter 1. And the COVID-19 pandemic has shown that the government can intervene in our daily lives in unprecedented ways on the scale of days and weeks, not decades and lifetimes. All of this means that we can (and must) make real changes in public safety in the here and now, alongside seeding bolder transformations with a longer time horizon. With all that in mind, I close by offering not specific policy recommendations, but a set of four lessons learned from Minneapolis—and then some thoughts on how we might translate these lessons into policy proposals. Inevitably, these suggestions will be too simple. But I hope they provide the start of a better conversation.

First, police reform can "work"—but only if we define the outcomes narrowly. As traced in *The Minneapolis Reckoning*, real and meaningful changes have happened in policing throughout the city's history and substantial efforts continue to this day. There is also initial evidence that BLM protests between 2014 and 2019 spurred reforms to police training, oversight, and practices that reduced the number of Black Americans killed by law enforcement in cities with protest mobilization (even as the national total changed little).[28] Homing in on specific reforms in Minneapolis and elsewhere, research documents that training programs can successfully reorient officers' attitudes about their role in the community and residents' perceptions of local law enforcement.[29] Accountability changes, including stronger policies and internal and external oversight, can reduce officers' use-of-force rates if designed and implemented thoughtfully.[30] These wins, which don't *end* but can *reduce* police violence, are prone to failures and back-sliding. But they can be important harm reduction strategies.

Second, given these limits, we must do more than simply continue to "reform" the police. Moving beyond the political tug-of-war over violence means that instead of arguing for more regulations around police violence and more funding for the police, we should instead call for transforming policing while *shrinking its scale* to reduce its impact in the daily lives of Americans. In particular, we should work to reduce the constant friction between police and poor communities of color by supporting community thriving and developing an array of alternative models of preventing and responding to harm. In addition, we should roll back the aggressive policies of the "War on Drugs" era that fueled biased police stops and constant surveillance and harassment, reducing the kinds of "proactive" policing emblematized in New York City's stop-and-frisk regime.[31] None of this means neglecting public safety, but instead paying careful attention to reducing the harms imposed by law enforcement. Whatever the (limited) benefits of hiring more police and such "proactive" strategies on deterring crime, they come with substantial social, emotional, and political costs, especially for young men of color.[32] Building alternative models, outside and inside of policing, could thus bring us more safety *and* justice.

Third, any kinds of alternative approaches we develop need to reckon with the reality that police violence in America is fundamentally tied to the high rates of lethal violence in the community. And urban violence is primarily a story of *gun violence*.[33] Police kill more people here than in any other Western democracy—but our citizens kill each other at unrivaled rates, too, in part because of the easy availability of guns in poor urban neighborhoods.[34] Not surprisingly, countries with the highest homicide rates in the community and the greatest economic inequality see the most residents killed by officers.[35] Homicide rates and gun prevalence shape not only real risks for officers, but also their perceptions of dangerousness. Indeed, the threat of guns and gun violence undergirds officers' sense of a "danger imperative," fueling police violence against residents and shielding officers from later accountability, as sociologist Michael Sierra-Arévalo's work shows.[36] All of this means that redressing police violence will require changing police culture and policies, yes, but also the broader culture of violence and its drivers.

The final key lesson is that cities cannot solve the racialized inequality underlying urban violence and police violence alone. Truly reckoning with that violence means fighting racism and working toward full social, political, and economic inclusion of all Americans. It means a reimagining of what is required to create a thriving multiracial democracy.[37] That reimagining will not come cheap. Spending to improve public welfare through broad-access programs, which benefit a majority of Americans, will always cost more than the concentrated surveilling and punishing of the most marginalized.[38] And yet, being "cheap on crime" costs the country tremendously in lives lost and the ripple effects of those losses. To really get to the heart of the problem, the country will need transformative state and federal investments. And to do that, we'll need to change our politics.

So, what might meaningful changes that take these lessons to heart look like? We don't have to start from scratch. Abolitionists *and* reformers have already begun to envision and enact alternative prevention and response systems—from the REP hotline, alternative responders to 911 calls, and violence interruption programs described in chapter 6, to restorative justice models that bring together victims and perpetrators of harm.[39] There are other models too, like strategic non-response to biased police calls, diverting 911 calls to social workers or sending case managers directly to impacted areas (e.g., encampments for unhoused people) to triage service needs, and, crucially, expanding community capacity for low-barrier housing and other vital resources.[40] Similarly, cities are starting to ask whether we need law enforcement agents to regulate traffic and traffic accidents, or if this work can be shifted to other agencies and/or technological alternatives like traffic cameras (though these, too, come with a set of collateral consequences as well as important privacy concerns).[41]

We will also have to work to scale up these programs while thinking carefully about what accountability means.[42] Simply hiring volunteers from the community, for example, is not enough to make sure that alternative responses are less violent than the police.[43] (Picture a community patrol composed of George Zimmermans and Kyle Rittenhouses.) The state, in other words, has no monopoly on unjust violence in the name of "security." But by reducing police-citizen contact, we can potentially intervene to reduce lethal (and non-lethal) police violence. And it can reduce the slow violence of policing,[44] including the rate at which people in poor communities get saddled with the burden of arrest and conviction for low-level offenses that punish poverty.[45] It can also free up police department resources to respond to and investigate serious crimes—which in turn may improve community trust in law enforcement.[46] And, at the level of city politics, in a future where different agencies, with varying personal and professional identities and understandings of crime, are responsible for public safety, we stand a better chance of a more just form of policing.

There are also physical public safety investments we can make that do not require new agencies or workforces. One of the big drivers of proactive police stops was the "broken windows" thesis, which posited that the visible presence of disorder in a neighborhood could signal that crime and violence were tolerated, thus increasing the risk of serious victimization. The answer, police and policing scholars decided, was to crack down on lower-level offenses and disreputable people on the streets (such as the iconic "squeegee men" in New York City).[47] As a result, police forces increasingly invaded the daily lives of community members, especially young men of color. Ironically, few stopped to consider the literal *broken windows*. What if the lesson was *actually* about neighborhood infrastructure? Could fixing these physical markers of disorder reduce crime? Promising evidence suggests yes.[48] Addressing abandoned buildings, creating welcoming community spaces, and increasing lighting in high-crime areas can all improve the quality of life for residents, including by reducing opportunities for victimization.[49] And it does so while sending public money into coffers other than the police department.

Scaling up also means addressing the "broken windows" in our social safety net. We know that expanding access to housing, health care, food stamps, and other social supports can reduce criminal victimization and offending.[50] This means that the kinds of social investments required for a broad conception of safety must go so far beyond what would fit into a single department (or its budget). Housing policy, through this lens, is crime policy. Welfare assistance and health insurance are crime policies. Education is crime policy. Not only are they crime prevention, but building out these kinds of safety nets are also *police prevention*. That's why criminologist Elliot Currie's account of how to reckon with the persistently high rates of lethal violence in poor Black communities ends with a call for solutions largely *outside* of the criminal justice system. In addition to meaningful gun control, Currie envisions a world with full, dignified, and appropriately compensated employment, which would allow us to build the caring capacity of our schools, hospitals, and other public amenities in communities across the country.[51] You don't have to be a police abolitionist to imagine so many better ways to respond to and prevent violence.

None of these pathways will be easy to accomplish given the current fractured state of our politics. There are, of course, a substantial share of Americans who continue to "back the blue" and defend police against all critique. It's these same Americans fueling the manufactured panic over critical race theory, a predictable backlash to the summer of racial reckoning.[52] By September 2021 just under half (47 percent) of white Americans—and only 19 percent of Republicans—told pollsters that they "somewhat" to "strongly" supported Black Lives Matter. (In contrast, 83 percent of Black Americans continue to report support for the movement.[53]) The white majority's fickle political support, especially outside of left-leaning cities, is what most deeply constrains elected officials' willingness to drive change at the state and federal levels in redistributive and social policies, creating the binds cities then struggle to respond to. All of this means it is not enough to reimagine local politics; change has to go so much farther to resolve the vastly unequal life chances of Black and white Americans.

A liberatory future—and the paths toward it—is often difficult to imagine from where we stand in the present. There are no simple fixes for these systems of injustice. But our country has not always looked the way it does now, and it does not have to look this way in the future.

I BEGAN THINKING about this project in 2016, in the early years of BLM protests and on the heels of publishing a book, *Breaking the Pendulum: The Long Struggle over Criminal Justice*, with Joshua Page and Philip Goodman.[1] We had written the book to explain the gap between national rhetoric on criminal justice and what we saw happening on the ground. Whereas many scholars and popular commentators described these powerful pendulum swings between punitive and rehabilitative eras across history, we instead saw continuities across time and divergences across place. Even during the heyday of tough punishment in the 1990s, for example, there were people championing less punitive approaches in cities and states across the country. So, too, were elements of imprisonment deeply cruel and punishing even at the zenith of the rehabilitative ideal. That's because punishment always braids both logics, with the weave shaped not just by the national mood or trends in demographics, the economy, or other macro-level forces, but by the struggles of individual people fighting to define crime and punishment.[2] Those actors, we argued, made penal history.

As we were finishing *Breaking the Pendulum*, it became clear that the organizers and protesters fighting under the Black Lives Matter banner had become important players in this struggle. Like so many scholars in that moment, we came to understand policing as a critical entry-point into the criminal justice system and an important institution of punishment in its own right. Unlike the politics of mass incarceration, however, which are primarily about state and national contests, political struggles over policing predominantly operate at the local level, in city halls crisscrossing the country. And so as police killings and protests roiled Minneapolis, I started to map out who was shaping policing here.

Rather than a clear plan for my research questions and design, I entered the field with a set of open-ended questions and approaches that evolved as I learned more, developing what my colleague Douglas Hartmann describes as an *emergent* case study.[3] My first questions were about the arrangement of actors in the policing field, or the set of organizers, community representatives, journalists, city leaders and staff, the MPD and its officers, police oversight commissions, and others involved in shaping law enforcement in Minneapolis. I wanted to understand how each group perceived the problems in policing and how those views translated into their proposed solutions. That led me to begin an oral history of recent efforts to challenge police violence in Minneapolis, reaching out to key players in as many different spaces as possible over months and then years to conduct interviews.[4] I also talked to police, from department leadership to officers working Northside's beats who took me on ride-alongs, though few of those observations made it onto the page.

As I waded into this research, students began coming to my office wanting to know more about—and do more to change—policing in Minneapolis. It was my first student on the project, Santino Reynolds, then an undergraduate, who steered us toward talking to residents in North Minneapolis, still reeling from the 2015 killing of Jamar Clark. Eventually, more students would join that piece of the project, conducting and analyzing the interviews.[5] This team also assisted with a set of ethnographic observations between 2017 and 2019, witnessing public policy debates, protests for the victims of police violence, and meetings of relevant activist groups. Still more students joined to help me work through the interviews I conducted with activists that appear in chapter 2. This book thus emerged from a set of team projects; each left their mark on the project, pushing me to ask new and richer questions.

By 2019 I had wrapped up the various pieces of data collection for the project—or so I thought. We felt we had reached theoretical saturation (the moment when no new key themes are emerging across interviews). But as I was in the midst of analyzing the Northside interviews with my chapter 3 coauthors, police murdered George Floyd. The day after the news broke, we were scheduled to hold a research meeting. We shifted course, using the time to process. Like the rest of the city, we were in mourning. Just as quickly, however, I realized this was a moment of reckoning—one I couldn't, for the sake of this project, set aside or work through. I'd have to abandon my plan and start anew to understand the consequences of George Floyd's murder for policing (and its politics) in Minneapolis.

Of course, I never imagined this new pivot in 2020, or that it would take place in the midst of a global pandemic. Due to restrictions at the university and city hall, much of my fieldwork after the murder shifted to digital ethnography.[6] I watched hearings, community meetings, and the court trials online; followed posts and discussions from activists and city leaders on social media (Facebook, Twitter, and Instagram); and kept a close eye on multiple local media sources as they covered policing-related stories. In the end, from 2017 to 2023 we collected observations from over fifty-five events and public hearings and recorded over 2,500 social media posts and media articles—just a fraction of which made it onto the pages of this book, but all of which shaped my thinking. I also began looking to the past, searching for histories of Minneapolis and the MPD. Finally, in spring 2022 I restarted in-person fieldwork one last time, conducting interviews with the organizers and staffers developing the new models of safety profiled in chapter 6.

Only in the last two years of writing would I put all the pieces of the puzzle together, joining the historical research (chapter 1), interviews with local activists and police reformers (chapter 2), interviews with North-side residents (chapter 3), and process tracing of the varied aftermaths of the murder of George Floyd (chapters 4–6). My hope is that by stitching together this patchwork of archival, digital, ethnographic, and interview data, the book provides a sociological account of what happened in Minneapolis and how it matters for American policing.

Positionality: Getting Proximal

In recent years, sociologists have grown more reflexive, asking how our own identities intersect with the kinds of questions we develop, how we answer them, and the information we are able to collect. Pushing back against traditional scholarly norms that value objectivity and distance, a new generation has argued that embodied knowledge and human closeness can enrich our scholarship. In the words of Reuben Miller, we must seek *proximity*: "The point is not just to empathize . . . The point is to walk alongside the people you spend time with and to do your best to learn from and communicate something about their lives with all the tools you have."[7] Only by standing close can we stand a chance at getting the picture right. In this framework, emotions, stories, and contradictions are all important forms of *data*, helping us to build a richer understanding of the social world.

In that spirit, let me say at the outset that this project was not simply a professional endeavor. The process was also deeply personal, as debates over the future of public safety in Minneapolis came to dominate not just my research but my life as a teacher, friend, neighbor, wife, and mother. My pathways to and across the city, for example, were marked by vigils to the victims of police violence. When Jamar Clark was shot and killed in 2015, I had lived in the city for two years, having recently moved to Minneapolis to start a job as an assistant professor of sociology at the University of Minnesota. His death jump-started local Black Lives Matter organizing and led me to start thinking more deeply about policing. When Justine

Damond was shot and killed two years later, it happened just across Lake Harriet from where I then lived, on a route I would later use to take my kids to and from their preschool. And when George Floyd was murdered in 2020 at 38th and Chicago, it was just two miles north of my home and on a corner I visited often.

For years, it seemed like everywhere I went, I saw and heard the consequences of police violence. Any time I biked across town or opened the newspaper or logged onto social media, people were talking about the police. Teaching undergraduate and graduate courses in these months and years, I struggled to make sense of these tragedies and their fallout in real time. In the final years of the project, I increasingly became a participant in the news-making process, providing an academic perspective in coverage on policing in the city. As I started to write this book in earnest, what I realized was that all of these conversations—with my team, the students in my classes, friends and family, and reporters—were data. And they had all led me not only to the questions I asked, and how I asked them, but also to the answers.

And I went through that process not as some disembodied "everywoman," but as a straight white woman, married with young kids and benefiting from many privileges, including a reliable income and a home in a safe neighborhood. With the notable exception of Justine Damond (a friend of a friend), most of the people killed by the police in Minneapolis did not look like me, my husband, or my children. When I saw the procession of Black men killed by officers—and revisited those tapes in the classroom and on the record with journalists—it continually evoked deep hurt and loss. But no matter how attuned I might have become to racialized police violence, it can never be the same as watching people who look like you, or who look like your children or partner, being killed on camera. And it can never be the same as watching those videos after directly experiencing the cops pulling you over for no reason, or stopping your family members, and routinely treating you and your loved ones with disrespect—a set of experiences that happened to me exactly zero times over the decade I lived in Minneapolis.

My whiteness meant that I needed to be reflective and reach beyond my own racial subjectivity with a lot of compassion, respect, and humility. One of the ways I did this was talking with residents, activists, and community leaders who had different lived experiences from my own. I was also fortunate to have many students of color come knocking on my door, and I prioritized hiring students for this project who understood the harms of police violence through the lens of their own lives. In addition to learning from the data and my students' reflections, I looked toward the Black and other minoritized scholars who have pioneered scholarship on race, policing, and the state. It is this work that provides much of the best empirical and theoretical innovation in the field, and it informed my perspective throughout the book. I tried, in other words, to get proximal.

Navigating Space, Negotiating Race

For white scholars, however, getting proximal is often not enough. Indeed, my visible whiteness, at times, led to tensions in the field. Though suspicion toward me, my research, and the University of Minnesota emerged at several points in the life of the project, it was nowhere clearer than in the reaction to the 2019 public forum my team held in North Minneapolis described briefly in chapter 3. The goal of the forum was to present a draft of our results in preparation for releasing a public report. We wanted to come back to the community to transparently share our data, confirm our findings, and see whether there were new ideas for policy recommendations. Like the forum held by Councilmember Ellison that opens that chapter, we held our event at the University of Minnesota's Urban Research and Outreach-Engagement Center, posting an announcement on the center's website and on Facebook to spread the word. We called our interview participants to invite them too, though many of the phone numbers we had from earlier years were now out of service.

The event announcement garnered the attention of a particular group of North Minneapolis residents, who began to raise concerns on the Facebook event page about the project's methods, ethics, and funding. Some of the comments implied that we had chosen a biased set of participants, or even fabricated the data altogether. Others accused us of draining resources that might have instead gone to the community. Frankly unprepared for this reaction, I turned to colleagues and friends for advice: Should I cancel the event? Broker a meeting beforehand? One veteran organizer told me this kind of reaction was why they held such sessions on an invite-only basis; the chance of doing harm was too high in open-invite forums. Others encouraged me to "take the lumps," facing the forum as a kind of critical accountability process. Mulling it over with my research team, I decided to hold the event, attempting to respond to the concerns in advance online. We owed it to our participants and the community to show up, we concluded. We also asked a trusted community leader in Northside to step in as the event moderator to help guide a meaningful conversation.

The audience thus was a mix of people, including a handful of our participants, some residents who came to the forum deeply mistrustful about the research project, and Northsiders who attended such events at the center. The night was, predictably, a disaster. We anxiously rushed through our presentation, coming across as self-aggrandizing. The question-and-answer session was the most intense period of public scrutiny I'd ever experienced, before or since, as we weathered a barrage of questions about the data collection process (*Who did we talk to and why? When and where had we posted these supposed recruitment flyers?*), community access (*Who had invited us to study Northside?*), forum structure (*Why did we not invite city leaders or the police chief, who could actually do something, to the event?*), and finances (*What had we done with the funding, and why didn't this money go to community?*). Most poignantly, audience members asked why we were putting ourselves on stage to tell them what they already knew—that the MPD had inflicted a great deal of harm on Black Northsiders, while failing to protect them from staggeringly high rates of community violence, marking their boys and young men as *an endangered species*. The presentation, one person commented, had left them feeling "hopeless."

Though I shared the presentation of our results with my coauthors, the fact that the team was led by a white woman was a particular point of pain. Some in the audience understood me not to be sharing the stage, but using the student researchers (and the community moderator) as "Black shields" against critique. White scholars, they argued, took resources from the community; they were extractors. And, perhaps worse, these white Minnesotans were often *wrong*—they were listening *selectively* to (the wrong) Black voices and, in the process, wreaking damage. As Lisa Clemons, one of the anti-violence organizers described in chapter 6 and a community member who raised concerns about the project, would later tell a reporter about support for the charter amendment: "I think what's at issue is the White progressives' belief that they're helping us . . . [when] oftentimes they are hurting us."[8] These residents perceived me not as a white reactionary, but another misguided, paternalistic white progressive, attacking the police instead of doing something to address the urgent issue of community violence in Northside.

The forum was a critical lesson for me in how my whiteness shaped community perceptions of the project and its goals. It took me and the rest of the team (who were positioned differently) time to process—work that is in some ways still ongoing. Yet we also took away from the event important empirical and theoretical conclusions. The audience reaction to our findings, the critical comments about our methods and ethics, and our own response to those critiques all told us something about the world, including how absolutely ignored many people in Northside felt by the public conversation on police violence, and their pain at the lack of city response to what they understood as a dire emergency. This feedback deeply informed how we wrote up our findings, both in the public report we later released and in our academic work. And the critiques about selective attention to certain Black community voices, as well as accusations that it was white people in Minneapolis who were pushing radical change, also became key analytical foci for chapter 5.

Beyond these thematic lessons, the forum also pushed me in a deeper way to think about my role in both academia and the broader world. The forum was part of why I hesitated about whether I would write this book—by early 2020, it didn't seem like we would learn that much from another academic book on residents' attitudes about the police, or on BLM activism, especially one written from the perspective of a white academic. I was working on the report and some papers with the students on the research team, and at the time, that felt like the natural end of the project. What changed for me after George Floyd's murder, and why I ultimately wrote the book you're reading, was realizing that the story was not about reducing the complex racial politics of policing to a simple narrative, but instead, understanding how a diverse set of voices were deployed by a multiracial cast of city leaders to challenge *and* defend the Minneapolis Police Department. And central to that was really listening deeply to residents' concerns about community violence. It was these contested politics of policing, and the story of Minneapolis's attempt to reckon with the murder, that made the analysis more than a rehashing of what we already knew. The data I had collected earlier, in retrospect, became preamble for a story I did not know yet that I would be telling.

With a bit more distance, I also now find myself persuaded by many of the community members' critiques of our academic research. Scholars, and especially white researchers, *should* be hesitant to ask marginalized communities to share their trauma, especially when the research covers well-trod ground. We should develop such studies cautiously, respectfully, and in conversation with the community and previous scholarship by scholars of color. For some, the answer will be moving toward participatory action research frameworks that make the community a core research partner from the start, housing research projects within existing community groups or organizations, and/or developing deeper relationships of trust, rapport, and accountability before entering the field. We should also expect (rather than be surprised by) community mistrust, fueled in part by the very real ways universities contribute to inequality.[9]

Finally, we need to develop better ways to systematically give back to community, including sharing knowledge but also resources. That means making our work public, at a minimum, and also finding ways to partner with other groups and organizations to support community thriving. As a small step toward that goal, the royalties from this book will go to community organizations who continue to fight for justice in Minneapolis. But the real changes we need must go deeper, in reevaluating how we design, structure, and reward academic labor. In short, scholarship can (and has) made powerful interventions in the world, but it is also important to think bigger about how our departments, universities, and disciplines can help today.

A Police-Free Future?

As I wrote *The Minneapolis Reckoning*, I tried to be as transparent as possible in how I learned what I knew. In a traditional ethnography, part of that work appears in the moments when the author becomes a subject in their account. But in part because of my whiteness, it often seemed important *not* to center my own experiences or emotions directly in the book. As the methodology turned to digital ethnography, writing myself into the story became even more clumsy. Digital ethnography gets us closer, in some ways, to being the proverbial fly on the wall as our bodies remain at a distance.

But here, at the very end of the story, I want to linger for a minute in my own experiences of the summer of reckoning. After the murder of George Floyd, it felt like everyone in my social network was suddenly a police abolitionist.[10] How could we not be—had we not "seen enough"? The country, especially the hyper-online, had seen the murder, filmed on a teenager's cell phone. We had seen the explosion of police violence *at protests against police violence* across the country. Military tanks had rolled down our streets, attacking neighbors on their porches. During the unrest, my husband and I spent several late nights outside our own home, watching the street as our kids slept, glued to live streams of protests across the city. When the Target on Lake Street was being looted, and the 3rd Precinct sat moldering with flames, I went and served as witness. In the daytime, we took our kids (home because of the pandemic) to protest outside the governor's mansion. I biked to the protest that would end up at Mayor Frey's doorstep, marching alongside friends in what was one of our first meet-ups since the start of the pandemic. And, exhausted, I attempted to make sense of all of this to my far-flung friends and the reporters who were suddenly interested in Minneapolis.

In addition to what so many of us in Minneapolis experienced over those days of rage, the tragedy struck a hideously personal chord in my department. It turned out the two rookie officers responsible for George Floyd's murder (Lane and Kueng) had completed their bachelor's degrees in sociology at the University of Minnesota. The flagship University of Minnesota campus in the Twin Cities had once housed a criminal justice program, which was merged with the Sociology Department long before my time, becoming a track within the major. That meant that we had some students who wanted to go into law enforcement careers, a pathway that was featured prominently on career brochures. Lane and Kueng had taken our classes. Had we failed them, and the city? As the department reeled from the news, many of our PhD students banded together to take a stand: the department (and sociology as a discipline) could not be complicit, they argued, but instead must divest from policing. That meant rethinking the department's undergraduate track in criminology.

The conversation propelled a critical self-reflection of the program, led by graduate students and some of my colleagues, on our classrooms and scholarship. What was the program offering to students interested in criminal justice careers, and what did it mean to provide those courses ethically? What should be the role (if any) of law enforcement as guest speakers in our classes? Could we do better to make the pains of racism in the world clearer, for example, by diversifying the kinds of scholars and scholarship prized in our curriculum? And could we better embolden our students to fight for change, whatever their future career path, and illustrate the resistance struggles that have come before and provide *hope* today for the future? It was not enough just to show the trauma, pain, and structural constraints of the present—we had to, like abolitionists, engage in radical imagination. Maybe sociology could help train the future leaders who would take on the mantle of developing new models of safety.

In the years since the murder, I've kept these lessons in how I think about my teaching and research close to my heart. And yet, inside and outside of the classroom, I never quite came to call myself a police abolitionist. Depending on the day, time, and place, I exist somewhere in an in-between space that, judging from the conversations I often have in the classroom and the community, seems to contain so many of us. And that too was data. Experiencing viscerally the critique that the sociology program I poured so much of myself into might be part of the problem, for example, gave me new insights into why and how city leaders and police resist change. And there was much to be learned from trying to answer students' sharp critiques. *The Minneapolis Reckoning* is a long start to an answer for these questions, to connect the voice in my head that believes in some vision of abolition and the voice that says we will always have some kind of policing.

The depth and complexity of racism today, inside and outside of policing, is sometimes immobilizing—there is *so much* to change, and so many barriers. Sometimes when I describe my work to well-meaning white friends, they conclude that it's all too "complicated." I am haunted by the voice of Sheila, one of the white Northsiders described in chapter 2, who reminds me of many of my undergraduate students. Sheila's homegrown sociological vision of police violence was disempowering; it seemed, to her, that every route to change was set up to fail. The problem ran too deep to fix. But sociology, as the visionary W.E.B. Du Bois believed, can be *emancipatory* as well.[11] If we better understand the roots of a problem, we stand a better chance of making meaningful transformations.

The deep structural roots of the problem also mean that there are a lot of places to start doing the work—in intimate moments in our everyday lives, building up community, protecting the right to vote and growing the diversity of who gets a say in our politics, filling the streets with protest, and otherwise working toward cultural, political, and structural change in America.[12] The first question, then, need not be whether you believe in a police-free future, but what you can do here and now to work toward creating more justice for everyone. Within that framing, there is abolitionist work for all of us.

LIST OF ACRONYMS

BCR   Behavioral Crisis Response

BLM   Black Lives Matter

BLMM / M4BL   Black Lives Matter Movement / Movement for Black Lives

CPAC   Civilian Police Accountability Council

CUAPB   Communities United Against Police Brutality

DOJ   Department of Justice

GFS   George Floyd Square

MDHR   Minnesota Department of Human Rights

MPD   Minneapolis Police Department

OPCR   Office of Police Conduct Review

OVP   Office of Violence Prevention

PCOC   Police Conduct Oversight Commission

REP   Relationships Evolving Possibilities

TCC4J   Twin Cities Coalition for Justice for Jamar

TIMELINE OF KEY EVENTS IN MINNEAPOLIS

1867   Minneapolis incorporated

1934   Battle of Deputy Run and Bloody Friday

1967   Plymouth Avenue riot and National Guard deployment

1989   Smalley-Weiss fatal SWAT raid

1992   Murder of officer Jerome "Jerry" Haaf

2007   Mill City 5 lawsuit against the MPD for racial discrimination against officers

2010   MPD officers kill David Smith

2015   MPD begins reforms under the National Initiative

2015   MPD officers kill Jamar Clark; 4th Precinct occupation

2017   MPD officers kill Justine (Ruszczyk) Damond

2017   MPD150 releases report on MPD and begins organizing for a "police-free future"

2018   City creates the Office of Violence Prevention (OVP)

2020   MPD officers kill George Floyd; 3rd Precinct torched

2021   Charter amendment election

2022   All four officers involved in Floyd murder are convicted and sentenced

2023   Consent decree with MDHR entered; DOJ report released

ACKNOWLEDGMENTS

PEOPLE OFTEN THINK about writing as a solitary endeavor. But we never really write alone. In our heads is often a crowd: scholars we've read, people in the community we've talked to, imagined readers of the book, guests at our dinner table (and on our social media feeds), and more. And, if we're lucky, we have a team of support at every stage. I was very lucky.

As I noted earlier in the book, this all began as a team project. My first debt of gratitude, then, is to my many student collaborators. Santino Reynolds, then an undergraduate student on a Ronald E. McNair summer fellowship under my mentorship, was first to join the project in 2017, initiating the Northside interviews. AshLee Smith and De Andre' Beadle, both PhD students at the time, soon grew the team, adding their insights. By 2018 Amber Joy Powell, then a PhD student, began as a project manager (funded through grants from the University of Minnesota, including the Center for Urban and Regional Affairs), completing roughly half of our Northside interviews and many of the event observations. Amber's expertise with qualitative interviews, and the care she brought to those conversations, truly made the project. Paige Olson and Maya Smith later assisted with transcribing these interviews. Christopher Robertson, also a PhD student, joined the team as we were completing the Northside interviews, working with Amber and me to analyze the transcripts. Though Amber and Chris are formally coauthors on only chapter 3, our conversations together throughout the years were invaluable in shaping my thinking across the book.

Other students joined the project to assist with the other data collection and analysis efforts, providing their wisdom along the way. Anneliese Ward used my interviews with players in the policing field in her senior undergraduate honors thesis, later joining me and PhD student Dwjuan Frazier on a related publication. Dwjuan also began some of the historical research included in chapter 1. Daniel Cueto-Villalobos, the last PhD student to join the project, worked through the racial politics of the charter amendment debates with me in an article-in-progress that extends some of the findings in chapter 4. Undergraduates Yusra Hassan and Khadija Ba and PhD candidates Ryan Steel and Caity Curry assisted with the unglamorous but critical job of formatting footnotes and fact-checking. Ryan also provided generous comments, critiques, and line edits throughout an early draft. Finally, thanks to students in my Policing America class in fall 2022 for their comments and to Eric Seligman for building the index.

A team of professionals shepherded this book from start to finish. Writing coach Michelle Niemann was invaluable in speeding along the initial book drafting. She was my first reader on every page of writing and made the process of revising infinitely easier. Editor extraordinaire Letta Page came to my rescue at the end, helping to streamline and clean the prose throughout. I'm grateful to call this wonderful page-smith my friend as well as my editor. David Van Riper, director of spatial analysis at the Minnesota Population Center, created the terrific maps you see in the book. And, of course, none of this would have been possible without Princeton University Press sociology editor Meagan Levinson and assistant editor Erik Beranek. Meagan "got" this book from our very first meeting, and I'm deeply grateful for her support. Thanks too to the two anonymous peer reviewers, who provided both support and smart critiques.

I benefited from many conversations with academic friends and colleagues over the years. I will no doubt miss important names here, but my gratitude is enormous, especially for those generous souls who read the full manuscript when it was much too long: Monica Bell, Andrea Leverentz, Amber Joy Powell, and Patrick Sharkey. All provided crucial feedback, sharpened my focus, and inspired me with their scholarship. Susanna Blumenthal, Douglas Hartmann, David Thacher, Fergus McNeill, Jeremy Levine, and Tony Cheng each read parts of the book, providing incisive comments. Michael Lansing and Will Cooley deserve special thanks for helping me develop the historical chapter; their scholarship and advice were foundational. Will was also part of a terrific writing group, organized by William Jones with Malinda Lindquist and Michael Walker, that provided comments on an early book proposal, as did Jennifer Carlson. Victor Ray helped talk me off a cliff at a key moment in the publishing process. While we lost Devah Pager, my PhD advisor, much too soon, the lessons she taught me years ago still made it to these pages, too.

The University of Minnesota has been a wonderful home for the past decade. Kathy Hull, current department chair in sociology, and the department staff, have been terrific supporters. My colleague Josh Page has the honor of having taught my very first punishment class back when I was an undergraduate and he was a graduate student (it's all his fault) and has been an invaluable mentor and friend since. Thanks, too, to Christopher Uggen, a stalwart mentor as far back as my graduate school days and with whom unexpected hallway conversations on the tenth floor are always insightful (and very often funny). I first met Joe Soss when I interviewed at Minnesota, and he quickly became an invaluable mentor, with a knack for pointing me toward just the right article or book at pivotal moments. Thanks also to the Institute of Advanced Study, which provided an enriching and much-needed semester of teaching relief and interdisciplinary conversation. My co-fellows Tracey Deutsch, Fayola Jacobs, and Shaden Tageldin wrote with me most Tuesday mornings during that semester, providing company and helping to shape the book in its early stages.

The Minneapolis Reckoning is intended to go beyond academia—and people in the community were just as critical in shaping its pages. My deepest thanks go to everyone who took time out of their busy lives to talk to me and my team throughout the years. Though many of these contributors remain anonymous in the text, their thoughts and experiences were foundational. Thanks also to the many advocates in Minneapolis who are named in the book, some of whom made time in their busy schedules to talk with me, read work-in-progress, and provide thoughtful comments and advice over the years. As I wrote, Justin Terrell and Katie Remington Cunningham at the Minnesota Justice Research Center provided a source of inspiration in their efforts to make bold structural changes in policy and practice; both also provided thoughtful feedback on chapter 6. In addition, I am deeply grateful to the many local journalists who covered the policing beat in Minneapolis and whose reporting was essential to this project. (Support your local news outlets!) Lastly, Chuck Turchick, a regular community auditor of my classes and zealous citizen participant in the politics of policing in Minneapolis, read the book from cover to cover, catching the errors only he would be able to see.

My final set of acknowledgments goes to my family, especially my husband, Dan Myers, who listened to me narrate these words for years before I tried to write them down. We joked many times about starting a podcast, but, truly, his efforts to explain the finer points of the American political system saved me much embarrassment. Dan also faithfully reads a "dead tree" version of the local newspaper every morning, and, for years, dutifully set aside articles relevant to the project. That's love. Our kids, Theo and Ivy, provided a daily source of joyful chaos. Ivy has the privilege of having been present, in utero and as a newborn, for some of the fieldwork (even, at one point, behind a bullet-proof vest). Thanks too to my mother, Yvonne Phelps, who has been my loudest and most indefatigable cheerleader since my birth and was always ready to hop on a plane when Dan and I (frequently) needed help. Lastly, my thanks go to my in-laws,

Chuck and Julie Myers, who not only raised one of my favorite people but provided loving support to me, Dan, and the kids. Their path showed me it was possible to balance academic work, kids, and a marriage with verve. As I was writing, we lost Julie, adding another layer of grief to the story. I'm grateful to be surrounded by her children and grandchildren, working to honor her legacy.

To everyone on and off these pages, I offer my deepest gratitude; I hope the book does you justice.

Preface

1. Kim Barker et al., "Officers Charged in George Floyd's Death Not Likely to Present United Front," *New York Times*, June 4, 2020, https://www.nytimes.com/2020 /06/04/us/george-floyd-police-records-chauvin.html.

2. David Garland, "Penal Excess and Surplus Meaning: Public Torture Lynchings in Twentieth Century America," *Law and Society Review* 39, no. 4 (2005): 793–833.

3. Some of the exact wording of the pledge looked slightly different on the boards held up by activists during the event from what was read and later distributed. The language included here is copied from a press release issued by Reclaim the Block (June 7, 2020), available at https://www.reclaimtheblock.org/home/#resources.

4. On the Ferguson protest movement, see Andrea S. Boyles, *You Can't Stop the Revolution: Community Disorder and Social Ties in Post-Ferguson America* (Oakland: University of California Press, 2019); and Jennifer E. Cobbina, *Hands Up, Don't Shoot: Why the Protests in Ferguson and Baltimore Matter, and How They Changed America* (New York: New York University Press, 2019). For a summary and critique of police reform in the 2010s, see Monica C. Bell, "Police Reform and the Dismantling of Legal Estrangement," *Yale Law Journal* 126 (2017): 2054–150.

5. See, e.g., Alex S. Vitale, *The End of Policing* (New York: Verso, 2017); Mariame Kaba and Andrea J. Ritchie, *No More Police: A Case for Abolition* (New York: New Press, 2022).

6. Bring Me the News, "After Another Child Shot, MPD Chief Decries Gun Violence 'Epidemic' in Minneapolis," *Bring Me the News*, July 11, 2021, https://bringmethenews .com/minnesota-news/after-another-child-shot-mpd-chief-decries-gun-violence -epidemic-in-minneapolis.

7. See, e.g., Robert M. Fogelson, *Big-City Police* (Boston: Harvard University Press, 1977); Benjamin Bowling, Robert Reiner, and James W. E. Sheptycki, *The Politics of Police*, 5th ed. (New York: Oxford University Press, 2019).

8. Simon Balto and Max Felker-Kantor, "Police and Crime in the American City, 1800–2020," *Oxford Research Encyclopedia of American History* (2022).

Introduction

1. In 2020, 59 percent of Minneapolis residents identified as white, compared to 19 percent Black or African American, 6 percent Asian or Pacific Islander, 10 percent Hispanic or Latino/a/x, 5 percent multiracial, and 1 percent American Indian or Native. Statistics compiled from https://www.mncompass.org/profiles/city /minneapolis (last accessed May 25, 2022).

2. On the construction of the "community," see Jeremy R. Levine, *Constructing Community* (Princeton, NJ: Princeton University Press, 2021); Zakiya Luna, "Who

Speaks for Whom? (Mis)Representation and Authenticity in Social Movements," *Mobilization: An International Quarterly* 22, no. 4 (2017): 435–50.

3. This is a standard story for social movements. For examples outside of policing, see Deborah Stone, *Policy Paradox: The Art of Political Decision Making*, 3rd ed. (New York: W. W. Norton, 2012); David S. Meyers, *How Social Movements (Sometimes) Matter* (Cambridge: Polity Press, 2021). As movements scholar Sidney Tarrow concludes, "Although cycles of contention . . . can produce temporary coalitions for reform, they are usually too brief, too divided, and too dependent on temporary opportunities to provide permanent support once the fear of disorder disappears." See *Power in Movement: Social Movements and Contentious Politics*, 3rd ed. (New York: Cambridge University Press, 2011), 220.

4. Elizabeth Hinton and DeAnza Cook, "The Mass Criminalization of Black Americans: A Historical Overview," *Annual Review of Criminology* 4 (2021): 261–86.

5. Robin D. G. Kelley, *Freedom Dreams: The Black Radical Imagination* (Boston: Beacon Press, 2022).

6. This ambivalence about the role of state protection in visions of Black freedom is not just a contemporary phenomenon. W.E.B. Du Bois, in his classic account of Reconstruction, argued that Black freedom required substantial investments in state protection (via the military) to shield Black Americans from white supremacist violence. Freedom for Du Bois was not freedom from state violence, but instead the deployment of state violence "to empower the powerless." See Quinn Lester, "Whose Democracy in Which State?: Abolition Democracy from Angela Davis to W.E.B. Du Bois," *Social Science Quarterly* 102, no. 7 (2021): 3085. Similarly, Black movements in the 1960s articulated varied understandings of liberation. While the canonical civil rights movements fought for equality under the law, some of the more radical movements called for Black separatism instead. Groups like the Black Panther Party called for community control of the police. Thus, there has never been just one vision of liberation, or the ideal relationship between Black Americans and the state, but instead many. See Michael C. Dawson, *Black Visions: The Roots of Contemporary African-American Political Ideologies* (Chicago: University of Chicago Press, 2001).

7. On the disparate policing services provided across neighborhoods, see Daanika Gordon, *Policing the Racial Divide: Urban Growth Politics and the Remaking of Segregation* (New York: New York University Press, 2022).

8. Or, as scholar-activist Ruth Wilson Gilmore writes, we must "change everything." See Ruth Wilson Gilmore, *Change Everything: Racial Capitalism and the Case for Abolition* (Chicago: Haymarket Books, 2023).

9. David R. Johnson, *American Law Enforcement: A History* (St. Louis: Forum Press, 1981).

10. Eric H. Monkkonen, *Police in Urban America, 1860–1920* (Cambridge: Cambridge University Press).

11. George L. Kelling and Mark H. Moore, "The Evolving Strategy of Policing," *Perspectives on Policing* 4 (1988): 1–16.

12. David M. Oshinsky, *Worse than Slavery: Parchman Farm and the Ordeal of Jim Crow Justice* (New York: Free Press, 1996).

13. Khalil Gibran Muhammad, *The Condemnation of Blackness: Race, Crime, and the Making of Modern America* (Cambridge, MA: Harvard University Press, 2011).

14. On the role of police violence at protests in shaping public opinion and policy, see Omar Wasow, "Agenda Seeding: How 1960s Black Protests Moved Elites, Public Opinion and Voting," *American Political Science Review* 114, no. 3 (2020): 638–59.

15. See Hinton and Cook, "Mass Criminalization"; Simon Balto and Max Felker-Kantor, "Police and Crime in the American City, 1800–2020," *Oxford Research Encyclopedia of American History* (2022). On policing as "violence work," see Micol Seigel, *Violence Work: State Power and the Limits of Police* (Durham, NC: Duke University Press, 2018).

16. Simon Balto, *Occupied Territory: Policing Black Chicago from Red Summer to Black Power* (Chapel Hill: University of North Carolina Press, 2020).

17. Balto and Felkor-Cantor, "Police and Crime."

18. *Washington Post*, "Fatal Force," https://www.washingtonpost.com/graphics /investigations/police-shootings-database (last accessed March 24, 2023); see also Franklin Zimring, *When Police Kill* (Boston: Harvard University Press, 2018).

19. Frank Edwards, Hedwig Lee, and Michael Esposito, "Risk of Being Killed by Police Use of Force in the United States by Age, Race-Ethnicity, and Sex," *Proceedings of the National Academy of Sciences of the United States of America* 116, no. 34 (2019): 16793–98.

20. Reed T. DeAngelis, "Systemic Racism in Police Killings: New Evidence from the Mapping Police Violence Database, 2013–2021," *Race and Justice* (2021), https:// doi.org/10.1177/21533687211047943; Jeffrey Fagan and Alexis D. Campbell, "Race and Reasonableness in Police Killings," *Boston University Law Review* 100 (2020): 951–1015.

21. Susannah N. Tapp and Elizabeth J. Davis, "Contacts between Police and the Public, 2020," Report, 2022, https://bjs.ojp.gov/sites/g/files/xyckuh236/files/media /document/cbpp20.pdf.

22. See, e.g., Joscha Legewie, "Racial Profiling and Use of Force in Police Stops: How Local Events Trigger Periods of Increased Discrimination," *American Journal of Sociology* 122 (2016): 379–424; Justin Nix et al., "A Bird's Eye View of Civilians Killed by Police in 2015: Further Evidence of Implicit Bias," *Criminology & Public Policy* 16, no. 1 (2017): 309–40; Jeffrey Rojek, Richard Rosenfeld, and Scott H. Decker, "Policing Race: The Racial Stratification of Race in Police Traffic Stops," *Criminology* 50 (2012): 993–1024; Rob Voigt et al., "Language from Police Body Camera Footage Shows Racial Disparities in Officer Respect," *PNAS* 114, no. 25 (2017): 6521–26.

23. Monica C. Bell, "Police Reform and the Dismantling of Legal Estrangement," *Yale Law Journal* 126 (2017): 2054–150; see also Joe Soss and Vesla M. Weaver, "Police Are Our Government: Politics, Political Science, and the Policing of Race-Class Subjugated Communities," *Annual Review of Political Science* 20 (2017): 565–91.

24. Bell, "Dismantling Legal Estrangement"; Elliot Currie, *A Peculiar Indifference: The Neglected Toll of Violence on Black America* (New York: Metropolitan Books, 2020).

25. FBI UCR, "Crime in the U.S., 2019," Expanded Homicide Data Table 1, https:// ucr.fbi.gov/crime-in-the-u.s/2019/crime-in-the-u.s.-2019/tables/expanded-homicide -data-table-1.xls (last accessed March 20, 2023).

26. Centers for Disease Control and Prevention, "Leading Causes of Death—Males—Non-Hispanic Black—United States, 2018," https://www.cdc.gov/minorityhealth/lcod /men/2018/nonhispanic-black/index.htm (last updated March 2, 2022).

27. Monica C. Bell, "Situational Trust: How Disadvantaged Mothers Reconceive Legal Cynicism," *Law and Society Review* 50, no. 2 (2016): 314–47; Susan Clampet-Lundquist, Patrick J. Carr, and Maria J. Kefalas, "The Sliding Scale of Snitching: A Qualitative Examination of Snitching in Three Philadelphia Communities," *Sociological Forum* 30, no. 2 (2015): 265–85; John Hagan et al., "Dual-Process Theory of Racial Isolation, Legal Cynicism, and Reported Crime," *Proceedings of the National Academy of Sciences* 115, no. 28 (2018): 7190–99; Lonnie M. Schaible and Lorine A. Hughes, "Neighborhood Disadvantage and Reliance on the Police," *Crime and Delinquency* 58, no. 2 (2012): 245–74.

28. Michael Javen Fortner, *Reconstructing Justice: Race, Generational Divides, and the Fight over "Defund the Police"* (Washington, DC: Niskanen Center, 2020), 33, https://www.niskanencenter.org/wp-content/uploads/2020/10/Reconstructing-Justice-Final.pdf; see also Paige E. Vaughn, Kyle Peyton, and Gregory A. Huber, "Mass Support for Proposals to Reshape Policing Depends on the Implications for Crime and Safety," *Criminology & Public Policy* 21, no. 1 (2022): 125–46.

29. In *Black Silent Majority: The Rockefeller Drug Laws and the Politics of Punishment* (Cambridge, MA: Harvard University Press, 2015), Michael Javen Forner argues that Black advocacy and support drove the establishment of the punitive New York drug laws.

30. Jill Leovy, *Ghettoside: A True Story of Murder in America* (New York: Spiegel & Grau, 2015).

31. See Bell, "Dismantling Legal Estrangement"; Monica C. Bell, "Anti-Segregation Policing," *NYU Law Review* 95, no. 3 (2020): 650–755; Andrea S. Boyles, *You Can't Stop the Revolution: Community Disorder and Social Ties in Post-Ferguson America* (Oakland: University of California Press, 2019).

32. Lisa Miller describes this as "racialized state failure"; see Lisa L. Miller, "Racialized State Failure and the Violent Death of Michael Brown," *Theory and Event* 17, no. 3 (2014), https://muse-jhu-edu.ezp2.lib.umn.edu/pub/1/article/559374. For a comparative account, see Lisa L. Miller, *The Myth of Mob Rule: Violent Crime and Democratic Politics* (Oxford: Oxford University Press, 2018).

33. Currie, *Peculiar Indifference*; see also Ruth D. Peterson and Lauren J. Krivo, *Divergent Social Worlds: Neighborhood Crime and the Racial-Spatial Divide* (New York: Russell Sage Foundation, 2010); Robert J. Sampson, William Julius Wilson, and Hanna Katz, "Reassessing 'Toward a Theory of Race, Crime, and Urban Inequality': Enduring and New Challenges in 21st Century America," *Du Bois Review* 15, no. 1 (2018): 13–34; Patrick Sharkey, *Uneasy Peace: The Great Crime Decline, the Renewal of City Life, and the Next War on Violence* (New York: W. W. Norton, 2018); David Garland, "The Current Crisis of American Criminal Justice: A Structural Analysis," *Annual Review of Criminology* 6 (2023): 43–63.

34. While this term is today understood as a racist dog whistle, it was initially used within the Black community to fight for more protection from intra-community victimization. See James Forman Jr., *Locking Up Our Own: Crime and Punishment in Black America* (New York: Farrar, Straus & Giroux, 2017).

35. Our exceptionalism is not in overall rates of violence but in *lethal* violence, fueled primarily by gun violence. See Kevin R. Reitz, "Introduction," in *American Exceptionalism in Crime and Punishment*, ed. Kevin R. Reitz (New York: Oxford University Press, 2017), 1–52.

36. Lisa L. Miller, *The Perils of Federalism: Race, Poverty, and the Politics of Crime Control* (New York: Oxford Academic, 2008).

37. Paul E. Peterson, *City Limits* (Chicago: University of Chicago Press, 1981).

38. I adopt the "cheap on crime" phrasing from Hadar Aviram's work on the 2008 financial crisis. While the phrase was developed in a different context, it also works well to explain cities' responses to inequality and crime during a longer historical period of fiscal austerity. See Hadar Aviram, *Cheap on Crime: Recession-Era Politics and the Transformation of American Punishment* (Oakland: University of California Press, 2015).

39. John Clegg and Adaner Usmani, "The Economic Origins of Mass Incarceration," *Catalyst* 3, no. 3 (2019).

40. Egon Bittner, *Aspects of Police Work* (Boston: Northeastern University Press, 1990).

41. Weihua Li and Jamiles Lartey, "As Murders Spiked, Police Solved About Half in 2020," *The Marshall Project*, January 12, 2022, https://www.themarshallproject.org/2022/01/12/as-murders-spiked-police-solved-about-half-in-2020.

42. Rory Kramer and Brianna Remster, "The Slow Violence of Contemporary Policing," *Annual Review of Criminology* 5 (2022): 43–66.

43. Sharkey, *Uneasy Peace*.

44. Forman Jr., *Locking Up Our Own*.

45. White elites were also deeply influential in calling for these punitive resources. See, e.g., Katherine Beckett, *Making Crime Pay: Law and Order in Contemporary American Politics* (New York: Oxford University Press, 1999); Jonathan Simon, *Governing through Crime: How the War on Crime Transformed American Democracy and Created a Culture of Fear* (New York: Oxford University Press, 2007).

46. Elizabeth Hinton, Julilly Kohler-Hausmann, and Vesla M. Weaver, "Did Blacks Really Endorse the 1994 Crime Bill?," *New York Times*, April 13, 2016, https://www.nytimes.com/2016/04/13/opinion/did-blacks-really-endorse-the-1994-crime-bill.html.

47. Forman Jr., *Locking Up Our Own*.

48. Keeanga-Yamahtta Taylor, *From #BlackLivesMatter to Black Liberation* (Chicago: Haymarket Books, 2016).

49. Pamela E. Oliver, "Repression and Crime Control: Why Social Movement Scholars Should Pay Attention to Mass Incarceration as a Form of Repression," *Mobilization: An International Quarterly* 13, no. 1 (2008): 1–24; Pamela E. Oliver, "Resisting Repression: The Black Lives Movement in Context," in *Racialized Protest and the State: Resistance and Repression in a Divided America*, ed. Hank Johnston and Pamela Oliver (New York: Routledge, 2020); Hannah L. Walker, *Mobilized by Injustice: Criminal Justice Contact, Political Participation, and Race* (New York: Oxford University Press, 2020).

50. Michelle Alexander, *The New Jim Crow: Mass Incarceration in the Age of Colorblindness* (New York: New Press, 2010).

51. Aurélie Ouss and John Rappaport, "Is Police Behavior Getting Worse? Data Selection and the Measurement of Policing Harms," *Journal of Legal Studies* 49, no. 1 (2020): 153–98.

52. Deva R. Woodly, *Reckoning: Black Lives Matter and the Democratic Necessity of Social Movements* (New York: Oxford University Press, 2021).

53. Oliver, "Resisting Repression"; Barbara Ransby, *Making All Black Lives Matter* (Oakland: University of California Press, 2018); Alvin B. Tillery, "What Kind of Movement Is Black Lives Matter? The View from Twitter," *Journal of Race, Ethnicity and Politics* 4, no. 2 (2019): 297–323.

54. Boyles, *Can't Stop the Revolution*; Jennifer E. Cobbina, *Hands Up, Don't Shoot: Why the Protests in Ferguson and Baltimore Matter, and How They Changed America* (New York: New York University Press, 2019); Vanessa Williamson, Kris-Stella Trump, and Katherine Levine Einstein, "Black Lives Matter: Evidence That Police-Caused Deaths Predict Protest Activity," *Perspectives on Politics* 16, no. 2 (2018): 400–415.

55. For histories of the national movement, see Ransby, *Black Lives Matter*, and Woodly, *Reckoning*.

56. Movement leaders describe this as racial capitalism. See Ransby, *Black Lives Matter*. On racial capitalism and policing, see Michael Javen Fortner, "Racial Capitalism and City Politics: Toward a Theoretical Synthesis," *Urban Affairs Review* 59, no. 2 (2023): 630–53; Robert Vargas, "Postscript: Four Ways Race and Capitalism Can Advance Urban Sociology," *City & Community* 21, no. 3 (2022): 256–62.

57. Woodly, *Reckoning*.

58. See Campaign Zero, "What We Do," https://campaignzero.org/about/what-we-do (last accessed March 23, 2023).

59. See Movement for Black Lives, "The Movement for Black Lives," https://m4bl.org (last accessed March 23, 2023).

60. Mariame Kaba, *We Do This 'til We Free Us: Abolitionist Organizing and Transforming Justice* (Chicago: Haymarket Books, 2021).

61. Author's calculations, using data from Bureau of Justice Statistics, Law Enforcement Management and Administrative Statistics (LEMAS), 2020, https://www.icpsr.umich.edu/web/NACJD/studies/38651#.

62. Jeffery T. Manuel and Andrew Urban, "'You Can't Legislate the Heart': Minneapolis Mayor Charles Stenvig and the Politics of Law and Order," *American Studies* 49, no. 3/4 (2008): 195–219.

63. Deena Winter, "Critics Say Proposed Police Contract Doesn't Rein in Out-of-Control MPD," *Minnesota Reformer*, March 17, 2022, https://minnesotareformer.com/2022/03/17/critics-say-proposed-police-contract-doesnt-rein-in-out-of-control-mpd.

64. Mapping Police Violence Database, https://mappingpoliceviolence.us/cities (last accessed September 25, 2022).

65. See University of Minnesota Libraries, "Mapping Prejudice," https://mappingprejudice.umn.edu (last accessed February 13, 2023).

66. All community demographics reported from the Minnesota Compass website, which summarizes American Community Survey data from 2016 to 2020. Data for North Minneapolis were aggregated for the Near North (https://www.mncompass.org/profiles/city/minneapolis/near-north) and Camden (https://www.mncompass.org/profiles/city/minneapolis/camden) community areas, compared to the city of Minneapolis as a whole (https://www.mncompass.org/profiles/city/minneapolis) (last accessed May 25, 2022).

67. In 2020 the MPD reported eighty-four cases of murder and nonnegligent manslaughter, of which thirty-eight happened in the 4th Precinct (home to just 16 percent of the city's 430,000 residents). Author's calculations, using the

US 2020 Decennial Census and MPD Crime Dashboard, available at: https://www
.minneapolismn.gov/government/government-data/datasource/crime-dashboard
(last accessed March 20, 2023).

68. Philip Goodman, Joshua Page, and Michelle Phelps, *Breaking the Pendulum: The Long Struggle over Criminal Justice* (New York: Oxford University Press, 2017).

69. Balto and Felkor-Cantor, "Police and Crime." On how police cultivate and filter citizen demands, see Tony Cheng, *The Policing Machine: Enforcement, Endorsements, and the Illusion of Public Input* (Chicago: University of Chicago Press, 2024).

70. Bowling, Reiner, and Sheptycki's classic Britain-centric text uses "the politics of the police" to refer to the totality of scholarship on policing, including the functions and effects of police, policing history, policing in different political arrangements (e.g., democratic vs. authoritarian policing), police oversight and accountability mechanisms, private policing, cop culture, etc. See Benjamin Bowling, Robert Reiner, and James W. E. Sheptycki, *The Politics of Police*, 5th ed. (New York: Oxford University Press, 2019). I use the phrase "the politics of policing" more narrowly to refer to the set of actors and institutions that shape how a municipal police force operates in a specific time and place. For a contemporary example of the contentious racial politics of policing in another US city (Chicago), see Jan Doering, *Us versus Them: Race, Crime, and Gentrification in Chicago Neighborhoods* (New York: Oxford University Press, 2020).

71. For a critical account of the role of the media in shaping perceptions of crime, see Stuart Hall, Chas Critcher, Tony Jefferson, John Clarke, and Brian Roberts, *Policing the Crisis: Mugging, the State, and Law & Order* (London: Palgrave Macmillan, 2017).

72. Woodly, *Reckoning*. See also Danielle K. Brown and Rachel Mourão, "No Reckoning for the Right: How Political Ideology, Protest Tolerance and News Consumption Affect Support Black Lives Matter Protests," *Political Communication* 39, no. 6 (2022), 737–54.

73. For more on the emergent case study method, see "Author's Note."

74. I note in the text whether quotes are from the interviews conducted by my team or reporters. For quotes from public records, the original source is noted in endnotes. On digital ethnography, see Jeffrey Lane and Jessa Lingel, "Digital Ethnography for Sociology: Craft, Rigor, and Creativity," *Qualitative Sociology* 45 (2022): 319–26.

75. Riffing off Nina Simone's iconic song, several artists described George Floyd's murder and its aftermath with the elegy "Minnesota Goddamn." See, e.g., Louise Erdrich, *The Sentence* (New York: Harper Collins Publishers, 2021); MONICO, "MINNESOTA GODDAMN," https://www.youtube.com/watch?v=Pdl9qovl91A (last accessed March 22, 2023).

Chapter One

1. Samuel L. Myers Jr., "The Minnesota Paradox," in *Sparked: George Floyd, Racism, and the Progressive Illusion*, ed. Walter L. Jacobs (St. Paul: Minnesota Historical Society Press, 2021).

2. Christopher Ingraham, "Racial Inequality in Minneapolis Is among the Worst in the Nation," *Washington Post*, May 30, 2020, https://www.washingtonpost.com /business/2020/05/30/minneapolis-racial-inequality.

3. Another way to summarize their results was that while Black residents comprised only 19 percent of the city's population, they represented nearly 60 percent of those arrested. Native American residents represented just 2 percent of the city's population but 6 percent of arrests. See American Civil Liberties Union, *Picking Up the Pieces: A Minneapolis Case Study*, Report, 2015, https://www.aclu.org/issues/racial -justice/race-and-criminal-justice/picking-pieces.

4. Richard A. Oppel Jr. and Lazaro Gaio, "Minneapolis Police Use Force against Black People at 7 Times the Rate of Whites," *New York Times*, June 3, 2020, https:// www.nytimes.com/interactive/2020/06/03/us/minneapolis-police-use-of-force.html.

5. Andy Mannix, "Gunfire Disproportionately Claiming Black Victims in Minneapolis, New Data Show," *Star Tribune*, August 12, 2022, https://www.startribune .com/gunfire-disproportionately-claiming-black-victims-in-minneapolis-new-data -show/600197896.

6. Thomas D. Peacock and Donald R. Day, "Nations within a Nation: The Dakota and Ojibwe of Minnesota," *Daedalus* 129, no. 3 (2000): 137–59.

7. In addition, white landowners in Minnesota invited their Southern counterparts to buy land and support businesses in the North Star State, creating financial entanglements between the Midwest and South that benefited white landowners in both regions in the period. See Christopher P. Lehman, *Slavery's Reach: Southern Slaveholders in the North Star State* (St. Paul: Minnesota Historical Society Press, 2019).

8. Lincoln Steffens, "The Shame of Minneapolis: The Ruin and Redemption of a City That Was Sold Out," *McClure's Magazine*, January 1903, 9.

9. Isaac Atwater, *History of the City of Minneapolis* (New York: Munsell, 1893), 3, 887, 1000; see also Augustine E. Costello, *History of the Fire and Police Departments of Minneapolis* (Minneapolis: Relief Association Publishing Co., 1890).

10. Robert M. Fogelson, *Big-City Police* (Boston: Harvard University Press, 1977), 112.

11. Iric Nathanson, *Minneapolis in the Twentieth Century: The Growth of an American City* (St. Paul: Minnesota Historical Society Press, 2010). In Northeastern cities, early police forces were often run by local aldermen. Part of the early wave of professionalizing reforms was to consolidate police power at the municipal level. See Fogelson, *Big-City Police*. Today it is typical for city police departments to be overseen by either the mayor or a city manager. Some cities also appoint a board of commissioners to determine department policies.

12. Costello, *History of Minneapolis*, 316.

13. Costello, *History of Minneapolis*, 314.

14. For example, in 1887, during Ames's third term, the Minnesota Legislature would wrestle control of the MPD away from Ames, who had appointed his lackeys (or "crooks" in the terms of his opponents) as the department's officers, putting the department in the hands of a new Board of Police Commissioners. The new structure was abolished just three years later.

15. Erik Rivenes, *Dirty Doc Ames and the Scandal That Shook Minneapolis* (St. Paul: Minnesota Historical Society Press, 2018).

16. Steffens, "Shame of Minneapolis," 9.

17. Matthew Frye Jacobson, *Whiteness of a Different Color: European Immigrants and the Alchemy of Race* (Cambridge, MA: Harvard University Press, 1998); see also David R. Roediger, *The Wages of Whiteness: Race and the Making of the*

American Working Class (New York: Verso Books, 2007). Note that many Progressive Era reformers also supported eugenics, a part of the movement seemingly forgotten in twenty-first century invocations of the "progressive" label, designed to signify more radical commitment in contrast to the term's 1990s precursor, "liberal." See, e.g., Thomas C. Leonard, *Illiberal Reformers: Race, Eugenics, and American Economics in the Progressive Era* (Princeton, NJ: Princeton University Press, 2016).

18. Fogelson, *Big-City Police.*

19. National Commission on Law Observance and Enforcement, "Wickersham Report on Police," *American Journal of Police Science* 2, no. 4 (1931): 344.

20. Sarah A. Seo, *Policing the Open Road: How Cars Transformed American Freedom* (Cambridge, MA: Harvard University Press, 2019).

21. David Thacher and Jessica Gillooly, "How the Public Became the Caller: The Emergence of Reactive Policing, 1880–1970" (conference presentation, Law and Society Association, June 1–4, 2023).

22. Michael J. Lansing, "From Wheat to Wheaties: Minneapolis, the Great Plains, and the Transformation of American Food," in *The Greater Plains: Rethinking a Region's Environmental Histories*, ed. B. Frehner and K. A. Brosnan (Lincoln: University of Nebraska Press, 2021).

23. Michael Fossum, *History of the Minneapolis Police Department* (Minneapolis: n.p., 1996).

24. For more on the strike, see William Millikan, "Maintaining 'Law and Order': The Minneapolis Citizen's Alliance in the 1920s," *Minnesota History* 51, no. 6 (1989): 219–33; Charles Rumford Walker, *American City: A Rank-and-File History of Minneapolis* (New York: Farrar & Rinehart, 1937); Tom Weber, *Minneapolis: An Urban Biography* (St. Paul: Minnesota Historical Society Press, 2020).

25. Nathanson, *Minneapolis in the Twentieth Century*, 90.

26. Quoted in Nathanson, *Minneapolis in the Twentieth Century*, 84.

27. Fossum, *History of Minneapolis Police*, 13.

28. Jennifer Delton, *Making Minnesota Liberal: Civil Rights and the Transformation of the Democratic Party* (Minneapolis: University of Minnesota Press, 2002), 61.

29. Delton, *Making Minnesota Liberal.*

30. Humbert H. Humphrey, *The Education of a Public Man: My Life and Politics* (Minneapolis: University of Minnesota Press, 1976), 94, cited in Nathanson, *Minneapolis in the Twentieth Century*, 60–61.

31. Delton, *Making Minnesota Liberal*; see also Samuel G. Freedman, *Into the Bright Sunshine: Young Hubert Humphrey and the Fight for Civil Rights* (New York: Oxford University Press, 2023).

32. Michael Brenes, "Police Reform Doesn't Work," *Boston Review*, April 26, 2021, https://www.bostonreview.net/articles/police-reform-doesnt-work.

33. Michael J. Lansing, "Policing Politics: Labor, Race, and the Police Officers Federation of Minneapolis, 1945–1972," *Minnesota History* 67, no. 5 (2021): 226–38.

34. Lansing, "Policing Politics." On similar claims made by the Los Angeles Police Department on staffing rates, see Max Felker-Kantor, *Policing Los Angeles: Race, Resistance, and the Rise of the LAPD* (Chapel Hill: University of North Carolina Press, 2018), 21.

35. David Vassar Taylor, *African Americans in Minnesota* (St. Paul: Minnesota Historical Society Press, 2002), 51. On the Great Migration more broadly, see Isabel Wilkerson, *The Warmth of Other Suns: The Epic Story of America's Great Migration* (New York: Vintage Books, 2010).

36. Rose Helper, *Racial Policies and Practices of Real Estate Brokers* (Minneapolis: University of Minnesota Press, 1969); see also https://mappingprejudice.umn.edu (last accessed February 13, 2023).

37. Richard Rothstein, *The Color of Law: A Forgotten History of How Our Government Segregated America* (New York: Liveright, 2017).

38. Human Toll: A Public History of 35W, https://humantoll35w.org (last accessed May 30, 2023).

39. Taylor, *African Americans in Minnesota*; Kirsten Delegard and Michael J. Lansing, "Prince and the Making of Minneapolis Mystique," *Middle West Review* 5, no. 1 (2018): 1–24.

40. Lansing, "Policing Politics," 230.

41. David Hugill, *Settler Colonial City: Racism and Inequity in Postwar Minneapolis* (Minneapolis: University of Minnesota Press, 2021).

42. Lansing, "Policing Politics," 8. The Minneapolis NAACP chapter was founded in 1914 and had been fighting against racist violence for decades by the 1960s, including protests in 1922 following a beating meted out by MPD officers. Those protests happened against the backdrop of the Ku Klux Klan attempting a revival and opening chapters in Minnesota. See Kirsten Delegard, "'A Demand for Justice and Law Enforcement': A History of Police and the Near North Side," *The Historyapolis Project*, November 30, 2015, http://historyapolis.com/blog/2015/11/20/a-demand-for-justice-and-law-enforcement-a-history-of-police-and-the-near-north-side.

43. Frank Premack, "Mayor Denies Any Serious Race Bias among Policemen," *Minneapolis Morning Tribune*, June 19, 1963, 1, cited in Lansing, "Policing Politics," 238.

44. MPD150, "Enough Is Enough," 74.

45. US Commission on Civil Rights, "Report on Police-Community Relations in Minneapolis and St. Paul," 1965, 6.

46. Elizabeth Hinton, *America on Fire: The Untold History of Police Violence and Black Rebellion since the 1960s* (New York: Liveright, 2021).

47. Sarah Jayne Paulsen, "Black Power and Neighborhood Organizing in Minneapolis, Minnesota: The Way Community Center, 1966–1971" (master's thesis, University of South Carolina, 2018), https://scholarcommons.sc.edu/etd/4793.

48. Nathanson, *Minneapolis in the Twentieth Century*.

49. Jelani Cobb, ed., *The Essential Kerner Commission Report* (New York: W. W. Norton, 2021), 8.

50. Cobb, *Essential Kerner Commission Report*, 7.

51. Andrea M. Headley and James E. Wright II, "National Police Reform Commissions: Evidence-Based Practices or Unfulfilled Promises?," *Review of Black Political Economy* 46, no. 4 (2019): 277–305.

52. Hinton, *America on Fire*.

53. The term "ghetto" initially referred to the segregated neighborhoods of European Jews, but later the term came to refer to hyper-segregated, low-income, predominantly Black neighborhoods. See Mitchell Duneier, *Ghetto: The Invention of a Place, the History of an Idea* (New York: Farrar, Straus & Giroux, 2016).

54. Robert J. Sampson, William Julius Wilson, and Hanna Katz, "Reassessing 'Toward a Theory of Race, Crime, and Urban Inequality': Enduring and New Challenges in 21st Century America," *Du Bois Review* 15, no. 1 (2018): 13–34.

55. Khalil Gibran Muhammad, *The Condemnation of Blackness: Race, Crime, and the Making of Modern America* (Cambridge, MA: Harvard University Press, 2011).

56. John Clegg and Adaner Usmani, "The Economic Origins of Mass Incarceration," *Catalyst* 3, no. 3 (2019).

57. Bruce Western, *Punishment and Inequality in America* (New York: Russell Sage Foundation, 2007); Reuben Jonathan Miller, *Halfway Home: Race, Punishment, and the Afterlife of Mass Incarceration* (New York: Little, Brown, 2021).

58. Pamela E. Oliver, "Repression and Crime Control: Why Social Movement Scholars Should Pay Attention to Mass Incarceration as a Form of Repression," *Mobilization: An International Quarterly* 13, no. 1 (2008): 1–24; Pamela E. Oliver, "Introduction: Black Lives Matter in Context," *Mobilization: An International Quarterly* 26, no. 4 (2021): 391–99.

59. Brenes, "Police Reform Doesn't Work."

60. Lansing, "Policing Politics."

61. Nathanson, *Minneapolis in the Twentieth Century.*

62. Jeffery T. Manuel and Andrew Urban, "'You Can't Legislate the Heart': Minneapolis Mayor Charles Stenvig and the Politics of Law and Order," *American Studies* 49, no. 3/4 (2008): 195–219. Francis "Frank" Rizzo ran a similar (and more high-profile) campaign in Philadelphia. See Timothy J. Lombardo, *Blue-Collar Conservatism: Frank Rizzo's Philadelphia and Populist Politics* (Philadelphia: University of Pennsylvania Press, 2018).

63. Manuel and Urban, "Legislate the Heart."

64. Kirsten Swanson, "How a 1971 Arrest Laid the Groundwork for the State Investigation into Minneapolis Police," KTSP, July 27, 2022, https://kstp.com/5-investigates/how-a-1971-arrest-laid-the-groundwork-for-the-state-investigation-into-minneapolis-police.

65. Paulsen, "Black Power." See also Hugill, *Settler Colonial City.*

66. As James Forman Jr. writes in *Locking Up Our Own: Crime and Punishment in Black America* (New York: Farrar, Straus & Giroux, 2017), these kinds of interventions across the country were framed as a "Marshall Plan" for Black America, riffing off the plan to rebuild Europe in the wake of world war. In 1967 Senator Humphrey would make the same call for the Marshall Plan for cities in the run-up to declaring his intention to enter the presidential race. See Nathanson, *Minneapolis in the Twentieth Century,* 120–30.

67. Delegard and Lansing, "Prince Minneapolis Mystique," 1–24.

68. "A Police State: Episode 1, 1975," Overpoliced & Underprotected in MSP and Twin Cities Public Television, 2022, https://www.overpolicedmsp.org/documentary.

69. Quoted in Nelson Oramas, "Drug Enforcement in Minority Communities: The Minneapolis Police Department, 1985–1990" (Washington, DC: Police Executive Research Forum, 1994), 7. On the concept of the "asshole" and its role in policing, see John Van Maanen, "The Asshole," in *Policing: A View from the Street,* ed. Peter K. Manning and John Van Maanen (Santa Monica, CA: Goodyear Publishing, 1978), 221–37.

70. Will Cooley, "Minneapolis: The Rise of the 'Thumpers,'" *The Nation,* June 1, 2020, https://www.thenation.com/article/society/minneapolis-police-brutality-racism.

71. On police militarization, see Peter B. Kraska, *Militarizing the American Criminal Justice System: The Changing Role of the Armed Forces and the Police* (Boston: Northeastern University Press, 2001); Radley Balko, *Rise of the Warrior Cop: The Militarization of America's Police Forces* (New York: Public Affairs, 2014); Stuart Schrader, *Badges without Borders: How Global Counterinsurgency Transformed American Policing* (Berkeley: University of California Press, 2019).

72. Karen Mills, "City Image Tarnished by Allegations of Police Racism," Associated Press, March 21, 1989, https://apnews.com/article/962eed0dea6d4ccdadbbe151564 b7413.

73. Oramas, "Drug Enforcement," 7.

74. Cooley, "Rise of the 'Thumpers.'"

75. See the "Minneapolis: Civilian Review" section in Human Rights Watch, "Shielded from Justice: Police Brutality and Accountability in the United States," 1998, https://www.hrw.org/legacy/reports98/police/uspo87.htm.

76. Human Rights Watch, "Shielded from Justice."

77. Author's calculations, using data from Bureau of Justice Statistics (BJS), Law Enforcement Management and Administrative Statistics (LEMAS), 1990, https://www.icpsr.umich.edu/web/NACJD/series/92.

78. Oramas, "Drug Enforcement," 24.

79. Art Hughes, "'Officer Down': Remembering Jerry Haaf," Minnesota Public Radio, September 25, 2002, http://news.minnesota.publicradio.org/features/200209 /25_hughesa_haaf.

80. According to local lore, the moniker was coined by a gun-shop owner who sold "Murderapolis" T-shirts.

81. Homicide totals generated from the Federal Bureau of Investigation, Crime Data Explorer, available at https://cde.ucr.cjis.gov (v. 23.4.1).

82. Author's calculations, using BJS LEMAS, 1997, https://www.icpsr.umich.edu /web/NACJD/series/92.

83. Michelle Alexander, *The New Jim Crow: Mass Incarceration in the Age of Colorblindness* (New York: New Press, 2010).

84. On the role of sexual policing of women in fueling gentrification, see Anne Gray Fischer, *The Streets Belong to Us: Sex, Race, and Police Power from Segregation to Gentrification* (Chapel Hill: University of North Carolina Press, 2022).

85. On the role of police in maintaining racial segregation and fueling urban growth, see Daanika Gordon, *Policing the Racial Divide: Urban Growth Politics and the Remaking of Segregation* (New York: New York University Press, 2022).

86. Libor Jany, "Minneapolis Chief Open to Revisiting 2003 Agreement to Improve Police-Community Relations," *Star Tribune*, October 18, 2017, https://www .startribune.com/minneapolis-chief-open-to-revisiting-agreement-to-improve-police -community-relations/451524163.

87. Laura Collins, "Minneapolis Police Union Chief . . . Accused of Being Racist," *Daily Mail*, June 10, 2020, https://www.dailymail.co.uk/news/article-8399211/Minneapolis -Police-Union-Chief-accused-racism-2007-lawsuit-brought-five-officers.html.

88. Tim Nelson, "Gang Strike Force Victims Reach $3M Settlement," *MPR News*, August 25, 2010, https://www.mprnews.org/story/2010/08/25/strike-force -settlement; Randy Furst, "Payouts Reveal Brutal, Rogue Metro Gang Strike Force,"

Star Tribune, August 5, 2012, https://www.startribune.com/payouts-reveal-brutal-rogue-metro-gang-strike-force/165028086.

89. Unusual for its time, Smith's fatal encounter was captured fully on video through the YMCA's surveillance footage and a pen camera one of the officers carried on his uniform. See Neena Satija, "How Minneapolis Police Handled the In-Custody Death of a Black Man 10 Years before George Floyd," *Washington Post*, August 29, 2020, https://www.washingtonpost.com/investigations/2020/08/29/david-smith-death-minneapolis-police-kneeling.

90. Satija, "How Minneapolis Police Handled."

91. Federal Bureau of Investigation, Crime Data Explorer.

92. Author's calculations, using BJS LEMAS, 2016. Note that by 2016 the gap between the authorized force size (862) versus payroll totals (841) had widened, leading to a staffing ratio of 2.1 per 1,000 residents on the books, but 2.0 in practice.

93. In 2013 the chief asked the Office of Justice Programs' Diagnostic Center to provide reform recommendations. One of its suggestions was to improve the disciplinary system, including implementing an early intervention system for officers—another reform suggestion that would return in 2020, with the department seeming to have made little progress in the intervening years. See Office of Justice Programs, Office of Juvenile Justice and Delinquency Prevention, "Diagnostic Analysis of Minneapolis Police Department, MN: Opportunities for Evidence-Based Technical Assistance," US Department of Justice, January 2015.

94. Later investigations by Franklin's family argued that the SWAT officers who killed Franklin had orchestrated a cover-up of an execution. See Mike Padden, *The Minneapolis Police Department: Blue Code of Silence: The True Story of the Terrance Franklin Murder* (independently published, 2020).

95. Betsy Hodges, "As Mayor of Minneapolis, I Saw How White Liberals Block Change," *New York Times*, July 9, 2020, https://www.nytimes.com/2020/07/09/opinion/minneapolis-hodges-racism.html.

Chapter Two

1. Hennepin County Attorney's Office, "Freeman Declines Charges in Clark Shooting," 2016, https://www.hennepinattorney.org/news/news/2016/March/cao-clark-decision-3-30-2016.

2. Adding injury to this case, the lot that precinct was built on had previously housed a beloved community center. See Sarah Jayne Paulsen, "Black Power and Neighborhood Organizing in Minneapolis, Minnesota: The Way Community Center, 1966–1971" (master's thesis, University of South Carolina, 2018), https://scholarcommons.sc.edu/etd/4793.

3. Department of Justice, "Federal Officials Decline Prosecution in the Death of Jamar Clark," 2016, https://www.justice.gov/opa/pr/federal-officials-decline-prosecution-death-jamar-clark.

4. Libor Jany, "Minneapolis City Council Trims Police Budget Increase to Fund Anti-Violence Efforts," *Star Tribune*, November 30, 2018, https://www.startribune.com/minneapolis-council-trims-police-budget-increase-to-fund-anti-violence-efforts/501681431.

5. Some of the material in chapter 2 was previously published in Michelle S. Phelps, Anneliese Ward, and Dwjuan Frazier, "From Police Reform to Police Abolition? How Minneapolis Activists Fought to Make Black Lives Matter," *Mobilization: An International Quarterly* 26, no. 4 (2021): 421–41.

6. Kellie Carter Jackson, *Force and Freedom: Black Abolitionists and the Politics of Violence* (Philadelphia: University of Pennsylvania Press, 2019).

7. Louise Seamster and Victor Ray, "Against Teleology in the Study of Race: Toward the Abolition of the Progress Paradigm," *Sociological Theory* 36, no. 4 (2018): 315–42. In this respect, racial justice struggles look much like change and contestation in criminal justice practices. See Philip Goodman, Joshua Page, and Michelle Phelps, *Breaking the Pendulum: The Long Struggle over Criminal Justice* (New York: Oxford University Press, 2017).

8. Social movements represent "collective, organized, sustained, and noninstitutional challenge to authorities, power-holders, or cultural beliefs and practices." See Jeff Goodwin and James M. Jasper, eds., *The Social Movements Reader: Cases and Concepts* (Malden, MA: Wiley Blackwell, 2015), 4–5.

9. Aldon D. Morris, *The Origins of the Civil Rights Movement: Black Communities Organizing for Change* (New York: Free Press, 1984).

10. Sidney Tarrow, *Power in Movement: Social Movements and Contentious Politics*, 3rd ed. (New York: Cambridge University Press, 2011), 220.

11. Glenn E. Bracey II, "Black Movements Need Black Theorizing: Exposing Implicit Whiteness in Political Process Theory," *Sociological Focus* 49, no. 1 (2016): 11–27; Elizabeth Hinton, *America on Fire: The Untold History of Police Violence and Black Rebellion since the 1960s* (New York: Liveright, 2021).

12. Joshua Bloom and Waldo E. Martin Jr., *Black against Empire: The History and Politics of the Black Panther Party* (Oakland: University of California Press, 2016).

13. Verta Taylor describes these as periods of "abeyance." See "Social Movement Continuity: The Women's Movement in Abeyance," *American Journal of Sociology* 54, no. 5 (1989): 761–75. For more on the precursors to the BLM movement, see Pamela E. Oliver, "Resisting Repression: The Black Lives Movement in Context," in *Racialized Protest and the State: Resistance and Repression in a Divided America*, ed. Hank Johnston and Pamela Oliver (New York: Routledge, 2020); Barbara Ransby, *Making All Black Lives Matter* (Oakland: University of California Press, 2018).

14. Michelle Alexander, *The New Jim Crow: Mass Incarceration in the Age of Colorblindness* (New York: New Press, 2010).

15. See, e.g., the Abolitions Conference, organized by Tanya Golash-Boza and Whitney Pirtle, May 2023. A description of the conference's focus on abolitions can be found at https://sites.google.com/view/abolitions (last accessed April 5, 2023).

16. Patrick Sharkey, Keeanga-Yamahtta Taylor, and Yaryna Serkez, "The Gaps between White and Black America, in Charts," *New York Times,* June 19, 2020, https://www.nytimes.com/interactive/2020/06/19/opinion/politics/opportunity-gaps-race-inequality.html.

17. These decisions were tied in part to inconsistent eyewitness testimony about Brown's final moments. See US Department of Justice, "Department of Justice Report Regarding the Criminal Investigation into the Shooting Death of Michael Brown by Ferguson, Missouri Police Officer Darren Wilson," Report, 2015, https://www.justice

.gov/sites/default/files/opa/press-releases/attachments/2015/03/04/doj_report_on _shooting_of_michael_brown_1.pdf.

18. Keeanga-Yamahtta Taylor, *From #BlackLivesMatter to Black Liberation* (Chicago: Haymarket Books, 2016); Chloe N. Thurston, "Black Lives Matter, American Political Development, and the Politics of Visibility," *Politics, Groups, and Identities* 6, no. 1 (2018): 162–70; Allissa V. Richardson, *Bearing Witness while Black: African Americans, Smartphones, and the New Protest #Journalism* (New York: Oxford University Press, 2020). On the goals of radical movement discourse, see Myra Marx Ferree, "Resonance and Radicalism: Feminist Framing in the Abortion Debates of the United States and Germany," *American Journal of Sociology* 109, no. 2 (2003): 304–44.

19. Robin D. G. Kelley, *Freedom Dreams: The Black Radical Imagination* (Boston: Beacon Press, 2022). This kind of radical imagination, scholars posit, is one of the most important challenges activists can make to the status quo. See also Iris Marion Young, "Activist Challenges to Deliberative Democracy," *Political Theory* 29, no. 5 (2001): 670–90.

20. On the role of Black women in freedom struggles, see Treva B. Lindsey, *America, Goddam: Violence, Black Women, and the Struggle for Justice* (Oakland: University of California Press, 2022).

21. Ransby, *Making All Black Lives Matter.*

22. Deva R. Woodly, *Reckoning: Black Lives Matter and the Democratic Necessity of Social Movements* (New York: Oxford University Press, 2021), 161. *Reckoning* draws on Woodly's earlier work on how social movements reshape common sense. See Deva R. Woodly, *The Politics of Common Sense: How Social Movements Use Public Discourse to Change Politics and Win Acceptance* (New York: Oxford University Press, 2015).

23. Clarissa Rile Hayward, "Disruption: What Is It Good For?," *Journal of Politics* 82, no. 2 (2020): 448–59; Daniel Q. Gillion, *The Loud Minority: Why Protests Matter in American Democracy* (Princeton, NJ: Princeton University Press, 2020).

24. Woodly, *Reckoning,* 166–67.

25. Enid Logan, "Anger Management," *RSA Journal* 162, no. 5566 (2016): 26–29.

26. Ransby, *Making All Black Lives Matter,* 124.

27. Randy Furst, "Michelle Gross and the Minnesota Group She Leads Seek to Hold Police Accountable," *Star Tribune,* February 23, 2022, https://www.startribune .com/a-survivor-herself-michelle-gross-and-the-group-she-leads-seek-to-hold-bad -cops-accountable/600148717.

28. This text is from the coalition's description on a local resource page. See Resist Twin Cities, "Twin Cities Coalition for Justice 4 Jamar," https://resisttwincities.org /listing/united-states/minnesota/minneapolis/organization/twin-cities-coalition-for -justice-4-jamar (last accessed September 24, 2022).

29. See also Aleshia Faust et al., "Black Lives Matter and the Movement for Black Lives," in *Social Movements, 1768–2018,* 4th ed., ed. Charles Tilly, Ernesto Castañeda, and Lesley J. Wood (New York: Routledge, 2019).

30. Hennepin County Attorney's Office, "Clark Shooting."

31. MPR News Staff, "Mpls. Police: Internal Probe Clears Cops in Jamar Clark Shooting," *MPR News,* October 21, 2016, https://www.mprnews.org/story/2016/10/21 /jamar-clark-minneapolis-police-shooting-internal-investigation.

32. Ricardo Lopez, "How Gov. Dayton Got to His Statement on Race after Philando Castile Was Shot," July 17, 2016, https://www.startribune.com/how-dayton-got-to-his-statement-on-race-after-castile-was-shot/387094161.

33. Steven W. Thrasher, "Police Hunt and Kill Black People Like Philando Castile. There's No Justice," *The Guardian*, June 19, 2017, https://www.theguardian.com/commentisfree/2017/jun/19/philando-castile-police-violence-black-americans.

34. Pat Pheifer, "Settlement for Philando Castile's Girlfriend Will Be $800K," *Star Tribune*, November 29, 2017, https://www.startribune.com/st-anthony-council-discusses-settlement-with-castile-s-girlfriend/460640413.

35. Mitch Smith, "Minneapolis Police Chief Forced Out after Fatal Shooting of Australian Woman," *New York Times*, July 21, 2017, https://www.nytimes.com/2017/07/21/us/minneapolis-police-chief-resigns-days-after-officer-fatally-shot-a-woman.html.

36. His sentence was later reduced to five years after the Minnesota Supreme Court overturned the third-degree murder conviction. See Jon Collins and Matt Sepic, "Ex-Cop Noor Set for June Release after Resentence in Ruszczyk Killing," *MPR News*, October 21, 2021, https://www.mprnews.org/story/2021/10/21/judge-sentence-noor-in-killing-of-justine-ruszczyk.

37. Andy Mannix, "Minneapolis Agrees to Pay $20 Million in Death of Justine Ruszczyk Damond," May 4, 2019, https://www.startribune.com/minneapolis-agrees-to-pay-20-million-in-fatal-police-shooting-of-justine-ruszczyk-damond/509438812.

38. Hennepin County Attorney's Office, "No Charges against Police in Shooting Death of Marquez-Heraldes," 2016, https://www.hennepinattorney.org/news/news/2016/november/cao-marquez-heraldes-11-7-2016.

39. Hennepin County Attorney's Office, "No Charges against Police in North Minneapolis Fatal Shooting," 2020, https://www.hennepinattorney.org/news/news/2020/december/vue-case-12-21-2020.

40. See Jocelyn Fontaine et al., "Updated: Views of the Police and Neighborhood Conditions: Evidence of Change in Six Cities Participating in the National Initiative for Building Community Trust and Justice" (Washington, DC: Urban Institute, 2019), https://www.urban.org/research/publication/updated-views-police-and-neighborhood-conditions; Daniel S. Lawrence et al., "Impact of the National Initiative for Building Community Trust and Justice on Police Administrative Outcomes" (Washington, DC: Urban Institute, 2019), https://www.urban.org/sites/default/files/publication/100707/impact_of_the_national_initiative_for_building_community_trust_and_justice_on_police_administrative_outcomes_2.pdf; Jesse Jannetta et al., "Learning to Build Police-Community Trust: Implementation Assessment Findings from the Evaluation of the National Initiative for Building Community Trust and Justice" (Washington, DC: Urban Institute, 2019), https://www.urban.org/research/publication/learning-build-police-community-trust.

41. John Eligon and Mitch Smith, "Woman Shot by Minneapolis Officer 'Didn't Have to Die,'" Police Chief Says," *New York Times*, June 20, 2017, https://www.nytimes.com/2017/07/20/us/police-shooting-minneapolis-body-cameras.html.

42. Jannetta et al., "Community Trust and Justice," 25.

43. Fontaine et al., "Police and Neighborhood Conditions," 21.

44. Lawrence et al., "Police Administrative Outcomes."

45. Both the *Star Tribune*'s police-involved deaths database (which focuses only on deaths from direct physical force used by officers) and CUAPB's "Stolen Lives" records (which also includes deaths in custody and fatalities during vehicular chases) indicate that police killings in Minneapolis were somewhat higher in the mid-2000s compared to the 2010s. But between 2015 and 2019, neither shows measurable improvement.

46. Jesse Jannetta, "It Wasn't Enough: The Limits of Police-Community Trust-Building Reform in Minneapolis," in Urban Institute, *Urban Wire*, 2020, https://www .urban.org/urban-wire/it-wasnt-enough-limits-police-community-trust-building -reform-minneapolis.

47. Travis Campbell, "Black Lives Matter's Effect on Police Lethal Use-of-Force," Working Paper, 2021, https://doi.org/10.2139/ssrn.3767097.

48. Woodly, *Reckoning*; Samuel Sinyangwe, "Police Are Killing Fewer People in Big Cities, but More in Suburban and Rural America," *FiveThirtyEight*, June 1, 2020, https://fivethirtyeight.com/features/police-are-killing-fewer-people-in-big-cities-but -more-in-suburban-and-rural-america.

49. See, e.g., Stephen A. Crockett Jr., "Head of Minneapolis Police Union: 'Black Lives Matter Is a Terrorist Organization,'" *The Root*, June 2, 2016, https://www.theroot .com/head-of-minneapolis-police-union-black-lives-matter-i-1790855508.

50. Randy Furst, "Mayor Hodges Blasts 'Jackass Remarks' by Police Union Chief over Lynx Police Walkout," *Star Tribune*, July 13, 2016, https://www.startribune .com/minneapolis-police-chief-criticizes-officers-for-walking-off-job-at-lynx-game /386506061.

51. Jennifer Bjorhus and MaryJo Webster, "Convicted, but Still Policing," *Star Tribune*, October 1, 2017, https://www.startribune.com/convicted-of-serious-crimes-but -still-on-the-beat/437687453.

52. CBS Minnesota Staff, "'Body-Worn Cameras Must Be On': Mpls. Officials Announce MPD Policy Changes," CBS Minnesota, 2017, https://minnesota.cbslocal .com/2017/07/26/mpls-body-cam-policy-changes.

53. The mayor tepidly countered, telling reporters that officers could be disciplined for training that conflicted with MPD policy. But Kroll and his union had clearly won this round. See "Police Union Defies Mpls. Mayor, Offers Free 'Warrior' Training," KARE, April 24, 2019, https://www.kare11.com/article/news/police-union -defies-mpls-mayor-offers-free-warrior-training/89-4cc14458-a471-47c5-8f80 -8f2b2386bc3e.

54. One point of tension was that the chief was on vacation, hiking in the mountains, and did not immediately return to Minneapolis. From there, things went from bad to worse. An after-action report by the Department of Justice would show that power struggles between the chief and mayor hindered an effective response. See Frank Straub et al., "Maintaining First Amendment Rights and Public Safety in North Minneapolis" (Washington, DC: US Department of Justice's Office of Community Oriented Policing Services, 2017), https://cops.usdoj.gov/ric/Publications/cops -w0836-pub.pdf.

55. Peter Callaghan, "Hodges and Her Discontents: A Guide to the Five Contenders in the Minneapolis Mayor's Race," *MinnPost*, October 30, 2017, https://www .minnpost.com/politics-policy/2017/10/hodges-and-her-discontents-guide-five -contenders-minneapolis-mayors-race.

56. Camille J. Gage, "Swaggerapolis: Is It What We Really Need?" *Medium*, October 11, 2017, https://camillejgage.medium.com/swaggerapolis-is-it-what-we-really-need-fbb0ccc89620.

57. Michelle Ruiz, "'This Is a Time That Changed Me Forever': Inside the Political Debut of Minneapolis Mayor Jacob Frey," *Vogue*, January 31, 2022, https://www.vogue.com/article/minneapolis-mayor-jacob-frey-profile.

58. Adam Belz, "Police Reform Debate Surges in Minneapolis Mayoral Race after Justine Damond Shooting," *Star Tribune*, July 25, 2017, https://www.startribune.com/police-reform-debate-surges-in-minneapolis-mayoral-race-after-justine-damond-shooting/436615103.

59. Cody Nelson, "Levy-Pounds Announces She's Running for MPLS. Mayor," *MPR News*, November 15, 2016, https://www.mprnews.org/story/2016/11/14/nekima-levy-pounds-minneapolis-mayor-run.

60. Pollen Midwest, "2017 MPLS Voter Guide," 2017, https://www.pollenmidwest.org/voter-guide.

61. Emma Nelson and Adam Belz, "Downtown Minneapolis Groups Criticize Candidates Who Said They Could Envision a City without Police," *Star Tribune*, October 5, 2017, https://www.startribune.com/downtown-minneapolis-groups-criticize-candidates-who-said-they-could-envision-a-city-without-police/449647563.

62. City of Minneapolis, "2017 Election Results," last updated October 16, 2020, https://vote.minneapolismn.gov/results-data/election-results/2017.

63. Nelson and Belz, "Downtown Minneapolis Criticize Candidates."

64. Erin Golden, "Despite Criticism, Minneapolis City Council President Barb Johnson Says She Advocates for Her Ward," *Star Tribune*, July 5, 2015, https://www.startribune.com/despite-criticism-minneapolis-council-president-barb-johnson-says-she-advocates-for-her-ward/311647801.

65. In the ranked-choice tabulation process, Johnson garnered more first-choice votes, with Cunningham taking the lead only after consolidating all the non-Johnson votes, winning by a margin of 175 votes. See City of Minneapolis, "2017 Election Results."

66. For a collection of pivotal essays on abolition, see Mariame Kaba, *We Do This 'Til We Free Us: Abolitionist Organizing and Transforming Justice* (Chicago: Haymarket Books, 2021).

67. Kristoffer Tigue, "Frustration Fuels Calls for More Far-Reaching Police Reforms," *MinnPost*, October 18, 2016, https://www.minnpost.com/community-sketchbook/2016/10/frustration-fuels-calls-more-far-reaching-police-reform.

68. Jenna Wortham, "How a New Wave of Black Activists Changed the Conversation," *New York Times*, August 25, 2020, https://www.nytimes.com/2020/08/25/magazine/black-visions-collective.html.

69. On this kind of racial trauma, see Angela Onwuachi-Willig, "The Trauma of the Routine: Lessons on Cultural Trauma from the Emmett Till Verdict," *Sociological Theory* 34, no. 4 (2016): 335–57.

70. This group was initially called Black Visions Collective but later shortened the name.

71. MPD150, "Enough Is Enough: A 150-Year Performance Review of the Minneapolis Police Department," 2017, 3. An expanded version of the report released in 2020 is available at https://www.mpd150.com.

72. MPD150, "Enough Is Enough," 21.

73. MPD150, "Enough Is Enough," 3.

74. Wortham, "New Wave."

75. Jany, "Council Trims Police Budget."

76. Reclaim the Block, "In Disrupted Budget Address, Mayor Frey Talks Safety beyond Policing but Sticks with Status Quo Solutions in Requesting New Officers and More Money for MPD," press release, 2019.

77. Jessica Lee, "What We Learned from Minneapolis's 2020 Budget," *MinnPost*, December 12, 2019, https://www.minnpost.com/metro/2019/12/what-we-learned -from-minneapolis-2020-budget.

78. For another example of this tension between some abolitionists and the idea of community control of the police, see Pan-African Community Action, "The Radical Practicality of Community Control over Policing: A Reply to Our Critics," *Spectre Journal*, February 18, 2021, https://spectrejournal.com/the-radical-practicality-of -community-control-over-policing.

Chapter Three

1. All quotes from this event were transcribed by the lead author from a video of the demonstration live-streamed on Facebook by the Twin Cities Coalition for Justice 4 Jamar on November 15, 2018, available at https://www.facebook.com/watch/live/ ?ref=watch_permalink&v=2142792959370803.

2. Andrea S. Boyles, *You Can't Stop the Revolution: Community Disorder and Social Ties in Post-Ferguson America* (Oakland: University of California Press, 2019).

3. Jeremy R. Levine, *Constructing Community* (Princeton, NJ: Princeton University Press, 2021), 189.

4. Zakiya Luna, "Who Speaks for Whom? (Mis)Representation and Authenticity in Social Movements," *Mobilization: An International Quarterly* 22, no. 4 (2017): 435–50.

5. We also financially compensated people for their time with a $30 payment. A cash incentive can help to acknowledge the expertise of participants and the costs they incur by taking time to speak with researchers (e.g., missed work, childcare, etc.).

6. Some of the material in chapter 3 was previously published in academic articles. See Michelle S. Phelps, Christopher E. Robertson, and Amber Joy Powell, "'We're Still Dying Quicker Than We Can Effect Change': #BlackLivesMatter and the Limits of 21st-Century Policing Reform," *American Journal of Sociology* 127, no. 3 (2021): 867–903; Amber Joy Powell and Michelle S. Phelps, "Gendered Racial Vulnerability: How Women Confront Crime and Criminalization," *Law & Society Review* 55, no. 4 (2021): 429–51.

7. The vast majority of our participants currently lived in North Minneapolis, but a few had recently moved out of the neighborhood and/or lived elsewhere but frequently spent time in Northside.

8. Michelle S. Phelps, Amber Joy Powell, and Christopher E. Robinson, "Over-Policed and Under-Protected: Public Safety in North Minneapolis," *CURA Reporter*, November 17, 2020, https://www.cura.umn.edu/research/over-policed-and-under -protected-public-safety-north-minneapolis.

9. Monica C. Bell, "Police Reform and the Dismantling of Legal Estrangement," *Yale Law Journal* 126 (2017): 2054–150.

10. Bell, "Legal Estrangement," 2054.

11. Joe Soss and Vesla M. Weaver, "Police Are Our Government: Politics, Political Science, and the Policing of Race-Class Subjugated Communities," *Annual Review of Political Science* 20 (2017): 565–91.

12. All of the names used in this chapter for residents are pseudonyms, assigned to protect participants' confidentiality.

13. Charles R. Epp, Steven Maynard-Moody, and Donald P. Haider-Markel, *Pulled Over: How Police Stops Define Race and Citizenship* (Chicago: University of Chicago Press, 2014).

14. Vesla M. Weaver, "Policing Narratives and the Black Counterpublic," in *The Ethics of Policing: New Perspectives on Law Enforcement*, ed. B. Jones and E. Mendieta (New York: New York University Press, 2021), 149–78.

15. The cases of police violence that went viral during the BLM era themselves built on earlier scandals, e.g., the 1991 beating of Rodney King, as well as violence that rarely made the national news but was widely known in the community, e.g., Jon Burge's torture unit in Chicago. See, e.g., John Hagan, Bill McCarthy, and Daniel Herda, *Chicago's Reckoning: Racism, Politics, and the Deep History of Policing in an American City* (New York: Oxford University Press, 2022).

16. Some research finds that police killings of unarmed Black men increase mental health symptoms in Black communities, though other scholars find null effects. See, e.g., Jacob Bor et al., "Police Killings and Their Spillover Effects on the Mental Health of Black Americans: A Population-Based, Quasi-Experimental Study," *Lancet* 392, no. 10144 (2018): 302–10; Justin Nix and M. J. Lozada, "Police Killings of Unarmed Black Americans: A Reassessment of Community Mental Health Spillover Effects," *Police Practice and Research* 22, no. 3 (2021): 1330–39.

17. See William T. Armaline, Claudio G. Vera Sanchez, and Mark Correia, "'The Biggest Gang in Oakland': Re-Thinking Police Legitimacy," *Contemporary Justice Review* 17, no. 3 (2014): 375–99.

18. Cameron identified as non-binary on our survey but at several points in the interview referred to themself as a woman.

19. See also Dawn Marie Dow, "The Deadly Challenges of Raising African American Boys: Navigating the Controlling Image of the 'Thug,'" *Gender and Society* 30, no. 2 (2016): 161–88; Sinikka Elliott and Megan Reid, "Low-Income Black Mothers Parenting Adolescents in the Mass Incarceration Era: The Long Reach of Criminalization," *American Sociological Review* 84, no. 2 (2019): 197–219; Shannon Malone Gonzalez, "Making It Home: An Intersectional Analysis of the Police Talk," *Gender and Society* 33, no. 3 (2019): 363–86.

20. Beth Richie describes this as the violence matrix, in which women of color are simultaneously burdened by community, gender-based, and police violence. See Beth E. Richie, *Arrested Justice: Black Women, Violence, and America's Prison Nation* (New York: New York University Press, 2012). See also Treva B. Lindsey, *America, Goddam: Violence, Black Women, and the Struggle for Justice* (Oakland: University of California Press, 2022).

21. Justin T. Pickett, Amanda Graham, and Francis T. Cullen, "The American Racial Divide in Fear of the Police," *Criminology* 60, no. 2 (2022): 291–320.

22. On positive experiences with police, see Wesley G. Skogan, *Police and Community in Chicago: A Tale of Three Cities* (Oxford: Oxford University Press, 2006);

Monica C. Bell, "Situational Trust: How Disadvantaged Mothers Reconceive Legal Cynicism," *Law and Society Review* 50, no. 2 (2016): 314–47; and Rebecca L. Fix, Dylan B. Jackson, and Monique Jindal, "Examining the Nuance in Adolescents' Police Encounters: Positive, Negative, or Both?," *Journal of Community Psychology* 51, no. 1 (2022): 1–16.

23. On community policing as reputation management, see Wayne Rivera-Cuadrado, "Crafting Charismatic Cops: Community Policing and the Faulty Reputations Paradigm," *Social Problems* 70, no. 2 (2021), https://doi.org/10.1093/socpro/spab054.

24. On these tensions in other studies, see Holly Campeau, Ron Levi, and Todd Foglesong, "Policing, Recognition, and the Bind of Legal Cynicism," *Social Problems* 68, no. 3 (2021): 658–74; Tracey L. Meares and Gwen Prowse, "Policing as a Public Good: Reflecting on the Term 'To Protect and Serve' as Dialogues of Abolition," *Florida Law Review* 73, no. 1 (2021): 1–30.

25. Boyles, *Can't Stop the Revolution*.

26. On Black communities' support for reformist efforts, see Bell, "Legal Estrangement"; Matthew Clair, "Criminalized Subjectivity: Du Boisian Sociology and Visions for Legal Change," *Du Bois Review: Social Science Research on Race* 18, no. 2 (2021), https://doi.org/10.1017/S1742058X21000217; James Forman Jr., *Locking Up Our Own: Crime and Punishment in Black America* (New York: Farrar, Straus & Giroux, 2017); Meares and Prowse, "Policing as Public Good."

27. See also Rashawn Ray, Kris Marsh, and Connor Powelson, "Can Cameras Stop the Killings? Racial Differences in Perceptions of the Effectiveness of Body-Worn Cameras in Police Encounters," *Sociological Forum* 32, no. 1 (2017): 1032–50.

28. Derrick Bell, *Faces at the Bottom of the Well: The Permanence of Racism* (New York: Basic Books, 1992).

29. On this theme in other studies, see Vesla M. Weaver, Gwen Prowse, and Spencer Piston, "Withdrawing or Drawing In? Political Discourse in Policed Communities," *Journal of Race, Ethnicity, Politics* 5, no. 3 (2020): 1–44.

30. Pew Research Center, "Black Americans Have a Clear Vision for Reducing Racism but Little Hope It Will Happen," 2022, https://www.pewresearch.org/race-ethnicity/2022/08/30/black-americans-have-a-clear-vision-for-reducing-racism-but-little-hope-it-will-happen.

31. See, e.g., Susan Clampet-Lundquist, Patrick J. Carr, and Maria J. Kefalas, "The Sliding Scale of Snitching: A Qualitative Examination of Snitching in Three Philadelphia Communities," *Sociological Forum* 30, no. 2 (2015): 265–85; Patrick J. Carr, Laura Napolitano, and Jessica Keating, "We Never Call the Cops and Here Is Why: A Qualitative Examination of Legal Cynicism in Three Philadelphia Neighborhoods," *Criminology* 45 (2007): 701–36; Hagan et al., *Chicago's Reckoning*.

32. See also Bell, "Situational Trust"; Jennifer E. Cobbina, Jody Miller, and Rod K. Brunson, "Gender, Neighborhood Danger, and Risk-Avoidance Strategies among Urban African-American Youths," *Criminology* 46, no. 3 (2008): 673–709.

33. National survey data shows that Black and Hispanic Americans are *less* likely to use the term "anti-racist" to describe themselves than white Americans. The term is most common among people who identify as "very liberal," but also those who ascribe to a "color-blind" perspective. See Samuel L. Perry, Kenneth E. Frantz, and Joshua B.

Grubbs, "Identifies as Anti-Racist? Racial Identity, Color-Blindness, and Generic Liberalism," *Socius* 7 (2021).

34. See also Geneva Cole, "Types of White Identification and Attitudes about Black Lives Matter," *Social Science Quarterly* 101, no. 4 (2020): 1627–33.

35. On these kinds of community meetings and their role in police legitimacy, see Jan Doering, *Us versus Them: Race, Crime, and Gentrification in Chicago Neighborhoods* (New York: Oxford University Press, 2020); Tony Cheng, *The Policing Machine: Enforcement, Endorsements, and the Illusion of Public Input* (Chicago: University of Chicago Press, 2024); Luis Daniel Gascón and Aaron Roussell, *The Limits of Community Policing: Civilian Power and Police Accountability in Black and Brown Los Angeles* (New York: New York University Press, 2019); and Steve Herbert, *Citizens, Cops, and Power: Recognizing the Limits of Community* (Chicago: Chicago University Press, 2006).

36. Allissa V. Richardson, *Bearing Witness while Black: African Americans, Smartphones, and the New Protest #Journalism* (New York: Oxford University Press, 2020).

37. Jennifer Chudy, "Racial Sympathy and Its Political Consequences," *Journal of Politics* 83, no. 1 (2021): 123.

38. Eduardo Bonilla-Silva, *Racism without Racists: Color-Blind Racism and the Persistence of Racial Inequality in America*, 3rd ed. (Lanham, MD: Rowman & Littlefield, 2009).

39. For other accounts of resistance to the BLM movement, see Jennifer E. Cobbina, *Hands Up, Don't Shoot: Why the Protests in Ferguson and Baltimore Matter, and How They Changed America* (New York: New York University Press, 2019); Barbara Ransby, *Making All Black Lives Matter* (Oakland: University of California Press, 2018); and Deva R. Woodly, *Reckoning: Black Lives Matter and the Democratic Necessity of Social Movements* (New York: Oxford University Press, 2021).

40. Castile was ostensibly pulled over because of a broken taillight. However, police radio transcripts from the stop also document that the officer believed Castile matched the description of a robbery suspect from several days prior because of his "wide-set nose." See Andy Mannix, "Police Audio: Officer Stopped Philando Castile on Robbery Suspicion: Police Recording Doesn't Cover Shooting Itself," *Star Tribune*, July 12, 2016, https://www.startribune.com/police-audio-officer-stopped-philando-castile-on-robbery-suspicion/386344001.

41. On the concept of racial realism, see Bell, *Faces at the Bottom*.

Chapter Four

1. Video available at the author's personal website, https://kimberlylatricejones.com/about (last accessed July 13, 2023).

2. Larry Buchanan, Quoctrung Bui, and Jugal K. Patel, "Black Lives Matter May Be the Largest Movement in U.S. History," *New York Times*, July 3, 2020, https://www.nytimes.com/interactive/2020/07/03/us/george-floyd-protests-crowd-size.html.

3. The title of this chapter is adapted from a tweet by Wesley Lowery, one of the journalists who created the *Washington Post*'s Fatal Force database. Responding to public statements by police chiefs condemning the murder, Wesley Lowery tweeted on May 28, 2020: "I imagine what my activist sources will say: words after the fact

are nice. George Floyd is still dead." The post has since been deleted, but a screenshot is on file with the author.

4. Maya Rao, "Some Minneapolis Black Leaders Speak Out against City Council's Moves to Defund Police," *Star Tribune*, July 2, 2020, https://www.startribune.com /some-minneapolis-black-leaders-speak-out-against-city-council-s-moves-to-defund -police/571594012.

5. Nekima Levy Armstrong, "Black Voters Want Better Policing, Not Posturing by Progressives," *New York Times*, November 9, 2021, https://www.nytimes.com/2021/11 /09/opinion/minneapolis-police-defund.html.

6. Elizabeth Wrigley-Field et al., "Racial Disparities in COVID-19 and Excess Mortality in Minnesota," *Socius*, 2020, https://doi.org/10.1177/2378023120980918.

7. Details of Floyd's life and death are drawn from Robert Samuels and Toluse Olorunnipa, *His Name Is George Floyd: One Man's Life and the Struggle for Racial Justice* (New York: Viking, 2022).

8. Chauvin also worked security at one of the same clubs in 2019. While early news coverage suggested perhaps the two men knew one another, the club owner later reported that it was unlikely.

9. Harmeet Kaur and Nicole Chavez, "What We Know about the 3 Ex-Police Officers on Trial This Week for George Floyd's Death," CNN, January 24, 2022, https:// www.cnn.com/2022/01/24/us/minneapolis-officers-background-george-floyd/index .html.

10. The officers, in fact, had earned their undergraduate degrees from my own department. See this book's author's note.

11. Buchanan et al., "Largest Movement."

12. Buchanan et al., "Largest Movement."

13. An after-action report commissioned by the city would conclude that the city and the MPD failed to follow the emergency protocols, leaving individual precincts and officers to make tactical decisions with little guidance or oversight. See Hillard Heintze, "City of Minneapolis: An After-Action Review of City Agencies' Responses to Activities Directly following George Floyd's Death on May 25, 2020," March 7, 2022, https://lims.minneapolismn.gov/Download/RCAV2/26623/2020-Civil-Unrest-After -Action-Review-Report.pdf.

14. Liz Navratil, Anna Boone, and James Eli Shiffer, "The Siege, Evacuation and Destruction of a Minneapolis Police Station," *Star Tribune*, August 11, 2020, https:// www.startribune.com/minneapolis-third-precinct-george-floyd-emails-public -records-reveal-what-happened-before-abandoned-mayor-frey/566290701.

15. Steven W. Thrasher, "Proportionate Response: When Destroying a Police Precinct Is a Reasonable Reaction," *Slate*, May 30, 2020, https://slate.com/news-and -politics/2020/05/george-floyd-protests-minneapolis-police-fires.html.

16. Kimberly Jones, https://kimberlylatricejones.com/about.

17. Anonymous, "The Siege of the Third Precinct in Minneapolis: An Account and Analysis," June 10, 2020, https://crimethinc.com/2020/06/10/the-siege-of-the-third -precinct-in-minneapolis-an-account-and-analysis.

18. On the militarization of police at protests for social justice, see Paul A. Passavant, *Policing Protest: The Post-Democratic State and the Figure of Black Insurrection* (Durham, NC: Duke University Press, 2021).

19. Erika A. Kaske et al., "Injuries from Less-Lethal Weapons during the George Floyd Protests in Minneapolis," *New England Journal of Medicine* 384 (2021): 774–75.

20. Deena Winter, "Bodycam Video: MPD Beat Jaleel Stallings after He Fired on Officers in Self Defense," *Minnesota Reformer*, September 2, 2021, https://minnesotareformer.com/2021/09/02/bodycam-video-mpd-beat-jaleel-stallings-after-he-fired-on-officers-in-self-defense.

21. Jamelle Bouie, "The Police Are Rioting. We Need to Talk About It," *New York Times*, June 5, 2020, https://www.nytimes.com/2020/06/05/opinion/sunday/police-riots.html.

22. Charmaine Chua, "Abolition Is A Constant Struggle: Five Lessons from Minneapolis," *Theory & Event* 23, no. 4 Supplement (2020): S127–47.

23. See Anna DalCortivo and Alyssa Oursler, "'We Learned Violence from You': Discursive Pacification and Framing Contests during the Minneapolis Uprising," *Mobilization: An International Quarterly* 26, no. 4 (2021): 457–74.

24. "MPD Chief Arradondo: 4 Police Officers Fired following Death of George Floyd," CBS Minnesota, May 26, 2020, https://minnesota.cbslocal.com/2020/05/26/mpd-chief-arradondo-4-police-officers-fired-following-death-of-george-floyd.

25. "'We Have to Do This Right': Hennepin County Attorney Mike Freeman Says George Floyd Investigation Will Take Time," CBS Minnesota, May 28, 2020, https://minnesota.cbslocal.com/2020/05/28/we-have-to-do-this-right-hennepin-county-attorney-mike-freeman-says-george-floyd-investigation-will-take-time. Part of the early conflict over the criminal charges revolved around the first autopsy report, which initially described "no physical findings" consistent with traumatic asphyxiation as the cause of death. See Ann Crawford-Roberts et al., "George Floyd's Autopsy and the Structural Gaslighting of America," *Scientific American*, June 6, 2020, https://blogs.scientificamerican.com/voices/george-floyds-autopsy-and-the-structural-gaslighting-of-america.

26. Ricardo Lopez, "Police Union President Bob Kroll Blasts Walz, Defends Officers Tied to George Floyd Killing," *Minnesota Reformer*, June 1, 2020, https://minnesotareformer.com/2020/06/01/police-union-president-bob-kroll-blasts-walz-defends-officers-who-killed-george-floyd.

27. Barbara Sprunt, "The History behind 'When the Looting Starts, the Shooting Starts,'" NPR, May 29, 2020, https://www.npr.org/2020/05/29/864818368/the-history-behind-when-the-looting-starts-the-shooting-starts.

28. People initially wondered on social media if this person was an off-duty cop; police later released a search warrant that identified him as a member of the Hells Angels Motorcycle Club, though the man was never charged with a crime. See Deena Winter, "What's Up with 'Umbrella Man'?," *Minnesota Reformer*, June 2, 2021, https://minnesotareformer.com/2021/06/02/whats-up-with-umbrella-man.

29. Matt Sepic, "Texas Man, 24, Admits Shooting at Minneapolis Police Station during Riot," *MPR News*, September 30, 2021, https://www.mprnews.org/story/2021/09/30/texas-man-24-admits-shooting-at-minneapolis-police-station-during-riot.

30. Scott Pham, "Police Arrested More Than 11,000 People at Protests across the US," *Buzzfeed News*, June 2, 2020, https://www.buzzfeednews.com/article/scottpham/floyd-protests-number-of-police-arrests.

31. This is broadly consistent with research that shows police repression of protests grew less violent after the 1960s, in large part because of the changing character

of protest tactics. See Thomas Elliott et al., "Softer Policing or the Institutionalization of Protest? Decomposing Changes in Observed Protest Policing over Time," *American Journal of Sociology* 127, no. 4 (January 2022): 1311–65; Sarah Soule and Christian Davenport, "Velvet Glove, Iron Fist, or Even Hand? Protest Policing in the United States, 1960–1990," *Mobilization: An International Quarterly* 14, no. 1 (April 15, 2009): 1–22.

32. Maya Rao and Jeffery Meitrodt, "Insurance Payouts Fall Far Short of What's Needed to Rebuild Twin Cities," *Star Tribune*, August 8, 2020, https://www.startribune.com/insurance-payouts-fall-far-short-of-what-s-needed-to-rebuild-twin-cities/572054742; Susan Du, "A Better Lake Street? A Daring Hope for Riot-Torn Corridor," *Star Tribune*, May 21, 2022, https://www.startribune.com/lake-street-fights-on-minneapolis-george-floyd-riot/600174854.

33. Dan J. Wang and Alessandro Piazza, "The Use of Disruptive Tactics in Protest as a Trade-Off: The Role of Social Movement Claims," *Social Forces* 94, no. 4 (2016): 1675–710.

34. Clarissa Rile Hayward, "Disruption: What Is It Good For?," *Journal of Politics* 82, no. 2 (2020): 448–59.

35. Daniel Q. Gillion, *The Loud Minority: Why Protests Matter in American Democracy* (Princeton, NJ: Princeton University Press, 2020).

36. Omar Wasow, "Agenda Seeding: How 1960s Black Protests Moved Elites, Public Opinion and Voting," *American Political Science Review* 114, no. 3 (2020): 638–59. For a contemporary example, see Joshua Bloom, *Contested Legitimacy in Ferguson: Nine Hours on Canfield Drive* (New York: Cambridge University Press, 2022).

37. Elizabeth Hinton, *America on Fire: The Untold History of Police Violence and Black Rebellion since the 1960s* (New York: Liveright, 2021).

38. Ryan D. Enos, Aaron R. Kaufman, and Melissa L. Sands, "Can Violent Protest Change Local Policy Support? Evidence from the Aftermath of the 1992 Los Angeles Riot," *American Political Science Review* 113, no. 4 (2019): 1012–28.

39. Glenn E. Bracey II, "Black Movements Need Black Theorizing: Exposing Implicit Whiteness in Political Process Theory," *Sociological Focus* 49, no. 1 (2016): 11–27.

40. Wasow, "Agenda Seeding."

41. Pamela E. Oliver, "Repression and Crime Control: Why Social Movement Scholars Should Pay Attention to Mass Incarceration as a Form of Repression," *Mobilization: An International Quarterly* 13, no. 1 (2008): 1–24.

42. Jenna Wortham, "How a New Wave of Black Activists Changed the Conversation," *New York Times*, August 25, 2020, https://www.nytimes.com/2020/08/25/magazine/black-visions-collective.html.

43. Miski Noor and Kandace Montgomery, "Foreword," in Mariame Kaba and Andrea J. Ritchie, *No More Police: A Case for Abolition* (New York: New Press, 2022).

44. Michael L. Levenson, "For Mayor Jacob Frey of Minneapolis, a Walk of Shame," *New York Times*, June 7, 2020. Note that both the title and the body text of this article were revised to be less sensational in subsequent digital and print editions of the paper. For the archived original version, see https://web.archive.org/web/20200607050003/https://www.nytimes.com/2020/06/07/us/minneapolis-mayor-jacob-frey-walk-of-shame.html.

45. Dionne Searcey and John Eligon, "Minneapolis Will Dismantle Its Police Force, Council Members Pledge," *New York Times*, June 7, 2020, https://www.nytimes.com/2020/06/07/us/minneapolis-police-abolish.html.

46. City of Minneapolis, "Transforming Community Safety Resolution," June 20, 2020, https://lims.minneapolismn.gov/Download/MetaData/23730/2020R-152_Id _23730.pdf.

47. Mariame Kaba, "Yes, We Mean Literally Abolish the Police," *New York Times*, June 12, 2020, https://www.nytimes.com/2020/06/12/opinion/sunday/floyd-abolish -defund-police.html.

48. For an example of the latter, see Matthew Yglesias, "The End of Policing Left Me Convinced We Still Need Policing," *Vox*, June 18, 2020, https://www.vox.com /2020/6/18/21293784/alex-vitale-end-of-policing-review.

49. Liz Navratil, "Most of Minneapolis City Council Pledges to 'Begin the Process of Ending' Police Department," *Star Tribune*, June 8, 2020, https://www.startribune .com/mpls-council-majority-backs-dismantling-police-department/571088302.

50. City of Minneapolis, "City Charter and Code of Ordinances," last amended November 5, 2013, https://www2.minneapolismn.gov/government/charter-ordinances -policies.

51. Michael J. Lansing, "Policing Politics: Labor, Race, and the Police Officers Federation of Minneapolis, 1945–1972," *Minnesota History* 67, no. 5 (2021): 226–38.

52. City of Minneapolis, "Amending Article VII of the City Charter," June 24, 2020, https://lims.minneapolismn.gov/Download/FileV2/22277/MPD-Charter -Amendment-Articles-VII-and-Article-VIII.pdf.

53. Astead W. Herndon, "How a Pledge to Dismantle the Minneapolis Police Collapsed," *New York Times*, September 26, 2020, https://www.nytimes.com/2020/09 /26/us/politics/minneapolis-defund-police.html.

54. For an abolitionist critique of the Camden story, see Brendan McQuade, "The 'Camden Model' Is Not a Model. It's an Obstacle to Real Change," *Jacobin Magazine*, July 4, 2020, https://jacobin.com/2020/07/camden-new-jersey-police-reform -surveillance. See also Brendan McQuade, *Pacifying the Homeland: Intelligence Fusion and Mass Supervision* (Oakland: University of California Press, 2019).

55. Deena Winter, "Abolishing the Police Won't Get Rid of the Police Union, under Court Ruling," *Minnesota Reformer*, August 11, 2020, https://minnesotareformer.com/2020 /08/11/abolishing-the-police-wont-get-rid-of-the-police-union-under-court-ruling.

56. Neal St. Anthony, "Minneapolis Business Groups Buy into Police Reform but Not Dismantlement," *Star Tribune*, July 14, 2020, https://www.startribune.com /minneapolis-business-groups-buy-into-police-reform-but-not-dismantlement /571699972.

57. Logan Carroll, "Emails Show Minneapolis Police Chief Coordinated with PR Pros to Fight Council, Protect Budget," *Minnesota Reformer*, May 24, 2021, https:// minnesotareformer.com/2021/05/24/with-budget-on-the-line-minneapolis-police -chief-coordinated-with-political-operatives-to-lobby-the-city-council-emails-show.

58. Jeremiah Jacobsen, "Poll: Most Minneapolis Residents Approve of Chief Arradondo, but Not MPD as a Whole," *Kare 11 News*, August 16, 2020, https://www .kare11.com/video/entertainment/television/programs/kare-saturday/89-be6bd610 -5c21-41bf-b60f-bbacf09b9f70; Emily Haavik, "Poll: Minneapolis Residents More Likely to Approve of Mayor than of City Council," *Kare 11 News*, August 15, 2020, https://www.kare11.com/article/news/local/minnesota-poll-views-on-mayor-jacob -frey-minneapolis-city-council-mpd/89-ed6665df-08f6-4219-ae65-3040a9d8f34d.

59. Ian Schwartz, "Minneapolis City Council President on Dismantling Police: Wanting to Call the Police 'Comes from a Place of Privilege,'" *RealClear Politics*, June 8, 2020, https://www.realclearpolitics.com/video/2020/06/08/minneapolis_city _council_president_on_dismantling_police_wanting_to_call_the_police_comes _from_a_place_of_privilege.html.

60. MPR News Staff, "Minneapolis Police Union Head Bob Kroll, Board Members Interview with MPR News," *MPR News*, June 23, 2020, https://www.youtube.com /watch?v=TxxqeKoH-Zk.

61. City of Minneapolis, "Minneapolis Police Department Crime Data," https:// tableau.minneapolismn.gov/views/MPDMStatCrimeData/CrimeDashboard-Home (last accessed May 3, 2023). Though there is a contested literature about whether police violence begets community violence, researchers have documented that the murder of George Floyd was associated with a spike in gun violence that disproportionately burdened Black neighborhoods in North Minneapolis. See Ryan P. Larson, N. Jeanie Santaularia, and Christopher Uggen, "Temporal and Spatial Shifts in Gun Violence, before and after a Historic Police Killing in Minneapolis," *Spatial and Spatio-temporal Epidemiology* 47 (2023), https://doi.org/10.1016/j.sste .2023.100602.

62. Jennifer Bjorhus and Liz Navratil, "'Staggering' Number of Minneapolis Cops Seeking Disability Benefits," *Star Tribune*, July 17, 2020, https://www.startribune.com /staggering-number-of-mpls-cops-are-filing-disability-claims/571809512.

63. Brad Heath, "After Floyd's Killing, Minneapolis Police Retreated, Data Shows," Reuters, September 13, 2021, https://www.reuters.com/investigates/special-report /usa-policing-minneapolis.

64. Rao, "Black Leaders Speak Out." On racial challenges in the politics of crime control, see Jan Doering, *Us versus Them: Race, Crime, and Gentrification in Chicago Neighborhoods* (New York: Oxford University Press, 2020).

65. Josiah Bates, "Minneapolis Residents Sue City over Alleged Police Department Rollbacks," *Time*, October 23, 2020, https://time.com/5902962/minneapolis -residents-sue-city-police-presence.

66. Sondra Samuels and Don Samuels, "Why We Northside Neighbors Are Suing Minneapolis," *Star Tribune*, September 24, 2020, https://www.startribune.com/why -we-northside-neighbors-are-suing-minneapolis/572210262.

67. Rao, "Black Leaders Speak Out."

68. CUAPB, "What Will It Take to End Police Violence? Recommendations for Reform," Report, 2020, https://d3n8a8pro7vhmx.cloudfront.net/cuapb/pages/1 /attachments/original/1591595256/WHAT_WILL_IT_TAKE_TO_END_POLICE _VIOLENCE_with_Appendices.pdf?1591595256.

69. CUAPB, "Understanding the Minneapolis City Council's Charter Amendment," Report, 2020, https://d3n8a8pro7vhmx.cloudfront.net/cuapb/pages/270/attachments /original/1595193284/Understanding_the_City_Council_Charter_Amendment_2020 .pdf?1595193284.

70. Sasha Cotton, "Transforming Community Safety Engagement Process: Phase 1 Update," Presentation to City Council, January 21, 2021, https://lims.minneapolismn .gov/Download/FileV2/23220/Transforming-Community-Safety-Engagement -Process-Presentation.pdf.

71. Eric Roper, "Poll: Cuts to Minneapolis Police Ranks Lack Majority Support," *Star Tribune*, August 15, 2020, https://www.startribune.com/poll-cuts-to-minneapolis-police-ranks-lack-majority-support/572119932.

72. See, e.g., Jessica Eaglin, "To 'Defund' the Police," *Stanford Law Review* 73, no. 1 (2021): 120–40; Jennifer Cobbina-Dungy et al., "'Defund the Police': Perceptions among Protesters in the 2020 March on Washington," *Criminology & Public Policy* 21, no. 1 (2022): 147–74; Michael Javen Fortner, *Reconstructing Justice: Race, Generational Divides, and the Fight over "Defund the Police"* (Washington, DC: Niskanen Center, 2020), https://www.niskanencenter.org/wp-content/uploads/2020/10/Reconstructing-Justice-Final.pdf; and Kevin H. Wozniak, *The Politics of Crime Prevention* (New York: NYU Press, 2023).

73. The city council's version of the 2021 ballot question specified that the new department would include a *mandatory* "Law Enforcement Services Division," a change council members attributed to citizen feedback on the first proposal.

74. Andy Mannix and Jeff Hargarten, "Minneapolis Closes in on Homicide Milestone at End of Violent Year," *Star Tribune*, December 30, 2021, https://www.startribune.com/a-most-violent-year-in-minneapolis/600131444.

75. The homicide statistics most comparable to present-day numbers only go back to 1960. In no period from 1960 to 2019, however, was such a dramatic one- or two-year upward swing visible.

76. Liz Sawyer and Jeff Hargarten, "Minneapolis Police Staffing Levels Reach Historic Lows amid Struggle for Recruitment, Retention," *Star Tribune*, September 16, 2023, https://www.startribune.com/a-most-violent-year-in-minneapolis/600131444.

77. For a recent analysis, see Aaron Chalfin et al., "Police Force Size and Civilian Race," *American Economic Review* 4, no. 2 (2022): 139–58. The authors estimate that every ten additional police officers prevented one homicide per year. Yet the benefits of this tactic were attenuated in majority-Black cities, and the costs of additional officers in additional low-level "quality of life" arrests were steepest for Black residents.

78. John Pfaff, "Can Criminal Justice Reform Survive a Wave of Violent Crime?," *New Republic*, June 21, 2021, https://newrepublic.com/article/162634/criminal-justice-reform-violent-crime.

79. Kim Hyatt, "Man Gets 37½-Year Sentence for Shooting That Killed Girl Jumping on Trampoline," *Star Tribune*, July 11, 2023, https://www.startribune.com/37-5-year-sentence-for-drive-by-gang-shooter-that-killed-girl-jumping-on-trampoline/600288889.

80. Rochelle Olson, "Frey Releases Public Safety Proposals for Minneapolis, Says City Must Make a Turn," *Star Tribune*, May 18, 2021, https://www.startribune.com/frey-releases-public-safety-proposals-for-minneapolis-says-city-must-make-a-turn/600058289.

81. Office of Minneapolis Mayor Jacob Frey, "A Minneapolis Model for Community Safety & Accountability," May 17, 2021, https://www.minneapolismn.gov/media/-www-content-assets/documents/Minneapolis-Model-for-Community-Safety-and-Accountability.pdf.

82. "After Another Child Shot, MPD Chief Decries Gun Violence 'Epidemic' in Minneapolis," *Bring Me the News*, July 11, 2021, https://bringmethenews.com/minnesota-news/after-another-child-shot-mpd-chief-decries-gun-violence-epidemic-in-minneapolis.

83. Alex Jokich, "Minneapolis City Leaders Appear Divided on How to Handle Violence in the City," *KSTP Eyewitness News,* June 1, 2021, https://kstp.com/kstp -news/top-news/minneapolis-city-leaders-appear-divided-on-how-to-handle -violence-in-the-city.

84. On the "turf wars" between politicians and gangs, see Robert Vargas, *Wounded City: Violent Turf Wars in a Chicago Barrio* (New York: Oxford University Press, 2016).

85. Jokich, "City Leaders Appear Divided."

86. "Yes for Minneapolis" raised a total of $4.9 million through small donations and some external support. "All of Minneapolis" raised substantially less, $1.6 million in total, mostly through large donations from local business interests. See Ballotpedia, "Minneapolis, Minnesota, Question 2," November 2021, https://ballotpedia .org/Minneapolis,_Minnesota,_Question_2,_Replace_Police_Department_with _Department_of_Public_Safety_Initiative_(November_2021).

87. See "Yes 4 Minneapolis," https://web.archive.org/web/20220131064719/https: //yes4minneapolis.org/about (last accessed using Wayback Machine on March 26, 2023). The city did not have a "police-only" response; 911 dispatchers could triage calls to police, the fire department, and ambulance services, for example. But what supporters of the charter amendment wanted was to have more of the 911 calls that were routed to police go to new first responders.

88. Jelani Cobb, "Derek Chauvin's Trial and George Floyd's City," *New Yorker,* July 2, 2021, https://www.newyorker.com/magazine/2021/07/12/derek-chauvins -trial-and-george-floyds-city.

89. "'I Would Take a Drawing on a Napkin': Chief Arradondo Says No Elected Official Has Spoken with Him about the Public Safety Ballot Question," CBS Minnesota, October 27, 2021, https://minnesota.cbslocal.com/2021/10/27/i-would-take -a-drawing-on-a-napkin-chief-arradondo-says-no-elected-official-has-spoken-with -him-about-the-public-safety-ballot-question.

90. This name was likely meant to imply that they represented the average city resident. See All of Mpls, "About All of Mpls," https://www.allofmpls.org/about-us (last accessed March 26, 2023). However, the coalition's nod to "all" of Minneapolis also echoed the discourse of "All Lives Matter," a slogan that was often invoked to rebut BLM's calls to think specifically about the cost of policing for Black Americans.

91. On authenticity claims in movements, see Zakiya Luna, "Who Speaks for Whom? (Mis)Representation and Authenticity in Social Movements," *Mobilization: An International Quarterly* 22, no. 4 (2017): 435–50.

92. Editorial Board, "Opinions on the 2021 Election: Star Tribune Editorial Board Endorsements," *Star Tribune,* October 30, 2021, https://www.startribune .com/opinions-on-the-2021-election-star-tribune-editorial-board-endorsements /600111589.

93. See, e.g., Pollen Midwest, "2021 MPLS Voter Guide," 2021, https://www .pollenmidwest.org/mplsisus; Reclaim the Block, "2021 Candidate Questionnaire," Reclaim the Block, 2021, https://www.reclaimtheblock.org/2021-candidate -questionnaire.

94. *The Minneapolis Uprising: Abolition and the Struggle for a Police-Free City,* UC Davis Humanities Institute, July 24, 2020, https://www.youtube.com/watch?v =S04q-WmcXMg.

95. Sheila Nezhad, "Minneapolis Doesn't Need a National Guard Occupation," *Star Tribune*, February 28, 2021, https://www.startribune.com/minneapolis-doesn't -need-a-national-guard-occupation/600028732.

96. In the local endorsement contest among Democratic–Farmer–Labor (DFL) voters, Nezhad earned the most votes, but failed to reach 60 percent, which meant that there was no official endorsement for the city's top seat. See Faiza Mahamud, "Minneapolis DFL Fails to Endorse in Mayor's Race, but Challenger Nezhad Finishes ahead of Frey," *Star Tribune*, June 17, 2021, https://www.startribune.com/minneapolis -dfl-fails-to-endorse-in-mayor-s-race-but-challenger-nezhad-finishes-ahead-of-frey /600069238.

97. "Building Community Safety and Transforming Policing Plan," Kate for Mpls, https://kateformpls.org/publicsafety (last accessed March 26, 2023).

98. His aunt was Alice Rainville, the city council's first woman president. Her daughter, Barbara "Barb" Johnson, would become a later council president, eventually ousted from the city council in 2017 by challenger Phillipe Cunningham.

99. Max Nesterak, "Minneapolis' Human Resources Office Tells Police They Won't Be Fired if Question 2 Passes," *Minnesota Reformer*, October 26, 2021, https:// minnesotareformer.com/briefs/minneapolis-human-resources-office-tells-police -they-wont-be-fired-if-question-2-passes.

100. City of Minneapolis, "2021 Ballot Questions," https://vote.minneapolismn.gov /results-data/election-results/2021/ballot-questions (last accessed March 26, 2023).

101. City of Minneapolis, "2021 Mayor," https://vote.minneapolismn.gov/results -data/election-results/2021/mayor (last accessed March 27, 2023).

102. City of Minneapolis, "Voter Turnout," https://vote.minneapolismn.gov/results -data/turnout (last accessed March 26, 2023).

103. Levy Armstrong, "Black Voters."

104. Rob Kuznia, "Once Nicknamed 'Murderapolis,'" CNN, September 25, 2022, https://www.cnn.com/2022/09/25/us/minneapolis-crime-defund-invs/index.html.

105. The question was worded as follows: "Do you support or oppose replacing the Minneapolis Police Department with a new Department of Public Safety, which may include police officers and will focus on public health, and giving the City Council more authority over public safety?"

106. Staff, "Minnesota Poll Results: Minneapolis Policing and Public Safety Charter Amendment," *Star Tribune*, September 18, 2021, https://www.startribune.com /minnesota-poll-public-safety-minneapolis-police-crime-charter-amendment-ballot -question/600097989.

107. On age and attitudes about police, see Rebecca Goldstein, "Senior Citizens as a Pro-Police Interest Group," *Journal of Political Institutions and Political Economy* 2, no. 2 (2021): 303–28.

108. Editorial Board, "Opinions on 2021 Election."

Chapter Five

1. This argument is a key component of critical race theory as well, which argues that our legal systems are designed to uphold (rather than upend) Black-white inequality. For a primer on critical race theory, see Victor Ray, *On Critical Race Theory: Why It Matters and Why You Should Care* (New York: Penguin Random House,

2022). On the myriad ways legal systems shield police from accountability, see Joanna Schwartz, *Shielded: How the Police Became Untouchable* (New York: Viking, 2023); Devon W. Carbado, *Unreasonable: Black Lives, Police Power, and the Fourth Amendment* (New York: New Press, 2022).

2. Keith L. Alexander, Steven Rich, and Hannah Thacker, "The Hidden Billion-Dollar Cost of Repeated Police Misconduct," *Washington Post*, March 9, 2022, https://www.washingtonpost.com/investigations/interactive/2022/police-misconduct-repeated-settlements.

3. As of June 12, 2023, the city's dashboard of reported police misconduct cases reported spending roughly $27 million in 2021, $11 million in 2022, and $10 million in the first half of 2023. See City of Minneapolis, Officer Payouts dashboard, https://www.minneapolismn.gov/government/government-data/datasource/officer-payouts-dashboard.

4. Chao Xiong and Rochelle Olson, "Juror Questionnaires in Derek Chauvin Trial Reveal Thoughts on Case, Race," *Star Tribune*, November 6, 2021, https://www.startribune.com/juror-questionnaires-in-derek-chauvin-trial-reveal-thoughts-on-case-race/600113714.

5. Prosecutors' arguments were well-honed. As Ellison later described in his memoir, they had run through several mock trials in extensive preparations for the case. See Keith Ellison, *Break the Wheel: Ending the Cycle of Police Violence* (New York: Hachette Book Group, Twelve Books, 2023).

6. Brooklyn Center's mayor then worked with the city council to pass a resolution that promised to implement all of the changes rival activists in Minneapolis had called for, including creating a new Department of Community Safety and Violence Prevention as well as revamping the misconduct review process. Two years later, however, Brooklyn Center had yet to implement much of the resolution, facing many of the same political and legal barriers as Minneapolis. See Torey Van Oot, "Slow Healing in Brooklyn Center as New Mayor Takes Office," *AXIOS Twin Cities*, January 9, 2023, https://www.axios.com/local/twin-cities/2023/01/09/brooklyn-center-mayor-april-graves-daunte-wright-police-reform.

7. Ben Crump Law, PLLC (@BenCrumpLaw), "National Civil Rights Attorney Ben Crump, Floyd Family, and Legal Team React to Sentencing of Derek Chauvin," Twitter, June 25, 2021, https://twitter.com/BenCrumpLaw/status/1408519744093929486.

8. Amy Forliti and Stephen Groves, "Floyd Family, Others See Inequality in Penalties for Ex-Cops," July 29, 2022, https://apnews.com/article/death-of-george-floyd-minneapolis-thomas-lane-sentencing-ac01ce5c70cb54acc5441d0182d0a66c.

9. Philip M. Stinson Sr. and Chloe A. Wentzlof, "On-Duty Shootings: Police Officers Charged with Murder or Manslaughter, 2005–2019" (Bowling Green State University, Research Brief One–Sheet No. 2019), https://www.bgsu.edu/content/dam/BGSU/health-and-human-services/document/Criminal-Justice-Program/policeintegritylostresearch/-9-On-Duty-Shootings-Police-Officers-Charged-with-Murder-or-Manslaughter.pdf.

10. See, e.g., Jeffrey Fagan and Alexis D. Campbell, "Race and Reasonableness in Police Killings," *Boston University Law Review* 100 (2020): 951–1015.

11. Somil Trivedi and Nicole Gonzalez Van Cleve, "To Serve and Protect Each Other: How Police-Prosecutor Codependence Enables Police Misconduct," *Boston University Law Review* 100 (2020): 895–933.

12. Erik Oritz, "More Officers Were Charged in Fatal Police Shootings in 2021. Not Everyone Sees Progress," NBC News, January 22, 2022, https://www.nbcnews.com/news/us-news/officers-charged-fatal-police-shootings-2021-not-everyone-sees-progres-rcna12799.

13. Sean Collins, "Why the Chauvin Verdict Didn't Feel Like Justice," *Vox*, April 23, 2021, https://www.vox.com/22395454/derek-chauvin-verdict-guilty-justice-prison-transformative-healing-defund-abolish-police.

14. This phrase came from the interview with an MPD150 organizer described in chapter 2.

15. City of Minneapolis, "City Budget," https://www.minneapolismn.gov/government/budget (last accessed March 26, 2023).

16. Vera Institute of Justice, "What Policing Costs: A Look at Spending in America's Biggest Cities," June 2020, https://www.vera.org/publications/what-policing-costs-in-americas-biggest-cities.

17. City of Minneapolis, "City Budget."

18. Estimates from the US Census Bureau Annual Survey of State and Local Government Finances. See Richard C. Auxier, "What Police Spending Data Can (and Cannot) Explain amid Calls to Defund the Police," Urban Institute, *Urban Wire*, June 9, 2020, https://www.urban.org/urban-wire/what-police-spending-data-can-and-cannot-explain-amid-calls-defund-police. A *New York Times* analysis using 2017 data from the 150 largest cities similarly found that Minneapolis hews close to the median among large cities. See Emily Badger and Quoctrung Bui, "Cities Grew Safer. Police Budgets Kept Growing," *New York Times*, June 12, 2020, https://www.nytimes.com/interactive/2020/06/12/upshot/cities-grew-safer-police-budgets-kept-growing.html.

19. Minneapolis Public Schools, "Building a Foundation for the Future: Minneapolis Public Schools 2019–20 Budget Book," https://financeandbudget.mpls.k12.mn.us/uploads/mps_budget_book_2019-2020.pdf (last accessed March 27, 2023).

20. Minneapolis Park and Recreation Board, "Minneapolis Park and Recreation Board Financial Status Report as of Year-End, 2019," https://www.minneapolisparks.org/wp-content/uploads/2020/04/2019_year-end_report.pdf (last accessed March 27, 2023).

21. Auxier, "Police Spending Data."

22. John Clegg and Adaner Usmani, "The Economic Origins of Mass Incarceration," *Catalyst* 3, no. 3 (2019). The limits of city budgets are particularly worrisome since local political fields are typically the spaces where residents from high-crime neighborhoods have the most access to the policy-making process. See Lisa L. Miller, *The Perils of Federalism: Race, Poverty, and the Politics of Crime Control* (New York: Oxford University Press, 2008).

23. See, e.g., Robert Vargas and Philip McHarris, "Race and State in City Police Spending Growth: 1980 to 2010," *Sociology of Race and Ethnicity* 3, no. 1 (2016): 96–112.

24. 2021 Mpls People's Budget, "Minneapolis City Council and Mayor Jacob Frey: Pass the People's Budget! We Can Thrive, Not Just Survive," https://docs.google.com/document/d/16-3SKF5E040Zax0nemxedPWRRsv3FJgStKO4s0lCeWw/edit (last accessed March 27, 2023).

25. Liz Navratil, "Two Big Compromises Helped Minneapolis Public Safety Plan Win Approval," *Star Tribune*, December 12, 2020, https://www.startribune.com/two-big-compromises-helped-minneapolis-public-safety-plan-win-approval/573378971.

26. City of Minneapolis, "City Budget."

27. Becky Z. Dernbach, "Mayor Jacob Frey Says He's Overhauling the Minneapolis Police Department. We Asked Him to Tell Us How," *Sahan Journal*, May 3, 2021, https://sahanjournal.com/policing-justice/minneapolis-mayor-frey-police-reform.

28. Liz Sawyer, Libor Jany, and Paul Walsh, "Minneapolis Police Insisted on 'No Knock' Warrant That Led to Amir Locke's Shooting Death," *Star Tribune*, February 5, 2020, https://www.startribune.com/minneapolis-police-insisted-on-no-knock-warrant -before-amir-locke-shooting-city-sets-moratorium/600143065.

29. Walker Orenstein and Solomon Gustavo, "Last Year, Minneapolis Police Announced a New Policy on No-Knock Warrants. Since Then, They've Asked for 90 of Them," *MinnPost*, September 3, 2021, https://www.minnpost.com/metro/2021/09 /last-year-minneapolis-police-announced-a-new-policy-on-no-knock-warrants-since -then-theyve-asked-for-90-of-them.

30. The ethics violation case would be found unwarranted, with Frey and his supporters claiming it had been a political stunt.

31. Deena Winter, "Mayor Frey Says His 2020 No-Knock Change Wasn't a Ban; Moratorium Still Has Exceptions," *Minnesota Reformer*, February 7, 2022, https:// minnesotareformer.com/briefs/mayor-frey-says-his-2020-no-knock-change-wasnt-a -ban-moratorium-still-has-exceptions.

32. "Every Police-Involved Death in Minnesota since 2000," *Star Tribune*, https:// www.startribune.com/every-police-involved-death-in-minnesota-since-2000 /502088871 (last updated January 12, 2023). The number of people killed during police contact is higher if you include people who died from car crashes related to police pursuits. In late 2020, three teens fleeing police in an alleged carjacking died when the driver crashed their vehicle. And in 2021 Leneal Frazier, the uncle of Darnella Frazier, the teen who filmed Floyd's death, was killed in North Minneapolis after an officer in a high-speed pursuit of a different vehicle blew through a red light and slammed into the side of Frazier's car.

33. Expansive changes in officers' obligation to report use of force in September 2020 made trends before and after this period difficult to compare. See Minneapolis Police Department, "Review of Crime Trends, Statistics, and Strategies in Response to Emerging Patterns," Presentation to Minneapolis City Council, 2021, https://lims.minneapolismn.gov/Download/FileV2/24316/CommunitySafetyUpdate _August262021.pdf. However, looking only at the year after the shift shows little in the way of improvement over time.

34. Jay Wong, "A Look at Racial Disparities in MPD Traffic Stops and Searches in 2020," Presentation to the Minneapolis Police Conduct Oversight Commission, April 22, 2021.

35. Lesley Stahl, "Minneapolis Police Chief Medaria Arradondo on George Floyd's Killing, Policies during Protests and Reform for His Department," CBS News, June 21, 2020, https://www.cbsnews.com/news/minneapolis-police-chief-medaria-arradondo -geroge-floyd-killing-60-minutes-2020-06-21.

36. Jon Collins, "MPLS Police Chief to Pull Out of Union Negotiations," *MPR News*, June 11, 2020, https://www.mprnews.org/story/2020/06/10/minneapolis -police-chief-to-pull-out-of-union-negotiations.

37. Jon Collins, "Half of Fired Minnesota Police Officers Get Their Jobs Back through Arbitration," *MPR News*, July 9, 2020, https://www.mprnews.org/story

/2020/07/09/half-of-fired-minnesota-police-officers-get-their-jobs-back-through
-arbitration.

38. MPLS For A Better Police Contract v. City of Minneapolis (Minn. 4th Judicial District, 2021). The group did ultimately win this battle, gaining access to the negotiations after the new contract was approved and making the city pay for their legal costs.

39. Deena Winter, "Critics Say Proposed Police Contract Doesn't Rein In Out-of-Control MPD," *Minnesota Reformer*, March 17, 2022, https://minnesotareformer.com/2022/03/17/critics-say-proposed-police-contract-doesnt-rein-in-out-of-control-mpd; Liz Navratil, "New Minneapolis Police Contract Makes Few Discipline Tweaks, Months after Election," *Star Tribune*, March 20, 2022, https://www.startribune.com/new-minneapolis-police-union-contract-few-discipline-tweaks-after-election-focusing-on-change/600157604.

40. Minnesota Department of Human Rights, "Investigation into the City of Minneapolis and the Minneapolis Police Department," April 27, 2022, 49, https://mn.gov/mdhr/mpd/agreement.

41. Theresa Rocha Beardall argues that citizen review boards are deliberately disempowered. See "Police Legitimacy Regimes and the Suppression of Citizen Oversight in Response to Police Violence," *Criminology* 60, no. 4 (2022): 740–65.

42. Minneapolis Office of Police Conduct Review, "Office of Police Conduct Review Data Portal," https://www.minneapolismn.gov/government/government-data/datasource/office-of-police-conduct-review-dashboard (last accessed June 10, 2022).

43. Libor Jany, "In Minneapolis, Civilian Police Oversight Group Strives to Be Heard," *Star Tribune*, August 15, 2016, https://www.startribune.com/in-minneapolis-civilian-oversight-group-still-wrestling-with-its-identity/390134621.

44. Max Nesterak, "Minneapolis Has Yet to Discipline a Single Officer for Misconduct during Summer's Unrest," *Minnesota Reformer*, January 28, 2021, https://minnesotareformer.com/2021/01/28/minneapolis-has-yet-to-discipline-a-single-officer-for-misconduct-during-summers-unrest. This lack of discipline had long been a problem in the department. See Max Nesterak and Tony Webster, "The Bad Cops: How Minneapolis Protects Its Worst Police Officers until It's Too Late," *Minnesota Reformer*, December 15, 2020, https://minnesotareformer.com/2020/12/15/the-bad-cops-how-minneapolis-protects-its-worst-police-officers-until-its-too-late.

45. Deena Winter, "Bodycam Video: MPD Beat Jaleel Stallings after He Fired on Officers in Self Defense," *Minnesota Reformer*, September 2, 2021, https://minnesotareformer.com/2021/09/02/bodycam-video-mpd-beat-jaleel-stallings-after-he-fired-on-officers-in-self-defense.

46. Deena Winter, "2 SWAT Team Members Involved in Jaleel Stallings Case Were Part of Locke Raid," *Minnesota Reformer*, February 4, 2022, https://minnesotareformer.com/2021/09/02/bodycam-video-mpd-beat-jaleel-stallings-after-he-fired-on-officers-in-self-defense; Andy Mannix, "Minneapolis to Pay $1.5 Million to Man Police Shot at with Less-Lethal Rounds from Unmarked Van," *Star Tribune*, May 17, 2022, https://www.startribune.com/minneapolis-to-pay-1-5-million-jaleel-stallings-police-shot-at-less-lethal-rounds-from-unmarked-van/600173976.

47. Hillard Heintze, "City of Minneapolis: An After-Action Review of City Agencies' Responses to Activities Directly following George Floyd's Death on May 25, 2020," March 7, 2022, https://lims.minneapolismn.gov/Download/RCAV2/26623/2020-Civil-Unrest-After-Action-Review-Report.pdf.

48. Maya Rao, "Black Citizens Recount Fear, Distrust as Complaints against Minneapolis Police Go Nowhere," *Star Tribune*, May 14, 2022, https://www.startribune.com/black-citizens-recount-fear-distrust-as-complaints-against-mpd-go-nowhere/60017333.

49. Minnesota Department of Human Rights, "Investigation into Minneapolis Police," 55.

50. Andy Mannix, "Only Minneapolis Police Officer Formally Disciplined for Misconduct Tied to the Department's Riot Response Has Left Job," *Star Tribune*, October 29, 2021, https://www.startribune.com/only-minneapolis-police-officer-formally-disciplined-for-misconduct-tied-to-the-department-s-riot-re/600111337.

51. Dwight Hobbes, "Art Knight Got Demoted for Saying We Don't Need the Same Old 'White Boys' on the Police Force. He Wasn't Wrong," *Minnesota Reformer*, November 11, 2020, https://minnesotareformer.com/2020/11/11/art-knight-got-demoted-for-saying-we-dont-need-the-same-old-white-boys-on-the-police-force-he-should-be-applauded.

52. Lisa Sawyer and Andy Mannix, "Minneapolis Agrees to Pay $200,000 to Settle Discrimination Complaints by Two Former Police Officers," *PBS Frontline*, https://www.pbs.org/wgbh/frontline/article/minneapolis-settle-discrimination-complaints-former-police-officers.

53. Deena Winter, "Mayor, Chief Quietly Codified Change to Discipline Policy in Police Manual," *Minnesota Reformer*, October 28, 2021, https://minnesotareformer.com/2021/10/28/mayor-chief-quietly-codified-change-to-discipline-policy-in-police-manual.

54. Formally known as the Peace Officer Discipline Procedures Act, Minnesota Statute 629.89, 2022, https://www.revisor.mn.gov/statutes/cite/626.89.

55. DeRay McKesson et al., "Police Union Contracts and Police Bill of Rights Analysis," Campaign Zero, June 29, 2016, https://campaignzero.org/research/police-union-contracts-police-bill-of-rights-analysis.

56. 2021 Minnesota Statutes, 626.89 Peace Officer Discipline Procedures Act, https://www.revisor.mn.gov/statutes/cite/626.89.

57. Emma Pederson, "Cop Authority and Use of Deadly Force: How Police Associations Shaped Minnesota Statute 609.066" (master's thesis, University of Minnesota, 2023).

58. Minnesota House Floor No. 1, 91st Legislature, 2020, 2nd Special Session, https://www.revisor.mn.gov/bills/text.php?number=HF1&type=bill&version=1&session=ls91&session_year=2020&session_number=2.

59. Randy Furst, "Once Viewed as a 'Paper Tiger,' POST Board Pursues New Reforms to Discipline Misbehaving Police," *Star Tribune*, May 22, 2022, https://www.startribune.com/once-viewed-as-a-paper-tiger-the-post-board-is-pursuing-new-reforms-to-discipline-misbehaving-police/600175524; see also Minnesota Justice Research Center, "Accountability in Policing: The Unexplored Power of the POST Board," 2022, https://www.mnjrc.org/_files/ugd/88fad1_df68d35de02140a7ba93c1541316531b.pdf.

60. Joshua Page, Heather Schoenfeld, and Michael Campbell, "To Defund the Police, We Have to Dethrone the Law Enforcement Lobby," *Jacobin*, July 4, 2020, https://jacobin.com/2020/07/defund-police-unions-law-enforcement-lobby.

61. Minnesota Senate Floor No. 2909, 93rd Legislature, 2023, https://www.revisor.mn.gov/bills/text.php?number=SF2909&version=4&session_year=2023&session_number=0.

62. Christopher Magan, "Guns Got All of the Attention, but There's More in the $880M Public Safety Bill," *Pioneer Press*, May 16, 2023, https://www.twincities.com /2023/05/16/guns-got-the-attention-but-theres-much-more-in-the-880-million -public-safety-bill.

63. Alex Gangitano, "Biden Signs Resolution Overturning DC Crime Bill," *The Hill*, March 20, 2023, https://thehill.com/homenews/3903352-biden-signs-resolution -overturning-dc-crime-bill.

64. Minnesota Department of Human Rights, "Stipulation and Order with the Minneapolis Police Department," June 8, 2020, https://mn.gov/mdhr/assets /Order%20signed%20by%20Judge%206.8.20_tcm1061-435169.pdf.

65. See Civil Rights Division, US Department of Justice, *The Civil Rights Division's Pattern and Practice Police Reform Work: 1994–Present* (Washington, DC, 2017).

66. Libor Jany and Randy Furst, "Amid Federal Probe, Police Reform Canvassers Say They've Gathered 1,100 Complaints against Minneapolis Police," *Star Tribune*, October 14, 2021, https://www.startribune.com/amid-federal-probe-police-reform -canvassers-say-they-ve-gathered-1-100-complaints-against-minneapoli/600106298.

67. Andy Mannix, "Justice Department to Probe Whether Minneapolis Police Have 'Pattern and Practice' of Misconduct," *Star Tribune*, April 21, 2021, https://www .startribune.com/justice-department-to-probe-whether-minneapolis-police-have -pattern-and-practice-of-misconduct/600048448.

68. Minnesota Department of Human Rights, "Investigation into Minneapolis Police."

69. Minnesota Justice Research Center, *Community Engagement: Shaping a Consent Decree in Minneapolis*, March 31, 2023, https://www.mnjrc.org/_files/ugd /88fad1_abc60d31b3bc47edbb2e68cc40095db6.pdf. Note that as a member of this organization's Research Steering Committee, I provided expert consulting on the report.

70. Minnesota Department of Human Rights, "Consent Decree," https://mn.gov /mdhr/mpd/agreement (last accessed April 29, 2023).

71. US Department of Justice Civil Rights Division and US Attorney's Office District of Minnesota Civil Division, "Investigation of the City of Minneapolis and the Minneapolis Police Department," June 16, 2023, https://www.justice.gov/opa/press -release/file/1587661.

72. Elizabeth Hinton, *America on Fire: The Untold History of Police Violence and Black Rebellion since the 1960s* (New York: Liveright, 2021).

73. Paul Butler, *Chokehold: Policing Black Men* (New York: New Press, 2017).

74. Tanaya Devi and Roland G. Fryer Jr., "Policing the Police: The Impact of 'Pattern-or-Practice' Investigations on Crime," *National Bureau of Economic Research, Working Paper* 27324 (2020), https://doi.org/10.3386/w27324.

Chapter Six

1. Whittier Cop Watch, "Field Guide to Twin Cities Collaborators," zine, June 5, 2021, archived at https://lib.edist.ro//field-guide-to-tc-collaborators-print.pdf.

2. See, e.g., Nikki Jones, *The Chosen Ones: Black Men and the Politics of Redemption* (Berkeley: University of California Press, 2018); Lisa L. Miller, *The Perils of Federalism: Race, Poverty, and the Politics of Crime Control* (New York: Oxford Academic, 2008).

3. Andrea S. Boyles, *You Can't Stop the Revolution: Community Disorder and Social Ties in Post-Ferguson America* (Oakland: University of California Press, 2019).

4. MAD DADS of Minneapolis, "Mission of MAD DADS," http://minneapolismaddads .org (last accessed March 27, 2023).

5. A Mother's Love Initiative, https://www.amothersloveinitiative.org (last accessed May 19, 2023).

6. James Varney, "Lisa Clemons, Mother's Love Initiative, Fights to Save Minneapolis Police Force," *Washington Times*, August 23, 2020, https://www.washingtontimes .com/news/2020/aug/23/lisa-clemons-mothers-love-initiative-fights-save-m.

7. Jones, *The Chosen Ones*.

8. Foreshadowing the critique of violence interrupters as sources of violence, in 2020 Smith would be ousted from the group after a series of sexual harassment allegations. See Tom Lyden, "MAD DADS Leader Accused of Harassment," FOX 9, December 27, 2020, https://www.fox9.com/news/mad-dads-leader-accused-of-harassment.

9. Varney, "Lisa Clemons."

10. Anton Jahn-Vavrus, Pablo Giebink Valbuena, and Ilyas Bouzouina, "At 38th and Chicago, Agape Movement Turns 'Street Energy into Community Energy,'" *MPR News*, December 31, 2020, https://www.mprnews.org/story/2020/12/30/at -38th-and-chicago-agape-movement-turns-street-energy-into-community-energy.

11. Janell Ross, "The Intersection Where George Floyd Died Has Become a Strange, Sacred Place. Will Its Legacy Endure?" *Time*, May 4, 2021, https://time.com /5954486/george-floyd-square.

12. Joshua Bloom and Waldo E. Martin Jr., *Black against Empire: The History and Politics of the Black Panther Party* (Oakland: University of California Press, 2016).

13. "Freedom Fighters Provide Security to Minneapolis Black Community," *Globe Post*, March 25, 2021, https://theglobepost.com/2021/03/25/minnesota-freedom -fighters.

14. Jessica Lee, "After Positive Results, Minneapolis Looks to Expand Anti-Violence Program," *MinnPost*, November 18, 2019, https://www.minnpost.com/metro /2019/11/after-positive-results-minneapolis-looks-to-expand-anti-violence-program.

15. Cure Violence's focus on norm-changing outside of coercive law enforcement actions differentiates it from the related "focused deterrence" strategy (sometimes known as the "CeaseFire" model). The focused deterrence model was intended to have a strong social norms and support component, but this was often underdeveloped compared to the law enforcement response. See Anthony A. Braga and David L. Weisburd, "Focused Deterrence and the Prevention of Violent Gun Injuries: Practice, Theoretical Principles, and Scientific Evidence," *Annual Review of Public Health* 36 (2015): 55–68; David M. Kennedy, *Don't Shoot: One Man, A Street Fellowship, and the End of Violence in Inner-City America* (New York: Bloomsbury, 2011).

16. Liz Navratil, "White House-Backed Coalition Aims to Support Minneapolis Violence Prevention Programs," *Star Tribune*, April 21, 2022, https://www.startribune .com/white-house-backed-coalition-aims-to-support-minneapolis-violence -prevention-programs/600166846.

17. Deena Winter, "With Violent Crime Up, Minneapolis Tries Something New: Violence Interrupters," *Minnesota Reformer*, December 9, 2020, https:// minnesotareformer.com/2020/12/09/with-violent-crime-up-minneapolis-tries

-something-new-violence-interrupters. The process of applying for city contracts is arduous, typically weeding out all but the most bureaucratized nonprofits. See Jones, *The Chosen Ones*; Douglas Hartmann, *Midnight Basketball: Race, Sports, and Neoliberal Social Policy* (Chicago: University of Chicago Press, 2016); and Robert Vargas, "Gangstering Grants: Bringing Power to Collective Efficacy Theory," *City & Community* 18, no. 1 (2019): 369–91. The OVP tried to ease these burdens for smaller community groups, which would later prompt a lawsuit from a community group demanding more information from the grantees.

18. City of Minneapolis, "MinneapolUS Strategic Outreach Initiative, 2021 End of Year Reports," June 8, 2022, https://lims.minneapolismn.gov/Download/RCAV2 /27677/Office-of-Violence-Prevention-Update-Presentation.pdf.

19. Patrick Sharkey, Gerard Torrats-Espinosa, and Delaram Takyar, "Community and the Crime Decline: The Causal Effect of Local Nonprofits on Violent Crime," *American Sociological Review* 82, no. 6 (2017): 1214–40.

20. Jeffrey A. Butts et al., "Cure Violence: A Public Health Model to Reduce Gun Violence," *Annual Review of Public Health* 36 (2015): 39–53.

21. On this theme, see Robert Vargas, *Wounded City: Violent Turf Wars in a Chicago Barrio* (New York: Oxford University Press, 2016); Jan Doering, *Us versus Them: Race, Crime, and Gentrification in Chicago Neighborhoods* (New York: Oxford University Press, 2020); and Daniel Gascón, "Uncomfortable Kinship: An Ethnography on the Professional World of Gang Experts and Street Outreach Workers in South Los Angeles," *Social Justice* 49, no. 1 (2023): 81–110.

22. On exposure to violence among interrupters, see David Hureau et al., "Exposure to Gun Violence among the Population of Chicago Community Violence Interventionists," Northwestern University: Institute of Social Policy Research, Working Papers, 2022, https://www.ipr.northwestern.edu/our-work/working-papers/2022/wp-22-12.html.

23. Boyd Huppert, "Looted and Burned, Northside Cub Returns with New Grocery Store Model," KARE 11, May 24, 2021, https://www.kare11.com/article/news /local/land-of-10000-stories/looted-and-burned-northside-cub-returns-with-new -store-model/89-36d8d07f-5351-4b7e-942e-131d5fe6b58e.

24. CUAPB, "Response Letter to Minnesota Reformer," July 13, 2021. On file with author.

25. On the lack of Fourth Amendment protections against search and seizure by police alternatives, see Shawn Fields, "The Fourth Amendment without Police," *University of Chicago Law Review* 90, no. 4 (2023), https://papers.ssrn.com/sol3/papers .cfm?abstract_id=4047011.

26. Rachel Weiher, "'We Can't Breathe': An Analysis of George Floyd Square" (master's thesis, University of St. Thomas, 2021).

27. GFS attracted national media attention, as did Seattle's "police-free" zone in Capitol Hill. The space in Seattle, however, imploded after a spate of violence that left a Black teenager dead at the hands of the zone's armed volunteer security force.

28. See, e.g., Nick Williams, "At George Floyd Square, 'All the Businesses . . . Are Still Struggling,'" *Star Tribune*, May 24, 2022, https://www.startribune.com/business -owners-at-george-floyd-square-just-want-things-back-to-normal/600176054.

29. Meet on the Streets, George Floyd Square, "What Does Justice Look Like?," Justice Resolution, August 7, 2020, https://healingmnstories.files.wordpress.com /2020/08/floyd-square-resolution.pdf.

30. Miguel Otárola, "When It Comes to Reopening 38th and Chicago, Minneapolis City Leaders and Community Members Find Themselves at an 'Impasse,'" *Star Tribune*, September 5, 2020, https://www.startribune.com/when-it-comes-to-reopening-38th-and-chicago-city-and-community-find-themselves-at-an-impasse/572330482.

31. US Press Freedom Tracker, "Individuals Steal Photojournalist's Camera Drone ahead of George Floyd Anniversary Demonstrations," May 25, 2021, https://pressfreedomtracker.us/all-incidents/individuals-steal-photojournalists-camera-drone-ahead-of-george-floyd-anniversary-demonstrations.

32. Carma Hassan, "Reports of Gunshots near George Floyd Square on the Anniversary of His Death," CNN, May 25, 2021, https://www.cnn.com/2021/05/25/us/minneapolis-george-floyd-square-shooting/index.html.

33. Libor Jany, "Relatives, Friends of Man Gunned Down at George Floyd Square Grieve His Loss," *Star Tribune*, April 1, 2021, https://www.startribune.com/relatives-friends-of-man-gunned-down-at-george-floyd-square-grieve-his-loss/600041027.

34. Deena Winter, "Minneapolis City Council Members Accuse Mayor of Skirting Law with Agape Contract," *Minnesota Reformer*, June 17, 2021, https://minnesotareformer.com/briefs/minneapolis-city-council-members-accuse-mayor-of-skirting-law-with-agape-contract.

35. On authenticity claims in movements, see Zakiya Luna, "Who Speaks for Whom? (Mis)Representation and Authenticity in Social Movements," *Mobilization: An International Quarterly* 22, no. 4 (2017): 435–50.

36. See Susan Du, "Minneapolis Survey: Strong Support for Creating Permanent Memorial at George Floyd Square," *Star Tribune*, April 1, 2021, https://www.startribune.com/minneapolis-survey-strong-support-for-creating-permanent-memorial-at-george-floyd-square/600041094.

37. Ben Hovland and J. D. Duggan, "Minneapolis Clears George Floyd Square at 4:00 A.M.," *Sahan Journal*, June 3, 2021, https://sahanjournal.com/race/george-floyd/minneaolis-george-floyd-square-reopened.

38. Niko Georgiades and Sam Richards, "Private Mercenary Group Targets, Assaults, & Detains Anti-Police Protesters in Uptown Minneapolis," *Unicorn Riot*, October 27, 2021, https://unicornriot.ninja/2021/private-mercenary-group-targets-assaults-detains-anti-police-protesters-in-uptown-minneapolis.

39. Indeed, violence prevention groups are often explicitly designed as collaborations with the police; see, e.g., Office of Justice Programs, Office of Juvenile Justice and Delinquency Prevention, "OJJDP FY 2021 Comprehensive Youth Violence Prevention and Reduction Program" (US Department of Justice, May 4, 2021), https://ojjdp.ojp.gov/funding/fy2021/O-OJJDP-2021-105001.

40. Deena Winter, "Public Safety Alternatives Are Untested, Viewed Skeptically by Anti-police Activists," *Minnesota Reformer*, July 12, 2021, https://minnesotareformer.com/2021/07/12/public-safety-alternatives-are-untested-viewed-skeptically-by-anti-police-activists.

41. Reid Forgrave, "Agape Movement Aims to Change Hearts in South Minneapolis," *Star Tribune*, May 21, 2022, https://www.startribune.com/agape-movement-aims-to-change-hearts-in-south-minneapolis/600175358.

42. See, e.g., "Tricks and Tensions," in Mariame Kaba and Andrea J. Ritchie, *No More Police: A Case for Abolition* (New York: New Press, 2022).

43. Jeff Asher and Ben Horwitz, "How Do the Police Actually Spend Their Time?," *New York Times*, June 19, 2020, https://www.nytimes.com/2020/06/19/upshot/unrest-police-time-violent-crime.html.

44. See table 6 in Zoë Thorkildsen et al., "Minneapolis Police Department and Emergency Communications Center Staffing and Operations Assessment & Review of Problem Nature Codes" (Arlington, VA: CNA, January 2022), https://lims.minneapolismn.gov/Download/RCAV2/26161/Minneapolis-Staffing-Operations-and-PNC-Assessment-FINAL.pdf. See also US Department of Justice Civil Rights Division and US Attorney's Office District of Minnesota Civil Division, "Investigation of the City of Minneapolis and the Minneapolis Police Department," June 16, 2023, https://www.justice.gov/opa/press-release/file/1587661.

45. Barry Friedman, "Disaggregating the Policing Function," *University of Pennsylvania Law Review* 169, no. 4 (2021): 925–99.

46. Egon Bittner, *Aspects of Police Work* (Boston: Northeastern University Press, 1990), 249, quoted in David Thacher, "Shrinking the Police Footprint," *Criminal Justice Ethics* 41, no. 1 (2022): 66.

47. Cynthia Lum, Christopher S. Koper, and Xiaoyun Wu, "Can We Really Defund the Police? A Nine-Agency Study of Police Response to Calls for Service," *Police Quarterly* 25, no. 3 (2022): 255–80.

48. On the expansion of these groups nationwide, see Ram Subramanian and Leily Arzy, "Rethinking How Law Enforcement Is Deployed," *Brennan Center for Justice*, November 17, 2022, https://www.brennancenter.org/our-work/research-reports/rethinking-how-law-enforcement-deployed.

49. City of Minneapolis, "Request for Proposals for Mobile Behavioral Health Crisis Response Teams," March 1, 2021, https://lims.minneapolismn.gov/Download/FileV2/23305/Mobile-Mental-Health-RFP.pdf.

50. See Jackson Beck, Melissa Reuland, and Leah Pope, "Case Study: CAHOOTS" (New York: Vera Institute of Justice, 2020), https://www.vera.org/behavioral-health-crisis-alternatives/cahoots.

51. See, e.g., City of Minneapolis, "Behavioral Crisis Response in Minneapolis," Infographic, February 22, 2022, https://www.minneapolismn.gov/media/-www-content-assets/documents/BCR-Infographic-2.2.22.pdf.

52. On ambulance services, see Josh Seim, *Bandage, Sort, and Hustle: Ambulance Crews on the Front Lines of Urban Suffering* (Oakland: University of California Press, 2020).

53. Quotes transcribed by author using a public recording of the hearing. See City of Minneapolis, "Public Health & Safety Committee," April 20, 2022, https://lims.minneapolismn.gov/MarkedAgenda/PHS/3152.

54. Amanda Agan, Jennifer L. Doleac, and Anna Harvey, "Prosecutorial Reform and Local Crime Rates," Paper Series (Law & Economics Center at George Mason University Scalia Law School Research, October 29, 2021), https://ssrn.com/abstract=3952764.

55. Emma Frankham, "Mental Illness Affects Police Fatal Shootings," *Contexts* 17, no. 2 (2018): 70–72. In Minnesota, see Jennifer Bjorhus, "A Cry for Help," *Star Tribune*, June 5, 2016, https://www.startribune.com/police-being-forced-to-front-lines-of-growing-mental-health-crisis/374510841.

56. Hennepin County Attorney's Office, "No Charges against Two Officers in Fatal Shooting of Travis Jordan," 2019, https://www.hennepinattorney.org/news/news

/2019/january/cao-jordan-case-1-3-2019. Note that all of these calls involve 911 call-takers as critical intermediaries between the public and police. On this theme, see Jessica Gillooly, "How 911 Callers and Call-Takers Impact Police Encounters with the Public: The Case of the Henry Louis Gates Jr. Arrest," *Criminology and Public Policy* 19, no. 3 (2020): 787–804.

57. I heard about this incident from the BCR staff, but a local crime watch group live-tweeted the call for help. See CrimeWatchMpls (@CrimeWatchMpls), "BCR help call (social workers), calling for police help, urgent," Twitter, May 27, 2022, https://twitter.com/CrimeWatchMpls/status/1530227821301440514.

58. Robert J. Sampson, "Collective Efficacy Theory: Lessons Learned and Directions for Future Inquiry," in *Taking Stock: The Status of Criminological Theory*, ed. Francis T. Cullen, John Paul Wright, and Kristie R. Blevins (New York: Routledge, 2017), 149–67.

59. Monica C. Bell, "Next-Generation Policing Research: Three Propositions," *Journal of Economic Perspectives* 35, no. 4 (2021): 29–48.

60. Jason Sole, *From Prison to Ph.D.: A Memoir of Hope, Resilience, and Second Chances* (Independently published, 2014).

61. The other three core members are Rox Anderson, Josina Manu Maltzman, and Susan Raffo.

62. Revolutionary Emergency Partners, "Our Work," https://repformn.org/revolutionary-emergency-partners (last accessed March 29, 2023).

63. One Million Experiments, "Episode 5 - REP with Signe Victoria Harriday," podcast, March 24, 2022, https://millionexperiments.com/podcast/season-1/podcast-episode-5.

64. One Million Experiments, "Signe Victoria Harriday."

65. Ella Fassler, "People in Minneapolis Are Calling Each Other Instead of the Cops," *Vice*, November 22, 2021, https://www.vice.com/en/article/qjb8z5/people-in-minneapolis-are-calling-each-other-instead-of-the-cops.

66. Thacher, "Shrinking the Police Footprint."

67. US DOJ, "Investigation of the MPD," 62.

68. Susan Du, "Minneapolis Public Safety Commissioner Says He Lacks Staff to Transform Public Safety," *Star Tribune*, July 1, 2023, https://www.startribune.com/minneapolis-public-safety-commissioner-says-he-lacks-staff-to-transform-public-safety/600286874.

69. See, e.g., Jocelyn Simonson, "Democratizing Criminal Justice through Contestation and Resistance," *Northwestern University Law Review* 111 (2017): 1609–24.

70. See also David Alan Sklansky, *Democracy and the Police* (Redwood City, CA: Stanford University Press, 2007); David Thacher, "Community Policing without the Police? The Limits of Order Maintenance by the Community," in *Community Policing and Peacekeeping*, ed. Peter Grabosky (Boca Raton, FL: CRC Press, 2009).

71. John Rappaport, "Some Doubts About 'Democratizing' Criminal Justice," *University of Chicago Law Review* 87 (2020): 711–813.

72. Ruth Wilson Gilmore, *Change Everything: Racial Capitalism and the Case for Abolition* (Chicago: Haymarket Books, 2022); see also Geo Mather, *A World without Police: How Strong Communities Make Cops Obsolete* (New York: Verso, 2021).

73. Roberto R. Aspholm, *Views from the Streets: The Transformation of Gangs and Violence on Chicago's South Side* (New York: Columbia University Press, 2020).

74. For an account of an innovative housing program for chronically unhoused people in Seattle, see Devin Collins, Katherine Beckett, and Marco Brydolf-Horwitz, "Pandemic Poverty Governance: Neoliberalism under Crisis," *City & Community* (2022), https://doi.org/10.1177/15356841221140078.

Conclusion

1. Hennepin County Attorney's Office, "Report of the Hennepin County Attorney's Office Regarding the Death of Andrew Tekle Sundberg," 2022, https://www.hennepinattorney.org/-/media/cao/news/2022/Report-of-the-Hennepin-County-Attorneys-Office-Regarding-the-Death-of-Andrew-Tekle-Sundberg.pdf.

2. Fox 9 live-streamed the protest. See Fox 9 Minneapolis–St. Paul, "Video: Mom Shot at by Tekle Sundberg Interrupts Rally, Expresses Outrage with Protestors," July 16, 2022, https://www.youtube.com/watch?v=-BbBSRACOKY.

3. For a national perspective on police killings where the victim is unarmed, see Nick Selby et al., *In Context: Understanding Police Killings of Unarmed Civilians* (St. Augustine, FL: Contextual Press, CIAI Press, 2016).

4. Rory Kramer and Brianna Remster, "The Slow Violence of Contemporary Policing," *Annual Review of Criminology* 5 (2022): 43–66.

5. Egon Bittner, *Aspects of Police Work* (Boston: Northeastern University Press, 1990).

6. Forrest Stuart, *Ballad of the Bullet: Gangs, Drill Music, and the Power of Online Infamy* (Princeton, NJ: Princeton University Press, 2020).

7. Rosa Brooks, *Tangled Up in Blue: Policing the American City* (New York: Penguin Books, 2021), 18.

8. Beth E. Richie, *Arrested Justice: Black Women, Violence, and America's Prison Nation* (New York: New York University Press, 2012).

9. See, e.g., Derecka Purnell, *Becoming Abolitionists: Police, Protests, and the Pursuit of Freedom* (New York: Astra House, 2021).

10. Michael Javen Forner, *Black Silent Majority: The Rockefeller Drug Laws and the Politics of Punishment* (Cambridge, MA: Harvard University Press, 2015).

11. See, e.g., Jasmine Linnea Kelekay, "'Black Lives Matter Here, Too': Policing Blackness in a Nordic Welfare State" (PhD diss., UC Santa Barbara, 2022), https://escholarship.org/uc/item/3p28b2pf#main.

12. Monica C. Bell suggests one way to link reform and abolition projects is to (re)imagine policing that would work *against* residential segregation. See Monica C. Bell, "Anti-Segregation Policing," *NYU Law Review* 95, no. 3 (2020). See also Amna Akbar, "An Abolitionist Horizon for (Police) Reform," *California Law Review* 108, no. 6 (2020): 101–68.

13. This question of whether the state can provide real justice without harm is an ongoing debate among abolitionists. See "Tricks and Tensions" in Mariame Kaba and Andrea J. Ritchie, *No More Police: A Case for Abolition* (New York: New Press, 2022).

14. Hence the tortured language in the amendment that the new department "could include licensed peace officers . . . if necessary."

15. Mariame Kaba, "Yes, We Mean Literally Abolish the Police," *New York Times*, June 12, 2020, https://www.nytimes.com/2020/06/12/opinion/sunday/floyd-abolish-defund-police.html.

16. See Joe Soss, "On Casing a Study versus Studying a Case," in *Rethinking Comparison: Innovative Methods for Qualitative Political Inquiry*, ed. Erica S. Simmons and Nicholas Rush Smith (Cambridge: Cambridge University Press, 2021).

17. Zeeshan Aleem, "New Data Shows Just How Wrong Democrats Are to Embrace Eric Adams," MSNBC, June 6, 2023, https://www.msnbc.com/opinion /msnbc-opinion/eric-adams-police-report-rcna87952.

18. Jordan Levy, "Three Commissioners Just Resigned in Protest from Philly's Police Oversight Board," *Billy Penn at WHYY*, May 30, 2023, https://billypenn.com /2023/05/30/philadelphia-police-oversight-commission-resignations.

19. Lakeidra Chavis and Geoff Hing, "The War on Gun Violence Has Failed," *The Marshall Project*, March 23, 2023, https://www.themarshallproject.org/2023/03/23 /gun-violence-possession-police-chicago.

20. Joshua Fechter, "Watch: Austin Police Chief Weighs In on City's Deadliest Year in Decades, Police Reform and 'Defunding' the Department," *Texas Tribune*, December 10, 2021, https://www.texastribune.org/2021/12/10/austin-police -homicides-spending.

21. Sean Keenan and Rick Rojas, "Atlanta City Council Approves 'Cop City' Funding Despite Protests," *New York Times*, June 6, 2023, https://www.nytimes.com/2023 /06/06/us/atlanta-cop-city-funding-vote.html.

22. Matt Dougherty, "Abolishing the Police Was Never the Plan in Ithaca," Ithaca .com, May 18, 2023, https://www.ithaca.com/news/ithaca/abolishing-the-police-was -never-the-plan-in-ithaca/article_b639deee-f52b-11ed-9d06-bfdaa4d74078 .html.

23. Samuel Sinyangwe, "Police Are Killing Fewer People in Big Cities, But More in Suburban and Rural America," *FiveThirtyEight*, June 1, 2020, https://fivethirtyeight .com/features/police-are-killing-fewer-people-in-big-cities-but-more-in-suburban -and-rural-america.

24. These cities were Mesa, AZ; Oklahoma City, OK; Virginia Beach, VA; Colorado Springs, CO; Jacksonville, FL; and Arlington, TX. See Chris Tausanovitch and Christopher Warshaw, "Representation in Municipal Government," *American Political Science Review* 108, no. 3 (2014): 605–41.

25. For these calculations, I used the Police Scorecard, https://policescorecard .org (last accessed June 12, 2023), which uses the Mapping Police Violence database (among others) to create police metrics for each city.

26. Rick Rouan, "Fact Check: No, Police Aren't Only Killing Black People in Blue States," *USA Today*, April 27, 2021, https://www.usatoday.com/story/news/factcheck /2021/04/27/fact-check-no-police-arent-killing-black-people-only-blue-states /4858626001.

27. In the words of Angela Davis, freedom is a constant struggle. See *Freedom Is a Constant Struggle: Ferguson, Palestine, and the Foundations of a Movement* (Chicago: Haymarket Books, 2016).

28. Deva R. Woodly, *Reckoning: Black Lives Matter and the Democratic Necessity of Social Movements* (New York: Oxford University Press, 2021); Travis Campbell, "Black Lives Matter's Effect on Police Lethal Use of Force" (July 2, 2023), http://dx .doi.org/10.2139/ssrn.3767097.

29. Jesse Jannetta et al., *Research Report: Learning to Build Police-Community Trust: Implementation Assessment Findings from the Evaluation of the National*

Initiative for Building Community Trust and Justice (Washington, DC: Urban Institute, 2019), https://www.urban.org/sites/default/files/publication/100705/learning_to_build_police-community_trust_3.pdf.

30. For empirical evaluations of these efforts and policy recommendations, see Samuel Walker and Carol A. Archbold, *The New World of Police Accountability*, 3rd ed. (Thousand Oaks, CA: Sage, 2019); Franklin E. Zimring, *When Police Kill* (Cambridge, MA: Harvard University Press, 2018); Joanna Schwartz, *Shielded: How the Police Became Untouchable* (New York: Viking, 2023).

31. Jeannine Bell, "Dead Canaries in the Coal Mines: The Symbolic Assailant Revisited," *Georgia State University Law Review* 34, no. 3 (2018): 513–79.

32. For a review of the literature on proactive policing, see National Academies of Sciences, Engineering, and Medicine, "Proactive Policing: Effects on Crime and Communities," Consensus Study Report, 2018, https://nap.nationalacademies.org/catalog/24928/proactive-policing-effects-on-crime-and-communities. For critical commentary on the report, see David Thacher, "The Aspiration of Scientific Policing," *Law & Social Inquiry* 44, no. 1 (2018): 273–97.

33. David M. Hureau, "Seeing Guns to See Urban Violence: Racial Inequality & Neighborhood Context," *Daedalus* (Winter 2022): 49–66.

34. Kevin R. Reitz, "Introduction," in *American Exceptionalism in Crime and Punishment*, ed. Kevin R. Reitz (New York: Oxford University Press, 2017), 1–52.

35. See Paul J. Hirschfield, "Exceptionally Lethal: American Police Killings in a Comparative Perspective," *Annual Review of Criminology*, 2023, https://doi.org/10.1146/annurev-criminol-030421-040247. Within the United States, county-level rates of violent crime and gun ownership also correlate with rates of fatal police shootings. See Keller G. Sheppard, Gregory M. Zimmerman, and Emma E. Fridel, "Examining the Relevance of Contextual Gun Ownership on Fatal Police Shootings," *Justice Quarterly* 39, no. 6 (2021): 1214–36.

36. Michael Sierra-Arévalo, "American Policing and the Danger Imperative," *Law & Society Review* 55, no. 1 (2021): 70–103. Brooks, *Tangled Up in Blue*, argues that part of the answer is for officers to accept a certain level of lethal risk as inherent to the job in order to prioritize residents' safety first.

37. Reuben Miller describes this as a reimagining of what we owe one another. See Reuben Jonathan Miller, *Halfway Home: Race, Punishment, and the Afterlife of Mass Incarceration* (New York: Little, Brown, 2021).

38. Christopher Lewis and Adaner Usmani, "The Injustice of Under-Policing in America," *American Journal of Law and Equality* 2 (2022): 85–106.

39. See, e.g., Ejeris Dixon and Leah Lakshimi Piepzna-Samarasinha, eds., *Beyond Survival: Strategies and Stories from the Transformative Justice Movement* (Chico, CA: AK Press, 2020); Danielle Sered, *Until We Reckon: Violence, Mass Incarceration, and a Road to Repair* (New York: New Press, 2019).

40. Katherine Beckett, Forrest Stuart, and Monica Bell, "From Crisis to Care," *Inquest*, 2021, https://inquest.org/from-crisis-to-care.

41. Sarah A. Seo, *Policing the Open Road: How Cars Transformed American Freedom* (Cambridge, MA: Harvard University Press, 2019). Traffic cameras, of course, carry other kinds of risks, and many activist coalitions on the left have argued that the widespread adoption of traffic cameras would extend the harms and costs of mass government surveillance.

42. Shawn Fields, "The Fourth Amendment without Police," *University of Chicago Law Review* 90, no. 4 (2023): 1023–93; Farhang Heydari, "The Private Role in Public Safety," *George Washington Law Review* 90, no. 3 (2022): 696–760.

43. See, e.g., Russell Brewer and Peter Grabosky, "The Unraveling of Public Security in the United States: The Dark Side of Police-Community Co-Production," *American Journal of Criminal Justice* 39, no. 1 (March 1, 2014): 139–54.

44. Kramer and Remster, "Slow Violence."

45. Alexandra Natapoff, *Punishment without Crime: How Our Massive Misdemeanor System Traps the Innocent and Makes America More Unequal* (New York: Basic Books, 2018); Issa Kohler-Hausmann, *Misdemeanorland: Criminal Courts and Social Control in an Age of Broken Windows Policing* (Princeton, NJ: Princeton University Press, 2018).

46. Jill Leovy, *Ghettoside: A True Story of Murder in America* (New York: Spiegel & Grau, 2015).

47. Kohler-Hausmann, *Misdemeanorland*.

48. Michelle C. Kondo et al., "A Difference-In-Differences Study of the Effects of a New Abandoned Building Remediation Strategy on Safety," *PLOS One* 10, no. 8 (2015), https://doi.org/10.1371/journal.pone.0136595.

49. John Jay College Research Advisory Group Preventing and Reducing Community Violence, "Reducing Violence without Police: A Review of Research Evidence" (New York: Research and Evaluation Center, 2020), https://johnjayrec.nyc/2020/11/09/av2020.

50. For recent reviews on this evidence, see Thea Sebastian et al., *A New Community Safety Blueprint: How the Federal Government Can Address Violence and Harm through a Public Health Approach* (Washington, DC: Brookings Institute, 2022); Elizabeth Glazer and Patrick Sharkey, "Social Fabric: A New Model for Public Safety and Vital Neighborhoods," *The Square One Project*, 2021, https://squareonejustice.org/wp-content/uploads/2021/04/CJLJ8743-Social-Fabric-Square-One-WEB-report-210406.pdf.

51. For an account of how to end persistent American poverty, see Matthew Desmond, *Poverty, by America* (New York: Penguin Random House, 2023).

52. Victor Ray, *On Critical Race Theory: Why It Matters and Why You Should Care* (New York: Penguin Random House, 2022).

53. Juliana Menasce Horowitz, *September 27* (Pew Research Center, 2021), https://www.pewresearch.org/fact-tank/2021/09/27/support-for-black-lives-matter-declined-after-george-floyd-protests-but-has-remained-unchanged-since.

Author's Note

1. Phillip Goodman, Joshua Page, and Michelle Phelps, *Breaking the Pendulum: The Long Struggle over Criminal Justice* (New York: Oxford University Press, 2017).

2. Drawing on Pierre Bourdieu's work, we argued that this struggle took place in the *penal field*, or the social and political space in which these actors fought to determine penal policies and practices. For more on the penal field concept, see Joshua Page, "Punishment and the Penal Field," in *The Sage Handbook of Punishment and Society*, ed. Richard Sparks and Jonathan Simon (London: Sage, 2013), 152–66. The policing field is one of several subfields of the penal field, shaping the policies and practices of local police departments.

3. See the methodological appendix in Douglas Hartmann, *Midnight Basketball: Race, Sports, and Neoliberal Social Policy* (Chicago: University of Chicago Press, 2016). This concept builds off Michael Burawoy's extended case method, which refers to extending from observations in the field to broader theoretical and historical insights. See Michael Burawoy, "The Extended Case Method," *Sociological Theory* 16, no. 1 (2002): 4–33.

4. For more on the methodology of these interviews, see Michelle S. Phelps, Anneliese Ward, and Dwjuan Frazier, "From Police Reform to Police Abolition? How Minneapolis Activists Fought to Make Black Lives Matter," *Mobilization: An International Quarterly* 26, no. 4 (2021): 421–41.

5. For more on the methodology on these interviews, see Michelle S. Phelps, Christopher E. Robertson, and Amber Joy Powell, "'We're Still Dying Quicker Than We Can Effect Change': #BlackLivesMatter and the Limits of 21st-Century Policing Reform," *American Journal of Sociology* 127, no. 3 (2021): 867–903.

6. Mario Luis Small, "Ethnography Upgraded," *Qualitative Sociology* 45 (2022): 477–82, https://link.springer.com/article/10.1007/s11133-022-09519-1.

7. Reuben Jonathan Miller, *Halfway Home: Race, Punishment, and the Afterlife of Mass Incarceration* (New York: Little, Brown, 2021), 291.

8. Rob Kuznia, "Once Nicknamed 'Murderapolis,'" CNN, September 25, 2022, https://www.cnn.com/2022/09/25/us/minneapolis-crime-defund-invs/index.html.

9. Davarian L. Baldwin, *In the Shadow of the Ivory Tower: How Universities Are Plundering Our Cities* (New York: Bold Type Books, 2021).

10. See, e.g., Derecka Purnell, *Becoming Abolitionists: Police, Protests, and the Pursuit of Freedom* (New York: Astra House, 2021).

11. Aldon Morris, "Alternative View of Modernity: The Subaltern Speaks," *American Sociological Review* 87, no. 1 (2022): 1–16.

12. Ruha Benjamin, *Viral Justice: How We Grow the World We Want* (Princeton, NJ: Princeton University Press, 2022).